Johan Lewi Jan Paredaens

Data Structures of Pascal, Algol 68, PL/1 and Ada

With 105 Figures

Springer-Verlag Berlin Heidelberg GmbH

Johan Lewi

Katholieke Universiteit Leuven
Department of Computer Science
Celestijnenlaan 200 A
3030 Leuven/Heverlee, Belgium

Jan Paredaens

University of Antwerp
Department of Computer Science
Universiteitsplein 1
2610 Antwerp/Wilrijk, Belgium

ISBN 978-3-642-70241-9

Library of Congress Cataloging-in-Publication Data. Lewi, Johan. Data structures of Pascal, Algol 68, PL/1 and Ada. Bibliography: p. Includes index. 1. Data structures (Computer science) 2. PASCAL (Computer program language) 3. ALGOL (Computer program language) 4. PL/I (Computer program language) 5. Ada (Computer program language) I. Paredaens, Jan. II. Title. QA76.9.D35L47 1986 005.7'3 86-15560
ISBN 978-3-642-70241-9 ISBN 978-3-642-70239-6 (eBook)
DOI 10.1007/978-3-642-70239-6

Originally published by Springer-Verlag Berlin Heidelberg New York in 1986

2145/3140-543210

SMALL is beautiful.
E. Schumacher, 1975.

To Dany and Nicole.

Preface

This book is intended as a text for a course in programming languages. The prerequisites for such a course are insight in structured programming and knowledge as well as practical experience of at least one (e.g., Pascal) of the programming languages treated in the book.

The emphasis is on language concepts rather than on syntactic details. The book covers a number of important language concepts that are related to data structures. The comparison of the programming languages Pascal, Algol 68, PL/1 and Ada consists in investigating how these concepts are supported by each of these languages. Interesting evaluation criteria are generality, simplicity, safety, readability and portability.

The study of programming languages is based on a simple model called SMALL. This model serves as a didactic vehicle for describing, comparing and evaluating data structures in various programming languages.

Each chapter centers around a specific language concept. It consists of a general discussion followed by a number of language sections, one for each of the languages Pascal, Algol 68, PL/1 and Ada. Each of these sections contains a number of illustrating program fragments written in the programming language concerned. For each program fragment in one language, there is an analogous fragment in the others.

The book can be read "vertically" so that the programming languages Pascal, Algol 68, PL/1 and Ada are encountered in that order several times. A "horizontal" reading of the book would consist in selecting only those sections which only concern one language.

The Appendix gives the syntax diagrams of Pascal, Algol 68, PL/1 and Ada. For PL/1 and Ada, only a subset is covered by the book.

J. Lewi
J. Paredaens

Contents

Chapter 0

INTRODUCTION

§0.1 Programming

Programming is a discipline that has various engineering and mathematical aspects. Although most of these aspects are interrelated, each of them covers a number of characteristics and goals which are very specific. The progress being made in teaching programming is reflected by the fact that most computer science curricula contain a broad spectrum of programming courses, each emphasizing a different aspect of programming.

Three important aspects are:

(1) programming methodologies and techniques,
(2) programming language concepts, and
(3) programming language notations.

The **first aspect** deals with methodologies and techniques for designing and developing algorithms. The main goals are readability, reliability and flexibility of programs. Examples illustrating this aspect are stepwise refinement, hierarchical and modular composition, verification and specification.

The **second aspect** is related to the fact that one must know exactly to what extent programming methodologies and techniques are supported by the language being used. In other words, one has to have a precise idea of the full power of the language. If the methodology under consideration is not completely supported or not at all covered by the language concepts available, then the underlying methodology must be made explicit by adequate program documentation. As an extreme case, using Fortran as a programming language does not mean that one must forget about concepts such as recursion at all the various stages of program design. One might also use a verification technique even where this technique is not supported by the programming language. It is the authors' conviction that the programmer must be aware not only of the power of the language to be used, but also of its shortcomings.

The **third aspect** concerns knowledge of the syntactic details of writing programs. Of course, this aspect is important if ultimately we want our programs to be executed by our computer.

The various aspects of programming have different priorities. It would be inconceivable nowadays that a particular notation should determine our way of thinking, as was the case with Fortran for many programmers in the past. Therefore, design methodologies and techniques must come first. Furthermore, the programmer must have a complete grasp of the power of the language at the level of language concepts, not merely at the level of, for example, writing semicolons in programs. Finally, it is obvious that the notation will always play a role in any aspect of programming. Clearly, one cannot teach methodologies, techniques and concepts without any form of notation.

There is a need for courses emphasizing different aspects of programming. If the notation is overemphasized, it can be very confusing for the programmer in the sense that language constructs which look completely different may in fact express the same concept. A typical example is the declaration of a based variable and the allocate statement in PL/1, as compared with the pointer type declaration and the new statement in Pascal, respectively.

§0.2 Language concepts

This book mainly covers one aspect of programming, namely **programming language concepts**. The importance of this topic is illustrated by the following points:

(1) The programmer has to know to what extent methodologies and techniques for program design are supported by the language. Therefore, he has to be aware not only of its power, but also of its shortcomings. As an example, the programmer has to know whether a concept is implemented in a safe way, or whether its use is unsafe because its effect is machine dependent or there is a loss of information, e.g. type control.

(2) Insight into programming language concepts and data structures facilitates and promotes the learning of new languages. It often turns out that language constructs which seem completely different in form actually express the same concept.

(3) Another aim of this study is the introduction of a well-suited terminology in

the field of programming languages. This need stems largely from the fact that most programmers write programs with a high degree of automatism. They claim to know the meaning of a language concept, but they often fail to explain it in an accurate way. Our concern is to make programmers conscious of the underlying concepts of the data structures they use. The introduction of an adequate terminology is a first step towards achieving this goal.

(4) The study of concepts of data structures serves the purpose of an evaluation of the current generation of programming languages, called the von Neumann languages. There are already signs of a new generation of programming languages but the widespread use of these languages seems still to be some time away. In the meantime, languages like Pascal, Algol 68, PL/1 and Ada must do the job. If we want to avoid the same design mistakes made by programming language designers of the past, we must have a clear understanding of what has gone before. Therefore, this study serves as a means of analyzing and evaluating the design decisions of existing programming languages.

§0.3 Programming languages

The starting point of our book was a systematic study of the programming language concepts available in Pascal. Later on, we decided to investigate how these concepts are handled in other languages such as Algol 68, PL/1 and Ada. A comparison of languages on the level of concepts gives a better understanding of the concepts themselves. Moreover, the Pascal-like subsets of Algol 68, PL/1 and Ada serve as an excellent basis for learning the languages and for managing their complexity.

Pascal and the Pascal-like subsets of Algol 68, PL/1 and Ada are described by means of syntax charts given in the appendix.

0.3.1 Pascal

Pascal is mainly the work of one person, N. Wirth. In Pascal, there is a well-balanced trade-off between language complexity and programming power. Clearly, this trade-off must be seen in the light of an early stage in the evolution of programming language concepts.

The fact that the success of Pascal exceeded the expectations of its designer is a strong indication of the need for simple software writing tools. Pascal was designed with the following principle in mind: "If our basic tool, the language in which we design and code our programs, is also complicated, the language itself becomes part of the problem rather than part of its solution", from "The Emperor's Old Clothes" [Hoare 1981].

The basic reference for the language Pascal as used in this book is

Pascal User Manual and Report
K. Jensen, N. Wirth
Springer-Verlag, New York, Heidelberg, Berlin (1974, 3rd ed. 1985).

0.3.2 Algol 68

Algol 68 was designed by a small team headed by A. van Wijngaarden. The work was sponsored by the IFIP Working Group 2.1.
Algol 68 is an excellent example of so-called orthogonal design, as described in [van Wijngaarden 1965], [Denvir 1979] and [Turski 1981]. Orthogonal design implies that one starts from a few basic features and constructs the language in such a way that the composition rules for deriving new features from existing ones contain a minimum of exception rules. As a consequence, the level of complexity of Algol 68 as a language (not to be confused with its reference description) is fairly low. The generality principle, which dictates that related concepts should be unified into a simple framework, is also nicely realised in Algol 68.

The reference description of Algol 68 used in this book is

Revised report on the Algorithmic Language Algol 68
van Wijngaarden, A. et al.
Springer-Verlag, Berlin, Heidelberg, New York (1976).

0.3.3 PL/1

Design work on PL/1, a product of IBM, was begun in the mid-60s. It was meant as a replacement for Fortran and Cobol and borrowed a number of features from Algol 60.

PL/1 has a huge variety of language features designed to satisfy the needs of a large class of programmers. Although each of these features may be very attractive on its own, the complexity of the language as a whole is so high that mastering the complete language becomes a real problem. One of the main lessons to be learned from this experience is that the complexity of a language can affect the readability, verifiability and maintenance of its programs.

PL/1 has been included in order to illustrate the fact that all the concepts covered in this book also apply to this language. This gives rise to a Pascal-like subset of PL/1, which seems to be an excellent start for novice programmers to learn PL/1 in an incremental way.

The authors are aware of the fact that a number of interesting features (such as exception handling, offsets and areas, external procedures) fall outside the scope of this subset.

The reference description of PL/1 used in this book is

> OS PL/1 Checkout and Optimizing Compilers:
> Language Reference Manual
> IBM GC33-0009-4
> 5th ed. (1976)

0.3.4 Ada

In the mid-70s, the United States Department of Defense decided to sponsor the development of a new programming language called Ada. Ada was designed for the domain of large, real-time, embedded systems, although it is expected to have an impact in many other areas. It contains a number of very attractive features, each of which seems to be nicely engineered.

In this book, only a Pascal-like subset of Ada is treated. Features such as packages, tasking and exception handling are outside the scope of this study.

The development of Ada is very new. There is not enough experience to judge whether or not the lessons of the past about the design of simple programming tools have been effectively learned.

The reference description for Ada is

> Reference Manual for the Ada Programming Language
> United States Department of Defense
> ANSI/MIL-STD 1815
> (January 1983)

Ada is a registered trademark of the U.S. Government, Ada Joint Program Office.

§0.4 A simple model

The study of programming languages in this book is based on a model called SMALL: a Simple data structure Model for Algorithmic Languages. This model serves as a didactic vehicle for describing, comparing and evaluating data structures in various programming languages. The emphasis is on illustrating significant differences and similarities between data structures, and no attempt is made to give complete descriptions of the programming languages involved. The detailed descriptions of these languages can be found in the existing reference manuals mentioned above.

SMALL is not meant as a formalism for describing exhaustively the semantics of programming languages. The SMALL approach can be considered a compromise between the purely intuitive and the purely formal (mathematically based) definition methods. Formal definitions such as denotational semantics [Gordon 1979] are very lengthy and require some mathematical background. The authors' hope is that the SMALL approach will be accessible to a wide audience and that it will smooth the way towards the study of more formal description methods.

§0.5 SMALL

In SMALL, we distinguish three kinds of objects: ***values***, ***expressions*** and ***types***. This gives rise to three abstract disjoint sets: the set of values, denoted by V, the set of expressions, denoted by E, and the set of types, denoted by T. For each set, there are a number of primitive objects and a number of composition rules producing composite objects within the set.

Values are objects that can be processed by an algorithm. Examples of values are numbers, characters, locations, routines, arrays and records. Values are sometimes called *internal* objects. They can be structured in various ways. In SMALL, the properties of values will be described by means of three basic functions: the ***contents function***, the ***selection function*** and the ***result function***.

Expressions are objects which are used to denote values. Examples are identifiers, constant denotations, procedure calls, selection and indexing constructs, declarations, statements and programs. Expressions are often called *external* objects. They have a so-called syntactic structure which is very much language dependent. In SMALL, the relationship between expressions and values is described by the *denotation function*. The evaluation of compound expressions is described in terms of three basic operators: the ***contents operator***, the ***selection operator*** and the ***result operator***.

Every expression has a type, which specifies certain properties of the values denoted by the expression. Type information may increase readability, reliability and ease of compilation. In SMALL, the association of expressions with types is described by the ***type function***. The properties of types will be defined by means of four basic functions: the ***reference function***, the ***structure function***, the ***type of selector function*** and the ***routine function***. Two additional functions will be discussed: the ***union function*** and the ***constraint function***.

The concepts covered by SMALL are illustrated by a large number of examples written in Pascal, Algol 68, PL/1 and Ada. The reader is assumed to have some knowledge of at least one of these languages. In the case of simple examples, reading the Pascal, PL/1, Algol 68 and Ada versions might be somewhat tedious. By systematically working through all four language versions of each example however, the reader is able to gradually get used to the notation of each language as he progresses through the book.

§0.6 Abbreviations and Conventions

List of abbreviations

V	set of Values
A	set of Atomic values
C	set of Composite values
D	set of data
L	set of Locations
R	set of Routine values
TR	set of TRansitions
CONF	set of CONFigurations
AD	set of Atomic Data
CD	set of Composite Data
AL	set of Atomic Locations
CL	set of Composite Locations
E	set of Expressions
N	set of Names
CE	set of Compound Expressions
T	set of Types

DEN	DENotation function
CONT	CONTents function
SEL	SELection function
RES	RESult function
TYP	TYPe function
REF	REFerence function
STRUCT	STRUCTure function
TOS	Type Of Selector function
ROUT	ROUTine function
UNION	UNION function
CONSTR	CONSTRaint function
M_{SEL}	SELection operator
M_{CONT}	CONTents operator
M_{RES}	RESult operator
$M_{DEUNION}$	DEUNION operator
M_{CONSTR}	CONSTRaint operator
M_s	type of transitions

List of conventions

The symbols on the left-hand side, possibly indexed, stand for an arbitrary object on the right-hand side.

μ	type (mode in Algol 68)
$\alpha, \beta, \gamma, \delta,$ $\varsigma, \eta, \phi, \omega, \rho,$	location
r	routine value
e	expression
s	transition or expression denoting a selector
v	value
s	selector
c	constraint
SEL_v	selector selecting a transitionless value
SEL_s	selector selecting a transition

Chapter 1

VALUES

One of the three basic sets of objects covered by SMALL is the set of *values*, denoted by V. Values are *internal objects* , also called *abstract* objects, and are processed by the actions specified in a program. The properties of values uniquely determine the kinds of actions that can be performed on them.

Our main purpose here is to study the fundamental properties of values. These properties are described in terms of a didactic model called SMALL and illustrated by examples in the languages Pascal, Algol 68, PL/1 and Ada. In SMALL, the properties of values are described by means of three basic functions : the *contents function* , the *selection function* and the *result function.*

The starting point of our analysis is the division of the class of values V into a number of subclasses, the elements of each subclass sharing common properties. First, we will give a rough description of this classification, which will then be analyzed in detail in the subsequent chapters.

We shall distinguish the following classes in V:

A: the set of Atomic values. These are the values that cannot be further decomposed into smaller units.

C: the set of Composite values. These are the values that can be decomposed into smaller component values. These components may be atomic or may in turn be composite.

D: the set of Data. These are the values that are of a read-only nature, i.e., one cannot speak about the contents of these values.

L: the set of Locations. These are the values which are locational in nature: i.e they represent storage which may contain other values.

R: the set of Routine values. These values represent algorithms specifying a number of actions, possibly in terms of formal parameters. A call of a routine value first binds the actual parameters to the corresponding formal parameters, then executes the algorithm and eventually returns a result. Routine values must be seen in a very general context. They can be expressed by procedures and functions, but also by statements and declarations.

TR: the set of TRansitions. To explain these, let us first introduce the notion of configuration. Intuitively, a configuration can be seen as a snapshot at a particular point of the execution of a program. Such a configuration contains all the information that would be necessary to halt the program at that point in its execution and to restart it some time later at the same point. The set of all configurations is called CONF. A transition is then a function from configurations to configurations. As will be explained later, a transition may be (part of) the result of the call of a routine value.

All these definitions will be treated in a more precise way in Chapter 6. Notice that the terms *datum* and *data* have a special meaning throughout this book. In particular, the property datum must be carefully distinguished from the property location, as we shall explain in more detail later.

As illustrated in Figure 1.1, the set V of values in SMALL is partitioned into six classes : AD, CD, AL, CL, R and TR. Each of these classes is characterized by means of a number of properties defining the basic operations (functions) applicable to the values of each class.

In SMALL there are three functions defined on values : the *contents function*, the *selection function*, and the *result function*.

1. The *contents function* : CONT. This function is defined on locations only. The contents function specifies which value is contained in a given location. In von Neumann programming languages such as Pascal, Algol 68, PL/1 and Ada, we can manipulate locations as well as their contents. The contents function is discussed in Chapters 3, 5 and 7.

2. The *selection function*: SEL. The selection function is defined on composite values only. This function specifies the component values of a given composite value. Typical examples are the indexing of elements in an array value and the selection of fields from a record value. The selection function is discussed in Chapters 4 and 5.

3. The *result function* : RES. This function is defined on routine values only. It specifies which value is the result of the execution of the routine value after the formal parameters have been correctly bound to the actual parameters. The result function is discussed in Chapter 6.

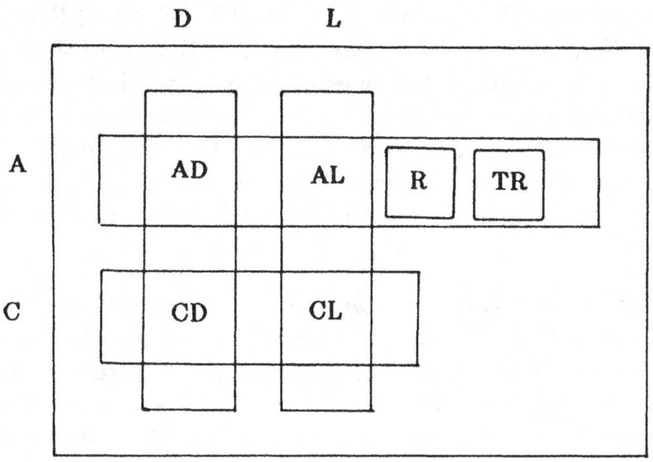

Figure 1.1.

	contents function CONT	selection function SEL	result function RES
AD			
TR			
CD		×	
AL	×		
CL	×	×	
R			×

Figure 1.2.

In fact, the partitioning of V into AD, CD, AL, CL, R and TR is guided by the basic functions CONT, SEL and RES. The basic functions and their corresponding domains are illustrated in Figure 1.2, where a cross ("x") indicates that the specified function is defined on that class of values. Observe from Figure 1.2 that the only two classes of values that are not distinguished by the functions CONT, SEL and RES are AD and TR. The difference between AD and TR is that transitions are functions on the set of configurations CONF. This will be clarified in Chapter 6.

Values are abstract objects (*internal objects*), for which we must have notations called *expressions (external objects)*. The set of expressions is denoted by E. An expression has a syntactic structure. It can be a name (atomic expression) or a compound expression. Examples of names are identifiers, constants and operators. Compound expressions are built up from names, but their structure is language dependent, i.e., it is part of the syntax of the language. The function specifying the value denoted by an expression is the *denotation function*, abbreviated DEN. The function DEN is discussed in Chapter 8.

Notice the fundamental difference between the name '1' and the value denoted by '1'. In SMALL, we will often use the notation shown in Figure 2.1 to refer to the value 1, whereas '1' is the name denoting it. Specifically, we will write DEN.1 to indicate the value 1. The function DEN is partly defined by the language and partly by the programmer. This gives rise to *language defined expressions* and *program defined expressions* respectively. This is discussed in more detail in Chapter 8.

Notice that a value may be denoted by several expressions. Examples of expressions which all denote the value DEN.1 are '1','I','one','f(3)','A[1]', where 'I' and 'one' are declared as constant identifiers denoting the value DEN.1,' f(3)' is a function call delivering the value DEN.1 and 'A' is declared as a constant integer vector having DEN.1 as its first element. The first three constructs are names, whereas the last two are compound expressions.

Clearly, the structure properties of values are completely different from the structure properties of expressions. The structure of values belongs to the semantic part of the language, whereas the structure of expressions belongs to its syntactic part. Clearly, a compound expression may denote an atomic value, and a name may denote a composite value.

Chapter 2

ATOMIC DATA

§2.1 Concept

The *atomic data* are values on which neither the *selection function* SEL, nor the *contents function* CONT, nor the *result function* RES is defined. The difference between atomic data and transitions will be clarified in Chapter 6.

Atomic data are the values with which we are mostly familiar in programming languages. They are often called scalar values. Examples of atomic data common to almost all programming languages are numbers, boolean values and characters.

We recall that 1 in a cloudlet (see Figure 2.1) means the internal object which can be denoted by the expression '1'. In SMALL we write DEN.1 to indicate this internal object. This atomic datum DEN.1 must not be confused with its location holding that datum, as is illustrated by examples on locations in Chapter 3. Notice also the difference between DEN.1 and DEN.'1'. The former is an integer atomic datum, whereas the latter is a character atomic datum. Actually, atomic data may be of different types. Types are introduced in Chapter 9.
In the sequel, we will give a few examples of the use of atomic data in Pascal, Algol 68, PL/1 and Ada. These examples illustrate that an atomic datum, such as DEN.3, can be denoted by various expressions having different syntactic structures, such as '3', 'a',{contents (vecint[3])}, 'fint(i)' and {contents (i)}.

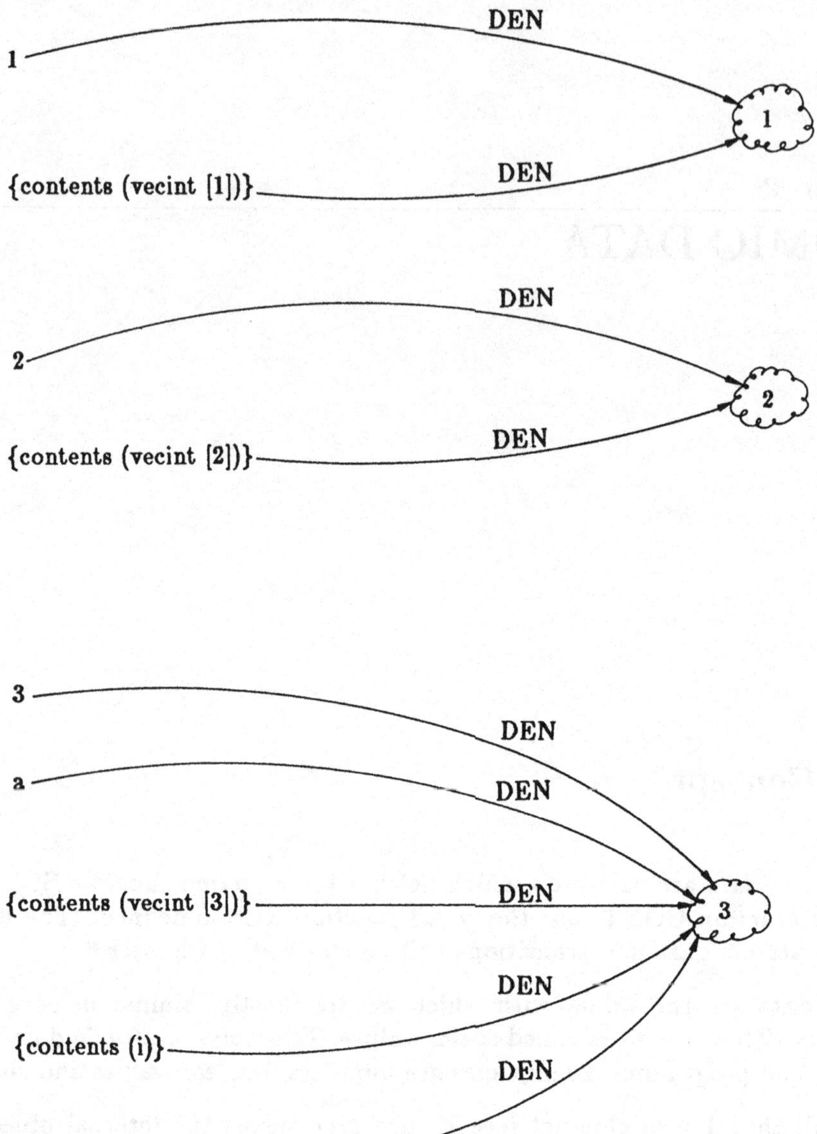
DEN
1
1
{contents (vecint [1])}
DEN
DEN
2
2
{contents (vecint [2])}
DEN
3
DEN
a
DEN
{contents (vecint [3])}
DEN
3
DEN
{contents (i)}
DEN
fint(i)

Figure 2.1.

§2.2 Atomic data in Pascal

Example

```
const a=3;
var i:integer;
    vecint:array[1..3] of integer;
function fint(x:integer):integer;
    <declarations>
    begin
       <statements>;
       fint:=x
    end{fint};
begin
    i:=3;
    vecint[1]:=1;
    vecint[2]:=2;
    vecint[3]:=3;
    ...fint(i)...
end
```

Just before the end of the above program we have the situation shown in Figure 2.1.

Figure 2.1 is called a value diagram. A value diagram is a graphical representation of a set of values V and a set of expressions E, together with the relations and the functions that are defined on these sets. For the moment the denotation function DEN is the only function that is represented in the value diagrams.

The value diagrams will be extended to include other functions and relations as soon as these are introduced. The notation {contents(i)} must always be read as "the contents of the variable i". As we will see in Chapter 3, there is a fundamental difference between the location denoted by 'i' and its contents. The notation {contents(i)} is not a legal Pascal expression. Unfortunately, in Pascal there is no way to specify explicitly the contents of the location denoted by 'i'. The contents operator can only be specified implicitly, i.e., by means of the context.

For instance, if the variable 'i' occurs on the right hand side of an assignment, or if it is an actual parameter of a procedure call where the parameter binding is a call by value, then 'i' stands for {contents(i)}. Implicit operations of this kind are also known as *automatic type conversions* in PL/1 or *coercions* in Algol 68. In Pascal, the second occurrence of i in the assignment 'i:=i+1' is implicitly combined by the contents operator. This operator is defined by the context.

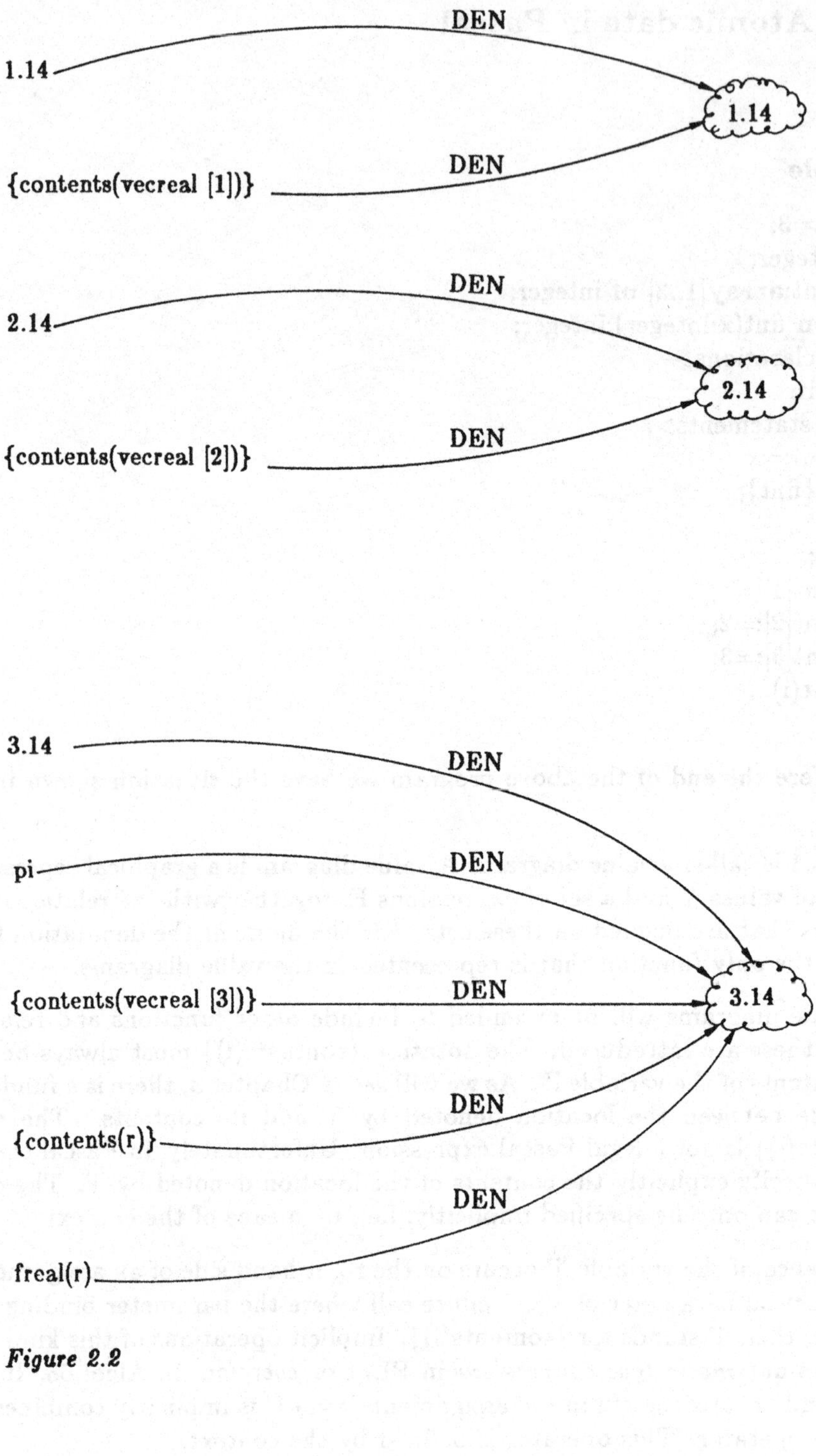
DEN
1.14
1.14
DEN
{contents(vecreal [1])}
DEN
2.14
2.14
DEN
{contents(vecreal [2])}
3.14
DEN
pi
DEN
{contents(vecreal [3])}
DEN
3.14
DEN
{contents(r)}
DEN
freal(r)

Figure 2.2

Example

```
const pi=3.14;
var r:real;
    vecreal:array[1..3] of real;
function freal (x:real):real;
    <declarations>
    begin
        <statements>;
        freal:=x
    end{freal};
begin
    r:=3.14;
    vecreal[1]:=1.14;
    vecreal[2]:=2.14;
    vecreal[3]:=3.14;
    ...freal(r)...
end
```

See Figure 2.2.

Example

```
const ok=true;
var b:boolean;
    vecbool:array[1..3] of boolean;
function fbool(x:boolean):boolean;
    <declarations>
    begin
        <statements>;
        fbool:=x
    end{fbool};
begin
    b:=true;
    vecbool[1]:=false;
    vecbool[2]:=true;
    vecbool[3]:=true;
    ...fbool(b)...
end
```

See Figure 2.3.

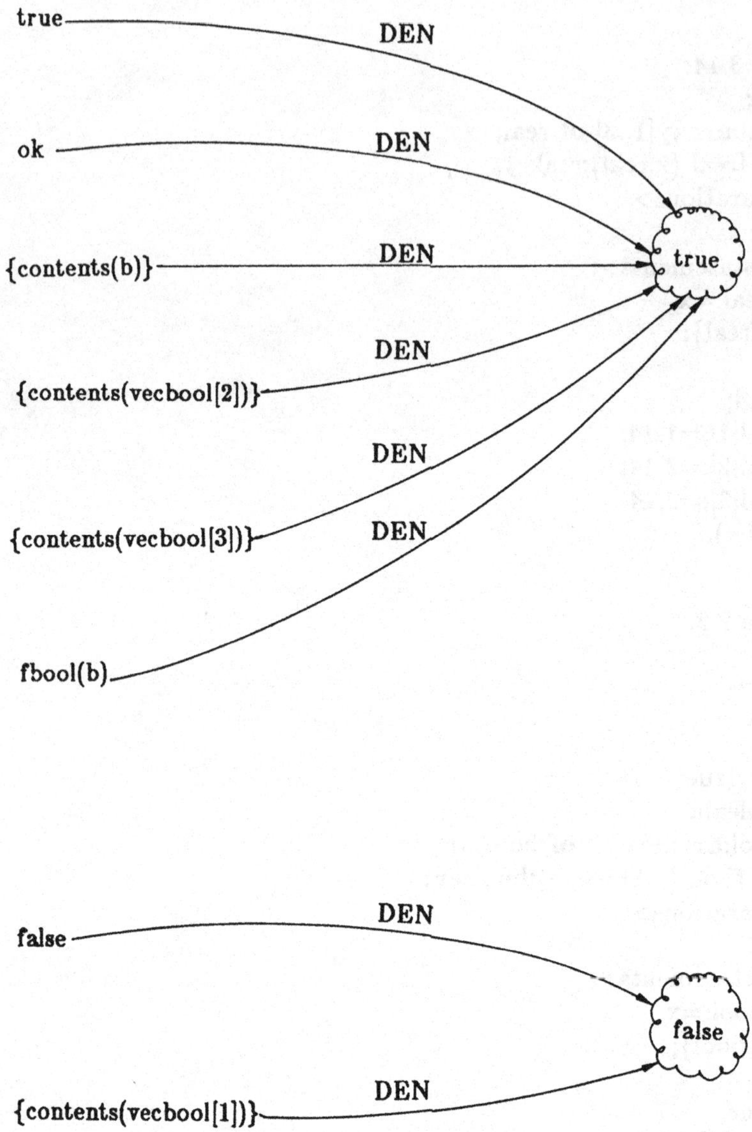
true
ok
{contents(b)}
{contents(vecbool[2])}
{contents(vecbool[3])}
fbool(b)
DEN
true
false
{contents(vecbool[1])}
false

Figure 2.3.

Example

```
const token='c';
var c:char;
    vecchar:array[1..3] of char;
function fchar(x:char):char;
    <declarations>
    begin
        <statements>;
        fchar:=x
    end{fchar};
begin
    c:='c';
    vecchar[1]:='a';
    vecchar[2]:='b';
    vecchar[3]:='c';
    ...fchar(c)...
end
```

See Figure 2.4.

Example

```
type color=(blue,indigo,purple,lilac);
var i:color;
    veccolor:array[color] of color;
function fcolor(x:color):color;
    <declarations>
    begin
        <statements>;
        fcolor:=x
    end{fcolor};
begin
    i:=indigo;
    veccolor[blue]:=indigo;
    veccolor[indigo]:=blue;
    veccolor[purple]:=lilac;
    veccolor[lilac]:=purple;
    ...fcolor(i)...
end
```

See Figure 2.5.

This example illustrates the use of an enumeration type,describing the set consisting of the values DEN.blue, DEN.indigo, DEN.purple and DEN.lilac.

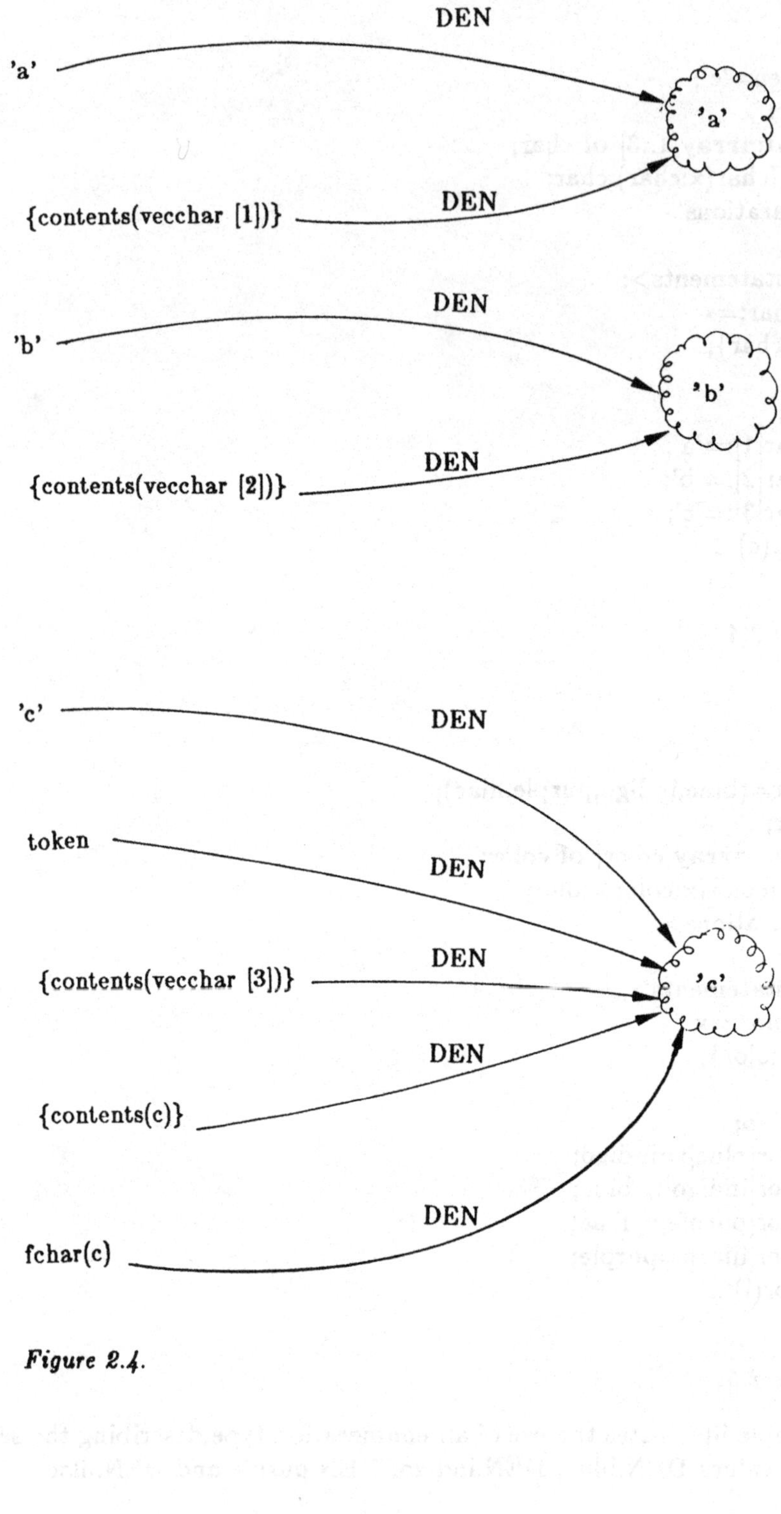
DEN
'a'
'a'
{contents(vecchar [1])}
DEN
DEN
'b'
'b'
{contents(vecchar [2])}
DEN
'c'
DEN
token
DEN
{contents(vecchar [3])}
DEN
'c'
DEN
{contents(c)}
DEN
fchar(c)

Figure 2.4.

§2.3 Atomic data in Algol 68

The Pascal examples in Section 2.2 can be translated almost literally into Algol 68 as follows :

Example

```
int a=3;
ref int i=loc int;
ref [ ] int vecint=loc[1:3]int;
proc(ref int) int fint=
    (ref int x)int:
        begin
            <declarations and statements>;
            x
        end co fint co;
begin
    i:=3;
    vecint[1]:=1;
    vecint[2]:=2;
    vecint[3]:=3;
    ...fint(i)...
end
```

Compare Figure 2.6 with Figure 2.1. In Figure 2.6, some expressions are preceded by the names of the languages to which they refer, whereas others are not, in which case the expressions refer to all the languages involved on that figure.

The notation '**int**(i)' is a legal Algol 68 expression and is called a cast construction. The notation '**int**(i)' specifies the contents of the location denoted by 'i'. The general format of a cast is μ_1 (< μ-expression>), where μ and μ_1 denote modes (types). The value denoted by the μ-expression is transformed (coerced) into a value of mode μ_1.

As an example, the value (which is a location) denoted by 'i' in '**int**(i)' is of mode '**ref int**'. This value is transformed (dereferenced) into a value of mode '**int**', i.e., its contents are taken. In the same way, '**int**(vecint[3])' means "the contents of the location denoted by vecint[3]". As we will see later, 'vecint[3]' is indeed of mode '**ref int**'.

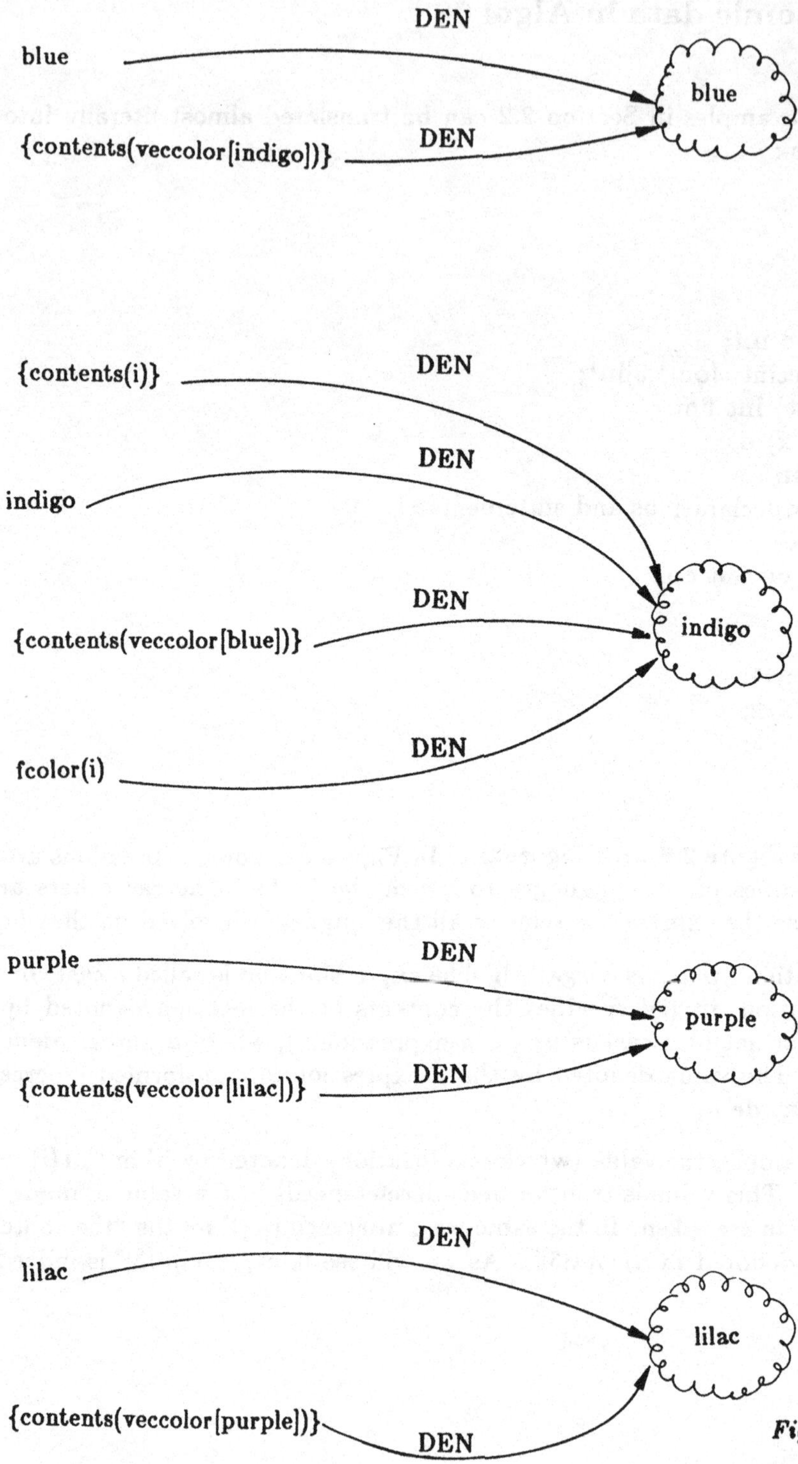
DEN
blue
blue
{contents(veccolor[indigo])}
DEN
{contents(i)}
DEN
DEN
indigo
DEN
{contents(veccolor[blue])}
indigo
fcolor(i)
DEN
purple
DEN
purple
{contents(veccolor[lilac])}
DEN
DEN
lilac
lilac
{contents(veccolor[purple])}
DEN

Figure 2.5.

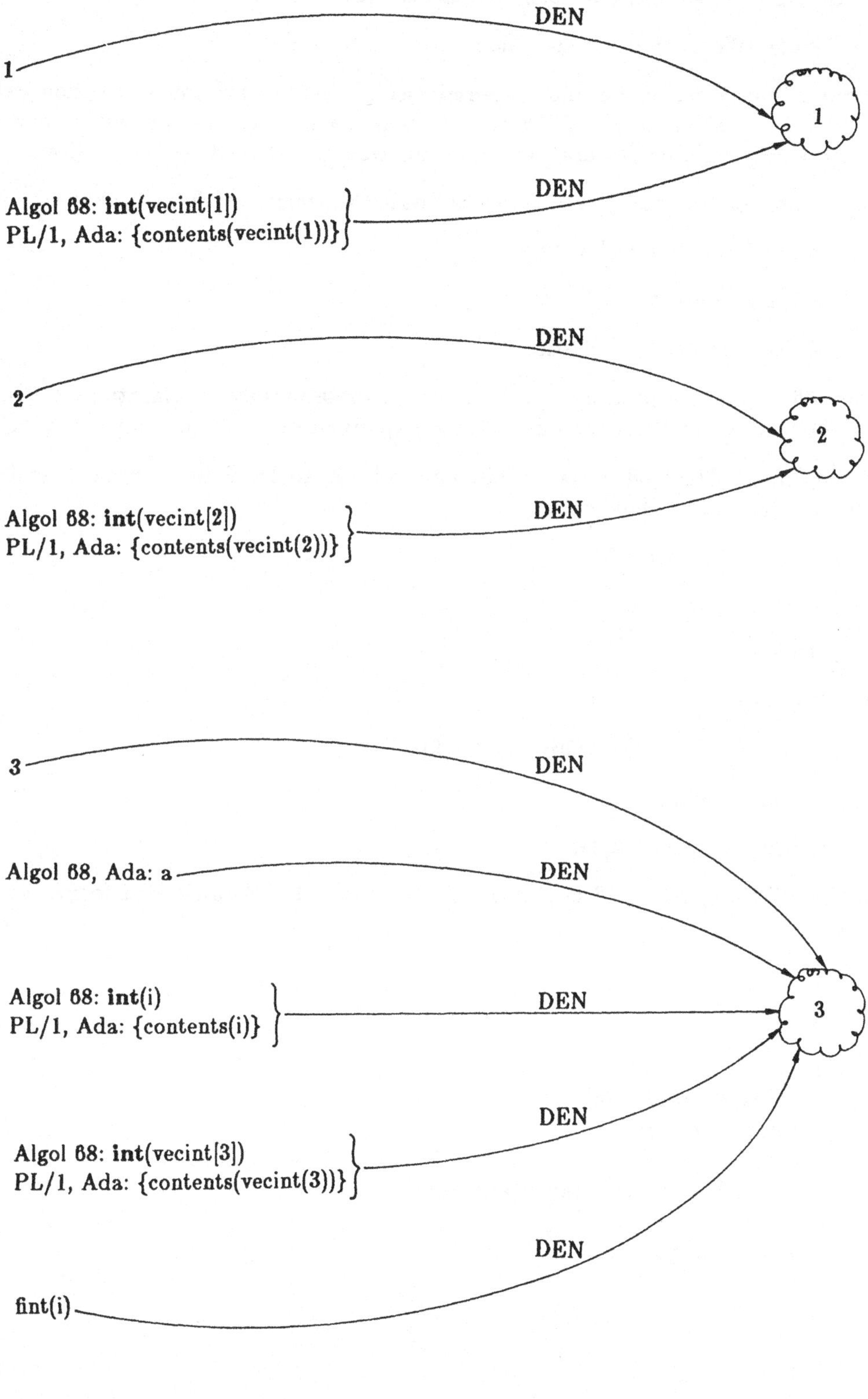
DEN
1
1
DEN
Algol 68: int(vecint[1])
PL/1, Ada: {contents(vecint(1))}
DEN
2
2
DEN
Algol 68: int(vecint[2])
PL/1, Ada: {contents(vecint(2))}
3
DEN
Algol 68, Ada: a
DEN
Algol 68: int(i)
PL/1, Ada: {contents(i)}
DEN
3
DEN
Algol 68: int(vecint[3])
PL/1, Ada: {contents(vecint(3))}
DEN
fint(i)

Figure 2.6.

In Algol 68, the general format of a declaration is

μ <identifier> = < μ-expression>

where μ specifies a mode and < μ-expression> stands for any expression delivering a value of mode μ. With this declaration format, we can write constant declarations, variable declarations, and function and procedure declarations.

An example of a constant declaration is '**int** a=3', which satisfies the above format.

Examples of variable declarations are

```
ref int i=loc int;
ref[ ]int vecint=loc[1:3]int;
```

Algol 68 allows the programmer to contract these variable declarations to '**int** i' and '[1:3]**int** vecint' respectively. This is explained in detail in Chapters 3 and 5.

Furthermore, Algol 68 allows declaration of variables to be combined with an initialization part. Thus we may write

```
ref int i=loc int:=3;
```

The contracted form is

```
int i:=3;
```

We also have

```
ref [ ]int vecint=loc[1:3]int:=(1,2,3);
```

whose contracted form is

```
[1:3]int vecint:=(1,2,3);
```

In the following Algol 68 examples, the contracted and initialized forms will be used.

Example

```
real pi=3.14;
proc (ref real) real freal=
    (ref real x)real:
        begin
            <declarations and statements>;
            x
        end co freal co;
```

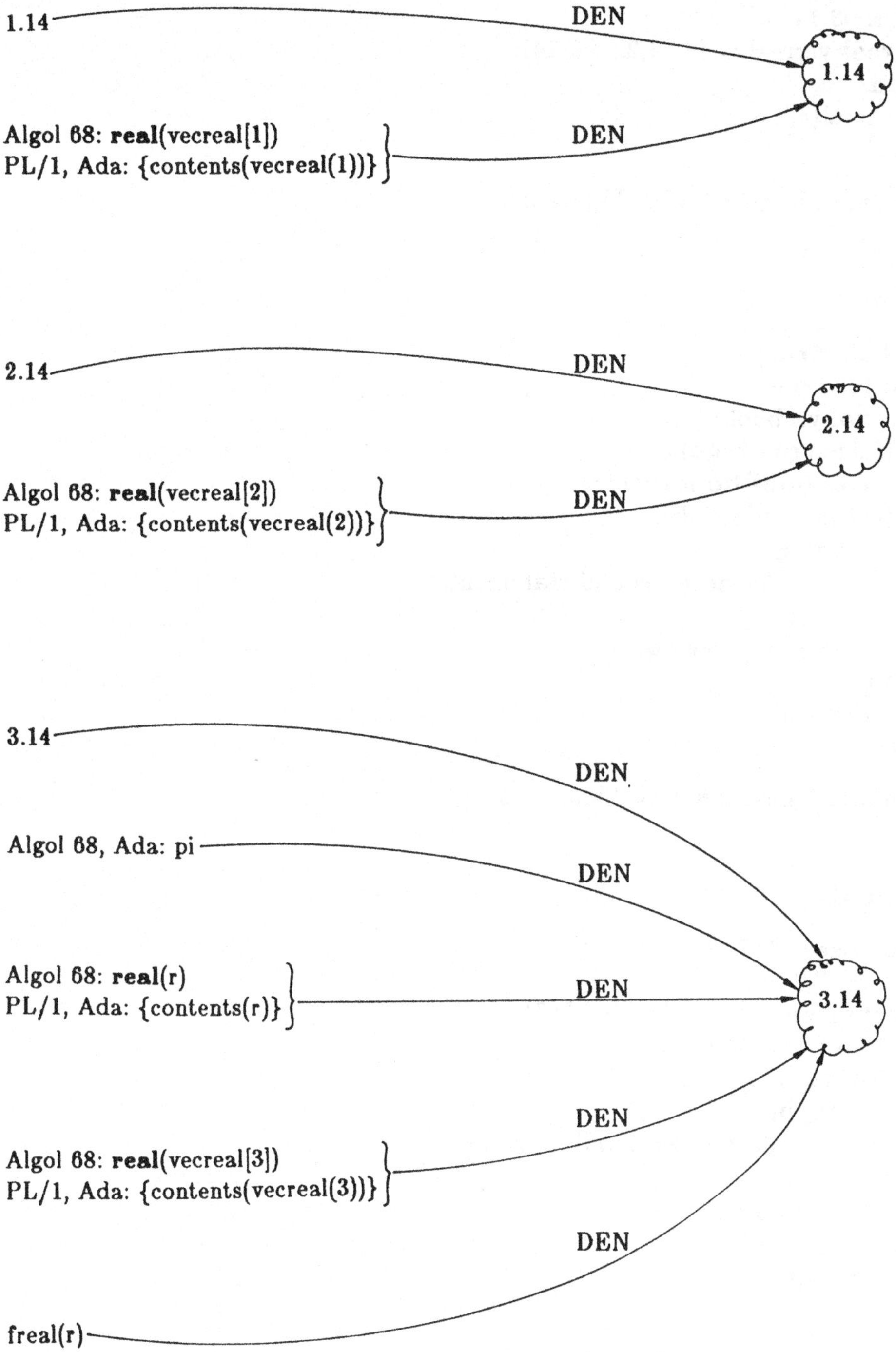
1.14
DEN
1.14
Algol 68: **real**(vecreal[1])
PL/1, Ada: {contents(vecreal(1))}
DEN
2.14
DEN
2.14
Algol 68: **real**(vecreal[2])
PL/1, Ada: {contents(vecreal(2))}
DEN
3.14
DEN
Algol 68, Ada: pi
DEN
Algol 68: **real**(r)
PL/1, Ada: {contents(r)}
DEN
3.14
DEN
Algol 68: **real**(vecreal[3])
PL/1, Ada: {contents(vecreal(3))}
DEN
freal(r)

Figure 2.7.

```
real r:=3.14;
[1:3]real vecreal:= (1.14,2.14,3.14);
begin
    ...freal(r)...
end
```

Compare Figure 2.7 with Figure 2.2.

Example

```
bool ok=true;
bool b:=true;
[1:3]bool vecbool:=
    (false,true,true);
proc (ref bool)bool fbool=
    (ref bool x)bool:
        begin
            <declarations and statements>;
            x
        end co fbool co;
begin
    ...fbool(b)...
end
```

Compare Figure 2.8 with Figure 2.3.

Example

```
char token="c";
char c:="c";
[1:3]char vecchar:= ("a","b","c");
proc (ref char)char fchar=
    (ref char x)char:
        begin
            <declarations and statements>;
            x
        end co fchar co;
begin
    ...fchar(c)...
end
```

Compare Figure 2.9 with Figure 2.4.

In Algol 68, the enumeration type as defined in Pascal and Ada does not exist.

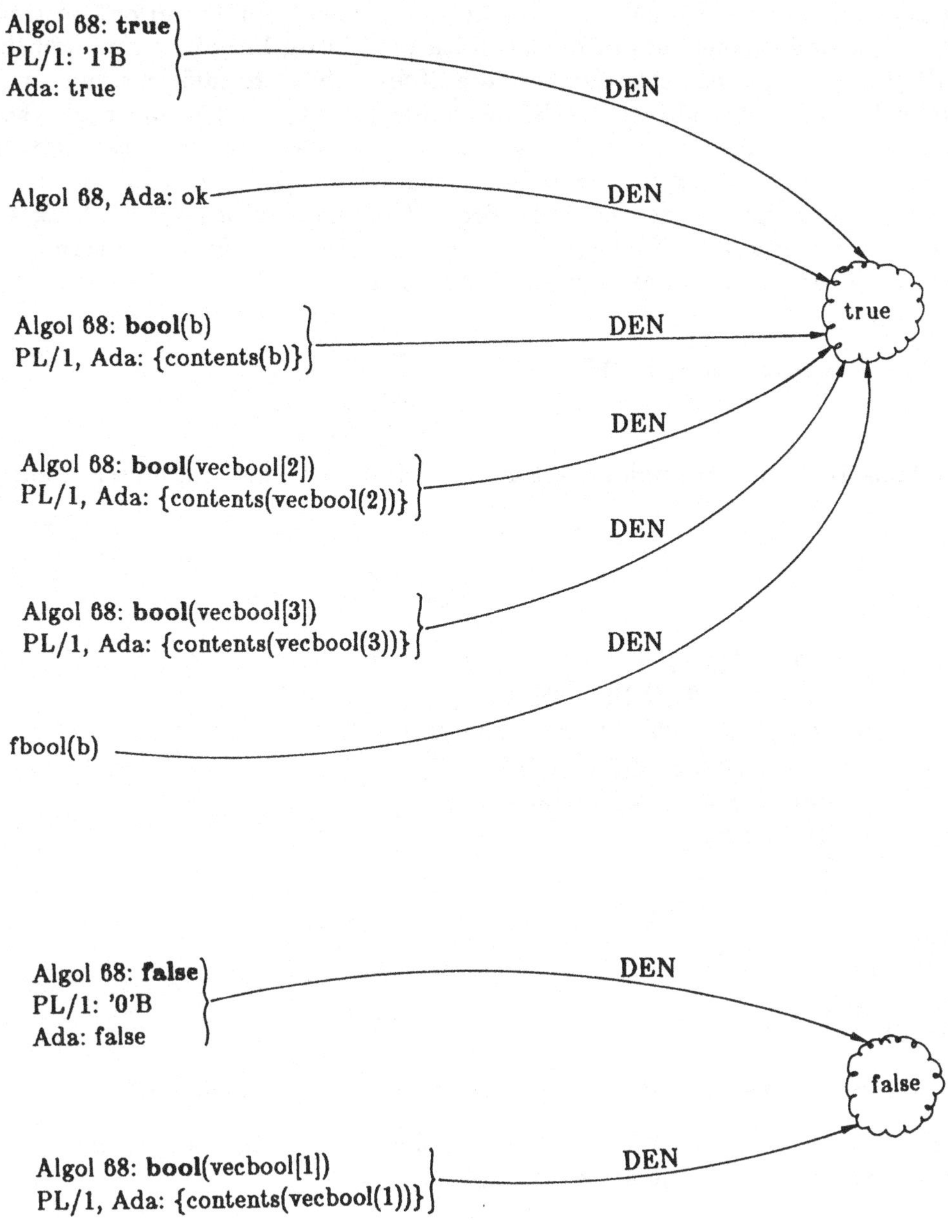

Algol 68: **true**
PL/1: '1'B
Ada: true
DEN
Algol 68, Ada: ok
DEN
true
Algol 68: **bool**(b)
PL/1, Ada: {contents(b)}
DEN
DEN
Algol 68: **bool**(vecbool[2])
PL/1, Ada: {contents(vecbool(2))}
DEN
Algol 68: **bool**(vecbool[3])
PL/1, Ada: {contents(vecbool(3))}
DEN
fbool(b)
Algol 68: **false**
PL/1: '0'B
Ada: false
DEN
false
Algol 68: **bool**(vecbool[1])
PL/1, Ada: {contents(vecbool(1))}
DEN

Figure 2.8.

For applications in which more bits are needed to handle an integer or a real value, Algol 68 allows atomic data of modes '**long int**', '**long long int**' etc., and '**long real**', '**long long real**', etc. Furthermore, if fewer bits are sufficient, one can use atomic data of modes '**short int**', '**short short int**' etc., and '**short real**', '**short short real**' etc. The number of bits (size) in each mode and also the maximum permitted number of **long**'s and **short**'s are implementation dependent. In Algol 68, the programmer has access to the size and the number of available **long**'s and **short**'s in his program. However, this does not greatly facilitate the transport of Algol 68 programs from one computer to another.

§2.4 Atomic data in PL/1

The following PL/1 examples are the literal translations of the Pascal examples in Section 2.2.

Example

```
DECLARE i BIN FIXED;
DECLARE vecint(1:3)BIN FIXED;
fint :  PROCEDURE(x)RETURNS(BIN FIXED);
            DECLARE x BIN FIXED;
            <declarations and statements>
            RETURN(x);
        END fint;
i=3;
vecint(1)=1;
vecint(2)=2;
vecint(3)=3;
...fint(i)...
```

See Figure 2.6. Notice that constant declarations do not exist in PL/1.

In PL/1, variable declarations may be combined with initialization parts. Thus, we may write in the above example

```
DECLARE i BIN FIXED INIT(3);

DECLARE vecint(1:3) BIN FIXED INIT(1,2,3);
```

In the following PL/1 examples, we shall use such initialization parts. The remark on the implicit contents operator in Pascal holds similarly for PL/1.

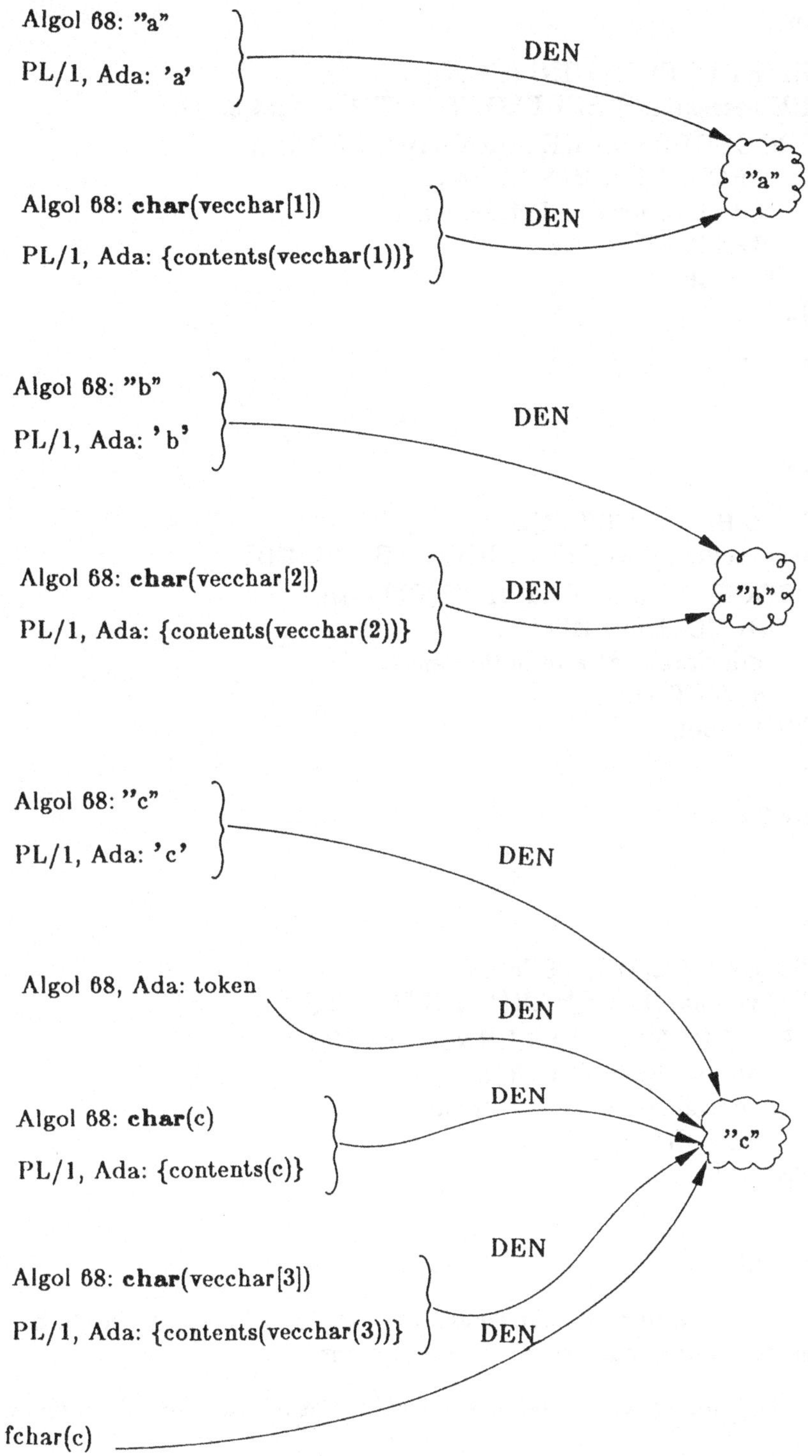
Algol 68: "a"
PL/1, Ada: 'a'
DEN
"a"
Algol 68: **char**(vecchar[1])
PL/1, Ada: {contents(vecchar(1))}
DEN
Algol 68: "b"
PL/1, Ada: 'b'
DEN
Algol 68: **char**(vecchar[2])
PL/1, Ada: {contents(vecchar(2))}
DEN
"b"
Algol 68: "c"
PL/1, Ada: 'c'
DEN
Algol 68, Ada: token
DEN
DEN
Algol 68: **char**(c)
PL/1, Ada: {contents(c)}
"c"
DEN
Algol 68: **char**(vecchar[3])
PL/1, Ada: {contents(vecchar(3))}
DEN
fchar(c)

Figure 2.9.

Example

```
DECLARE r BIN FLOAT INIT(3.14);
DECLARE vecreal(1:3) BIN FLOAT INIT(1.14,2.14,3.14);
freal : PROCEDURE(x) RETURNS(BIN FLOAT);
          DECLARE x BIN FLOAT;
          <declarations and statements>
          RETURN(x);
        END freal;
...freal(r)...
```

See Figure 2.7.

Example

```
DECLARE b BIT(1) INIT('1'B);
DECLARE vecbool(1:3) BIT(1) INIT('0'B,'1'B,'1'B);
fbool : PROCEDURE(x) RETURNS(BIT(1));
          DECLARE x BIT(1);
          <declarations and statements>
          RETURN(x);
        END fbool;
...fbool(b)...
```

See Figure 2.8.

Example

```
DECLARE c CHAR(1) INIT('c');
DECLARE vecchar(1:3) CHAR(1) INIT('a','b','c');
fchar : PROCEDURE(x) RETURNS(CHAR(1));
          DECLARE x CHAR(1);
          <declarations and statements>
          RETURN(x);
        END fchar;
...fchar(c)...
```

See Figure 2.9.

In PL/1, boolean values and characters are considered respectively to be bit strings and character strings consisting of one element.

In PL/1, the enumeration type as defined in Pascal and Ada does not exist.

Constant declarations can be simulated in PL/1 by means of preprocessor statements and declarations. Notice that this involves a textual replacement of the identifier by the corresponding constant throughout the program before compile time.

Examples

```
% DECLARE a FIXED;
% a=3;

% DECLARE pi FLOAT;
% pi=3.14;

% DECLARE token CHAR;
% token='c';
```

§2.5 Atomic data in Ada

The following Ada examples are the literal translations of the Pascal examples in Section 2.2.

Example

```
a:constant integer:=3;
i:integer;
vecint:array(1..3) of integer;
function fint(x:integer) return integer is
    <declarations>
    begin
        <statements>
        return x;
    end fint;
begin
    i:=3;
    vecint(1):=1;
    vecint(2):=2;
    vecint(3):=3; - - one may also write 'vecint:=(1,2,3)';
    ...fint(i)...
end
```

See Figure 2.6.

Example

```
pi:constant float:=3.14;
r:float:=3.14;
vecreal:array(1..3) of float:=(1.14,2.14,3.14);
function freal(x:float) return float is
    <declarations>
    begin
        <statements>
        return x;
    end freal;
begin
    ...freal(r)...
end
```

In this example, the initializations of 'r' and 'vecreal' are performed within the variable declarations.

See Figure 2.7.

Example

```
ok:constant boolean:=true;
b:boolean:=true;
vecbool:array(1..3) of boolean:=(false,true,true);
function fbool(x:boolean) return boolean is
    <declarations>
    begin
        <statements>
        return x;
    end fbool;
begin
    ...fbool(b)...
end
```

See Figure 2.8.

Example

```
token:constant character:='c';
c:character:='c';
vecchar:array(1..3) of character:=('a','b','c');
function fchar(x:character) return character is
    <declarations>
    begin
        <statements>
        return x;
    end fchar;
begin
    ...fchar(c)...
end
```

See Figure 2.9.

Example

```
type color is (blue,indigo,purple,lilac);
i:color;
veccolor:array(color) of color:=(indigo,blue,lilac,purple);
function fcolor(x:in color) return color is
    <declarations>
    begin
        <statements>
        return x;
    end fcolor;
begin
    i:=indigo;
    ...fcolor(i)...
end
```

The corresponding value diagram is as in Figure 2.5, with the square brackets in the indexing of the array "veccolor" replaced by round ones for Ada.

§2.6 Configurations

Later on, more precisely in Chapter 6, we will study the call of routine values, representing function calls, procedure calls, statements and declarations. The effect of a call of a routine value is a change in the state of the program.

A *configuration* (also called a state) of a program is a snapshot at a particular moment during the execution of the program. This snapshot contains all the information that would be necessary to halt the execution of the program at that particular moment and to restart it later on. The set of all possible configurations is denoted by CONF.

Throughout this book we will gradually define the notion of a configuration. Finally, in Section 9.5, we will give the precise definition. We will explain in Chapter 6 how the call of a routine value can change the configuration of a program. In Section 6.9 it is indicated that the execution of a statement and even the elaboration of a declaration are special cases of a call of a routine value, and hence they also induce a change in the configuration.

For the time being, a configuration consists only of the set of atomic data. In most programming languages, most of the atomic data are language defined. In some cases, atomic data can also be created by elaborating declarations and deleted by leaving specific program units. Examples of atomic data created in this way are data defined by enumeration types in Pascal and Ada.

Chapter 3

ATOMIC LOCATIONS

§3.1 Concept

The *atomic locations* are those values on which only the *contents function* CONT is defined. Hence neither the *selection function* SEL, nor the *result function* RES is defined on atomic locations.

An atomic location is an atomic value representing an indivisible part of memory, which in turn contains another value. The term *memory* must be interpreted in a broad sense here. It may be a sheet of paper, a computer memory or a blackboard. In SMALL, locations themselves are considered to be values. They can be processed like any other value, they can be transmitted as actual parameters to a routine value, they can result from the evaluation of a routine value, they can be components of a composite value and they can be stored as the contents of another location.

The contents function determines for each atomic location the value it contains. The contents of atomic locations can be atomic values (A), or composite locations (CL), but **not** composite data (CD). The reason for this restriction is discussed in detail in Chapter 7. The contents function is a mapping of the form

$$\text{CONT} : \text{AL} \rightarrow \text{V - CD}$$

Atomic locations must be denoted by means of expressions. This association is described by the *denotation function* DEN. In order to make the distinction between atomic locations (which are internal objects) and the expressions (which are external objects) denoting them, atomic locations are represented in SMALL by Greek letters.

There now follow a few definitions that are frequently used in the study of programming languages. Note however, that these definitions are not a part of SMALL.

In Pascal, Algol 68, PL/1 and Ada, the creation of atomic locations is either *static* or *dynamic*. *Static creation* of an atomic location means that the location is created by means of a variable declaration. Within a given program unit, excluding all inner program units, the number of such locations created in that unit is static, i.e. it is always known at compile time. *Dynamic creation* of an atomic location means that the location is created by means of a specific statement which can be executed dynamically. The number of such locations created within a given program unit is dynamic, i.e. in general it is only known at run time.

At this stage, we are able to describe only two kinds of relationships : the *contents function* CONT and the *denotation function* DEN. Notice that there also exist *type constraints* defining a relationship between the type of an atomic location and the type of its contents. In the following examples, the types of the expressions denoting the atomic values are not yet included in the value-diagrams. This will be done in Chapter 9.

The basic building blocks of structured programs in languages such as Pascal, Algol 68, PL/1 and Ada will be called *program units*.

Examples of program units are begin-end blocks, procedure and function blocks (termed subroutines and functions in PL/1, and subprograms in Ada), and Ada packages. A program unit consists of *declarations* and *statements*. A declaration in a program unit is said to be *local* to that program unit. The declaration establishes the name-value association by means of the function DEN.

The *scope of a declaration* of a name is the region of text over which the name-value association holds. In programming languages such as Pascal, PL/1, Algol 68 and Ada, the definition of the scope of a declaration of a name is based on the notion of program unit. With only a few exceptions, the scope of a declaration of a name effectively starts with its declaration and terminates at the end of the program unit to which the declaration is local.

Scopes of different declarations of the same name may overlap. This is the case when program units are nested and when names are overloaded, as will be explained later. A name-value association is said to be *visible* at a given point in the program text when an occurrence of the name at that point can refer to the value with which it is associated. Some suitable context may be required to realize this visibility. This will be explained in due course. The scope of name-value associations in a given programming language is defined by means of the ***visibility rules*** of the language.

The *scope of a value* is the program text determining the lifetime of that value. This means that during execution of this text the value exists, but elsewhere it does not exist. The scope of values will play an important role in the use of locations and routine values.

Any external (identifier) or internal access to a location whose storage space has already been released or whose storage space (or part of it) has been (unintentionally) reserved for other purposes, is considered a *dangling reference*. Notice that our definition of dangling reference is slightly more general than the one given in [Welsh 1977]. Dangling references can occur through absence of dynamic type checking, deallocation of locations, differences in lifetime of locations, overlays of locations, array locations with flexible length and uninitialized locations.

A completely safe solution would be to verify that the scope of a location will always be equal to or included in the scope of its contents. This verification, however, would complicate the run time organization of a compiler and would cause a significant overhead due to the additional run time checks. Dangling references will be discussed for each of the languages Pascal, Algol 68, PL/1 and Ada.

The notions of value scope and declaration scope are often confused. Consider a variable declaration associating the location α with a name x. The program unit defining the scope of the location α and the one determining the scope of the α-x association can be different.

§3.2 Atomic locations in Pascal

3.2.1 Static creation

Example

```
var x:integer;
begin
    x:=0;
    ...
end
```

The elaboration of the above piece of program consists of three steps :

(1) An atomic location, say α, is created statically. Its scope is the program unit to which the variable declaration is local.

(2) The name 'x' is associated with the atomic location α, so that

$$\text{DEN.x} = \alpha$$

Steps (1) and (2) are the result of the execution of the variable declaration '**var** x:integer'.

(3) The value denoted by the name '0' is stored as the contents of the atomic location α, so that

$$\text{CONT.}\alpha = \text{DEN.0}$$

The variable declaration in fact also causes a type to be associated with the name 'x'. For the moment, types are not included in the value diagrams. They will be introduced in Chapter 9.

We should observe that the three steps above actually represent transitions. Transitions and configurations are discussed in detail in Chapter 6.

In most programming languages, a name denoting a location is written as a sequence of letters and digits with the first element being a letter. Such a name is then called an *identifier.*

The value diagram, describing the situation after execution of steps (1), (2) and (3), is shown in Figure 3.1.

3.2.2 Dynamic creation

Example

```
var p:↑ integer;
begin
    new(p);
    p↑:=0;
    ...
end
```

The elaboration of the above piece of program consists of six steps :

(1) An atomic location, say ω, is created statically. Its scope is the program unit to which the variable declaration is local.

(2) The name 'p' is associated with the location ω so that

$$\text{DEN.p} = \omega$$

Steps (1) and (2) are the result of the execution of the variable declaration '**var** p:↑ integer'.

(3) An atomic location, say α, is created dynamically. Its lifetime is the whole program, unless it is explicitly freed during the program.

(4) The atomic location α is stored as the contents of ω, so that

$$\text{CONT}.\omega = \alpha$$

(5) The compound expression 'p↑', where '↑' is the contents operator, now denotes α. Hence we have

$$\text{DEN.p}\uparrow = \alpha$$

Steps (3), (4) and (5) are the result of the execution of the statement 'new(p)'.

(6) The value denoted by the name '0' is stored as the contents of α, so that we have

$$\text{CONT}.\alpha = \text{DEN.0}$$

Types are associated with each of the expressions as explained in Chapter 9.

The situation after execution of the six steps, is described by the value diagram in Figure 3.2.

Note that with the notation of Section 2.2 we can now write DEN.{contents(i)} as

CONT.DEN.i

and DEN.{contents(vecint[3])} as

CONT.DEN(vecint[3])

In Pascal, atomic locations may contain atomic data, atomic locations and composite locations. In contrast to Algol 68 and PL/1, however, Pascal and Ada do not allow atomic locations to contain either statically created locations or routine values(see Chapter 7). In none of the four languages may transition be contained in atomic locations.

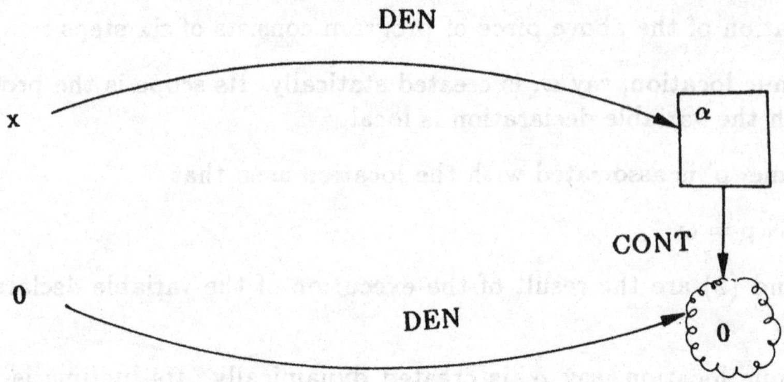

Figure 3.1.

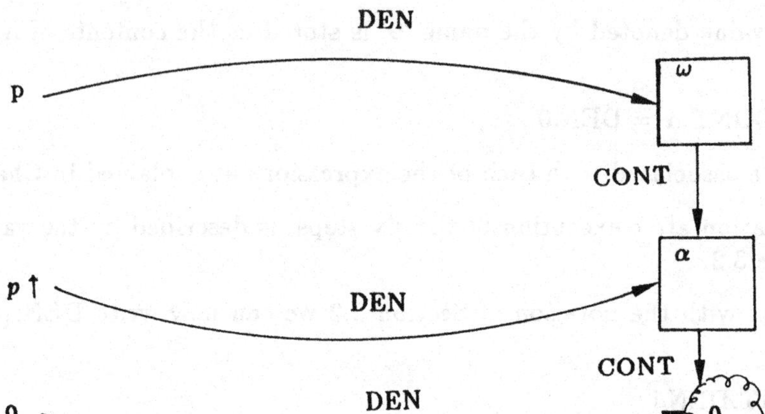

Figure 3.2.

Dangling references

There are two possible sources of dangling references in Pascal: the dispose statement and the record with variant fields. In Pascal, dynamically created locations can be freed on explicit request of the programmer by means of the dispose statement, as illustrated by the following example:

Example

```
var p:↑integer;
begin
    new(p);
    p↑:=0;
    ...
    dispose(p);
    ...p... {p denotes a location containing a dangling reference}
end
```

Records with variant fields are discussed in Section 9.7.1. The following example of dangling references arising from this construct is discussed in Chapter 10.

Example

```
type dangling =
    record
        case tag : (int, ref) of
            int : (i : integer);
            ref : (ptr : ↑ integer)
    end;
var x : dangling;
begin
    x.i := 100;
    ... x.ptr↑ ...{the access 'x.ptr↑' is a dangling reference}
end
```

§3.3 Atomic locations in Algol 68

3.3.1 Static creation

The following example is a literal translation of the Pascal example in Section 3.2.1.

Example

```
ref int x=loc int;
x:=0;
...
```

The elaboration of the above piece of program consists of the three steps described in Section 3.2.1. An attractive aspect of Algol 68 is that the creation of the atomic location is explicitly stated by means of the so-called generator '**loc int**', which means that an atomic location is created (to hold an integer value) with a scope which is the smallest program unit enclosing the generator.

In Algol 68, the variable declaration has the format

ref <mode> <identifier>=**loc** <amode>

The symbols <mode> and <amode> represent modes; <amode> can differ from <mode> in that <amode> may contain array bounds.

Variable declarations of the above format can always be contracted into

<mode> <identifier>

Contractions of this kind have been introduced for reasons of economic use of symbols. Especially when <mode> is a large expression, writing it only once reduces the probability of typing errors.

Contraction of variable declarations has been introduced on demand of the Algol 60 people, which asked for an analogous notation for their variable declarations. Note, however, that contracted declarations have turned out to be an important source of confusion for novice Algol 68 programmers, because of the existence of an implicit **ref**. For example, the identifier 'x' in the variable declaration '**int** x := 0', is of type **ref int**, whereas 'x' in the constant declaration **int** x = 0 is of type **int**.
The authors prefer the uncontracted form of variable declarations, because it nicely reflects the underlying programming concepts. The only reason why contractions of variable declarations are used in the examples is to make the reader familiar with them, as most textbooks on Algol 68 use these contracted forms.

In our example,

```
ref int x=loc int;
```

may be contracted to

```
int x;
```

Algol 68 also allows the initialization of a variable to be combined with its declaration, thus we have :

```
ref int x=loc int:=0;
```

or in contracted form

```
int x:=0;
```

The situation after elaboration of the example is as shown in Figure 3.1.

3.3.2 Dynamic creation

The following example is a literal translation of the first Pascal example in Section 3.2.2.

Example

```
ref ref int p=loc ref int;
p:=heap int;
ref int(p):=0;
...
```

The elaboration of the above piece of text consists of the six steps described in Section 3.2.2, with 'p↑' replaced by '**ref int**(p)'.

If we use the contracted and initialized forms of the variable declarations explained in Section 3.3.1, then we have the following possible combinations :

Examples

```
ref int p:=heap int:=0;
```

```
ref int p;
p:=heap int:=0;
```

```
ref int p:=heap int;
ref int(p):=0;
```

The situation after elaboration is described by the value diagram in Figure 3.3. Algol 68 also permits atomic locations to contain statically created locations:

Example

```
ref int x=loc int;
ref ref int p=loc ref int;
x:=0;
p:=x;
...
```

Other possible versions of the above example are:

Examples

```
ref int x=loc int:=0;
ref ref int p=loc ref int:=x;

int x:=0;
ref int p:=x;

int x;
ref int p;
x:=0;
p:=x;
```

Dangling references

Algol 68, in contast to PL/1 (see section 3.4), explicitly requires that the scope of the value of the right hand side of an assignment is equal to or includes the scope of the value of its left hand side. This (value) scope constraint avoids the situation of having access to some storage that has already been released. However, scope checking of values complicates the run time organization of Algol 68 compilers and represents a serious overhead in pointer handling.

The following examples illustrate the use of locations with different scopes.

Example

```
begin
    ref ref int p=loc ref int:=nil;
    begin
        ref int x=loc int:=0;
```

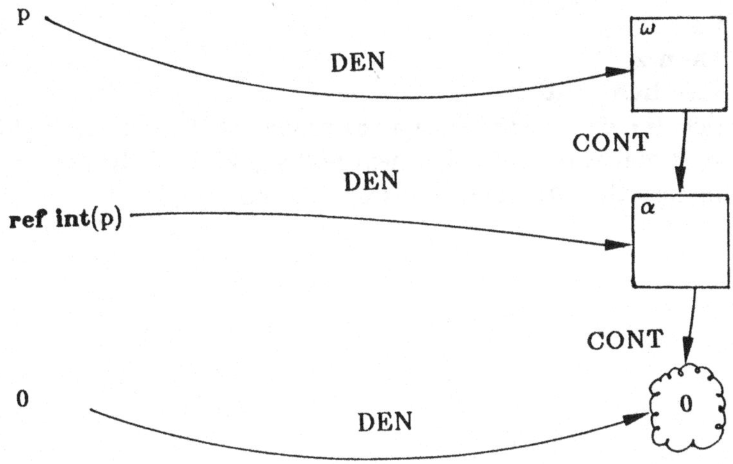

Figure 3.3.

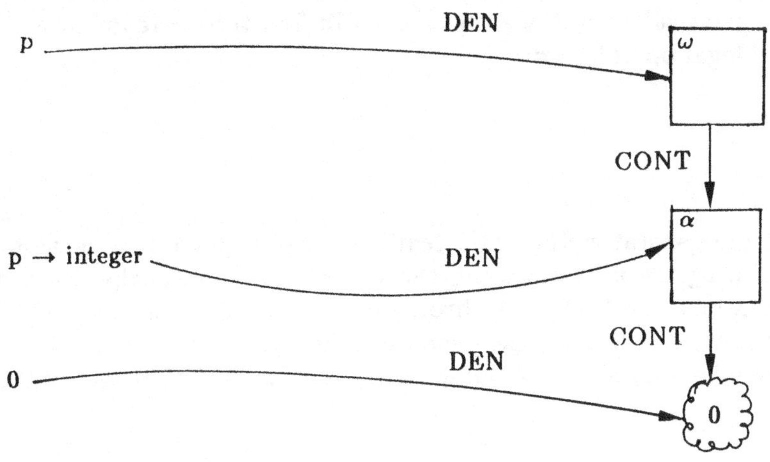

Figure 3.4.

```
        p:= if ...
                then x
                else heap int
              fi; co the dynamic check on the scopes of the left and right
                part values of the assignment will signal a run time error
                in case the then clause is executed co
    end;
    ...
end
```

Example

```
begin
    ...
    begin
        ref ref int p=loc ref int:=nil;
        ref int x=loc int:=0;
        ...
        p:= if ...
                then x
                else heap int
              fi; co the dynamic check on the scopes of the left and right
                part values of the assignment will find this assignment a
                legal operation co
        ...
    end
    ...
end
```

Notice that the generator '**loc int**' creates a location with a value scope which is the smallest program unit enclosing the generator, whereas the generator '**heap int**' creates a location that lives throughout the whole program. In the light of the orthogonality of Algol 68, the generators '**loc int**' and '**heap int**' can be used at any place where a location holding an integer is allowed by the context.

Example

```
ref int ptr; co 'ptr' is of type 'ref ref int' co
proc p = void :
    begin
        int i;
```

```
        ptr:=i;
            co this is an illegal assignment; a run time error is produced
              to ensure that the location denoted by 'ptr' cannot survive
              its contents, i.e., the location denoted by 'i' co
    end co p co;
p;
...ref int(prt) ...
```

§3.4 Atomic locations in PL/1

The definition of static and dynamic creation of locations must not be confused with the PL/1 definitions of static and dynamic allocation. In PL/1 terminology, allocation of a location for a given variable may take place statically, in which case it is allocated before execution of the program and remains allocated for the duration of the program.

3.4.1 Static creation

The following example is a literal translation of the Pascal example in Section 3.2.1.

Example

```
DECLARE x BIN FIXED;
x=0;
...
```

The elaboration of the above piece of program consists of the three steps described in Section 3.2.1.

PL/1 allows the programmer to combine the variable declaration with an initialization part. The example then becomes :

```
DECLARE x BIN FIXED INIT(0);
```

The situation after elaboration of the example is as shown in Figure 3.1.

In PL/1, the variable declaration

```
DECLARE x BIN FIXED;
```

has the default attribute *automatic*. Actually the declaration stands for

```
DECLARE x BIN FIXED AUTOMATIC;
```

This means that static creation of locations by means of variable declarations (as in Pascal, Algol 68 and Ada) corresponds to the PL/1 storage class AUTOMATIC. On the other hand, the PL/1 variable declaration

```
DECLARE x BIN FIXED STATIC;
```

would mean that storage is allocated before execution of the program and remains allocated throughout the duration of the program.

3.4.2 Dynamic creation

The following example is a literal translation of the first Pascal example in Section 3.2.2.

Example

```
DECLARE p POINTER;
DECLARE integer BIN FIXED BASED;
ALLOCATE integer SET(p);
p→integer=0;
...
```

The elaboration of the above piece of program consists of the six steps described in Section 3.2.2, with 'p↑' replaced by 'p→integer'. The atomic location α is created dynamically and stored within ω by means of the PL/1 allocate statement 'ALLOCATE integer SET(p)'. As we will see later, the name 'integer' plays the role of a type identifier. In PL/1 terminology, 'integer' is called a based variable. The storage class is termed BASED.

The situation after elaboration is described by the value diagram in Figure 3.4.

As in Algol 68, PL/1 also permits atomic locations to contain statically created atomic locations. The following example is a literal translation of the corresponding Algol 68 example in Section 3.3.2.

Example

```
DECLARE x BIN FIXED;
DECLARE p POINTER;
x=0;
p=ADDR(x);
...
```

Dangling references

Unlike Algol 68, PL/1 does not say a word about scope checking of locations and their contents. In PL/1 compilers, the situation in which the scope of the location on the right hand side of an assignment is enclosed by the scope of the location on the left hand side is not detected. This is illustrated by the following example:

Example

```
DECLARE p POINTER;
...
    DO;
        DECLARE x BIN FIXED INIT(0);
        ...
        p=ADDR(x);
        ...
    END;
...p... /*the location denoted by 'p' contains a dangling reference*/
```

Another possible source of dangling references in PL/1 is the FREE statement, whereby locations are freed explicitly by the programmer. The freeing of a location which is still accessible by a name or by other locations is not detected by PL/1 compilers. A dangling reference created in this way, is illustrated in the following example:

Example

```
DECLARE
    p POINTER,
    integer BIN FIXED BASED;
...
ALLOCATE integer SET(p);
...
p→integer=0;
...
FREE p→integer;
...p... /*'p' denotes a location that contains a dangling reference*/.
```

In PL/1, dangling references may also arise from the use of other features, such as the DEFINED feature and separate compilation.

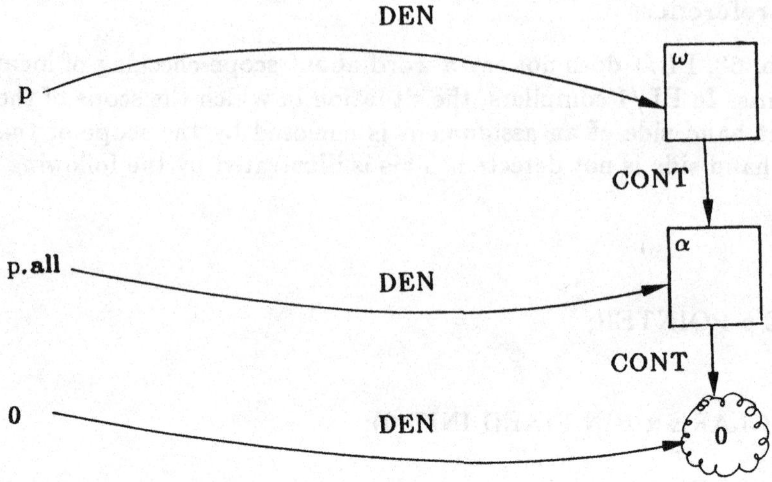

Figure 3.5.

§3.5 Atomic locations in Ada

3.5.1 Static creation

Example

```
x:integer;
begin
    x:=0;
    ...
end
```

This is a literal translation of the Pascal example in Section 3.2.1. Ada allows the initialization of the variable to be combined with its declaration as follows :

```
    x:integer:=0;
```

Once again, Figure 3.1 gives the corresponding value diagram.

3.5.2 Dynamic creation

Example

```
type pointertype is access integer;
p:pointertype;
begin
    p:=new integer;
    p.all:=0;
    ...
end
```

This is a literal translation of the first Pascal example in Section 3.2.2. The situation is described by the value diagram in Figure 3.5.

In contrast to Algol 68 and PL/1, atomic locations in Ada cannot contain statically created locations or routine values.

Dangling references

In Ada, there is no language defined deallocation instruction as in Pascal and PL/1. However, the programmer is able to define a deallocation procedure by making an instantiation of a language defined generic procedure 'unchecked-deallocation'. Its specification is:

```
generic
    type object is limited private;
    type name is access object;
    procedure unchecked-deallocation (x : in out name);
```

By making instances of this generic procedure, one can create special instructions to release dynamically created locations of a particular type.

By means of the generic parameters 'object' and 'name', the deallocation procedure can be tuned to a given type of location and to a given type of location variable. This technique allows the programmer to make the definition of the deallocation process local to a program unit so that dangling references can be turned off by simply suppressing the generic instantiation. This facility seems to be very important in the context of software maintenance.

```
declare
    type cell;
    type list is access cell;
    type cell is
        record
            atom : integer;
            next : list;
        end record;

    procedure free is
        new unchecked-deallocation (cell,list);

    ptr : list;
    ptr:=new cell'(0,null);
begin
    free(ptr);
    ...ptr.next ...
        {the access 'ptr.next' is a dangling reference}
end
```

In the absence of instances of the generic procedure 'unchecked-deallocation', there is no problem of dangling reference due to explicit freeing of storage or assignment of a location to another location with different value scope.

§3.6 Configurations

Two new concepts were introduced in this chapter : the set of atomic locations AL and the function CONT. We add them to the definition of a configuration. Hence, for the time being, a configuration is a triple (AD,AL,CONT). Initially, i.e., before elaboration of the declarations, the set AL is empty, at least in the four languages considered here, since in these languages no atomic locations are predefined. Atomic locations are created and added to AL by declarations of variables or by allocate statements, such as 'new' in Pascal and 'ALLOCATE' in PL/1. They are deleted from AL by leaving the scope of the locations or by deallocation statements, such as 'dispose' in Pascal and 'FREE' in PL/1.

Chapter 4

COMPOSITE DATA

§4.1 Concept

Composite data are those values on which only the *selection function* SEL is defined. Hence neither the *contents function* CONT, nor the *result function* RES is defined here.

A composite datum is a set of pairs, each pair consisting of a *selector* and a *component.*

Selectors are values used to select components from the composite datum; this will be expressed by the *selection function.* In SMALL, selectors are atomic data (AD). Components of composite data may be atomic values (A) or in turn composite values (C). As a result of this recursive definition of composite data, each composite datum has a hierarchical structure, or *data structure*, which can be represented in the form of a labeled tree, as in Figure 4.1. Such a data structure may have several *levels.* The label of each branch represents the selector and the label of the node at the end of the branch represents the corresponding component. Nonterminal nodes in the data structure correspond to composite values, whereas terminal nodes correspond to atomic values, i.e., values which cannot be decomposed any further.

The root A of the labelled tree in Figure 4.1. represents a composite datum with three components, a, B and C, having the selectors SEL_a, SEL_B and SEL_C respectively. The components B and C are themselves composite data. B is a composite datum with three components, b, c and d, having selectors SEL_b, SEL_c, SEL_d, and C is a composite datum with two components, e and f, having selectors SEL_e and SEL_f respectively. The relationship between a composite datum and its components is specified by the selection function. This function has two arguments; the first is a composite datum, and the second is a selector.

The selection function for composite data is a mapping of the form

$$SEL : CD \times AD \rightarrow V$$

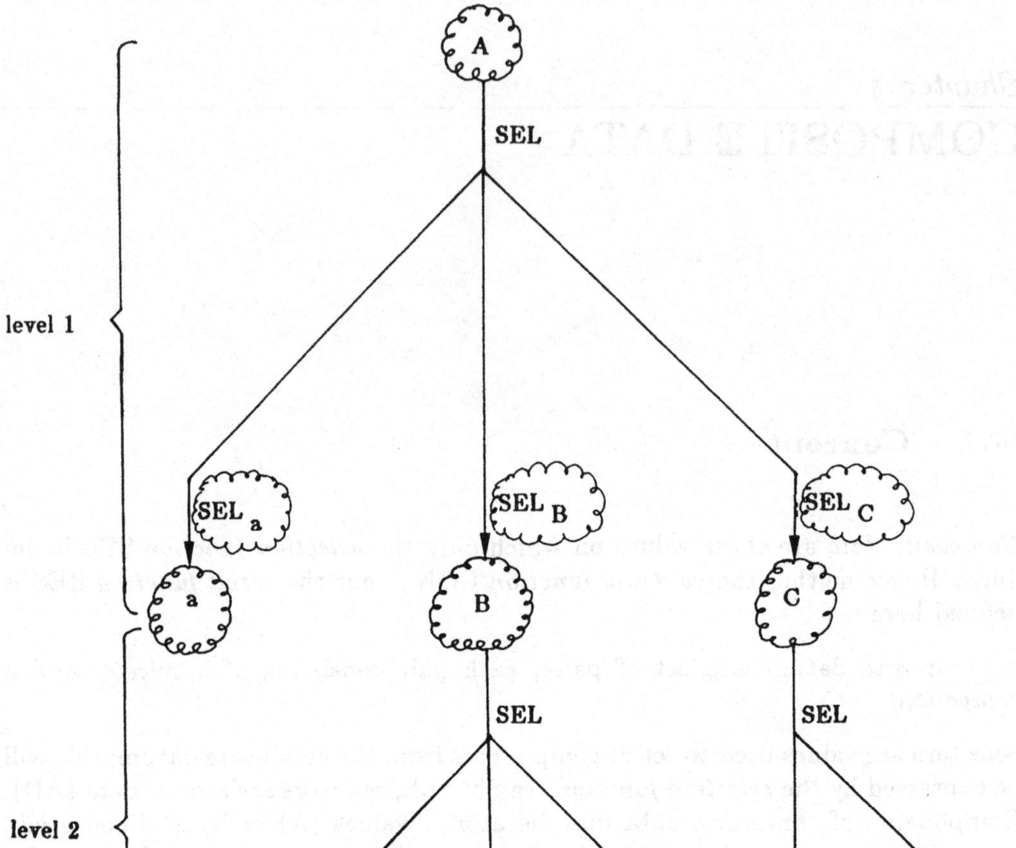
A
SEL
level 1
SEL a
SEL B
SEL C
a
B
C
SEL
SEL
level 2
SEL b
SEL c
SEL d
SEL e
SEL f
b
c
d
e
f

Figure 4.1.

Selection in a composite datum having a given data structure is performed by following a path in the data structure from the root to the leaves by scanning the selectors in a given order. The selection function associates with its arguments the component value determined by the specified selector.

As an illustration, consider the composite datum A, which consists of two composite data B and C with selectors DEN.1 and DEN.2 respectively. The composite datum B consists of three atomic data DEN.10, DEN.20 and DEN.30 with selectors DEN.1, DEN.2 and DEN.3 respectively, whereas the composite datum C consists of the atomic data DEN.40, DEN.50 and DEN.60 with selectors DEN.1, DEN.2 and DEN.3 respectively. The data structure of the composite datum A is shown in Figure 4.2, where the selected path for SEL(SEL(A,DEN.1),DEN.3) = DEN.30 is indicated.

Note that there is also a relationship between the type of the composite datum and the type of its components. This point is covered in Chapter 9.

A composite datum must not be confused with the name denoting it, since the former is an internal object whereas the latter is an external object. There is also a fundamental difference between a composite datum and a composite location. This will become clear in Chapter 5.

In most programming languages, composite data are divided into two classes: *array data* and *record data*. In general, components of array data are called *elements*, whereas components of record data are called *fields*. An important difference between array data and record data is that selection in array data is dynamic, i.e. a selector of an array datum is an atomic value denoted by some expression that calculates it, whereas selection in record data is static, i.e. the selectors can only be names whose values cannot be calculated. Another difference between array data and record data is related to the types of the components. Components of array data must be of the same type, whereas components of record data may have different types. Types are discussed in detail in Chapter 9.

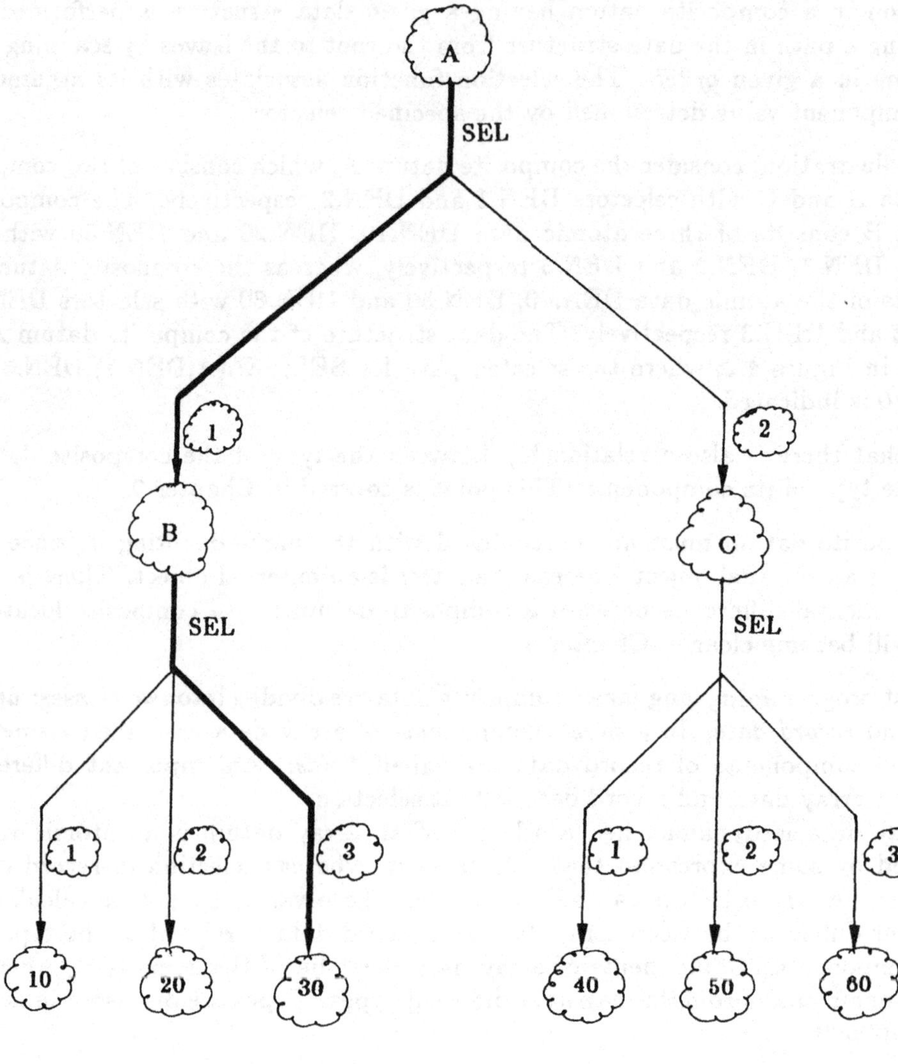

Figure 4.2.

§4.2 Array data in Pascal

Example

var matrix:**array**[1..2,1..3] **of** integer;
begin
    matrix[1,1]:=10; matrix[2,1]:=40;
    matrix[1,2]:=20; matrix[2,2]:=50;
    matrix[1,3]:=30; matrix[2,3]:=60;
    ...
end

After elaboration of the assignment statements, we have built an array datum as the contents of the array variable 'matrix'. This array datum will be denoted by {contents(matrix)} .

We have

SEL(SEL(DEN.{contents(matrix)},DEN.1),DEN.1) = DEN.10
SEL(SEL(DEN.{contents(matrix)},DEN.1),DEN.2) = DEN.20
SEL(SEL(DEN.{contents(matrix)},DEN.1),DEN.3) = DEN.30
SEL(SEL(DEN.{contents(matrix)},DEN.2),DEN.1) = DEN.40
SEL(SEL(DEN.{contents(matrix)},DEN.2),DEN.2) = DEN.50
SEL(SEL(DEN.{contents(matrix)},DEN.2),DEN.3) = DEN.60

The value diagram describing this situation is shown in Figure 4.3.

In Pascal, array data cannot be denoted directly as in Algol 68. As we will see in Chapter 5, 'matrix' denotes a composite location, the contents of which is an array datum. The array datum is denoted by the expression {contents (matrix)}, consisting of the contents operator and the operand 'matrix'. As we stated in section 2.2, there is no way in Pascal to express this contents operator explicitly, and it can only be expressed implicitly by the context. In the value diagrams of SMALL, we shall write {contents(matrix)} to denote the array datum in Pascal, although this is not a legal Pascal expression.

The selection of subarray data from array data is called *trimming*. Pascal allows a restricted form of trimming, as illustrated by the following example.

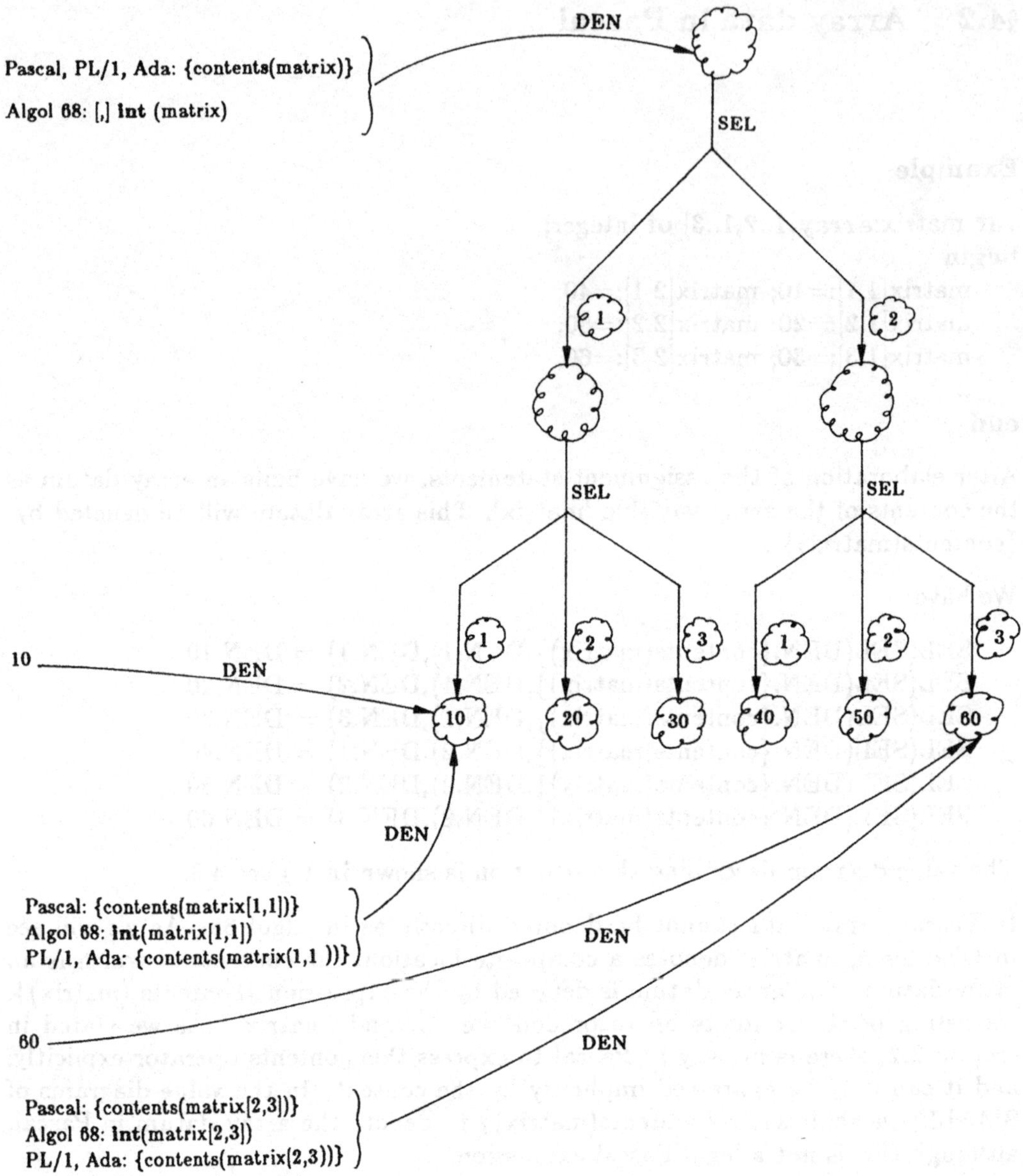
DEN
Pascal, PL/1, Ada: {contents(matrix)}
Algol 68: [,] int (matrix)
SEL
1
2
SEL
SEL
1
2
3
1
2
3
10
DEN
10
20
30
40
50
60
DEN
Pascal: {contents(matrix[1,1])}
Algol 68: int(matrix[1,1])
PL/1, Ada: {contents(matrix(1,1))}
DEN
60
DEN
Pascal: {contents(matrix[2,3])}
Algol 68: int(matrix[2,3])
PL/1, Ada: {contents(matrix(2,3))}

Figure 4.3.

Example

var matrix:**array**[1..2,1..3] **of** integer;
begin
    ...matrix[1]...
    ...matrix[2]...
end

Pascal allows the selection of subarray data from the array data {contents(matrix)} by writing {contents(matrix[1])} and {contents(matrix[2])} . This stems from the fact that in Pascal, the array type denoted by

array[1..2,1..3] **of** integer

can also be written as

array[1..2] **of array**[1..3] **of** integer.

Array data with dynamic length

A serious restriction in Pascal is that the number of elements of an array datum is static, i.e., known at compile time. This limitation stems from the fact that lower and upper bounds in index types of array types can only be denoted by constants.

Character string data

A special kind of array data in Pascal is character string data. The type for character strings in Pascal is expressed by ' **packed array** [T] **of** char', where T is a subrange type. Character string data possess additional properties not shared by other array data. These properties have to do with text files, relational operations and the pack-unpack operations for selecting individual components. The use of character strings is illustrated by the example below. Because of the lack of string locations with flexible length (see Algol 68 and PL/1), character string handling in Pascal is not an easy job. Character string constants are written as sequences of characters enclosed in single quotes.

Example

```
var i:integer;
    text_7:packed array[1..7] of char;
    vecchar:array[1..7] of char;
begin
    read(i);
    if i=1
        then text_7:='ok     '
        else text_7:='not ok ';
    write(text_7);
    ...
    vecchar:=unpack(text_7);
    vecchar[7]:='.';
    text_7:=pack(vecchar);
    write(text_7);
    ...
end
```

There is no semantics associated with packing, so the compiler writer is free to treat packed arrays as being identical to unpacked arrays. On the other hand, the compiler writer is free to store packed arrays of booleans (characters) within a simple machine word if the packed arrays are of the appropriate length. This means that although Pascal programs are portable as far as packed arrays are concerned, programs using packed arrays might run more efficiently on one machine than on another.

§4.3 Array data in Algol 68

The following example is a literal translation of the first Pascal example in Section 4.2.

Example

```
[1:2,1:3]int matrix;
matrix[1,1]:=10; matrix[2,1]:=40;
matrix[1,2]:=20; matrix[2,2]:=50;
matrix[1,3]:=30; matrix[2,3]:=60;
...
```

The array datum is denoted by an expression of the form '[,]**int**(matrix)'. Its data structure is as shown in Figure 4.2.

Algol 68 provides a means of constructing array data directly from its component values. This contruction will be called an ***array display*** (the Algol 68 term is ***row display***). The above example can then be rephrased as

[1:2,1:3]**int** matrix:=((10,20,30), (40,50,60));

The array display '((10,20,30), (40,50,60))' in the context of the type '[,]**int**' represents a two-dimensional array datum of integers. The value diagram for the Algol 68 program is shown in Figure 4.3.

In Algol 68, the contents operator corresponding to dereferencing can be written explicitly. The expression '[,]**int**(matrix)' specifies that the location denoted by 'matrix' must be dereferenced. 'matrix' is of type '**ref**[,]**int**' as we will see later.

In Algol 68, the array display

[,]**int**(((10,20,30), (40,50,60)))

can simply be written as

((10,20,30), (40,50,60))

in cases where the context of '[,]**int**' is strong enough.

Furthermore, it is possible to use array displays in constant declarations, such as

[,]**int** constmatrix=((10,20,30), (40,50,60));

Then we have

DEN.constmatrix = DEN.((10,20,30), (40,50,60))

Notice the difference between the denotations of 'constmatrix' and 'matrix'. Note further that DEN.((10,20,30),(40,50,60)) is language defined, while DEN. constmatrix is program defined.

Algol 68 permits the selection of subarray data of array data through a feature called *trimming*. By means of trimming a new array datum can be constructed out of the components of an old array datum.

Example

[,] **int** constmatrix=((10,20,30), (40,50,60));
...constmatrix [1:2 **at** 100, 2:3 **at** 200] ...
...constmatrix [1,2:3 **at** 1] ...

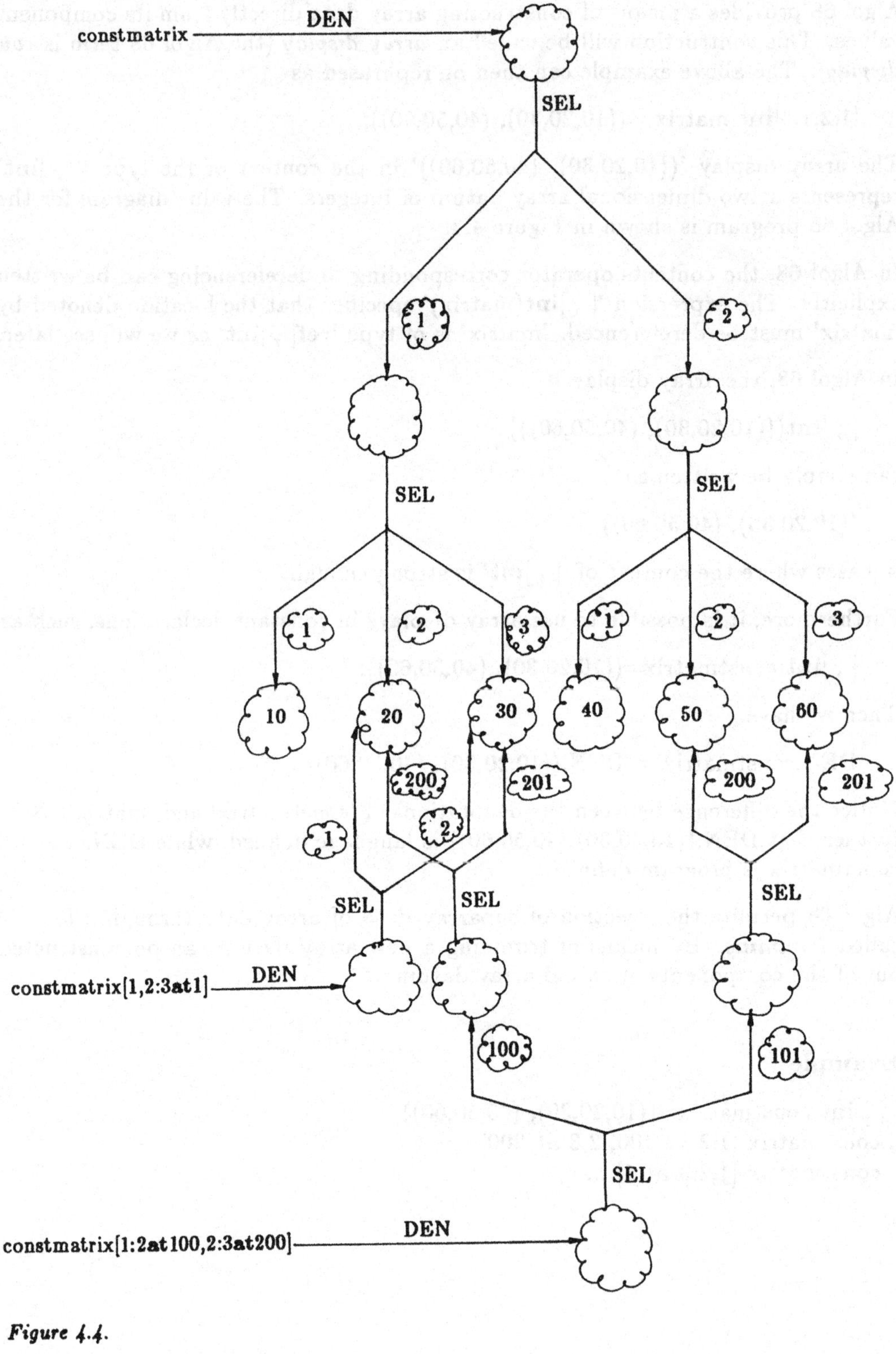
constmatrix
DEN
SEL
1
2
SEL
SEL
1
2
3
1
2
3
10
20
30
40
50
60
200
201
200
201
1
2
SEL
SEL
SEL
constmatrix[1,2:3at1]
DEN
100
101
SEL
constmatrix[1:2at100,2:3at200]
DEN

Figure 4.4.

The value diagram of the following array data is shown in Figure 4.4:

DEN.constmatrix

DEN.constmatrix[1:2 **at** 100, 2:3 **at** 200]

DEN.constmatrix[1,2:3 **at** 1]

The above-mentioned trimming is described in SMALL by

SEL(SEL(DEN.constmatrix[1:2 **at** 100,2:3 **at** 200],DEN.100),DEN.200) =
SEL(SEL(DEN.constmatrix,DEN.1),DEN.2)

SEL(SEL(DEN.constmatrix[1:2 **at** 100, 2:3 **at** 200],DEN.100),DEN.201) =
SEL(SEL(DEN.constmatrix,DEN.1),DEN.3)

SEL(SEL(DEN.constmatrix[1:2 **at** 100, 2:3 **at** 200],DEN.101),DEN.200) =
SEL(SEL(DEN.constmatrix,DEN.2),DEN.2)

SEL(SEL(DEN.constmatrix[1:2 **at** 100, 2:3 **at** 200],DEN.101),DEN.201) =
SEL(SEL(DEN.constmatrix,DEN.2),DEN.3)

SEL(DEN.constmatrix[1,2:3 **at** 1],DEN.1) =
SEL(SEL(DEN.constmatrix,DEN.1),DEN.2)

SEL(DEN.constmatrix[1,2:3 **at** 1],DEN.2) =
SEL(SEL(DEN.constmatrix,DEN.1),DEN.3)

Array data with dynamic length

In Algol 68, the length of array data is dynamic. This means that in general the number of elements of an array datum is only known at run time. The upper and lower bounds in the array types can be any integer expressions. The value of these expressions must be known at the time the array declaration is elaborated. The index type for array data in Algol 68 can only be an integer type. This is in contrast with the index type of array data in Pascal and Ada, which can be any discrete type, i.e., an integer type or an enumeration type.

Example

```
int n;
...
read(n);
...
[1:n,1:n]int matrix;
...
```

```
for i from 1 to n
    do for j from 1 to n
        do matrix[i , j]:=0 od
    od;
...
```

Algol 68 provides two operators, **lwb** and **upb**, which calculate the lower and upper bounds of an array datum. For instance, '1 **lwb** matrix' denotes the lower bound of the first dimension of the array datum contained in DEN.matrix, and '2 **upb** matrix' denotes the upper bound of the second dimension of the same array datum.

Bits and bytes data

Bits and bytes data in Algol 68 are special cases of boolean and character array data respectively. They correspond to contents of machine words. There are a number of language defined operations on bits and bytes data. Examples of operations on bits data are the shift operators, boolean operators, element selection and conversion operators between bits data and integers. There also exist **long** and **short** versions of the types **bits** and **bytes**, similar to those of **int** and **real**.

Since the number of bits (or bytes) in a bits (or bytes) datum is machine dependent, Algol 68 programs using these types may cause portability problems.

Character string data

Character strings are a special case of one-dimensional array data on which there are a number of language defined operations and for which a constant notation exists. The operations defined on character strings are the relational operators, concatenation and repetition. Character string constants in Algol 68 are denoted by sequences of characters enclosed in double quotes.

The type **string** is language defined as follows:

mode string=flex[1:0]**char**;

The keyword **flex** indicates that the memory space holding a value of type **string** can increase and decrease dynamically during the execution of the program. Locations of this type are called *array locations with flexible length* (see Section 5.3). This makes character string handling very attractive for the programmer if efficiency is not a major requirement.

Example

```
int i;
read(i);
...
string text;
...
text:=
    if i=0
        then "the input is 0"
        else "the input is different from 0"
    fi co the length of the string contained in 'text' can be expressed by 'upb
        text'. This length is either 14 or 19 depending on the value of the
        condition. co;
...
text:="we signal that"+text;
print(text);
...
text[1]:="i";
text[2]:=" ";
print(text);
...
```

The last two assignments can be contracted to

```
text[1:2]:="i ";
```

§4.4 Array data in PL/1

The following example is a literal translation of the first Pascal example in Section 4.2.

Example

```
DECLARE matrix(1:2,1:3) BIN FIXED;

...
matrix(1,1)=10; matrix(2,1)=40;
matrix(1,2)=20; matrix(2,2)=50;
matrix(1,3)=30; matrix(2,3)=60;
...
```

In PL/1, limited use may be made of array displays to construct array data directly from their components. The array display may only be used in the initialization part of an array variable declaration.

The above example can therefore be rephrased as :

DECLARE matrix(1:2,1:3) BIN FIXED INIT(10,20,30,40,50,60);

Notice that in PL/1, the two-level structure of the array data is not reflected in the array display.

The value diagram for the example is shown in Figure 4.3.

Trimming

In PL/1, a limited use of trimming is allowed. This is illustrated by the following example.

DECLARE matrix(1:2,1:3) BIN FIXED INIT(10,20,30,40,50,60);

... matrix(1,*) ...
... matrix(*,2) ...

The location denoted by 'matrix(1,*)' contains the array datum consisting of the elements denoted by '10', '20' and '30'. Similarly, the location denoted by 'matrix(*,2)' contains the array datum consisting of the elements denoted by '20' and '50'.

The value diagram of the following array data is shown in Figure 4.5:

DEN.{contents(matrix)}
DEN.{contents(matrix(1,*))}
DEN.{contents(matrix(*,2))}

The example above is described in SMALL by

SEL(DEN.{contents(matrix(1,*))},DEN.1) =
SEL(SEL(DEN.{contents(matrix)},DEN.1),DEN.1)

SEL(DEN.{contents(matrix(1,*))},DEN.2) =
SEL(SEL(DEN.{contents(matrix)},DEN.1),DEN.2)

SEL(DEN.{contents(matrix(1,*))},DEN.3) =
SEL(SEL(DEN.{contents(matrix)},DEN.1),DEN.3)

The reader is invited to draw the corresponding value diagram.

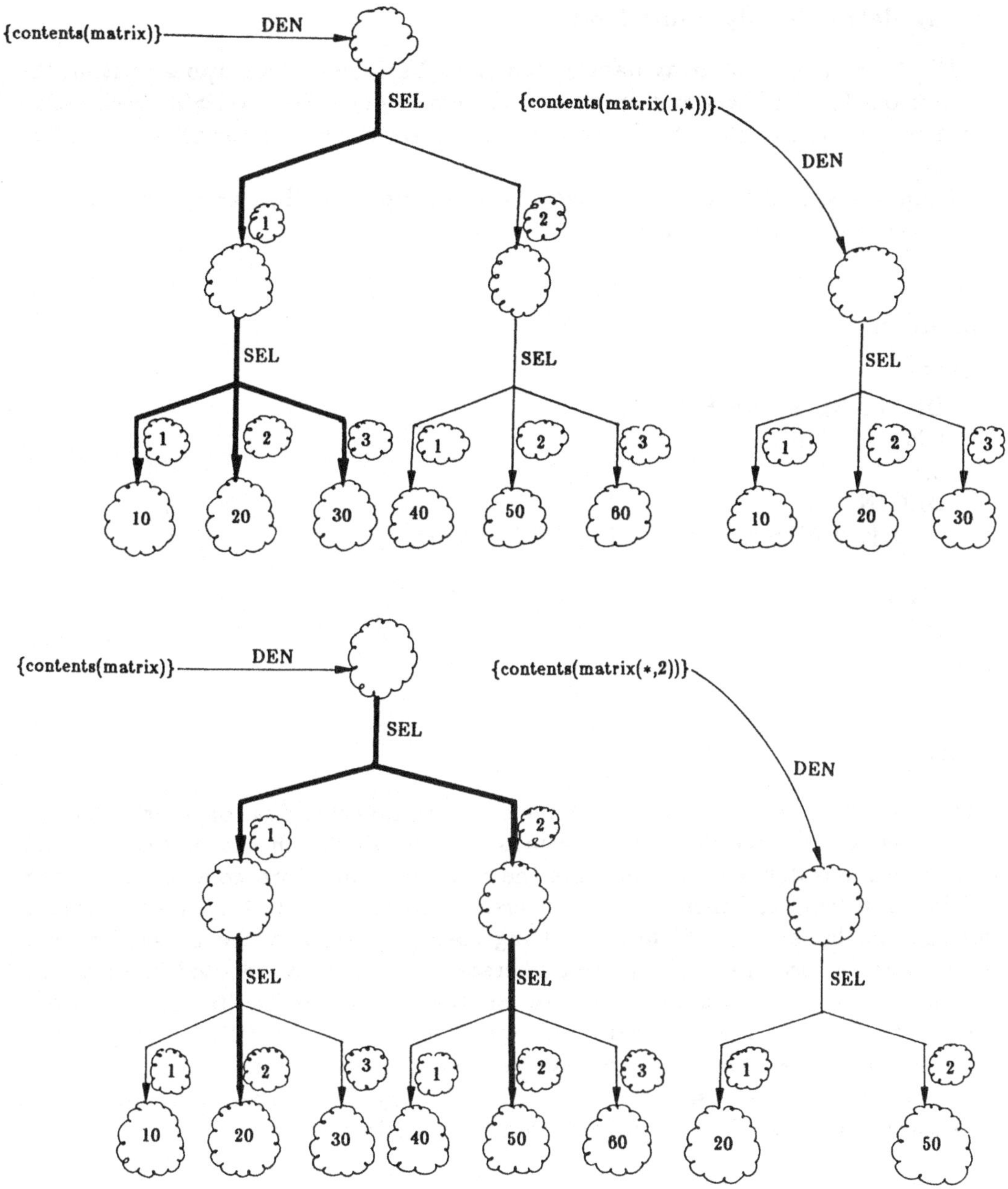
{contents(matrix)}
DEN
SEL
{contents(matrix(1,*))}
DEN
1
2
SEL
SEL
SEL
1
2
3
1
2
3
1
2
3
10
20
30
40
50
60
10
20
30
{contents(matrix)}
DEN
SEL
{contents(matrix(*,2))}
DEN
1
2
SEL
SEL
SEL
1
2
3
1
2
3
1
2
10
20
30
40
50
60
20
50

Figure 4.5.

Array data with dynamic length

In PL/1, the length of array data is dynamic. Variables which appear within the expressions for the lower and upper bounds in array types of a variable declaration must be declared in an outer block of the block to which that variable declaration is local.
Unfortunately, real types can be used as index types of PL/1 array data, but we do not consider this point here.

Example

```
BEGIN
    DECLARE n BIN FIXED;
    GET LIST(n);
    ...
    BEGIN
        DECLARE matrix(1:n,1:n) BIN FIXED;
        ...
    END;
    ...
END;
```

String data

Strings in PL/1 are a special case of one dimensional array data on which there are a number of language defined operations and for which constant notations exist. The operations defined on strings are the relational operators, concatenation, repetition, substring and various type conversion operations. PL/1 has both character strings and bit strings. Character string constants are denoted by sequences of characters enclosed in single quotes, whereas bit strings are denoted by sequences of 0's and 1's enclosed in quotes and terminated by the symbol 'B'. Character and bit string variables are declared with types 'CHAR(n)' and 'BIT(n)' respectively ($n \geq 0$) and contain character, respectively bit strings of length n. The strings are left adjusted. Left adjustment of bit strings is very unusual and may give rise to unexpected results when bit strings are converted into integers.

Example

```
DECLARE
   text_3 CHAR(3) INIT('JAN'),
   text_5 CHAR(5) INIT('JOHAN');
p : PROCEDURE(textformal);
         DECLARE textformal CHAR(*);
         <declarations and statements>
         /* the length of the string denoted by textformal is
             taken from the actual parameter. It is expressed by
             'LENGTH(textformal)'.*/
   END p;
...
CALL p(text_3);
...
CALL p(text_5);
...
```

The following declarations are all equivalent. Notice the use of a repetition factor for strings and an iteration factor for arrays.

```
DECLARE s(1:3) CHAR(5) INIT ('zzzzz','zzzzz','zzzzz');
DECLARE s(1:3) CHAR(5) INIT (3) 'zzzzz';
DECLARE s(1:3) CHAR(5) INIT ((5)'z',(5)'z',(5)'z');
DECLARE s(1:3) CHAR(5) INIT (3)(5)'z';
```

String variables in PL/1 may be of type 'CHAR(n) VARYING' or 'BIT(n) VARYING'. These variables contain strings of a length that may vary dynamically from 0 to n.

Locations of variables of type 'CHAR(n) VARYING' or 'BIT(n) VARYING' are of flexible length. The only difference compared to Algol 68 is that flexible locations in PL/1 have a maximum length.

Example

```
DECLARE i BIN FIXED;
GET LIST(i);
...
DECLARE text_100 CHAR(100);
DECLARE text CHAR(100) VARYING;
...
```

```
text_100='the input is an integer';
/*the string is left adjusted in the variable 'text_100' and filled with blanks*/
IF i=0
    THEN text='the input is 0';
    ELSE text='the input is different from 0';
    /* the length of the string containing in text is expressed by 'length
       (text)'. This length is either 14 or 19 depending on the value of the
       condition*/
...
text='we signal that' || text;
PUT LIST(text);
...
SUBSTR(text,1,2)='i ';
PUT LIST(text);
```

This example is an almost literal translation of the corresponding example in Section 4.3.

§4.5 Array data in Ada

The following example is a literal translation of the first Pascal example in Section 4.2.

Example

```
matrix:array(1..2,1..3) of integer;
begin
    matrix(1,1):=10; matrix(2,1):=40;
    matrix(1,2):=20; matrix(2,2):=50;
    matrix(1,3):=30; matrix(2,3):=60;
end
```

The array datum is denoted by {contents(matrix)}.

The value diagram for the example is shown in Figure 4.3.

Array aggregates

As in Algol 68, Ada array data can be directly expressed by means of array displays. Array displays in Ada are termed *array aggregates*. In positional array aggregates, the order in which the components are written is relevant.

Example

matrix:=((10,20,30), (40,50,60));

Array aggregates may also be written using naming.

Examples

matrix:=(1⇒(1⇒10,2⇒20,3⇒30),
        2⇒(1⇒40,2⇒50,3⇒60));

matrix:=(1⇒(1|2⇒0,3⇒1), 2⇒(1⇒0 **others** 1));

matrix :=(1..2⇒(1..3⇒0));

Initialization of variables

As in Algol 68 and PL/1, a variable declaration in Ada may be combined with the initialization of the variable.

Examples

matrix:**array**(1..2,1..3) **of** integer :=((10,20,30),(40,50,60));

matrix:**array**(1..2,1..3) **of** integer :=(1..2⇒(1..3⇒0));

Constant declarations

As in Algol 68, one may write in Ada something that is equivalent to a constant declaration.

Example

constmatrix:**constant array**(1..2,1..3) **of** integer :=((10,20,30), (40,50,60));

The array datum is denoted by constmatrix.

Trimming

Trimming of array data in Ada is limited to one dimensional arrays. The Ada term for trimming of one dimensional arrays is *slicing*.

Example

```
vec:constant array(1..4) of character :=('a','b','c','d');
begin
    ...vec(2..3)...
end
```

The expression 'vec(2..3)' denotes a one dimensional array consisting of two elements, DEN.'b' and DEN.'c'. The data structures and value diagrams are similar to those of Algol 68, as given in Section 4.3.

Index type

The index type of an array datum in Ada can be any discrete type, i.e., any enumeration type or any integer type.

Examples

```
type colortype is (blue,yellow,red,purple,black);
type vectype is array(colortype range<>) of integer;
        - -the bounds of the type 'vectype' are not specified.
        - -'vectype' is called an unconstrained array type
color:vectype (yellow..black);
        - -the bounds of the array variable are
        - -specified by means of an index constraint.
color1:array(yellow..black) of integer;
color2:array(colortype) of integer;
type vectype1 is array(integer range<>)of integer;
vec:vectype1(1..5);
vec1:array(1..5) of integer;
```

Array data with dynamic length

As in Algol 68 and PL/1, the length of array data in Ada is dynamic.

Example

```
n:integer;
...
vector:array(1..n) of integer;
...
```

Example

```
n:integer
...
type vectype is array(integer range<>)of integer;
vector:vectype(1..n);
...
```

Character string data

Character strings in Ada are a apecial case of array data on which concatenation and transput operations are defined and for which a constant notation exists. Character string constants are denoted by sequences of characters enclosed in double quotes. The language defined array type 'string' is given by:

```
subtype natural is integer range 1..integer'last;
type string is array(positive range<>) of character;
```

Variables of type 'string' can be defined by means of the type name 'string' and an index constraint.

```
text:string(1..20);
name:string(1..5):=(1..5=> '*');
```

The lack of string locations with flexible length (as defined in Algol 68 and PL/1) makes string handling in Ada rather difficult.

Example

```
with text_io; use text_io;

procedure p is
    i:integer;
    text_7:string(1..7);
    ...
begin
    if i=0
        then text_7:="ok     ";
        else text_7:="not ok";
    end if;
    put(text_7);
    ...
    text_7(7):=".";
    put(text_7);
    ...
end p;
```

§4.6 Record data in Pascal

Example

```
type rectype1=
      record
          first:boolean;
          second:char
      end;
type rectype=
      record
          first:integer;
          second:rectype1
      end;
var rec:rectype;
begin
   rec.first:=0;
   rec.second.first:=true;
   rec.second.second:='a';
   ...
end
```

In SMALL, {contents(rec)} denotes a record datum.

As in the case of array data in Pascal, there is no direct way of building record data from their components. Packed record data are analogous to packed array data (see Section 4.2).

The data structure of the record datum denoted by {contents(rec)} is shown in Figure 4.6

Figure 4.7 gives the value diagram for the above piece of Pascal program.

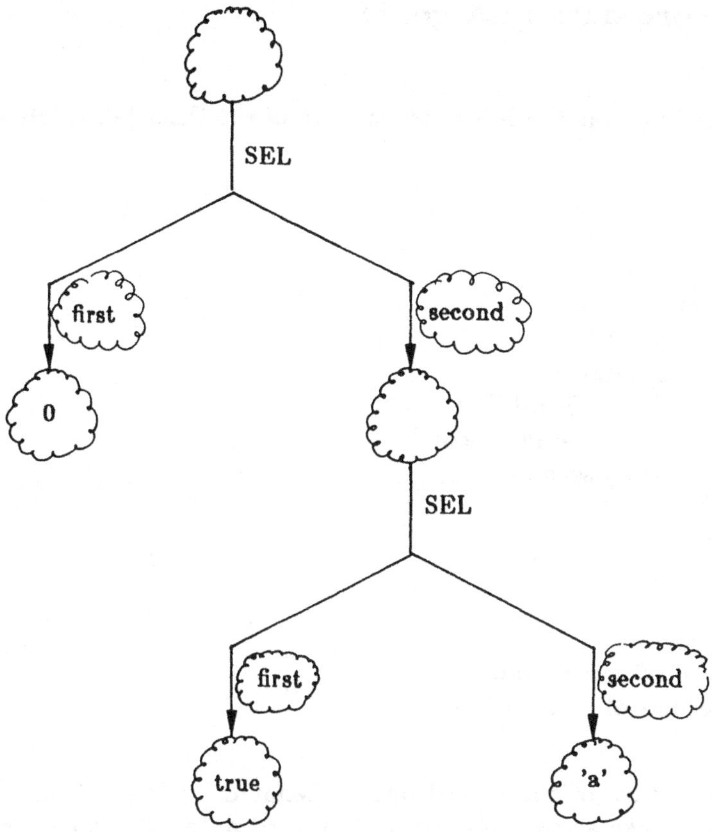

Figure 4.6.

§4.7 Record data in Algol 68

The following example is a literal translation of the Pascal example in Section 4.6.

Example

```
mode rectype=
        struct
            (  int first,
               struct
                   (  bool first,
                      char second
                   ) second
            );
rectype rec;
...

first of rec:=0;
first of second of rec:=true;
second of second of rec:="a";
...
```

The data structure of the record datum denoted by '**rectype**(rec)' is as shown in Figure 4.6. Like array data, Algol 68 record data can be constructed directly from their components by means of *record displays*. The Algol 68 term for record display is *structure display*. The above example can then be rephrased as follows :

rectype rec:=(0,(**true**,"a"));

The value diagram for the Algol 68 example is shown in Figure 4.8.

As in the case of array data, one may write a constant declaration as follows :

rectype constrec = (0,(**true**,"a"));

We then have

DEN.constrec = DEN.(0,(**true**,"a"))

Notice the difference between the denotations of the identifiers 'constrec' en 'rec'.

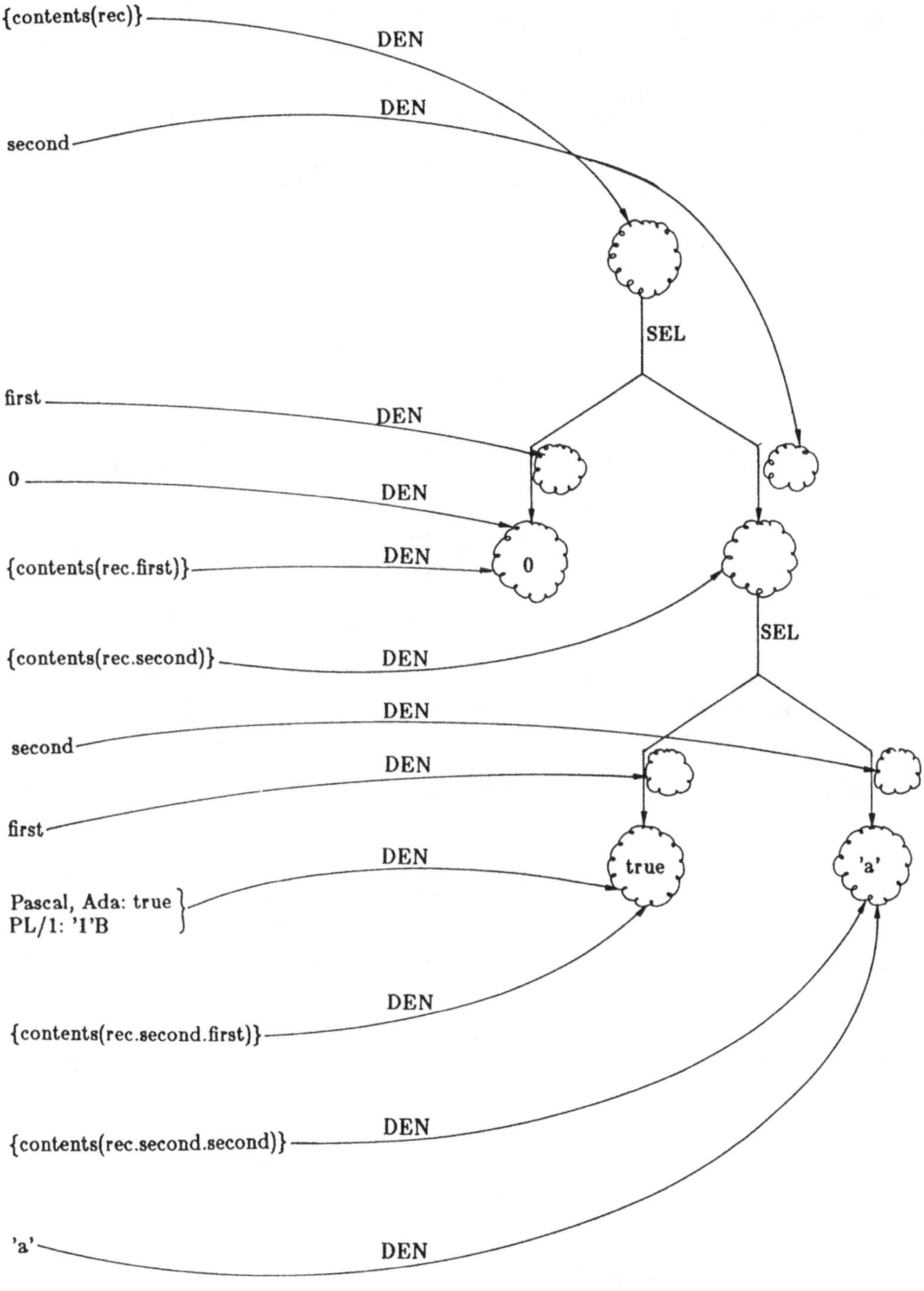
{contents(rec)}
DEN
second
DEN
SEL
first
DEN
0
DEN
{contents(rec.first)}
DEN
0
{contents(rec.second)}
DEN
SEL
second
DEN
first
DEN
true
'a'
Pascal, Ada: true
PL/1: '1'B
DEN
{contents(rec.second.first)}
DEN
{contents(rec.second.second)}
DEN
'a'
DEN

Figure 4.7.

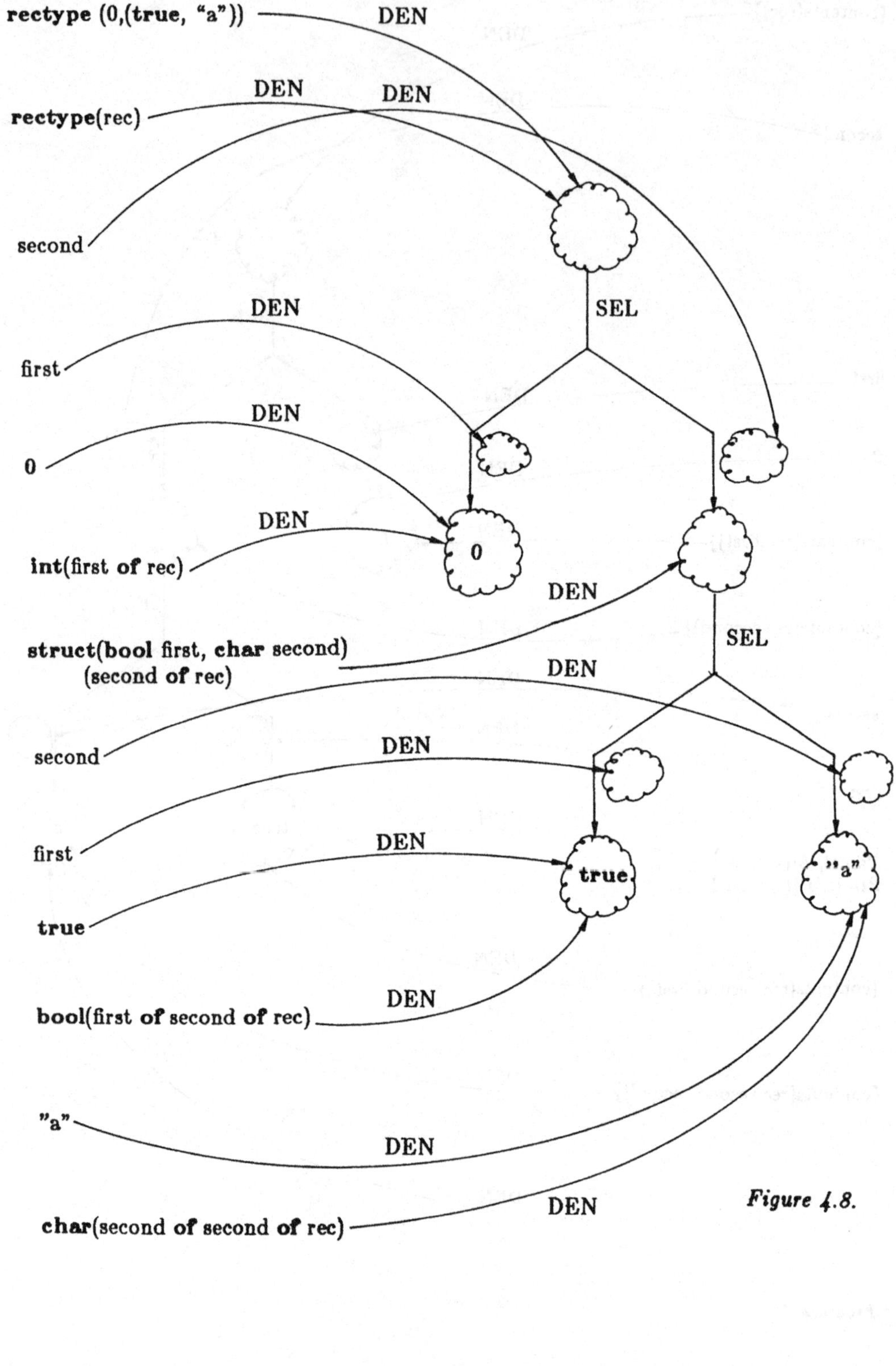
rectype (0,(true, "a"))
DEN
DEN
DEN
rectype(rec)
second
SEL
DEN
first
DEN
0
DEN
0
int(first of rec)
DEN
struct(bool first, char second)
(second of rec)
SEL
DEN
second
DEN
first
DEN
true
true
"a"
bool(first of second of rec)
DEN
"a"
DEN
DEN
char(second of second of rec)

Figure 4.8.

§4.8 Record data in PL/1

The following example is a literal translation of the Pascal example in Section 4.6.

Example

```
DECLARE
        1 rec,
            2 first BIN FIXED,
            2 second,
                3 first BIT(1),
                3 second CHAR(1);
...
rec.first=0;
rec.second.first='1'B;
rec.second.second='a';
...
```

As in the case of array variable declarations, the use of record displays in the initialization part of a record variable declaration is not possible. However, terminal nodes of the data structure can be initialized:

```
DECLARE
        1 rec,
            2 first BIN FIXED INIT(0),
            2 second,
                3 first BIT(1) INIT('1'B),
                3 second CHAR(1) INIT('a');
```

The value diagram for the PL/1 example is shown in Figure 4.7.

§4.9 Record data in Ada

The following example is a literal translation of the Pascal example in Section 4.6.

Example

```
type rectype1 is
        record
            first:boolean;
            second:character;
        end record;
```

```
type rectype is
        record
            first:integer;
            second:rectype1;
        end record;
rec:rectype;
begin
    rec.first:=0;
    rec.second.first:=true;
    rec.second.second:='a';
    ...
end
```

The record datum is denoted by {contents(rec)}. The value diagram for the Ada example is shown in Figure 4.7.

Record aggregates

As in Algol 68, Ada record data can be expressed directly by means of record displays. The Ada term for record display is ***record aggregate***. In positional record aggregates, the order in which the components are written is relevant.

Example

```
rec:=(0,(true,'a'));
```

Record aggregates may also be written using naming:

Example

```
rec:=(first⇒0, second⇒(first⇒true, second⇒'a'));
```

Initialization of variables

As in Algol 68 and PL/1, a variable declaration in Ada may be combined with the initialization of the variable.

Example

```
rec:rectype:=(0,(true,'a'));
```

Constant declarations

Example

constrec:**constant** rectype := (0,(true,'a'));

The record datum is denoted by 'constrec'.

§4.10 Mixed record and array data

Example in Pascal

```
type  vectype=array[1..3] of char;
       rectype=
           record
               first:integer;
               second:vectype
           end;
var arrayrec:array [1..2] of rectype;
...
begin
    arrayrec[1].first:=1;
    arrayrec[1].second[1]:='a';
    arrayrec[1].second[2]:='b';
    arrayrec[1].second[3]:='c';
    arrayrec[2].first:=2;
    arrayrec[2].second[1]:='x';
    arrayrec[2].second[2]:='y';
    arrayrec[2].second[3]:='z';
    ...
end
```

The composite datum A is built as the contents of the location denoted by 'arrayrec'. The data structure of A is shown in Figure 4.9.

We have for instance

SEL(A,DEN.1)=B
SEL(B,DEN.second)=C
SEL(C,DEN.3)=DEN.'c'
SEL(SEL(SEL(A,DEN.1),DEN.second),DEN.3)=DEN.'c'

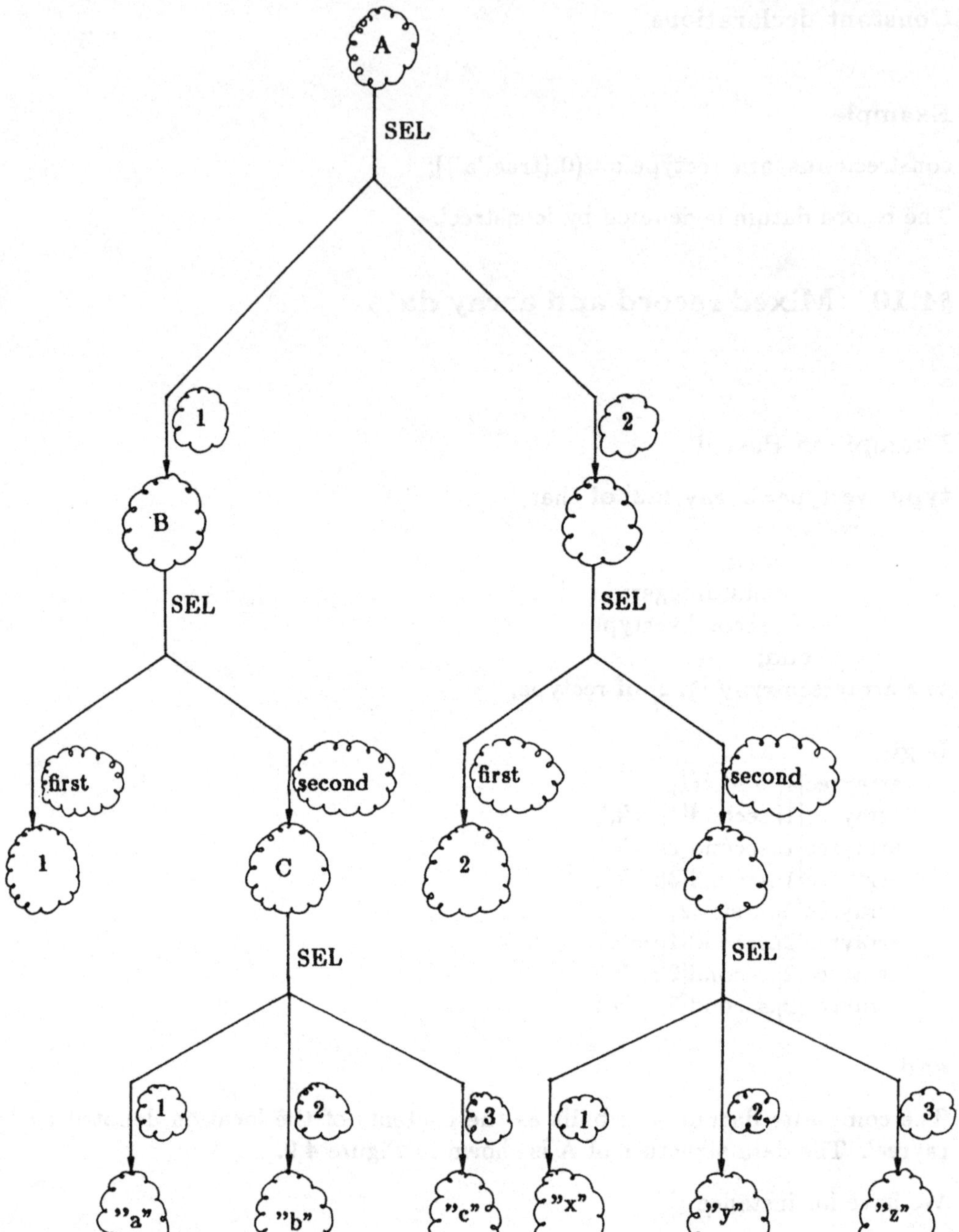
A
SEL
1
2
B
SEL
SEL
first
second
first
second
1
C
2
SEL
SEL
1
2
3
1
2
3
"a"
"b"
"c"
"x"
"y"
"z"

Figure 4.9.

We write

DEN.{contents(arrayrec[1].second[3])}=DEN.'c'

Example in Algol 68

```
[1:2]struct(int first,[1:3]char second) arrayrec
        =((1,("a","b","c")),(2,("x","y","z")));
```

We have

DEN((second of arrayrec[1])[3])=DEN."c"

Example in PL/1

```
DECLARE
        1 arrayrec(1:2),
            2 first BIN FIXED,
            2 second(1:3) CHAR(1);
...
arrayrec(1).first=1;
arrayrec(1).second(1)='a';
arrayrec(1).second(2)='b';
arrayrec(1).second(3)='c';
arrayrec(2).first=2;
arrayrec(2).second(1)='x';
arrayrec(2).second(2)='y';
arrayrec(2).second(3)='z';
...
```

We have

DEN.{contents(arrayrec(1).second(3))}=DEN.'c'

Example in Ada

```
type vectype is array (1..3) of character;
type rectype is
        record
            first:integer;
            second:vectype;
        end record;
arrayrec:constant array (1..2) of rectype
            :=((1,('a','b','c')),(2,('x','y','z')));
```

We have

DEN(arrayrec(1).second(3))=DEN.'c'

The reader is invited to draw the value diagrams of the above examples

§4.11 Configurations

Two new concepts were introduced in this chapter : the set of composite data CD and the function SEL. They are both added to the definition of a configuration. Hence, for the time being, a configuration is a 5-tuple (AD,AL,CD,CONT,SEL). In SMALL a composite datum is automatically included in CD as soon as its components and its selectors exist. For instance, since DEN.1 and DEN.2 are predefined in Algol 68, the following composite data automatically exist, amongst others:

DEN([1:2]**int** (1,2))
DEN([2:3]**int** (1,2))
DEN(**struct**(**int** a,b)(1,2))

For the function SEL the following relations hold, amongst others:

SEL(DEN([1:2]**int** (1,2)),DEN.1)=DEN.1
SEL(DEN([2:3]**int** (1,2)),DEN.3)=DEN.2
SEL(DEN(**struct**(**int** a,b) (1,2)),DEN.b)=DEN.2

Chapter 5

COMPOSITE LOCATIONS

§5.1 Concept

Composite locations are those values on which only the *selection function* SEL and the *contents function* CONT are defined. Hence the *result function* RES is not defined here. A composite location represents a part of the memory that is devided into several sublocations. Each sublocation is either atomic or in turn composite.

As in the case of composite data (see Chapter 4), a composite location is a set of selector-component pairs. The components of the composite locations are locations, which may be either atomic or composite. As a result of this recursive definition, a composite location has a hierarchical structure, or *location structure*, which can be represented in the form of a labeled tree. The branch labels in the tree represent the selectors, while the nodes represent the components. Nonterminal nodes correspond to composite locations, whereas terminal nodes correspond to atomic locations. This is analogous to the data structure of composite data, described in Section 4.1.

As in the case of composite data, the relationship between a composite location and its components is specified by the selection function SEL. This function has two arguments: the first is a composite location, while the second, the selector, is an atomic datum.

The selection function for composite locations is a mapping of the form

$$\text{SEL} : \text{CL x AD} \rightarrow \text{L}$$

The selection mechanism for composite locations is identical with that for composite data, described in Section 4.1.

The contents function specifies for each composite location the value it contains. In SMALL, this value must necessarily be a composite datum. The reason for this is explained in Chapter 7, where the contents function is analyzed in detail.

The contents function is then of the form

CONT : CL $\rightarrow$ CD

There is a strong interaction between the contents function and the selection function for composite locations. Indeed, if a composite location contains a composite datum, then every component of that datum is contained in a component of the composite location. This is explained in Chapter 7.

There is also a relationship between the type of the composite location, the type of its contents and the types of its components. This is discussed in Chapter 9.

In the languages Pascal, Algol 68, PL/1 and Ada, composite locations are divided into two classes : *array locations* and *record locations.* As in the case of composed data, selection in array locations is *dynamic*, whereas selection in record locations is *static.* Another difference between array locations and record locations is related to the types of their components. As we will see in Chapter 9, components of array locations must be of the same type, whereas components of record locations may have different types.

As in the case of atomic locations, composite locations in Pascal, Algol 68, PL/1 and Ada can be created either *statically* or *dynamically.* This was explained in Section 3.1. The definition of scope of a composite location is analogous to that for an atomic location given in Chapter 3. The remarks made there on dangling references for atomic locations in Pascal, Algol 68, PL/1 and Ada also hold for composite (array and record) locations.

§5.2 Array locations in Pascal

5.2.1 Static creation

Example

```
type vectype=array[1..3] of integer;
var vec:vectype;
begin
    vec[1]:=10;
```

```
    vec[2]:=20;
    vec[3]:=30;
    ...
end
```

The elaboration of the above piece of program consists of the following three steps:

(1) A composite location, say α, is created statically. Its scope is the program unit to which the variable declaration is local. At the same time, three sublocations of α are created statically. Let these sublocations be β, γ and δ. Then the selection function is defined on α so that

$$\text{SEL}(\alpha\text{n},\text{DEN.1}) = \beta$$
$$\text{SEL}(\alpha,\text{DEN.2}) = \gamma$$
$$\text{SEL}(\alpha,\text{DEN.3}) = \delta$$

(2) The name 'vec' is associated with the composite location α, so that

DEN.vec $= \alpha$.
At the same time, we have

$$\text{DEN.vec}[1] = \beta$$
$$\text{DEN.vec}[2] = \gamma$$
$$\text{DEN.vec}[3] = \delta$$

This is discussed in detail in Section 8.3.

(1) and (2) are the result of the execution of the variable declaration '**var** vec:vectype'.

(3) The contents CONT.α of the composite location α is set to the array datum consisting of the components DEN.10, DEN.20 and DEN.30 with which the selectors DEN.1, DEN.2 and DEN.3 are associated.

At the same time, we have

$$\text{CONT.}\beta = \text{DEN.10}$$
$$\text{CONT.}\gamma = \text{DEN.20}$$
$$\text{CONT.}\delta = \text{DEN.30}$$

Actually, we have here a composite location containing a composite datum. This is studied in a more general context in Section 7.6. As a result of the variable declaration, types are also associated with the expressions 'vec', 'vec[1]', 'vec[2]' and 'vec[3]' (see Chapter 9).

The location structure of the array location α is shown in Figure 5.1.

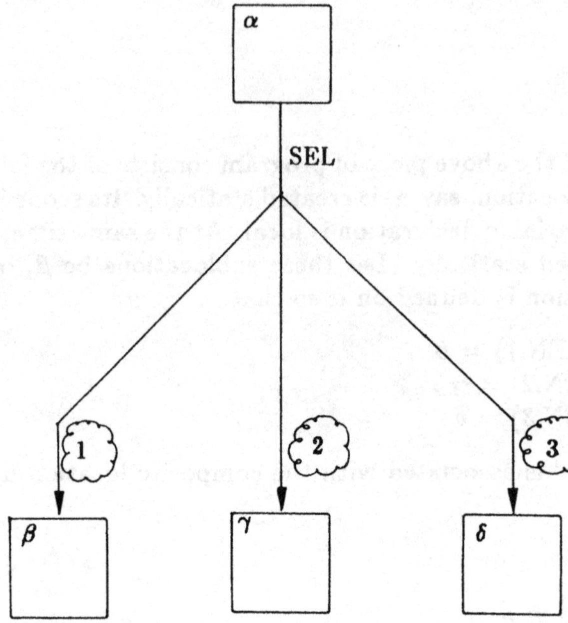

Figure 5.1.

We have

$$\text{SEL}(\alpha,\text{DEN}.1) = \beta$$
$$\text{SEL}(\alpha,\text{DEN}.2) = \gamma$$
$$\text{SEL}(\alpha,\text{DEN}.3) = \delta$$

The value diagram describing the situation after elaboration of the example is shown in Figure 5.2.

From this value diagram, we deduce for instance that

DEN.vec[1] = SEL(DEN.vec,DEN.1)
SEL(CONT.DEN.vec,DEN.1) = DEN.10
CONT.SEL(DEN.vec,DEN.1) = SEL(CONT.DEN.vec,DEN.1)

5.2.2 Dynamic creation

Example

```
type vectype=array[1..3] of integer;
   var ptr:↑vectype;
begin
   new(ptr);
   ptr↑[1]:=10;
   ptr↑[2]:=20;
   ptr↑[3]:=30;
   ...
end
```

The elaboration of the above piece of program consists of the following steps :

(1) An atomic location, say ω, is created statically. Its scope is the program unit to which the variable declaration is local.

(2) The name 'ptr' is associated with the location ω, so that DEN.ptr = ω.

(3) On execution of the statement 'new(ptr)', a composite location, say α, is created dynamically. At the same time, three sublocations of α are created dynamically. The scope of all these locations is the whole program. Let the sublocations be β, γ and δ. Then the selection function is defined so that

$$\text{SEL}(\alpha,\text{DEN}.1) = \beta$$
$$\text{SEL}(\alpha,\text{DEN}.2) = \gamma$$
$$\text{SEL}(\alpha,\text{DEN}.3) = \delta$$

(4) The composite location α is stored as the contents of ω, so that CONT.ω = α. This is studied in a more general context in Section 7.4.

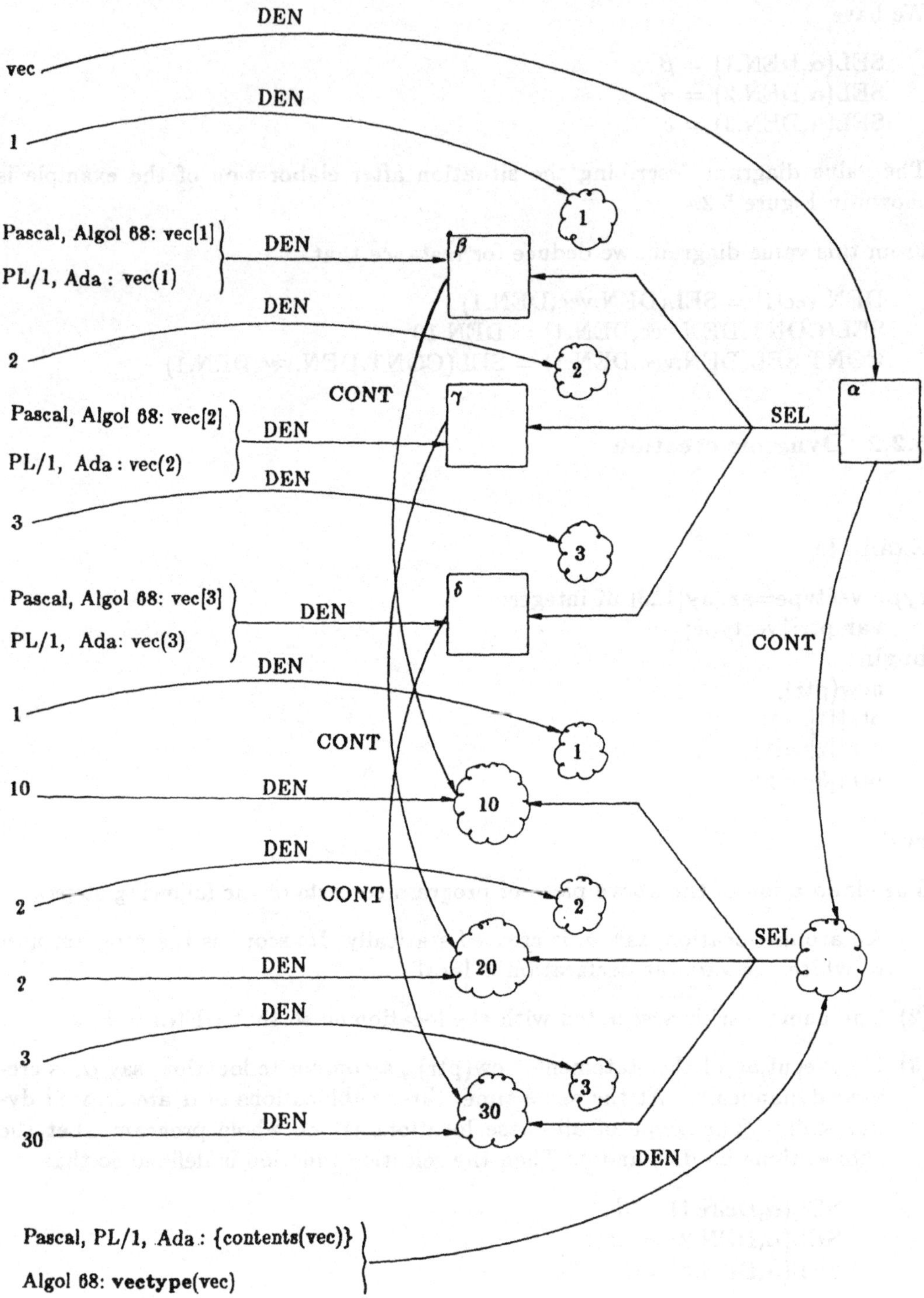
DEN
vec
DEN
1
1
Pascal, Algol 68: vec[1]
PL/1, Ada : vec(1)
DEN
β
DEN
2
2
CONT
γ
α
Pascal, Algol 68: vec[2]
PL/1, Ada : vec(2)
DEN
SEL
DEN
3
3
Pascal, Algol 68: vec[3]
PL/1, Ada: vec(3)
DEN
δ
CONT
DEN
1
1
CONT
10
DEN
10
DEN
2
CONT
2
SEL
2
DEN
20
DEN
3
3
30
DEN
30
DEN
Pascal, PL/1, Ada : {contents(vec)}
Algol 68: vectype(vec)

Figure 5.2.

(5) The compound expression 'ptr↑' now denotes α, so that DEN.ptr↑ = α.

At the same time, we have

DEN.ptr↑[1] = β
DEN.ptr↑[2] = γ
DEN.ptr↑[3] = δ

This is studied in detail in Section 8.3.

Steps (3), (4) and (5) are the result of the execution of the statement 'new(ptr)'.

(6) CONT.α is set to the array datum consisting of the components DEN.10, DEN.20, DEN.30, with selectors DEN.1, DEN.2 and DEN.3 respectively. We then also have

CONT.β = DEN.10
CONT.γ = DEN.20
CONT.δ = DEN.30

This is studied in detail in Section 7.6.

The location structure of the composite location α is shown in Figure 5.1.

Figure 5.3 gives the value diagram after execution of the example.

The reader may verify from Figure 5.3 that

DEN.ptr↑ = CONT.DEN.ptr
SEL(CONT.DEN.ptr↑,DEN.3)
= CONT.DEN.ptr↑[3]
= CONT.SEL(CONT.DEN.ptr,DEN.3)
= DEN.30

In contrast to PL/1, Algol 68 and Ada, the length of array locations in Pascal is static, i.e., the number of element locations must be known at compile time. As in the case of array data, this limitation stems from the fact that lower and upper bounds in index types of array types can only be constants. The absence of array locations with dynamic length causes problems in the construction of library routines for array handling, whereas the absence of array locations with flexible length makes string handling difficult.

Trimming

As explained in connection with array data, Pascal allows a restricted form of trimming of array locations.

Example

```
var matrix:array[1..2,1..3] of integer;
...
begin
    ...matrix[1]...
end
```

'matrix[1]' denotes a subarray location of the array location denoted by 'matrix'.

Character string locations

A special kind of array location in Pascal is the character string location. These locations can be created using the Pascal type '**packed array**[T] **of** char', where T is a subrange type. The role of packing in Pascal was discussed in Section 4.2.

§5.3 Array locations in Algol 68

5.3.1 Static creation

The following example is a translation of the Pascal example in Section 5.2.1.

Example

```
mode vectype=[1:3]int;
vectype vec;
begin
    ...
    vec[1]:=10;
    vec[2]:=20;
    vec[3]:=30;
    ...
end
```

The corresponding value diagram is as shown in Figure 5.2.

The declaration and initialization can be contracted to

```
    vectype vec:=(10,20,30);
```

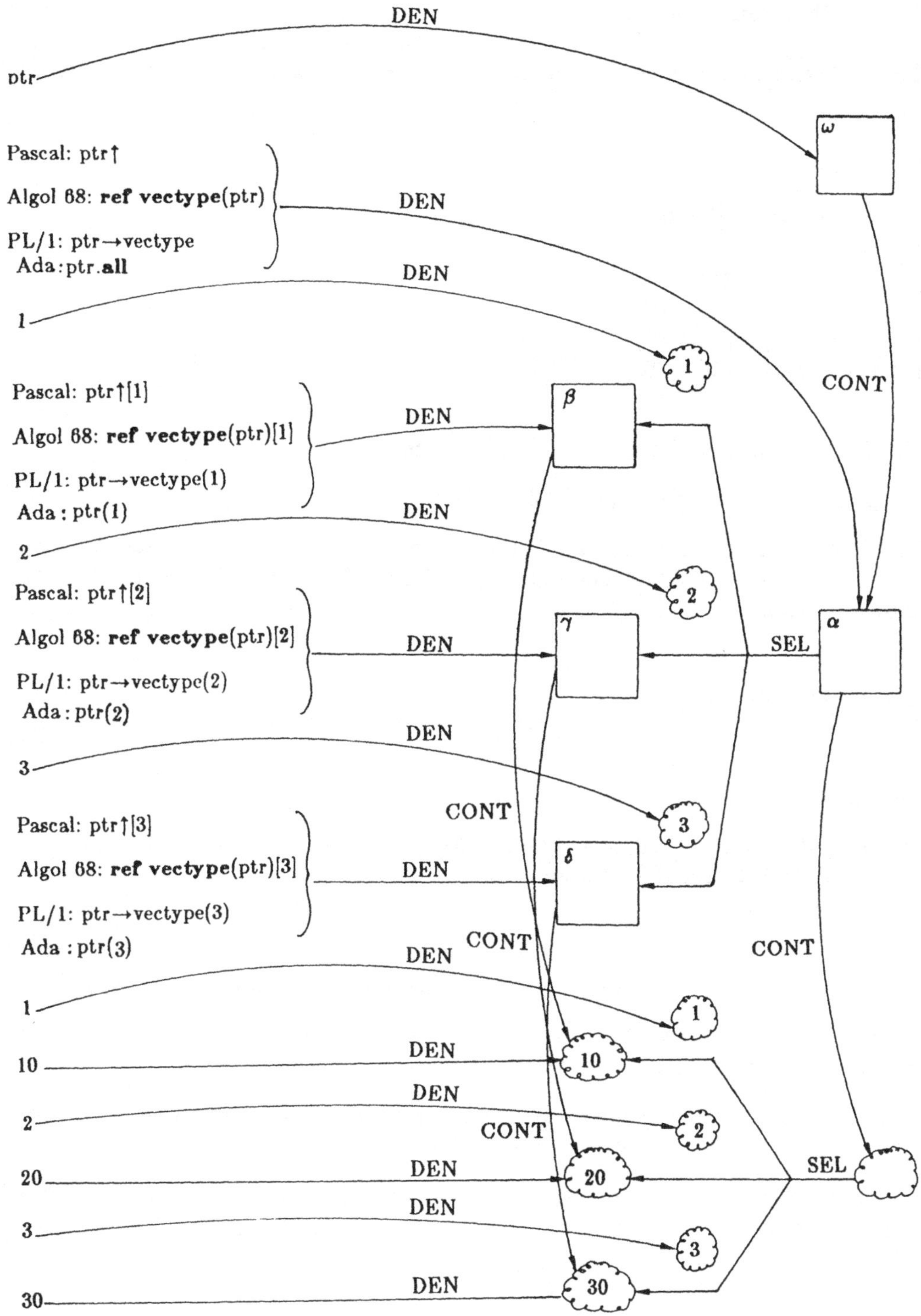
DEN
ptr
ω
Pascal: ptr↑
Algol 68: **ref vectype**(ptr)
PL/1: ptr→vectype
Ada: ptr.**all**
DEN
DEN
1
1
CONT
Pascal: ptr↑[1]
Algol 68: **ref vectype**(ptr)[1]
PL/1: ptr→vectype(1)
Ada: ptr(1)
β
DEN
DEN
2
2
Pascal: ptr↑[2]
Algol 68: **ref vectype**(ptr)[2]
PL/1: ptr→vectype(2)
Ada: ptr(2)
γ
DEN
SEL
α
DEN
3
3
CONT
Pascal: ptr↑[3]
Algol 68: **ref vectype**(ptr)[3]
PL/1: ptr→vectype(3)
Ada: ptr(3)
δ
DEN
CONT
DEN
CONT
1
1
10
DEN
10
2
DEN
2
CONT
SEL
20
DEN
20
3
DEN
3
30
DEN
30

Figure 5.3.

5.3.2 Dynamic creation

The following example is a translation of the Pascal example in Section 5.2.2.

Example

```
mode vectype=[1:3]int;
ref vectype ptr;
ptr:=heap vectype;
ref vectype(ptr)[1]:=10;
ref vectype(ptr)[2]:=20;
ref vectype(ptr)[3]:=30;
...
```

The last four lines of code can be replaced by

```
ptr:=heap vectype:=(10,20,30);
```

In Algol 68, '**ref vectype**(ptr)[1]' may be written as 'ptr[1]', because of the automatic type conversion (coercion) which is dereferencing .The value diagram is shown in Figure 5.3.

5.3.3 Trimming

Example

```
[1:2,1:3]int matrix:=((10,20,30),(40,50,60));
... matrix [1:2 at 100,2:3 at 200]...
... matrix [1,2:3 at 1]...
```

The name 'matrix' denotes a composite location, say α, with six component locations, say β, γ, δ, ς, η and θ. The value diagram is shown in Figure 5.4.

As in the case of array data (see Section 4.3), Algol 68 permits the selection of subarray locations of array locations by means of trimming.

The location structure of the array location ρ denoted by the expression 'matrix[1:2 **at** 100, 2:3 **at** 200]' is shown in Figure 5.5.

As another example, the coresponding diagram for array location ω denoted by the expression

'matrix[1,2:3 **at** 1]' is given in Figure 5.6.

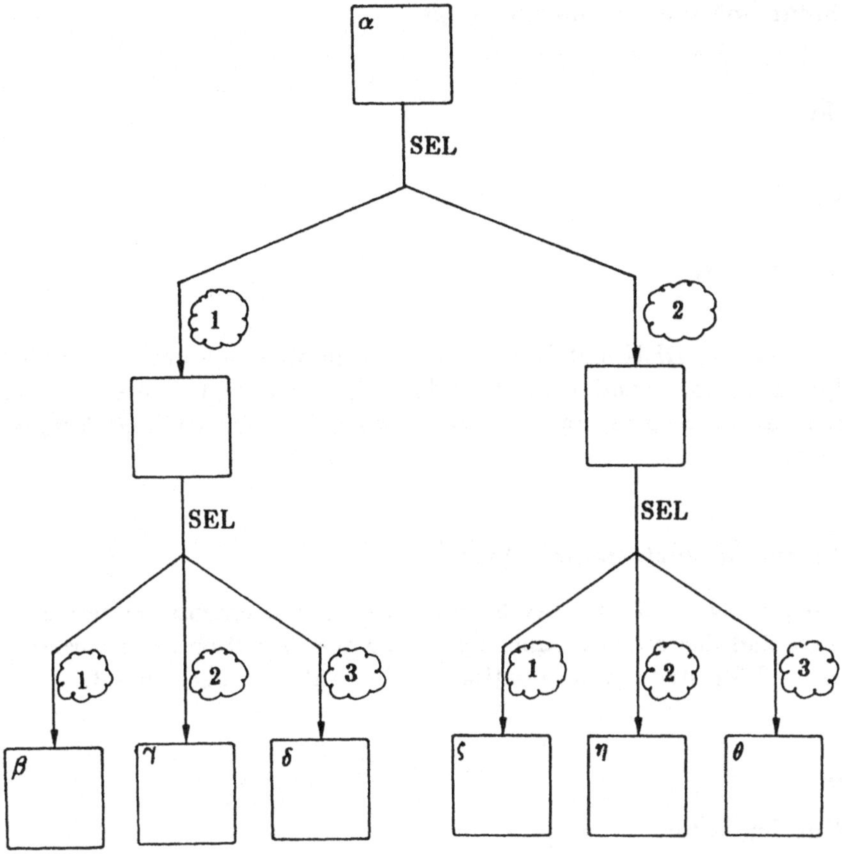

Figure 5.4.

Array locations with dynamic length

Example

int n;
read(n);
...
[1:n,1:n]**int** matrix;
...

The array location DEN.matrix consists of a number of elements (sublocations) that is dynamic. Lower and upper bounds of, for example, the second dimension of the array location are given by the expressions '2 **lwb** matrix' and '2 **upb** matrix' respectively.

Array locations with flexible length

In Algol 68, array locations may have a number of elements (sublocations) that can increase and decrease dynamically during the execution of the program. This feature is used for string manipulation, as illustrated in Section 4.3.

Example

flex[1:0]**int** flexvector;
    co DEN.flexvector has zero sublocations **co**
...
flexvector:=(1,2,3,4,5,6,7,8,9,10);
    co DEN.flexvector has ten sublocations **co**
...
flexvector:=10;
    co DEN.flexvector has one sublocation **co**
...
flexvector:=(100,200,300);
    co DEN.flexvector has three sublocations **co**.

Bits and bites locations

Bits and bytes locations in Algol 68 are special cases of boolean and character array locations respectively, and correspond to machine words. As in the case of bits and bytes data (see Section 4.3), Algol 68 programs using bits or bytes locations may cause portability problems.

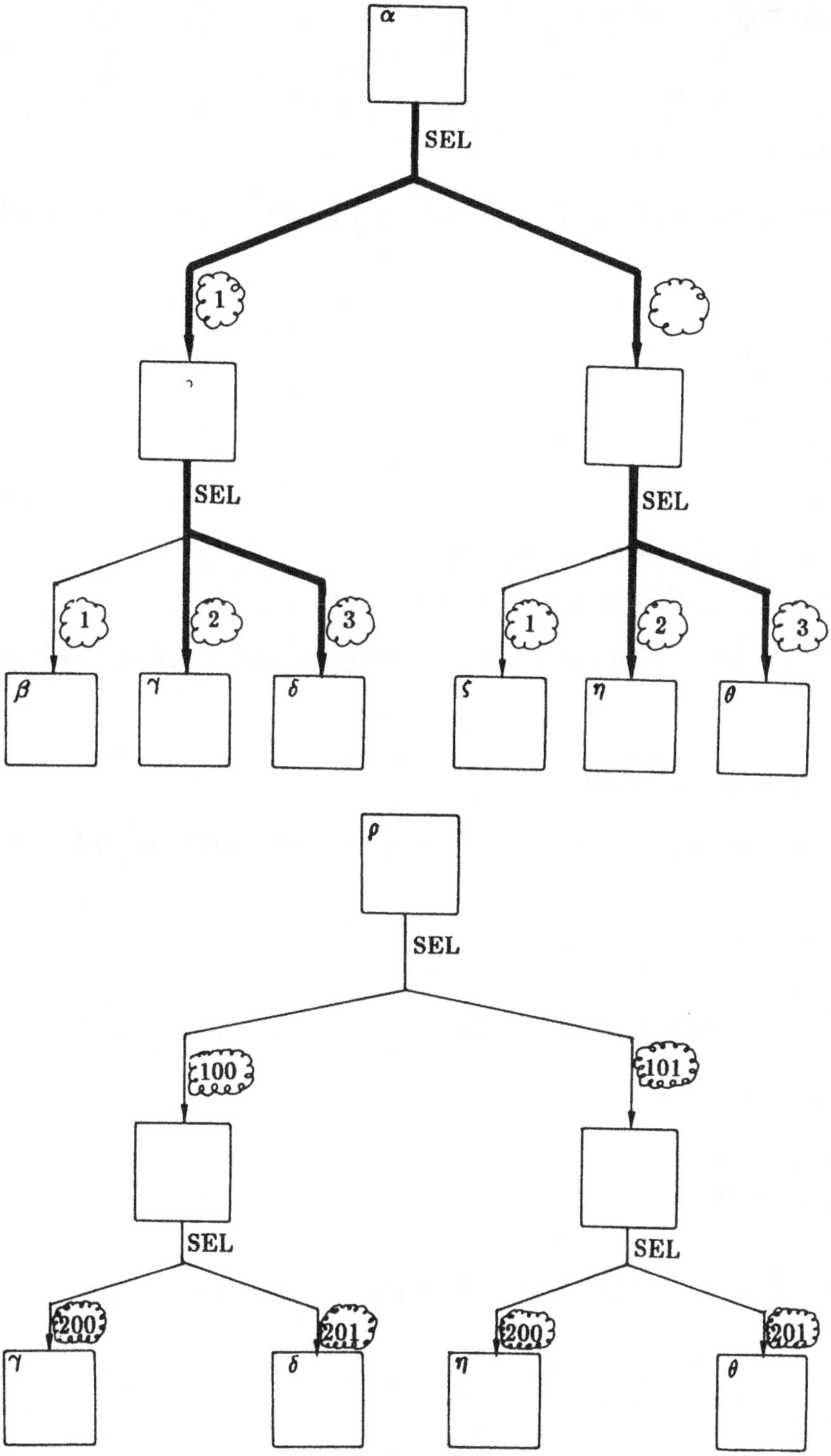
α
SEL
1
SEL
SEL
1
2
3
1
2
3
β
γ
δ
ς
η
θ
ρ
SEL
100
101
SEL
SEL
200
201
200
201
γ
δ
η
θ

Figure 5.5.

§5.4 Array records in PL/1

5.4.1 Static creation

The following example is a translation of the Pascal example in Section 5.2.1.

Example

```
DECLARE vec(1:3) BIN FIXED;
...
vec(1)=10;
vec(2)=20;
vec(3)=30;
```

These four lines of code can be replaced by

```
    DECLARE vec(1:3) BIN FIXED INIT (10,20,30);
```

The corresponding location structure and value diagram are shown in Figures 5.1 and 5.2.

5.4.2 Dynamic creation

The following example is a translation of the Pascal example in Section 5.2.2.

Example

```
DECLARE
    vectype(1:3) BIN FIXED BASED,
    ptr POINTER;
ALLOCATE vectype SET(ptr);
ptr→vectype(1)=10;
ptr→vectype(2)=20;
ptr→vectype(3)=30;
...
```

The value diagram is shown in Figure 5.3.

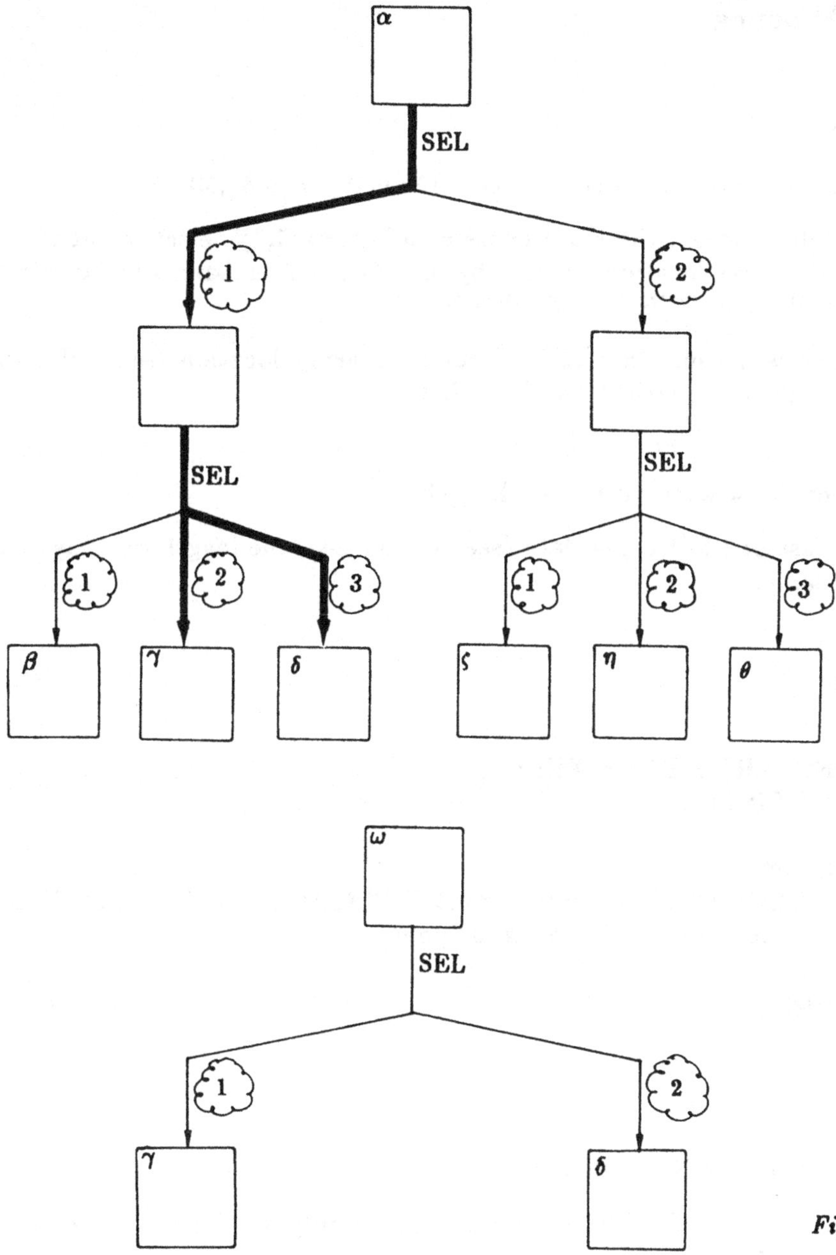

Figure 5.6.

5.4.3 Trimming

Example

DECLARE matrix(1:2,1:3) BIN FIXED INIT(10,20,30,40,50,60);

Given this declaration, the PL/1 expression 'matrix(1,*)' selects a subarray location from the array location denoted by 'matrix'. This subarray location contains the values DEN.10, DEN.20 and DEN.30.

In the same way, 'matrix (*,2)' selects a subarray location from DEN.matrix, containing the values DEN.20 and DEN.50.

Array locations with dynamic length

As in the case of PL/1 array data (see Section 4.4), the length of array locations can be dynamic.

Example

```
BEGIN;
      DECLARE n BIN FIXED;
      GET LIST(n);
      ...
      BEGIN;
         DECLARE matrix(1:n,1:n) BIN FIXED; /* the length of the array
            location DEN.matrix is dynamic */
         ...
      END;
      ...
END;
```

Array locations with a flexible length

Array locations with flexible length can be used only for character and bit strings (see Section 4.4).

String locations

As in the case of string data (see Section 4.4), string locations in PL/1 are a special case of one dimensional array locations and can be of two kinds: character or bit string locations. Examples can be found in Section 4.4.

§5.5 Array locations in Ada

5.5.1 Static creation

Example

```
type vectype is array(1..3) of integer;
vec:vectype;
begin
    vec(1):=10;
    vec(2):=20;
    vec(3):=30;
    ...
end
```

The variable declaration and the three assignment statements can be replaced by

```
vec:vectype:=(10,20,30);
```

This is analogous to Algol 68 (see Section 5.3.1).

The corresponding location structure and value diagram are shown in Figures 5.1 and 5.2.

In Ada, the array display can be specified either positionally, as above, or by naming, as follows:

```
vec:vectype:=(1=> 10,2=> 20,3=> 30);
```

5.5.2 Dynamic creation

Example

```
type vectype is array(1..3) of integer;
```

```
type pointertype is access vectype;
ptr:pointertype;
begin
    ptr:=new vectype;
    ptr(1):=10;
    ptr(2):=20;
    ptr(3):=30;
    ...
end
```

The variable declaration and the three assignment statements can be replaced by

```
    ptr:=new vectype'(10,20,30);
```

This is analogous to Algol 68 (see Section 5.3.2). However, in 'ptr(1)' there is as always an implicit dereferencing of DEN.ptr. The value diagram is shown in Figure 5.3.

5.5.3 Trimming

Example

```
vec:array(1..3) of character:=('a','b','c','d');
...
...vec(2..3)...
```

The expression 'vec(2..3)' in Ada denotes a subarray location of DEN.vec, containing the elements DEN.'b' and DEN.'c'. Trimming of array locations in Ada is limited to one dimensional array locations.

Array locations with dynamic length

In Ada, the length of array locations can be dynamic, as indicated in Section 4.5.

Character string locations

Character string locations are a special case of array locations which may hold character string data (see Section 4.5).

§5.6 Record locations in Pascal

5.6.1 Static creation

Example

```
type rectype=
        record
            first:integer;
            second:real
        end;
var rec:rectype;
begin
    rec.first:=1;
    rec.second:=3.14;
    ...
end
```

The elaboration of the above piece of program consists of three steps :

(1) A composite location, say α, is created statically. Its scope is the program unit to which the variable declaration is local. At the same time, two sublocations of α are created. Let these sublocations be β and γ. Then we have

$$\text{SEL}(\alpha,\text{DEN.first}) = \beta$$
$$\text{SEL}(\alpha,\text{DEN.second}) = \gamma$$

(2) The name 'rec' is associated with the composite location α, so that DEN.rec $= \alpha$. At the same time, we have

$$\text{DEN(rec.first)} = \beta$$
$$\text{DEN(rec.second)} = \gamma$$

This is studied in more detail in Section 8.3.

(3) The contents of the composite location α, CONT.α, is set to the record datum consisting of the components DEN.1 and DEN(3.14), with selectors first and second respectively.

At the same time, we have

$$\text{CONT}.\beta = \text{DEN}.1$$
$$\text{CONT}.\gamma = \text{DEN}(3.14)$$

Hence we have a composite location containing a composite datum. This is studied in a more general context in Section 7.7.

As a result of the variable declaration, types are also associated with the expressions 'rec', 'rec.first' and 'rec.second' (see Chapter 9).

The value diagram for the example is shown in Figure 5.7.

5.6.2 Dynamic creation

Example

```
type rectype=
        record
            first:integer;
            second:real
        end;
var ptr:↑rectype;
begin
    new(ptr);
    ptr↑.first:=1;
    ptr↑.second:=3.14;
    ...
end
```

The elaboration of the above piece of program consists of six steps :

(1) An atomic location, say ω, is created statically. Its scope is the program unit to which the variable declaration is local.

(2) The name 'ptr' is associated with the location ω, so that DEN.ptr $= \omega$.

(3) On execution of the statement 'new(ptr)', a composite location, say α, is created dynamically. Its scope is the whole program. At the same time, two sublocations of α are created dynamically, with the same scope. Let these sublocations be β and γ. Then we have

$$\text{SEL}(\alpha,\text{DEN.first}) = \beta$$
$$\text{SEL}(\alpha,\text{DEN.second}) = \gamma$$

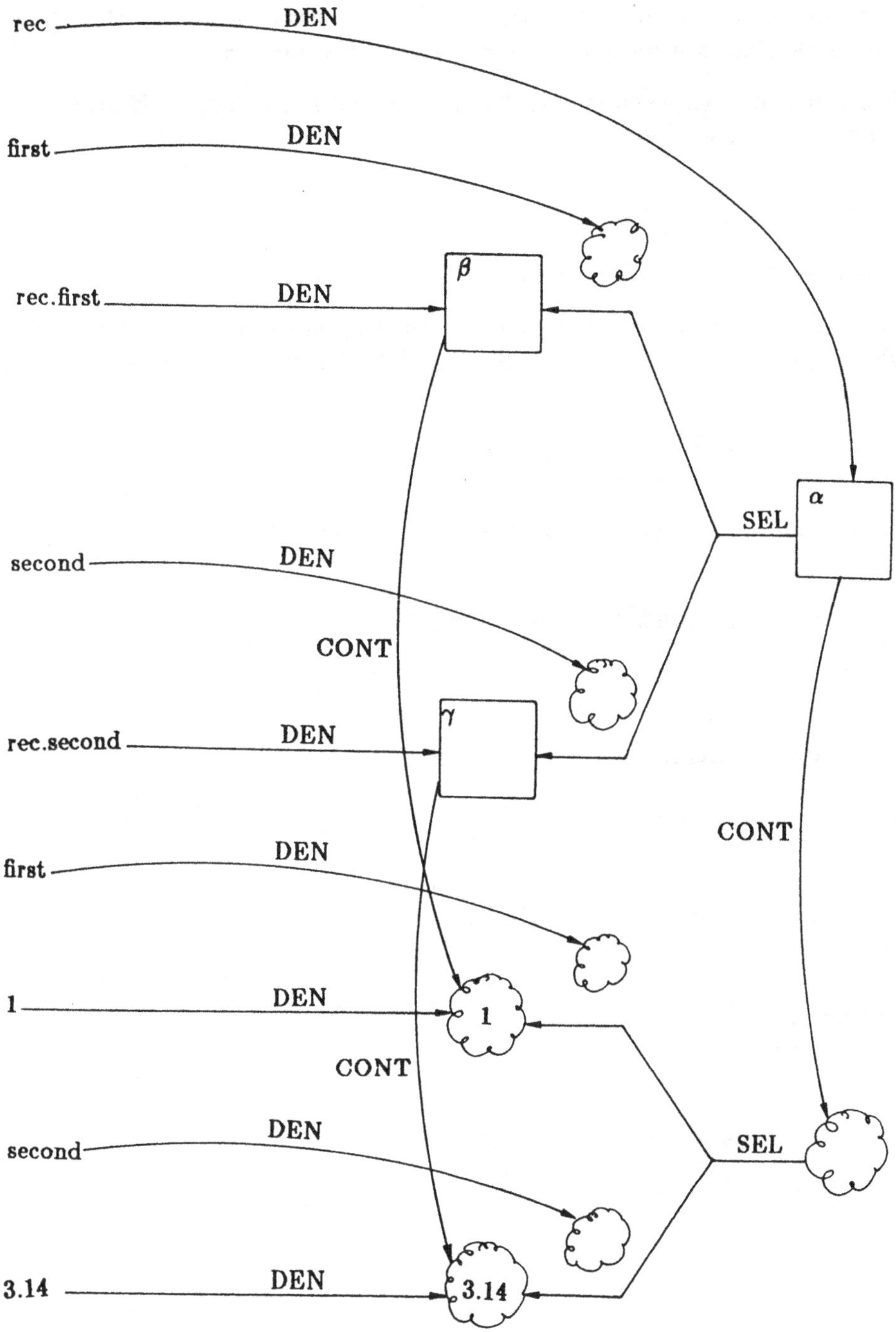
rec
DEN
first
DEN
rec.first
DEN
β
α
SEL
second
DEN
CONT
rec.second
DEN
γ
CONT
first
DEN
1
DEN
1
CONT
SEL
second
DEN
3.14
DEN
3.14

Figure 5.7.

(4) The composite location α is stored as the contents of ω so that CONT.$\omega = \alpha$. This is studied in a more general context in Section 7.4.

(5) The compound expression 'ptr↑' now denotes α, so that DEN.ptr↑ $= \alpha$. At the same time, we have

DEN(ptr↑.first) $= \beta$
DEN(ptr↑.second) $= \gamma$

This is studied in detail in Section 8.3.

(6) CONT.α is set to the record datum consisting of the components DEN.1 and DEN(3.14), with selectors DEN.first and DEN.second respectively. We then also have

CONT.β = DEN.1
CONT.γ = DEN.3.14

The value diagram for the example is shown in Figure 5.8.

§5.7 Record locations in Algol 68

5.7.1 Static creation

Example

```
mode rectype=struct(int first, real second);
rectype rec;
...
first of rec:=1;
second of rec:=3.14;
...
```

The last three lines of code can be replaced by

```
rectype rec:=(1,3.14);
```

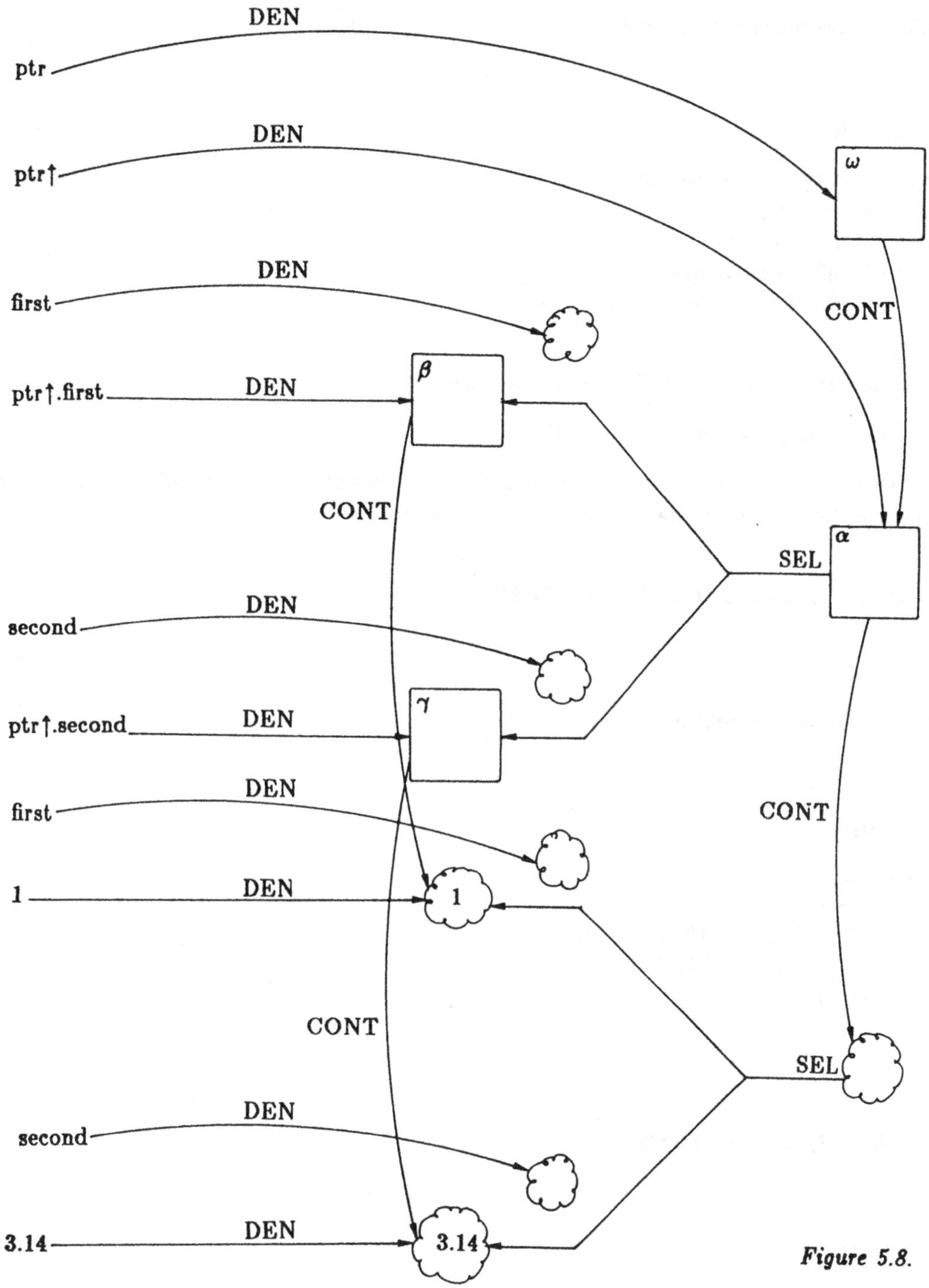
DEN
ptr
DEN
ptr↑
ω
DEN
first
CONT
β
ptr↑.first
DEN
CONT
α
SEL
DEN
second
γ
ptr↑.second
DEN
DEN
first
CONT
1
DEN
1
CONT
SEL
DEN
second
3.14
DEN
3.14

Figure 5.8.

5.7.2 Dynamic creation

Example

mode rectype=struct(int first, **real** second);
ref rectype ptr;
ptr:=**heap rectype;**
first **of ref rectype** (ptr):=1;
second **of ref rectype** (ptr):=3.14;
...

The last three lines of code can be replaced by

ptr:=**heap rectype**:=(1,3.14);

In Algol 68, one may write 'first **of ref rectype** (ptr)' as 'first **of** ptr', in which case implicit deferencing of DEN.ptr will occur.

§5.8 Record locations in PL/1

5.8.1 Static creation

Example

```
DECLARE
        1 rec,
            2 first BIN FIXED,
            2 second BIN FLOAT;
rec.first=1;
rec.second=3.14;
...
```

5.8.2 Dynamic creation

Example

```
DECLARE
        1 rectype BASED,
            2 first BIN FIXED,
            2 second BIN FLOAT,
```

```
        ptr POINTER;
ALLOCATE rectype SET(ptr);
ptr→rectype.first=1;
ptr→rectype.second=3.14;
...
```

§5.9 Record locations in Ada

5.9.1 Static creation

Example

```
type rectype is
        record
            first:integer;
            second:float;
        end record;
rec:rectype;
begin
    rec.first:=1;
    rec.second:=3.14;
    ...
end
```

The varable declaration and the two assignment statements can be replaced by

```
    rec:rectype:=(1,3.14);
```

5.9.2 Dynamic creation

Example

```
type rectype is
        record
            first:integer;
            second:float;
        end record;
type refrec is access rectype;
ptr:refrec;
begin
    ptr:=new rectype;
    ptr.first:=1;
    ptr.second:=3.14;
    ...
end
```

The variable declaration and the three assignment statements can be replaced by

```
ptr:= new rectype'(1,3.14);
```

§5.10 Configurations

One new set was introduced in this chapter : the set of composite locations CL. The function SEL was also extended to CL. We now add CL to the definition of a configuration, so that, for the time being, a configuration is a 6-tuple (AD,AL,CD,CL,CONT,SEL). In most programming languages there are no predefined composite locations. For programs written in these languages, CL is initially empty. Composite locations are created and added to CL by declarations of variables or by allocation statements. They are deleted from CL by deallocation statements or by leaving the program units delimiting their scope. This will be discussed further in Chapter 6.

Chapter 6

ROUTINE VALUES

§6.1 Concept

Routine values are those values on which only the *result function* RES is defined. Hence neither the *contents function* CONT, nor the *selection function* SEL is defined here. The set of routine values is called R.

A routine value represents an algorithm which describes a number of actions, possibly in terms of some formal parameters. The call or invocation of a routine value always first binds the actual parameters to the corresponding formal parameters, then executes the algorithm and finally returns the result.

The formal parameters of a routine value are *names* (N), whereas the actual parameters are *expressions* (E). Note that the formal parameters of the routine value and the actual parameters must agree in number and also in type (see Chapter 9).

In SMALL, the binding between an actual parameter (say the expression 'e') and its corresponding formal parameter (say the name 'x') consists of associating 'e' with 'x'. The actual form of this association depends on the parameter binding mechanism that is being considered. The parameter binding mechanisms in Pascal, Algol 68, PL/1 and Ada will be explained in terms of the binding in SMALL. This approach also simplifies the understanding of call mechanisms in programming languages in general.

A *transitionless value* is a value that is neither a transition, nor a composite value containing (possibly in a deeper level) a transition. In other words, a value is transitionless if it is either an atomic value or a composite value, all of whose components are transitionless values.

The result function is a function with n+1 arguments : a routine value and n other values, called the *actual parameters*, which are bound properly to the *formal parameters* of the routine value. The result function has the general form

$$\text{RES} : \text{R} \times \text{E} \times \ldots \times \text{E} \rightarrow \text{V}$$

The result function thus associates with its n+1 arguments a value, which is returned from the execution of the routine call after the actual parameters have been bound properly to the corresponding formal parameters.

Figure 6.1 shows how to represent the association

$$\text{RES}\ (r, e_1, e_2, ..., e_n) = b$$

where r is a routine value, the expressions $e_1, ..., e_n$ are the actual parameters and the value b is the result. In SMALL, result values of routines are restricted to transitions, transitionless values and composite values with only two components : a transition and a transitionless value. Note that in the diagrams routine values are always represented by the letter r, possibly indexed.

In SMALL, routine values themselves are considered to be values, i.e., they can be transmitted as parameters to other routine values, they can be components of composite data, they can be assigned to atomic locations and so on. Hence R is a subset of V, as illustrated in Figure 1.1.

§6.2 Transitions

Recall from Chapter 1 that a *configuration* can be seen as a snapshot at a particular moment during the execution of a program, containing all the information that would be necessary to restart the program at that point in its execution. The set of all the configurations was called CONF. We have partially defined the concept of configuration in the preceding chapters. A *transition* was defined in Chapter 1 to be a transformation between configurations; it is the result of the execution of a routine value. More precisely, a transition is a function from the set CONF to itself. In SMALL, transitions are considered to be values, so the set TR of transitions is a subset of V (see Figure 1.1).

Any program construction, whose execution may cause a transition is said to denote a routine value. Examples of such program constructions are declarations, statements, procedures, functions and programs. Hence the result of a program is a transition from an *initial configuration* to a *final configuration*. Notice that the set TR is not a component of the configurations since transitions do not augment the information contained in a configuration. Transitions are represented in diagrams by the letter s, possibly indexed.

Since a configuration is a tuple that contains sets and functions, a transition can be expressed as a transformation on sets and on functions. Each transition will be expressed in terms of three kinds of primitive actions:

1. Each time we want to add new objects (values, types, expressions) to a set, we write

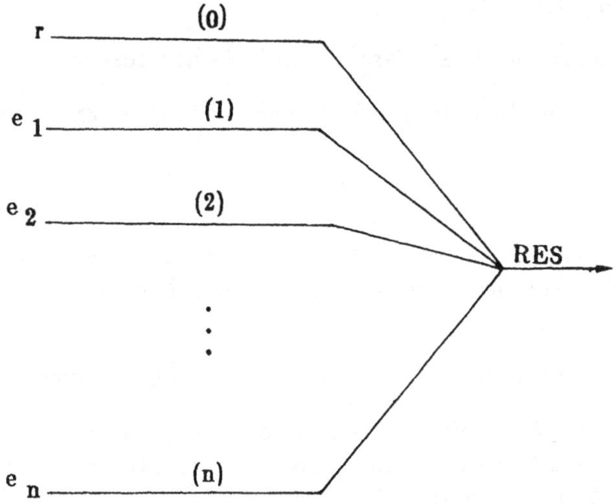

Figure 6.1.

$$S \leftarrow S \cup a_1 \cup \ldots \cup a_n$$

where S is the set and the a_i are the objects in question.

2. Each time we want to delete objects (values, types, expressions) from a set, we write

$$S \leftarrow S - a_1 - \ldots - a_n$$

3. Each time we want to alter a function at one point a of its domain with α, without altering the function at any other point, we write

$$F(a) \leftarrow \alpha$$

meaning that the function F evaluated at the point a now gives α.

Note that if an object a is deleted from the domain A of F then $F(a)$ is no longer defined. On the other hand it is only possible to create or alter the value of F at a if a belongs to A at that moment.

In the subsequent sections, we shall discuss a great number of examples on transitions. Here we just give two simple examples which will be explained in detail later.

Examples

Part of the transition induced by the variable declaration in Pascal

var v:**array**[1..2] **of** integer;

is

$$CL \leftarrow CL \cup \alpha$$
$$AL \leftarrow AL \cup \beta \cup \gamma$$
$$SEL(\alpha, DEN.1) \leftarrow \beta$$
$$SEL(\alpha, DEN.2) \leftarrow \gamma$$

The transition induced by the assignment statement

i:=1;

is CONT.DEN.i $\leftarrow$ DEN.1

§6.3 Functions and procedures

We distinguish two special classes of routine values r according to the kind of values returned by the function RES with r as its first argument.

r is called a *function value* if RES returns a transitionless value;

r is called a *procedure value* if RES returns a transition.

Notice that in SMALL a routine value for which RES returns a composite value with one transition component and one transitionless component is considered to be neither a function value nor a procedure value. Most programming languages allow functions to yield transitions. They are represented in SMALL by routine values, for which RES produces a composite value with two components, one component for the value that is returned and one component for the transition value (an example follows in Section 6.2).

Actually, there is no fundamental difference between a function identifier and an operator, except that an operator has either one or two formal parameters, whereas a function has zero or an arbitrary number of formal parameters. There is, however, a difference in the use of function identifiers and operators, i.e., function identifiers are used in prefix notation, whereas operators are used in infix notation. Notice that this difference is a property not of values but merely of notations, i.e., it is part of the syntactic sugar of programming languages. In the sequel we will not distinguish between a function and an operation.

In programming languages a routine value may be either language defined or program defined. Examples of language defined routine values are scalar operations (such as +, -, *, /, sin, cos, mod) and input-output operations. Program defined routine values are defined within the program.

There are a number of type relationships between the routine value, its result and its formal and actual parameters. These are discussed in Chapter 9.

Analogous to constants denoting atomic and composite values, a routine value is denoted by some kind of notation, termed *routine denotation.* A routine denotation is a piece of program that describes the corresponding algorithm. According to the current terminology in programming languages, routine denotations which denote procedure values are termed *procedures*, whereas any other routine denotation is termed a *function.* Notice, however, that a routine value yielding a composite value with a transition component and a transitionless component is **not** a function value in SMALL, although it is considered as a function in most programming languages.

Notice also that the term *function* is used in two different contexts : as a mathematical object and as a programming language construct. In the sequel this difference in meaning will only be made explicit if the context is not clear.

§6.4 Routine values in Pascal

6.4.1 Call by value

Call by value in functions

Example

```
var z:integer;
function f(x:integer):boolean;
    <declarations>;
    begin
        <statements>;
        f:=true
    end;
begin
    z:=3;
    ...f(z)...;
end
```

The execution of the above Pascal text consists of the following steps :

(1) An atomic location, say α, is created statically.

(2) The location α is denoted by 'z', so that DEN.z $= \alpha$.

(3) A routine value r with formal parameter 'x' is associated with the name 'f' so that DEN.f $= r$.

(4) The atomic location α is initialized to DEN.3, so that CONT.α = DEN.3.

(5) The binding of the actual parameter {contents(z)} to the formal parameter 'x' causes an atomic location, say β, to be created. It is denoted by 'x' and is initialized to DEN.{contents(z)}. Hence CONT.β = CONT.DEN.z. This parameter binding mechanism is termed ***call by value***.

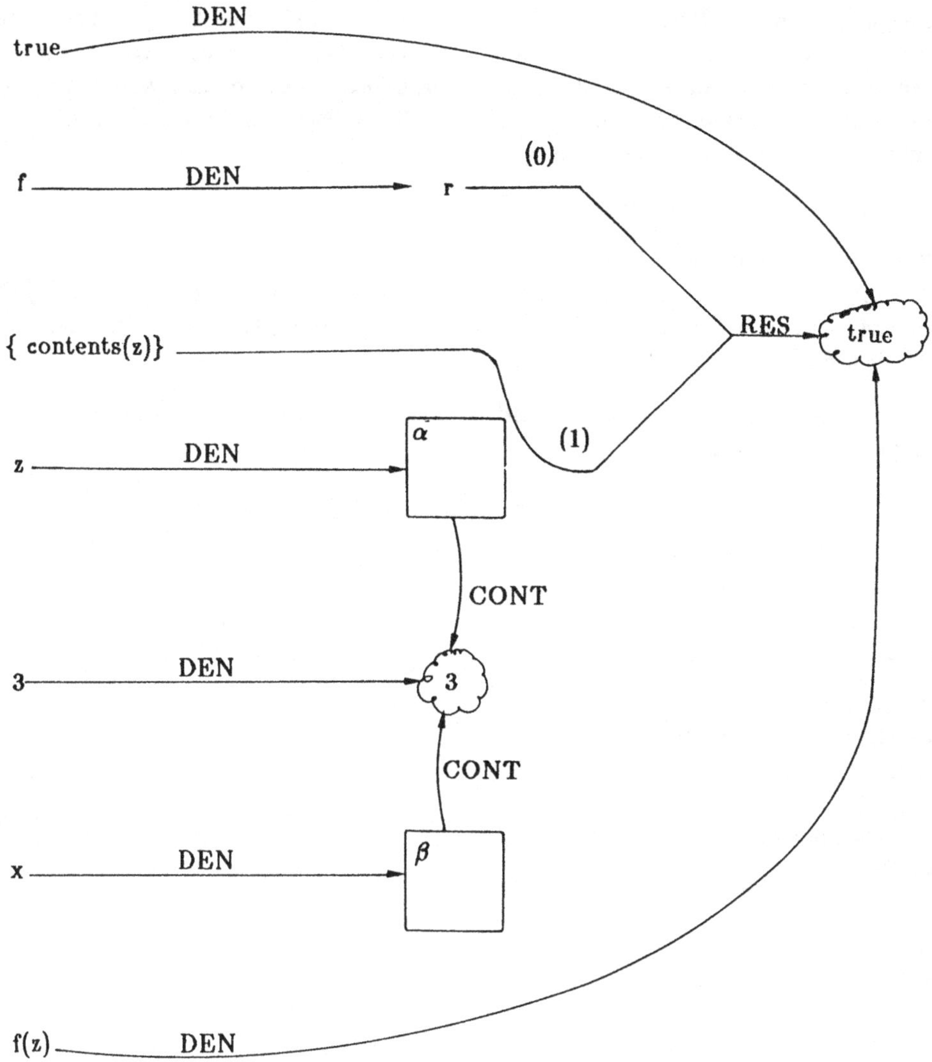
DEN
true
f
DEN
r
(0)
RES
true
{ contents(z)}
z
DEN
α
(1)
CONT
3
DEN
3
CONT
x
DEN
β
f(z)
DEN

Figure 6.2.

(6) The arguments of RES are DEN.f and {contents(z)}. The body of the routine value is executed. Within the body we have DEN.x = β. We assume that the body <statements> of the routine value does not contain any transitions. According to the definitions of Section 6.3, DEN.f is a function value. After execution of the body we have

RES(DEN.f,{contents(z)}) = DEN.true

(7) We have tph DEN.f(z) = DEN.true
Actually, 'f(z)' is a syntactic construct in Pascal standing for 'f({contents(z)})'. In SMALL, it is a compound expression representing the value DEN.true (see Section 8.3).

The value diagram just before the end of the execution of the function call 'f(z)' is shown in Figure 6.2.

Call by value in procedures

Example

```
var z:integer;
procedure p(x:integer);
    <declarations>;
    begin
        <statements>
    end;
begin
    z:=3;
    p(z);
    ...
end
```

This case is similar to call by value for functions, except that after execution of the body of the procedure, we have

RES(DEN.p,{contents(z)}) = s

where s represents a transition. Similarly we have

DEN.p(z) = s

A function call yielding a transition

Although the next example is a legal Pascal program, it is not considered to be an example of good programming practice.

Example

```
var a,x:integer;
function f(y:integer):integer;
    begin
        f:=y+1;
        x:=x+1
    end;
begin
    x:=0;
    ...
    a:=f(3);
    ...
end
```

In SMALL, the value RES(DEN.f,3) is a composite datum with two components: the first component is DEN.4 and the second is s, a transition which changes the contents of the location DEN.x.

As they are not explicitly defined in Pascal, we now define two selectors for composite data of the above kind: let SEL_v and SEL_s be the selectors which select the transitionless value and the transition respectively.

We then have

$$\text{SEL(RES(DEN.f,3)},SEL_v) = \text{DEN.4}$$
$$\text{SEL(RES(DEN.f,3)},SEL_s) = s$$

The transitions are expressed by

$$\text{CONT.DEN.x} \leftarrow \text{CONT.DEN.x} + \text{DEN.1}$$

The value diagram just before the end of the execution of the call 'f(3)' is shown in Figure 6.3. (Actually, the statement 'a:=f(3)' stands for something of the form 'a:=f(3).SEL_v'. This phenomenon is discussed further in Chapter 8.)

6.4.2 Call by variable

Call by variable always results in a transition, though this transition might not in fact change any value.

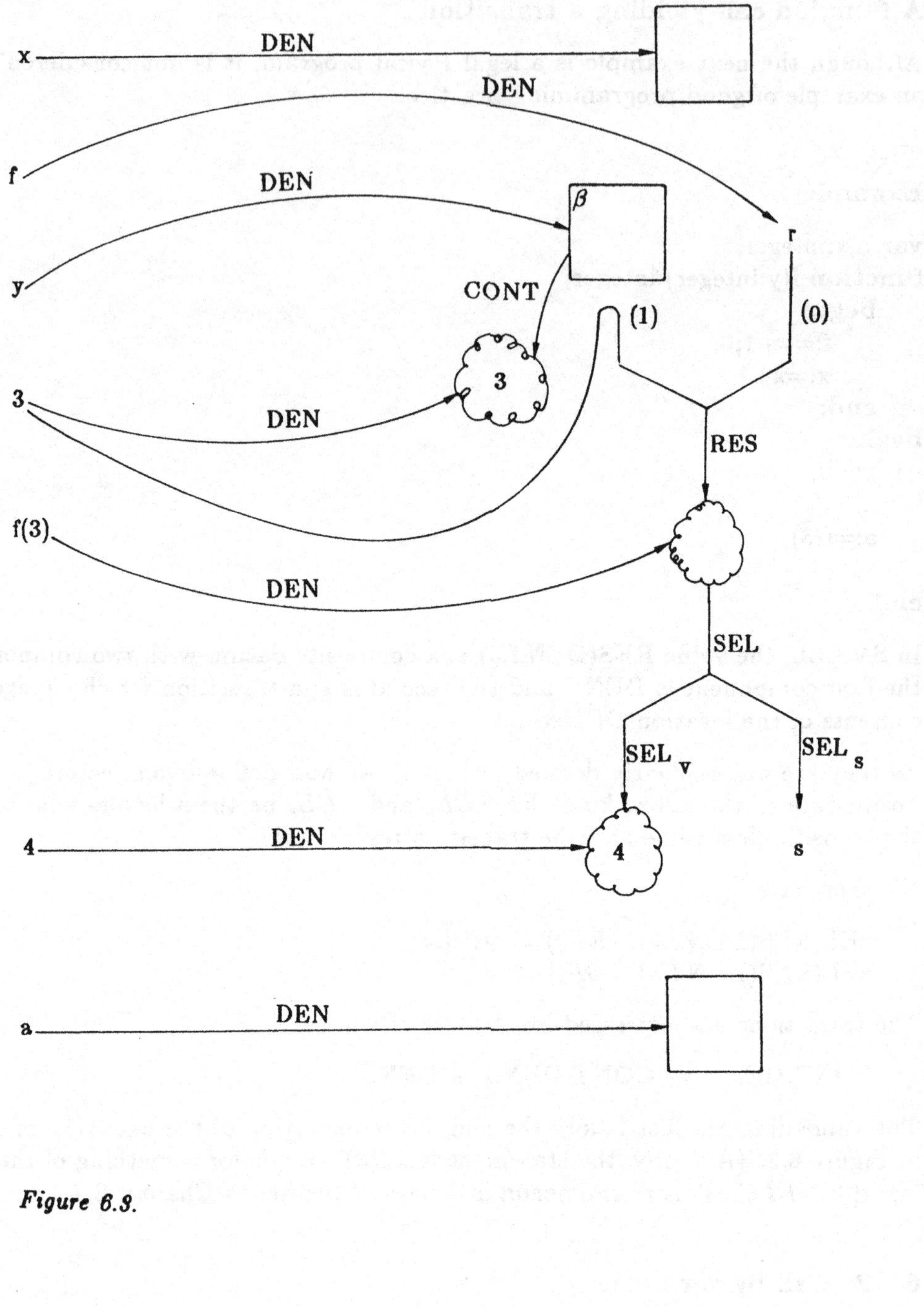
x
DEN
DEN
f
DEN
β
r
y
CONT
(1)
(0)
3
3
DEN
RES
f(3)
DEN
SEL
SEL v
SEL s
4
DEN
4
s
a
DEN

Figure 6.8.

Call by variable in functions

Example

```
var z:integer;
function f(var x:integer):boolean;
    <declarations>;
    begin
        <statements>;
        f:=true
    end;
begin
    z:=3;
    ...f(z)...;
end
```

The execution of the above Pascal text consists of the following six steps:

(1) An atomic location, say α, is created statically.

(2) The atomic location is denoted by 'z', so that DEN.z $= \alpha$.

(3) A routine value r with formal parameter 'x' is associated with the name 'f', so that DEN.f $= r$.

(4) The variable 'z' is initialized to DEN.3, so that CONT.α = DEN.3.

(5) The arguments of RES are DEN.f and 'z'. According to the parameter binding mechanism *call by variable*, the formal parameter 'x' and the actual parameter 'z' denote the same value. Hence, within the body of the routine value we have DEN.x = DEN.z. After execution of the body, RES(DEN.f,z) is a composite datum so that

$$\text{SEL}(\text{RES}(\text{DEN.f},\text{DEN.z}),SEL_v) = \text{DEN.true}$$
$$\text{SEL}(\text{RES}(\text{DEN.f},\text{DEN.z}),SEL_s) = s$$

where s is a transition.

(6) f(z) is a syntactic construct in Pascal. In SMALL, it is a compound expression representing a composite value consisting of the value DEN.true and a transition s as components. Hence we have

DEN.f(z) = RES(DEN.f,z)
See also Section 8.3, where this mechanism is described in a general framework.

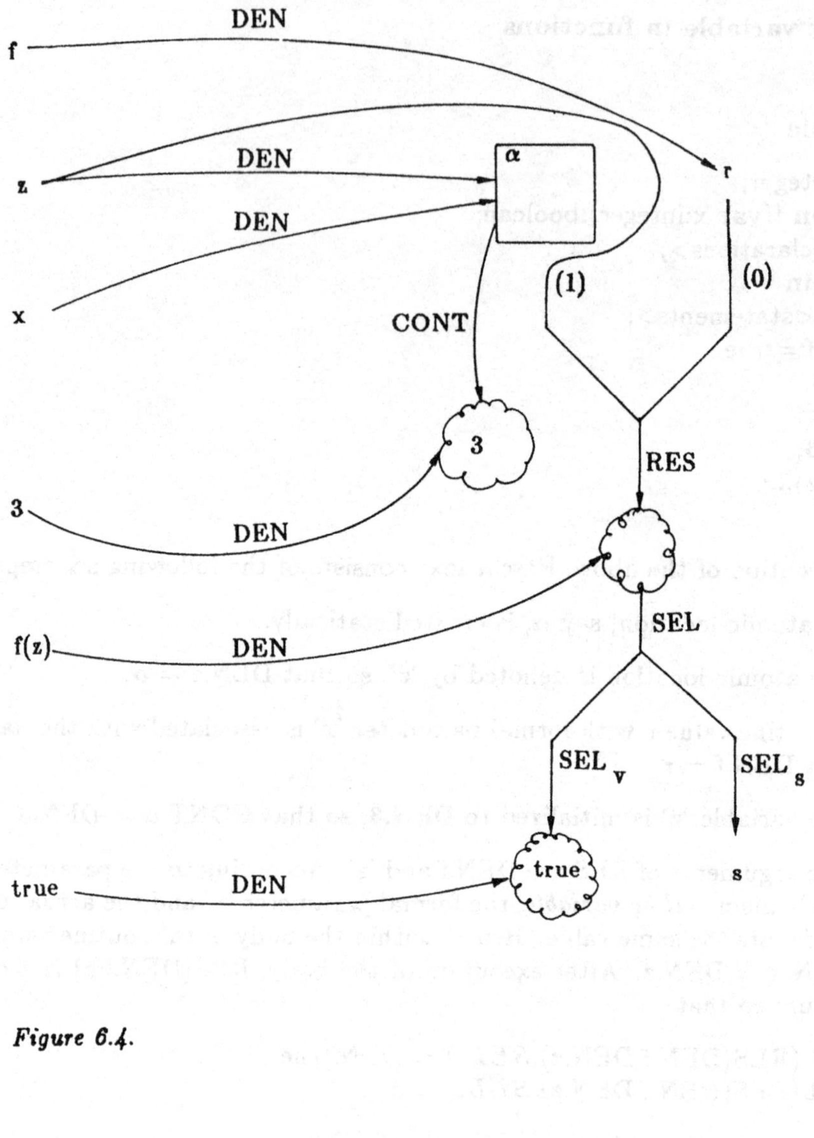
DEN
f
DEN
z
α
DEN
r
(1)
(0)
x
CONT
3
RES
3
DEN
SEL
f(z)
DEN
SEL v
SEL s
true
true
DEN
s

Figure 6.4.

The value diagram just before the end of the execution of the function call 'f(z)' is shown in Figure 6.4.

Call by reference in procedures

Example

```
var z:integer;
procedure p(var x:integer);
    <declarations>;
    begin
        <statements>
    end;
begin
    z:=3;
    p(z);
end
```

Call by variable in procedures is similar to call by variable in functions. The same six steps constitute the elaboration of the example, except that step (5) becomes RES(DEN.p,z) $= s$

where s stands for a transition, and step (6) becomes

DEN.p(z) $= s$

(see also Section 8.3)
The value diagram just before the end of the execution of the call 'p(z)' is shown in Figure 6.5.

Consider the following example in Pascal:

Example

```
var b:integer;
function f(var x:integer):integer;
    begin
        x:=x+1;
        f:=x+2
    end;
begin
    b:=0;
    ...f(b)+5...
end
```

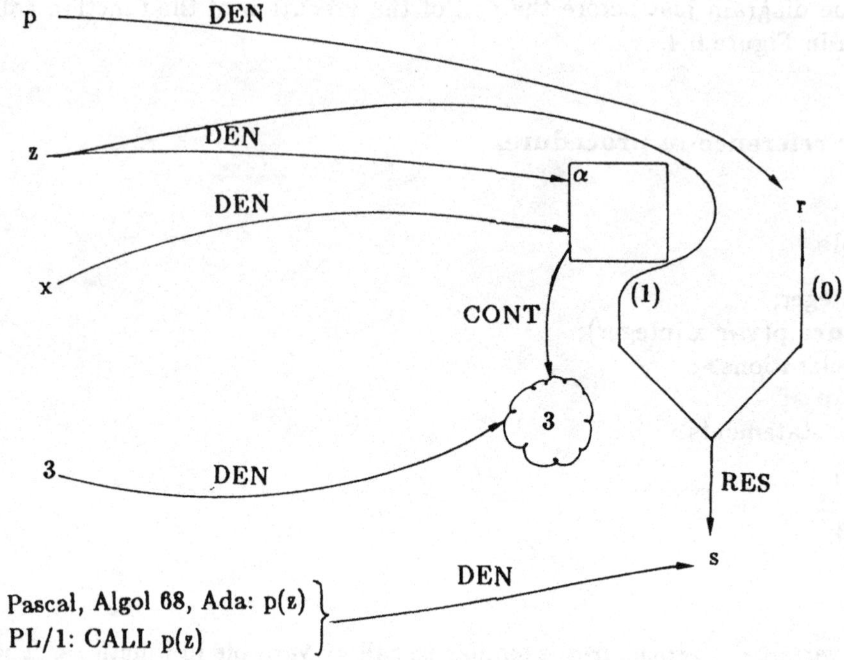
p
DEN
z
DEN
α
DEN
r
x
(1)
(0)
CONT
3
3
DEN
RES
s
DEN
Pascal, Algol 68, Ada: p(z)
PL/1: CALL p(z)

Figure 6.5.

The value diagram just before the end of the execution of the call 'f(b)' is shown in Figure 6.6. The value diagram just before the end of the execution of the part of the program given above is shown in Figure 6.7. Notice that RES(DEN.f,b) is a composite value with a transition component and a transitionless component.

The transition is expressed by

$$\text{CONT.DEN.b} \leftarrow \text{CONT.DEN.b} + \text{DEN.1}$$

while the transitionless component is DEN.3

6.4.3 Routine values as parameters

Example

```
function f(x:real):boolean;
    <declarations>;
    begin
        <statements>;
        f:=true
    end;
procedure p(function g(a:real):boolean);
    <declarations>;
    begin
        <statements>;
        ...g(3.14)...
    end;
begin
    ...
    p(f);
    ...
end
```

Suppose that 'f' yields a transitionless value, i.e., DEN.f is a function value. Then the execution of the above text consists of the following six steps :

(1) A function value r with one formal parameter 'x' is associated with 'f', so that DEN.f $= r$.

(2) A procedure value r_1 with one formal parameter 'g' is associated with 'p', so that DEN.p $= r_1$.

(3) The arguments of RES are DEN.p and f. The body of the procedure value DEN.p is executed after f has been bound to g so that within the body DEN.g = DEN.f. After execution of the body we have RES(DEN.p,f) = s.

(4) A compound expression 'p(f)' is created (cf. Section 8.3.) with DEN.p(f) = s.

(5) During the execution of the body of the procedure value r_1, the function value r is called and a 'call by value' binding between the formal parameter 'x' and the actual parameter '3.14' takes place. Hence an atomic location, say α, is created with CONT.α = DEN(3.14).

(6) The body of the routine value r is executed. We then have

RES(DEN.g,3.14) = DEN.true
DEN.g(3.14) = DEN.true

The value diagram just before the end of the execution of the call 'g(3.14)' is shown in Figure 6.8.

In Pascal, function values can be denoted by function identifiers and operators, whereas procedure values are denoted by procedure identifiers. Routine values cannot be stored in locations, they cannot be components of composite data and they cannot be the results of function values.

Pascal does not allow composite data (records and arrays) to be the results of function values. The results of function values may only be atomic data (AD) or locations (L).

6.4.4 Parameter binding for array values

In the following example, for any call of the procedure 'p', the actual parameter must be an array value with 1 as lower bound and 3 as upper bound. This is a consequence of the static bounds of Pascal arrays, as defined in standard Pascal in [Jensen 1975]. This is a serious restriction for Pascal users, especially in the construction of library routines.

Example

```
const maxvec=3;
type vectype=array[1..maxvec] of integer;
var vecactual:vectype;
procedure p(vecformal:vectype);
    <declarations>;
    begin
        <statements>
    end;
```

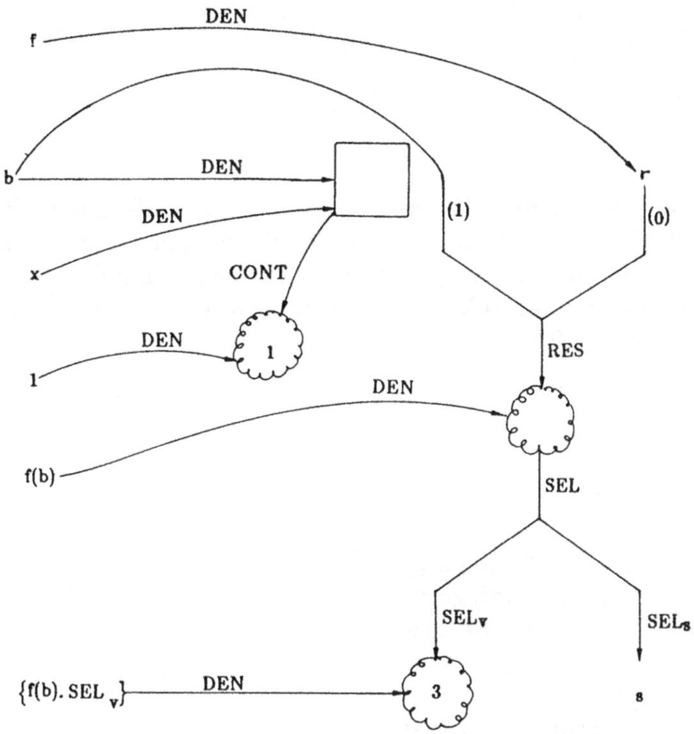

Figure 6.6.

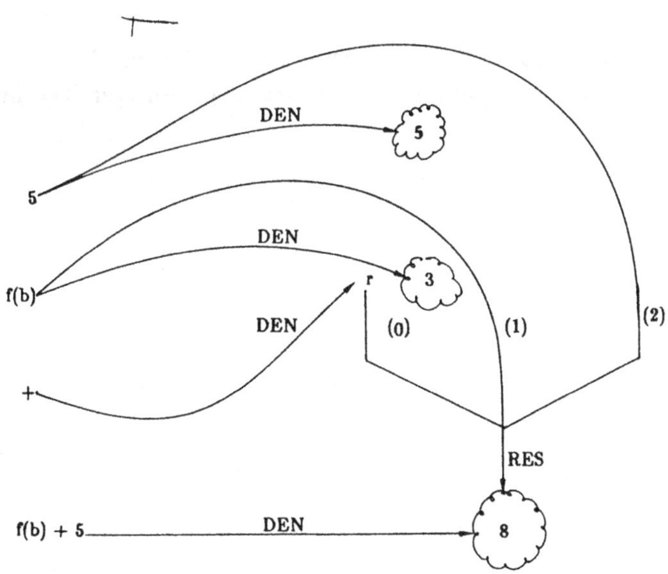

Figure 6.7.

```
begin
    ...
    p(vecactual);
    ...
end
```

The following example illustrates the use of the so-called conformant-array-schema, by means of which the array location denoted by the formal parameter assumes the bounds of the corresponding actual parameter. The conformant-array-schema may only be used with call by variable. It was first introduced in the Draft Proposal for Pascal in [Addyman 1980].

Example

```
type
    vectype_3=array[1..3] of integer;
    vectype_5=array[1..5] of integer;
    vectype = array[lwb..upb] of integer;
var vecactual_3:vectype_3;
    vecactual_5:vectype_5;
procedure p(var vecformal: vectype);
    <declarations>;
    begin
        <statements>

    {the identifiers 'lwb' and 'upb' denote the lower and upper bounds of the actual
    parameter which has been bound to the formal parameter 'vecformal'}
    end;
begin
    ...
    p(vecactual_3);
    ...
    p(vecactual_5);
    ...
end
```

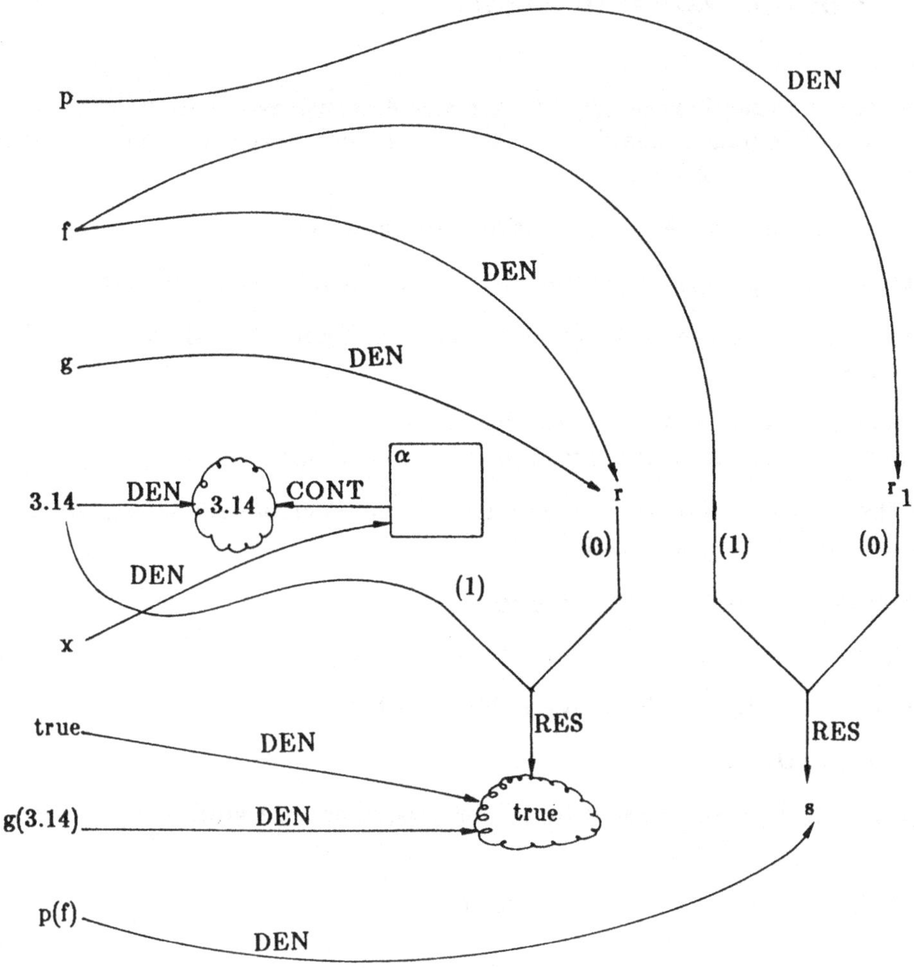
p
DEN
f
DEN
g
DEN
α
3.14
DEN
3.14
CONT
r
r_1
(0)
(1)
(0)
DEN
(1)
x
RES
RES
true
DEN
g(3.14)
DEN
true
s
p(f)
DEN

Figure 6.8.

§6.5 Routine values in Algol 68

Procedures and functions in Algol 68 are termed routines. There is only one type of parameter binding mechanism in Algol 68 (which covers the three parameter binding mechanisms of Pascal).

The general form of an Algol 68 routine declaration is

proc$(\mu_1,\ldots,\mu_i,\ldots,\mu_n)\mu$ <identifier>= $(\mu_1\delta_1,\ldots,\mu_i\delta_i,\ldots,\mu_n\delta_n)\mu$:<unit>

where the μ_i and μ are types (called modes in Algol 68) and the δ_i are *formal parameters.*

The general form of an Algol 68 routine call is
<**proc**$(\mu_1,\ldots,\mu_i,\ldots,\mu_n)\mu$ expression>$(e_1,\ldots,e_i,\ldots,e_n)$

where the e_i are expressions of type μ_i, denoting the *actual parameters.* We assume that all coercions in e_i are made explicit.

The parameter binding is expressed by :

$$\mu_i\delta_i = e_i$$

which is a legal Algol 68 declaration. We then have

$$\text{DEN}.\delta_i = \text{DEN}.e_i$$

Procedures in Algol 68 are said to deliver a value of type **void**.

6.5.1 Simulation of call by constant

Example

```
ref int z=loc int;
proc (int)bool f= (int x)bool:
    begin
        <declarations and statements>;
        true
    end;
z:=3;
...f(int(z))...
```

The execution of the above example consists of the following steps :

1) An atomic location, say α, is created.

2) The location α is denoted by 'z', so that DEN.z=α.

3) A routine value r with formal parameter 'x' is associated with the name 'f' so that DEN.f=r.

4) According to the parameter binding mechanism of Algol 68, the formal parameter 'x' is associated with the actual parameter '**int**(Z)', so that DEN.x=CONT.DEN.z

5) The arguments of RES are DEN.f and '**int**(z)'. The body of the routine value is executed. Notice that 'x' plays the role of a local constant in the body of the routine value.

6) After execution of the body we have

   DEN.f(z)=RES(DEN.f,**int**(z))=DEN.true

The parameter binding is described by '**int** x = **int**(z)', so that we have

DEN.x = DEN.**int**(z)

Here, the formal parameter 'x' is bound in such a way that 'x' plays the role of a local constant identifier in the body of the function. This binding is sometimes called *call by constant*. It is not allowed in Pascal and PL/1. Notice that instead of 'f(**int**(z))', one may write 'f(z)', in which case implicit dereferencing takes place.

The value diagram just before the end of the execution of the call 'f(**int**(z))' is shown in Figure 6.9.

6.5.2 Simulation of call by variable

Example

```
ref int z=loc int;
proc(ref int) void p=(ref int x) void:
    begin
        <declarations and statements>
    end;
z:=3;
...p(z)...;
```

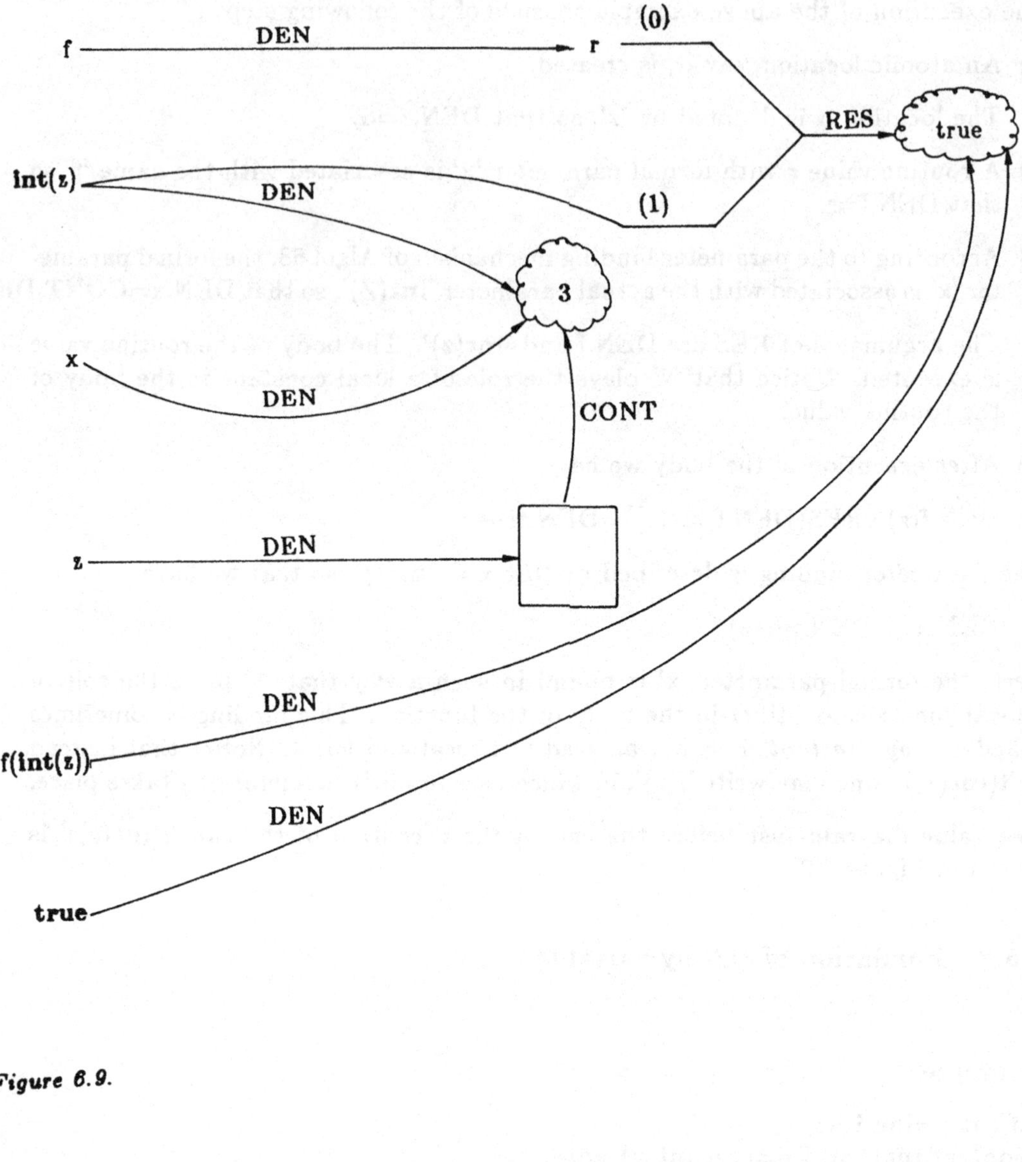

Figure 6.9.

The steps in the elaboration of this example and the corresponding value diagram can be found in Section 6.4.2. The parameter binding is described by the Algol 68 declaration:

ref int x=z; so that we have

DEN.x = DEN.z

6.5.3 Simulation of call by value

Example

```
ref int z=loc int;
proc (int) bool f=(int x) bool:
    begin
        ref int aux=loc int:=x;
        <declarations and statements>;
        true
    end;
z:=3;
... f(int(z))...
```

6.5.4 Routine values as parameters

Example

```
proc(real)bool f=
    (real x)bool:begin...;true end;
proc(proc(real)bool) void p=
    (proc(real)bool g) void:
        begin
            <declarations and statements>;
            ...g(3.14)...
        end;
...
p(f);
...
```

The elaboration of this example is as described in Section 6.4.3.

The parameter binding is described by the Algol 68 declaration

proc(real)bool g=f;

so that we have

DEN.g = DEN.f

6.5.5 Routine values as the contents of locations

Example

```
ref bool b=loc bool;
ref proc(int)bool fvar=loc proc(int)bool;
fvar:=
    if <boolean expression>
        then (int a)bool:begin...end
        else (int c)bool:begin...end
    fi;
b:=proc(int)bool(fvar)(3);
```

The same example can be rephrased using the contracted and initialized forms:

```
bool b;
proc(int)bool fvar:=
    if <boolean expression>
        then (int a)bool:begin...end
        else (int c)bool:begin...end
    fi;
b:='proc(int)bool (fvar)(3)'
```

The value diagram just before the end of the execution of the call 'fvar(3)' is shown in Figure 6.10.

Instead of '**proc(int)bool**(fvar)(3)' one may write 'fvar(3)' in the above context, in which case an implicit dereferencing of 'fvar' is assumed.

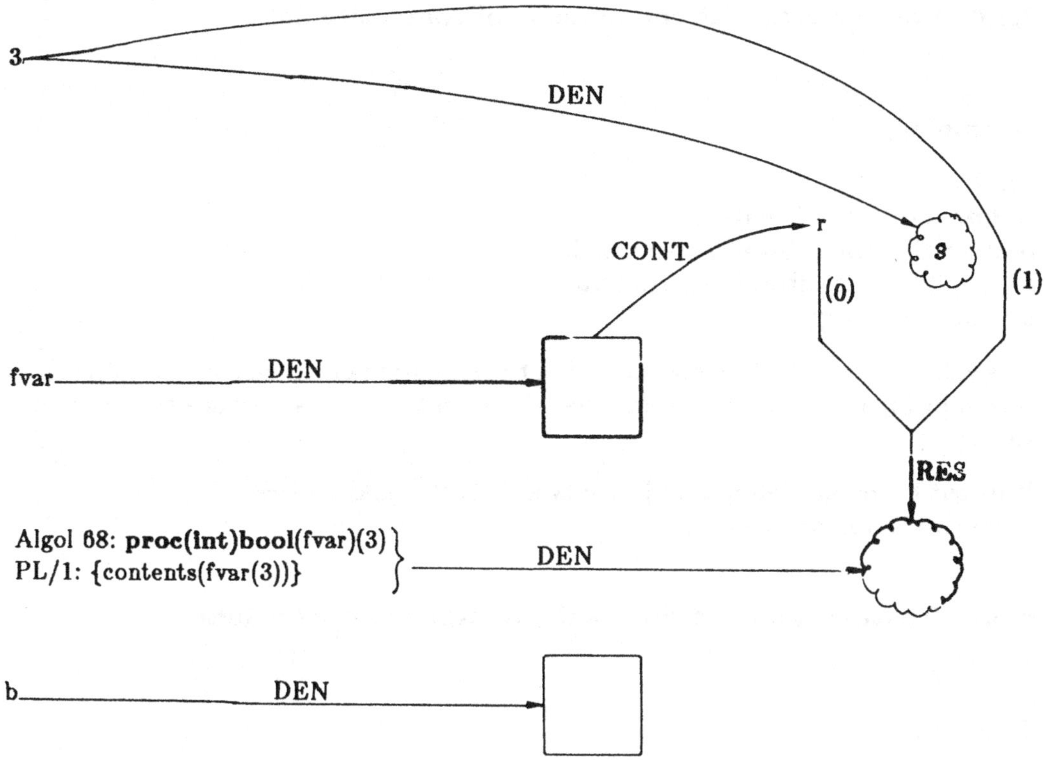
3
DEN
r
CONT
3
(0)
(1)
fvar
DEN
RES
Algol 68: **proc(int)bool**(fvar)(3)
PL/1: {contents(fvar(3))}
DEN
b
DEN

Figure 6.10

6.5.6 Routine values as components of composite data

Example

```
bool b;
[1:2]proc(int)bool routvec;
routvec[1]:=(int a)bool:begin...end;
routvec[2]:=(int c)bool:begin...end;
b:=routvec[2](10);
```

The value diagram just before the end of the execution of the call 'routvec[2](10)' is shown in Figure 6.11. We assume that these routine values produce transitionless values.

Without coercion (deferencing), 'routvec[2](10)' would be written '**proc**(**int**)**bool**(routvec[2])(10)'.

6.5.7 Routine values as the results of other routine values

Example

```
bool b;
proc(int)proc(real)bool f =
    (int a)proc(real)bool:
        begin
            <declarations and statements>;
            if <boolean expression>
                then (real c)bool:begin...end
                else (real d)bool:begin...end
            fi
        end;
b:=f(3)(3.14);
```

The value diagram just before the end of the execution of the function call 'f(3)(3.14)' is shown in Figure 6.12. We assume that these routine values do not produce a transition.

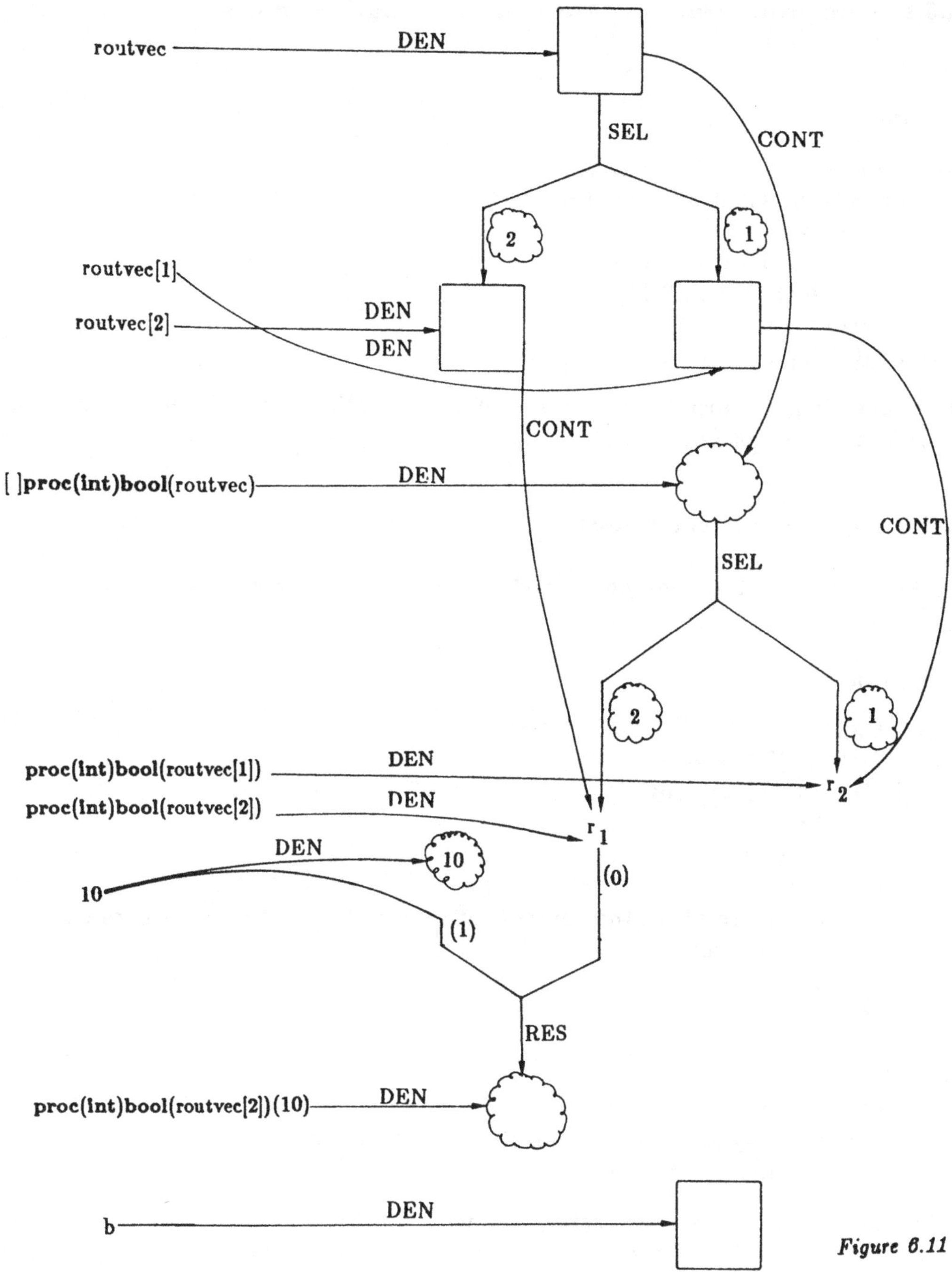

routvec
DEN
SEL
CONT
2
1
routvec[1]
routvec[2]
DEN
DEN
CONT
[ ]proc(int)bool(routvec)
DEN
CONT
SEL
2
1
proc(int)bool(routvec[1])
DEN
proc(int)bool(routvec[2])
DEN
r_2
r_1
DEN
10
10
(0)
(1)
RES
proc(int)bool(routvec[2])(10)
DEN
b
DEN

Figure 6.11

6.5.8 Composite values as the results of routine values

Examples

```
proc(int)struct(int a,[ ]real b) f=
    (int x)struct(int a,[ ]real b):
        begin
            <declarations and statements>;
            (0,(1.14,2.14,3.14))
        end;
...(b of f(1))[2]...;
```

The value diagram just before the end of the execution of the function call '(b of f(1))[2]' is shown in Figure 6.13.

6.5.9 Operator declarations

In Algol 68, operators may be defined by means of the operator declaration.

Example

```
[1:3]int a,b,c;
op([ ]int,[ ]int)[ ]int + =
    ([ ] int x,[ ]int y)[ ]int:
        begin
            flex[1:0]int z;
            ...
            co the result of the component-wise addition of x and y is calculated
                in z co;
            z
        end;
a:=(10,20,30);
b:=(40,50,60);
c:=[ ]int(a)+[ ]int(b);
        co one may also make use of the deferencing of 'a' and 'b' by
            writing 'c:=a+b' co
```

The atomic expression '+' is associated with a function value r, so that DEN.+ = r. The call of the function value is represented by '[ ]**int**(a) + [ ]**int**(b)'. The parameter binding can be expressed by the Algol 68 declarations

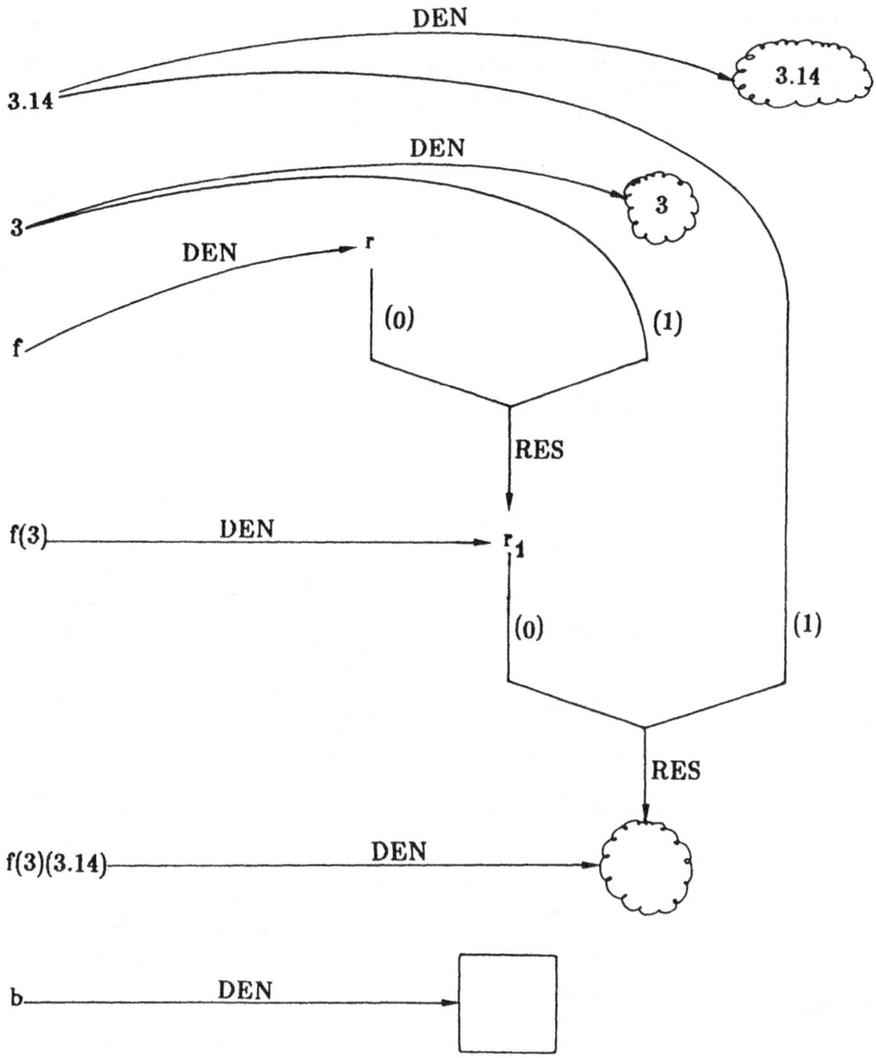

Figure 6.12

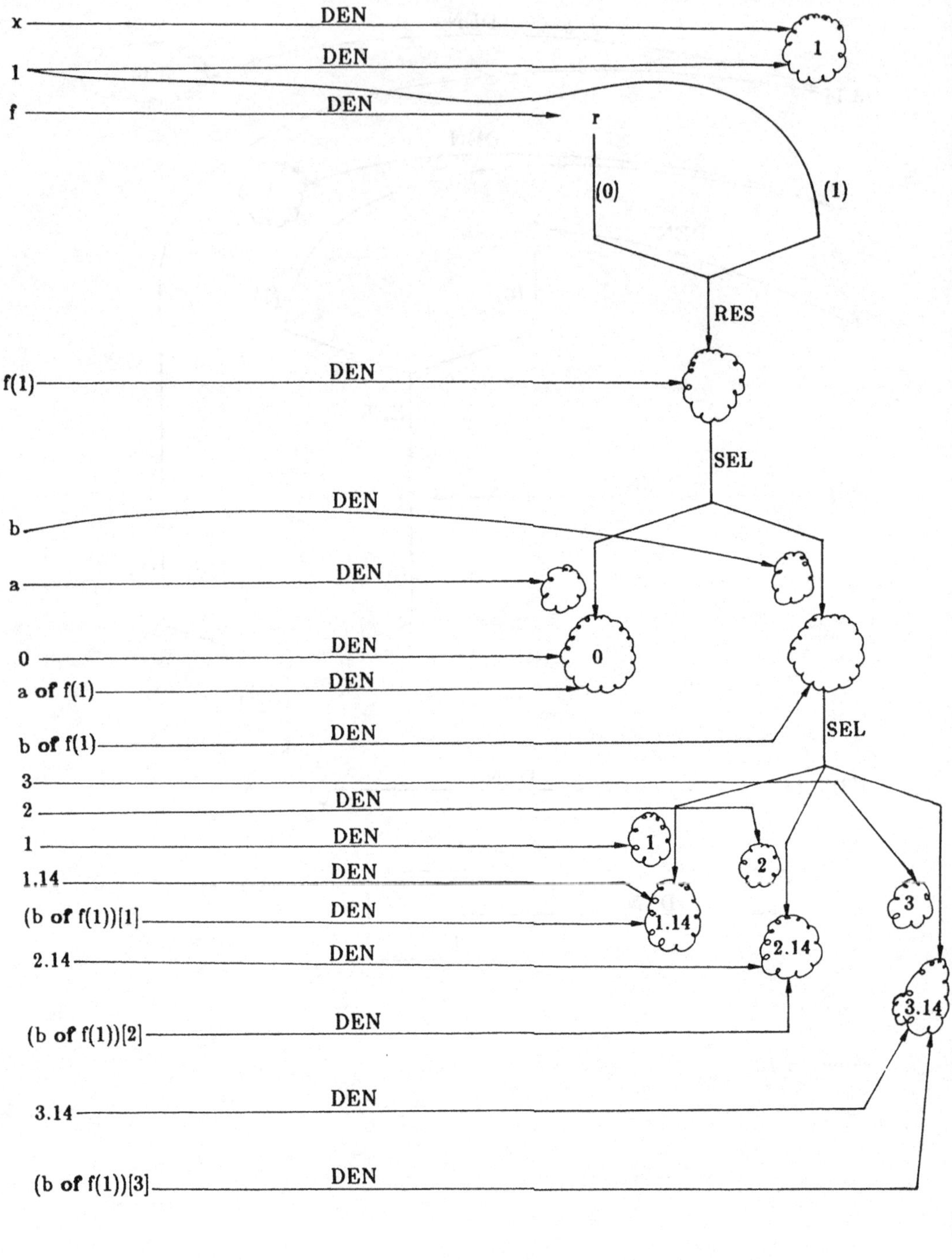
x
DEN
1
DEN
f
DEN
r
(0)
(1)
RES
f(1)
DEN
SEL
DEN
b
a
DEN
0
DEN
0
a of f(1)
DEN
b of f(1)
DEN
SEL
3
2
DEN
1
DEN
1
2
1.14
DEN
3
(b of f(1))[1]
DEN
1.14
2.14
DEN
2.14
3.14
(b of f(1))[2]
DEN
3.14
DEN
(b of f(1))[3]
DEN

Figure 6.13

[1:3]**int** x=[ ]**int**(a) and [1:3]**int** y=[ ]**int**(b)

This gives the relations

DEN.x = CONT.DEN.a and DEN.y = CONT.DEN.b

The call of the function value *r* then gives

RES(DEN.+,[ ]**int**(a),[ ]**int**(b)) = CONT.DEN.c
DEN([ ]**int**(a)+[ ]**int**(b))=CONT.DEN.c

The value diagram just before the end of execution of the call '[ ]**int**(a) + [ ]**int**(b)' is shown in Figure 6.14.

6.5.10 Parameter binding for array values

In contrast to Pascal, PL/1 and Ada, the parameter binding for array values in Algol 68 fits very well into the general concept of parameter binding.

Example

```
...
[1..3]int vecactual_3:=(1,2,3);
[1..5]int vecactual_5:=(1,2,3,4,5);
proc([ ]int)void p=([ ]int vecformal)void:
    begin
        <declarations and statements>
        co The bounds of the array datum denoted by 'vecformal' are those
            of the corresponding actual parameter. These bounds are
            expressed by 'lwb vecformal' and 'upb vecformal'
            respectively co
    end;
p(vecactual_3);
p(vecactual_5);
```

§6.6 Routine values in PL/1

6.6.1 Call by reference

Call by reference in functions

This case is similar to call by variable in functions in Pascal.

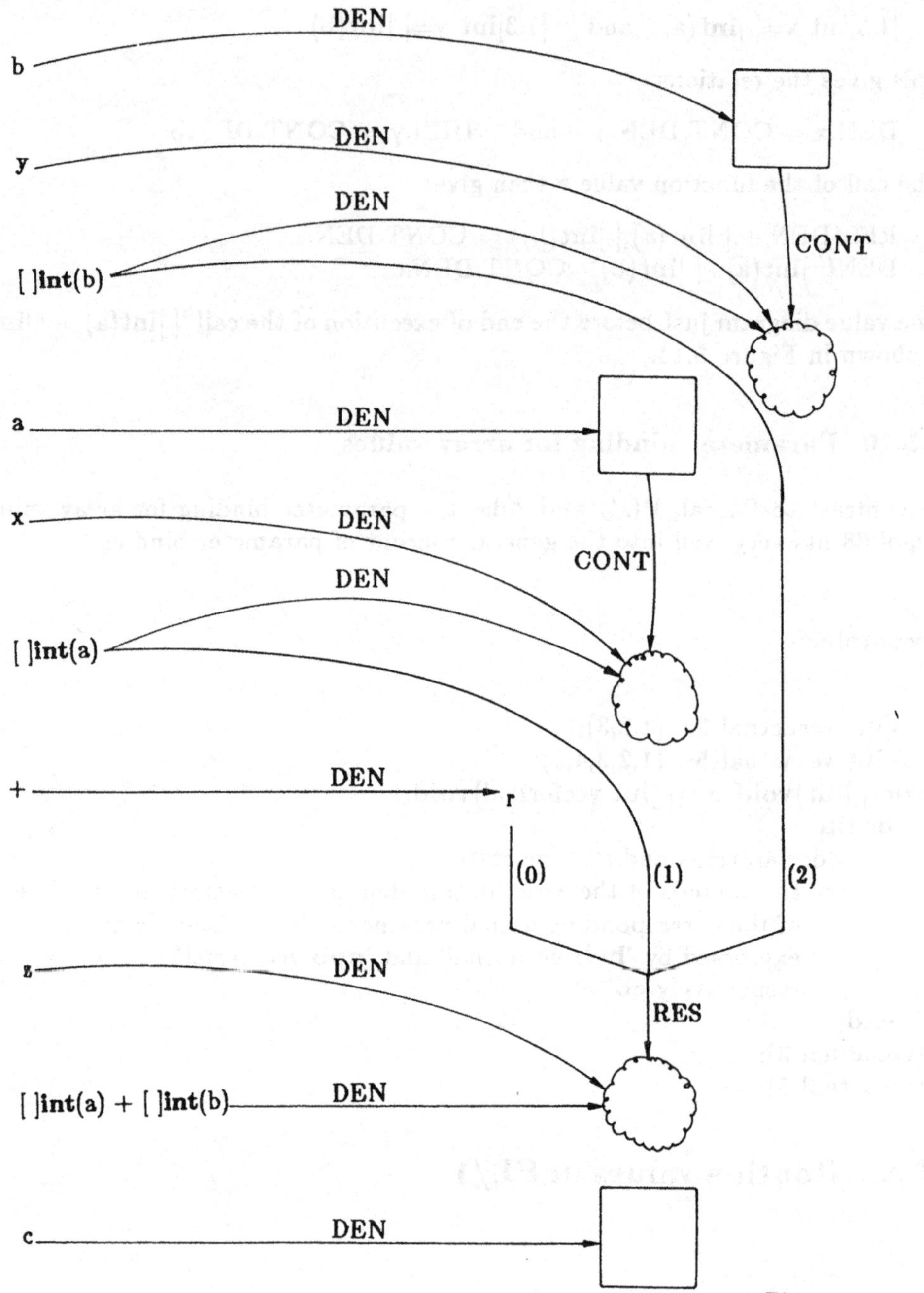
DEN
b
DEN
y
DEN
[ ]int(b)
CONT
a
DEN
x
DEN
CONT
DEN
[ ]int(a)
+
DEN
r
(0)
(1)
(2)
z
DEN
RES
[ ]int(a) + [ ]int(b)
DEN
c
DEN

Figure 6.14

Example

Recall the first example of Section 6.4.2. Its PL/1 translation is :

```
DECLARE z BIN FIXED;
f :  PROCEDURE(x) RETURNS(BIT(1));
        DECLARE x BIN FIXED;
        <declarations and statements>
        RETURN('1'B);
     END f;
z=3;
...f(z)...;
```

Call by reference in procedures

This case is similar to call by variable in procedures in Pascal.

Example

Recall the second example of Section 6.4.2. Its PL/1 translation is :

```
DECLARE z BIN FIXED;
p :  PROCEDURE(x);
        DECLARE x BIN FIXED;
        <declarations and statements>
     END p;
CALL p(z);
```

The execution of each of the two PL/1 programs given above consists of six steps which are identical to those specified for the Pascal call by variable in Section 6.4.2. The parameter binding is again DEN.x = DEN.z.
As in Pascal call by variable, the actual parameter must necessarily be a location.

The value diagrams of the two examples above are shown in Figures 6.4 and 6.5.

6.6.2 Call by dummy argument

Call by dummy argument in functions

This case is similar to call by value in functions in Pascal.

Example

```
DECLARE z BIN FIXED;
f : PROCEDURE(x) RETURNS (BIT(1));
      DECLARE x BIN FIXED;
      <declarations and statements>
      RETURN('1'B);
   END f;
z=3;
...f((z))...;
...f(5)...;
```

Call by dummy argument in procedures

This case is similar to call by value in procedures in Pascal.

Example

```
DECLARE z BIN FIXED;
f : PROCEDURE(x);
      DECLARE x BIN FIXED;
      <declarations and statements>
   END f;
z=3;
CALL f((z));
CALL f(5);
```

The execution of each of the above two PL/1 programs consists of seven steps which are identical to those given for the Pascal call by value examples in Section 6.4.1. As in the case of call by value, the formal parameter again plays the role of a variable local to the body of the routine value.

The PL/1 rules determining the parameter bindings call by reference and call by dummy argument are rather complex. We will give only those rules which are related to the features discussed in this book.

According to the PL/1 manual [IBM 1976], a dummy argument is created when the actual parameter expression is any of the following (actually, the list is much longer):

- a constant
- an expression involving operators
- an expression in parentheses
- a variable whose data attributes are different from the data attributes declared for the formal parameter
- a function reference with an argument list.

In contrast to Algol-like languages, the parameter binding mechanism is defined at the point of call of the routine value and not at its point of definition (declaration). This has an important consequence with respect to reliability of programs, which is discussed in Section 6.8.2.

6.6.3 Routine values as parameters

Example

```
f : PROCEDURE(x) RETURNS(BIT(1));
        DECLARE x BIN FLOAT;
        <declarations and statements>
        RETURN ('1'B);
    END f;
p : PROCEDURE(g);
        DECLARE g ENTRY (BIN FLOAT) RETURNS(BIT(1));
        <declarations and statements>
        ...g(3.14)...
    END p;
...
CALL p(f);
```

6.6.4 Routine values as the contents of locations

Example

```
DECLARE
    b BIT(1),
    fvar ENTRY(BIN FIXED) RETURNS (BIT(1));
f : PROCEDURE(a) RETURNS(BIT(1));
        DECLARE a BIN FIXED;
        <declarations and statements>
    END f;
```

```
g : PROCEDURE(b) RETURNS(BIT(1));
      DECLARE b BIN FIXED;
      <declarations and statements>
    END g;
IF <boolean expression>
    THEN fvar=f;
    ELSE fvar=g;
b=fvar(3);
```

This example is similar to the one given for Algol 68 in Section 6.5.5. The corresponding value diagram is given in Figure 6.10.

6.6.5 Routine values as components of composite data

Example

```
DECLARE
    b BIT(1),
    routvec(1:3) ENTRY(BIN FIXED) RETURNS(BIT(1));
f : PROCEDURE(a) RETURNS(BIT(1));
      DECLARE a BIN FIXED;
      <declarations and statements>
    END f;
g : PROCEDURE(b) RETURNS(BIT(1));
      DECLARE b BIN FIXED;
      <declarations and statements>
    END g;
h : PROCEDURE(c) RETURNS(BIT(1));
      DECLARE c BIN FIXED;
      <declarations and statements>
    END h;
routvec(1)=f;
routvec(2)=g;
routvec(3)=h;
IF <boolean expression>
    THEN b=routvec(1)(10);
    ELSE b=routvec(1)(20);
```

This example is similar to the one given for Algol 68 in Section 6.5.6. The value diagram is analogous to the one given in Figure 6.11.

6.6.6 Parameter binding for array values

Example

```
DECLARE vecactual(1:3) BIN FIXED INIT(1,2,3);
p : PROCEDURE(vecformal);
        DECLARE vecformal(1:3) BIN FIXED;
        <declarations and statements>
        /* the lower and upper bounds of the actual parameter must
        be 1 and 3 respectively */
    END p;
...
CALL p(vecactual);
...
```

Example

```
DECLARE
    vecactual_3(1:3) BIN FIXED INIT(1,2,3),
    vecactual_5(1:5) BIN FIXED INIT(1,2,3,4,5);
p : PROCEDURE(vecformal);
        DECLARE vecformal(*)BIN FIXED;
        <declarations and statements>
        /* the lower and upper bounds of the array location denoted by
        'vecformal' are taken from the actual parameter. They are
        expressed by 'HBOUND(vecformal,1)' and 'LBOUND(vecformal,1)'
        respectively */
    END  p;
...
CALL p(vecactual_3);
...
CALL p(vecactual_5);
```

§6.7 Routine values in Ada

Functions and procedures in Ada are called subprograms. The parameter binding mechanisms in Ada are called mode **in**, mode **out** and mode **in out**.

6.7.1 Mode in

Example

```
z:integer;
function f(x:in integer) return boolean is
    <declarations>
    begin
        <statements>
        return true;
    end f;
begin
    z:=3;
    ...f(z)...;
end
```

The Ada parameter binding mechanism mode **in** is identical to call by constant in Algol 68 (see Section 6.5.1).

Example

```
z:integer;
procedure p(x:in integer) is
    <declarations>
    begin
        <statements>
    end p;
z:=3;
p(z);
```

For the execution steps of the above two examples, see Section 6.5.1.

6.7.2 Mode out

Example

```
z:integer;
procedure p(x:out integer) is
    <declarations>
    begin
        <statements>
    end p;
z:=3;
p(z);
```

The execution of the above example consists of the following steps :

(1) An atomic location, say α, is created.

(2) The location α is denoted by 'z', so that DEN.z=α.

(3) A routine value r with formal parameter 'x' is associated with the name 'p', so that DEN.p=r.

(4) The atomic location α is initialized to DEN.3, so that CONT.α = DEN.3.

(5) According to the parameter binding mode **out** of Ada, the formal parameter 'x' is associated with the actual parameter 'z', and an atomic location, say β, is created and denoted by 'x', so that DEN.x = β

(6) The body <statements> of the routine value r is executed. A postlude action is added at the end of the body of the routine value, which consists of transferring the contents of DEN.x back into DEN.z. We therefore have CONT.α=CONT.β.

(7) After execution of the body we have

    DEN.p(z)=RES(DEN.p,z)=s

    where s is a transition.

The parameter binding mode **out** has no equivalent in Pascal, PL/1 or Algol 68. This mechanism is available in one of the early successors of Algol 60, namely Algol W [Wirth 1966], where it is termed *call by result.* The parameter binding mode **out** in Ada is not allowed for functions.

6.7.3 Mode in out

Example

```
z:integer;
procedure p(x:in out integer) is
    <declarations>
    begin
        <statements>
    end p;
z:=3;
p(z);
```

The execution of the above example consists of the following steps:

(1) An atomic location, say α, is created.

(2) The location α is denoted by 'z', so that DEN.z=α.

(3) A routine value τ with formal parameter 'x' is associated with the name 'p', so that DEN.p=τ.

(4) The atomic location α is initialized to DEN.3, so that CONT.α=DEN.3.

(5) According to the parameter binding mode **in out** of Ada, the formal parameter 'x' is associated with the actual parameter 'z', and an atomic location, say β, is created and denoted by 'x', so that DEN.x = β.

(6) A prelude action and a postlude action are added respectively before and after the body of the routine value. The prelude action consists of initializing the location DEN.x to the contents of DEN.z. We thus have CONT.β = CONT.α before the body of the routine value.
The postlude action consists of transferring the contents of DEN.x back into DEN.z. We therefore have CONT.α=CONT.β after the body.

The body of the routine value as modified above is executed.

(7) After execution of the body we have

DEN.p(z)=RES(DEN.p,z)=s

The parameter binding mode **in out** is not allowed for funcions.

Mode **in out** has no counterpart in Pascal, Algol 68 or PL/1. This mechanism is again available in Algol W, where it is termed *call by value result.*

The semantics of the parameter binding modes in Ada are defined in such a way that implementation both by value copying and by value sharing is possible. In the *value copying* implementation, the actual parameters are copied into the formal **in** or **in out** parameters on entering the body of the routine value. Similarly, the values of the formal **out** or **in out** parameters are copied back into the actual parameters on leaving the body of the routine value. In the *value sharing* implementation, the formal parameters are references to the actual parameters in the calling environment. Value sharing is only permitted for actual parameters which are arrays and records. Ada simply states that any program that relies on one of the two parameter binding implementations (copying or sharing) is erroneous.

6.7.4 Generic subprograms

In general, the parameter binding mechanism for routine values is one of the tools for grouping similarities within a class of computations into a common program structure. In this way, the abstraction of the computational behaviour can be better expressed.

The parameter binding mechanisms in Pascal, PL/1, Algol 68 and Ada discussed so far concern the binding between a name (formal parameter) and a value (actual parameter). This binding is *dynamic*, i.e., it occurs at run time.

The concept of generic subprograms introduces a parameter binding mechanism that can best be compared with the *call by name* of Algol 60. However, generic subprograms allow binding not only between a name and a value, but also between a name and a type. The binding for generic subprograms is *static*, i.e. it occurs at compile time.

In this section, we will only discuss generic subprograms where the generic formal parameters are bound to values. A discussion of type bindings is deferred to Chapter 9.

Notice already that in Ada the only way to parameterize subprograms by other subprograms is through the generic subprogram concept.

Parameter binding for atomic data

Example

```
        - - declaration of the global variables 'i', 'z' and 'b'
i:integer:=0;
z:float:=0.0;
b:boolean:=false;
        - - declaration of the generic subprogram 'f_generic'
        - - 'f_generic' does not denote a routine value
generic
   a:in integer;
   x:in out float;
function f_generic return boolean;

        - - the body of the generic specification of 'f_generic'
function f_generic return boolean is
   <declarations>
   begin
        <statements>
        ...a...; - - 'a' is used in the context of an integer
        ...x...; - - 'x' is used in the context of a location
                - - containing a floating point value.
        return true;
     end
        - -instantiation of the generic subprogram
        - -'f_instance' denotes a routine value
function f_instance is new f_generic(i+1,z);
        - -call of the routine value denoted by 'f_instance'
b:=f_instance;
```

The generic subprogram 'f_generic' describes a *pattern of routine values*, parametrized by the formal parameters 'a' and 'x'. Instances of 'f_generic' can be obtained by means of a so-called instantiation (see below), where the generic formal parameters 'a' and 'x' are bound to an integer value and a location holding a real value respectively. The parameter binding mechanism is made by *textual replacement* of the generic formal parameters by the expressions of the actual parameters in the instantiation. This parameter binding mechanism can best be compared with the call by name of Algol 60, except that here binding is static and is also valid for types.

As a result of the instantiation of the above generic subprogram, 'f_instance' denotes a routine value obtained from 'f_generic' by replacing each occurrence of 'a' by 'i+1' and 'x' by 'z'.

Parameter binding for routine values

Example

```
          - -declaration of the function 'f'
function f(x:in float) return boolean is
    <declarations>
    begin
        <statements>
        return true;
    end f;

          - -declaration of the generic procedure 'p_generic'
generic
        with function g(a:in float) return boolean;
procedure p_generic;

          - - the body of the generic specification of 'p_generic'
procedure p_generic is
        <declararations>
        begin
            <statements>
            ...g(3.14)...
        end p_generic;

        - -instantiation of the generic procedure 'p_ generic'
procedure p_user is new p_generic(f);

          - -call of the routine value denoted by 'p_user'
p_user;
```

6.7.5 More about routine values in Ada

As in Algol 68 (see Section 6.5.8), the result of a routine value in Ada may be a composite value.

Example

```
type rectype is
    record
        first:integer;
        second:array(1..3) of float;
    end record;
function f(x:in integer) return rectype is
    <declarations>
    begin
        <statements>
        return(0,(1.14,2.14,3.14));
    end f;
...
...f(1).second(2)...;
```

Like Algol 68 (see Section 6.5.9.), Ada allows the declaration of routine values denoted by operators.

Examples

```
type vectype is array(integer range <>)of integer;
a,b,c:vectype(1..3);
function "+"(x,y:in vectype) return vectype is
    z:vectype(x'first..x'last);
    begin
        <statements>
        return z;
    end "+";
a:=(10,20,30);
b:=(40,50,60);
c:=a+b;
```

6.7.6 Parameter binding for array values

Example

```
type vectype is array(1..3) of integer;
vecactual:vectype:=(1,2,3);
procedure p(vecformal:in vectype) is
    <declarations>
    begin
        <statements>
        - - the lower and upper bounds of the actual parameter
        - - must be exactly 1 and 3 respectively.
    end p;
p(vecactual);
```

Example

```
type vectype is array(positive range <>) of integer;
vecactual_3:vectype(1..3):=(1,2,3);
vecactual_5:vectype(1..5):=(1,2,3,4,5);
procedure p(vecformal:in vectype) is
    <declarations>
    begin
        <statements>
        - -the type of the formal parameter is an unconstrained
        - -array type. Therefore, the lower and upper bounds
        - -of the array datum denoted by 'vecformal' are taken
        - -from the actual parameter. They are expressed by
        - -'vecformal'first' and 'vecformal'last' respectively.
    end p;
p(vecactual_3);
p(vecactual_5);
```

§6.8 Evaluation of the parameter binding mechanisms

6.8.1 Protection of actual parameters

Suppose the actual parameter expression is a variable. In *call by value*, the contents of the variable are transmitted to the routine value, and it is as if there were a barrier around the variable protecting it from being overwritten during the elaboration of the body of the routine value. Call by value therefore seems to be an ideal parameter binding mechanism for transmitting *input values* to the routine value. If we look deeper into the mechanism of call by value, however, then we must admit that the protection aspect is worthless as soon as we have an actual parameter which is a location containing another location.

By means of *call by variable*, and the modes **out** and **in out**, the routine value is able to transmit *output values* into the environment of the call of the routine value. From the viewpoint of structured programming, however, these parameter binding mechanisms are far from ideal since the transmission is based on a transition. A nicer way of outputting values from a routine value is to make use of the result mechanism of functions. However, this solution does not work for composite data in Pascal and PL/1. Call by variable can sometimes be useful. This is the case when large composite data are to be transmitted, which for reasons of efficiency we do not want to be copied.

In Ada, it is up to the compiler designer to implement the **out** and **in out** modes for composite data by means of copying or sharing.

6.8.2 Place of definition of the type of parameter binding

The type of the parameter binding in PL/1 is specified at the point of call, whereas in Pascal, Algol 68 and Ada, the type is specified at the point of definition (declaration) of the routine value. Specifying the type of parameter binding at the point of call of the routine value has the following drawback : one may define a routine value that can have a completely different effect depending on the way the actual parameters are denoted in the call. Suppose a program is divided into a number of routines written by different programmers. From a software engineering point of view, it is not wise to define a routine that can be interpreted differently by its users. This situation will lead to unsafe programs that are difficult to read, verify and maintain. As far as maintenance is concerned, it can lead to programming errors that are difficult to locate and to correct.

Example in Algol 68

```
int z;
proc(ref int) void p=
   (ref int x) void:begin...end;
proc(int) void q =
   (int y) void:begin...end;
z:=3;
p(z);
q(z);
```

In the example above, the type of the formal parameter determines whether the location denoted by 'z' or its contents are bound. If this type is '**ref int** ', we have DEN.x=DEN.z(call by variable), whereas if it is '**int**', we have DEN.y = CONT.DEN.z (call by constant).

Example in Algol 68

```
int z;
proc(ref int) bool f =
   (ref int x) bool:
      begin
         <declarations and statements>;
         true
      end;
...
z:=3;
...f(z)...;co simulation of call by variable co
...f(loc int :=z)...;co simulation of call by value co
```

Due to the Algol 68 principle of orthogonality, which allows the use of the generator '**loc int**' at all places where a location holding an integer is expected, call by value can be directly simulated.

The parameter binding is described by DEN.x = DEN.z for the first function call, and DEN.x = DEN(**loc int**) = α for the second function call. In the latter case, we also have CONT.α = CONT.DEN.z. This is exactly call by value.

Note that in both cases the definition of the function is identical. Thus we obtain the same drawback as with PL/1, where the type of parameter binding is defined at the point of call. This example illustrates that orthogonality is not always the best solution.

Example in PL/1

```
DECLARE a BIN FIXED;
p : PROCEDURE(x);
        DECLARE x BIN FIXED;
        <declarations and statements>
        x=0;
        ...
    END p;
CALL p((a));/* the contents of the variable 'a' remain unchanged*/
CALL p(a);/* the contents of the variable 'a' are destroyed*/
```

Depending on the presence or the absence of one pair of parentheses in the call, the effect of the procedure call can be completely different.

Example in PL/1

```
DECLARE a BIN FIXED INIT(0);
p : PROCEDURE (x);
        DECLARE x BIN FLOAT;
        <declarations ans statements>
        x=...;
    END p;
...
CALL p(a);
```

Most programmers with little experience in PL/1 are surprised to learn that the actual parameter above is transmitted as a call by dummy argument. Notice that the (type) attributes of 'a' and 'x' differ, which is the reason for this phenomenon.

Example in PL/1

```
DECLARE i;
p : PROCEDURE(x);
        DECLARE x BIN FLOAT;
        <declarations and statements>
        x=...;
    END p;
...
CALL p(i);
```

The variable 'i' is declared by default with attribute BIN FIXED. Imagine what happens if, for one reason or another, one changes the name of the variable 'i' to 'z'! This is one of the reasons why certain PL/1 defaults are considered to be bad programming practice.

§6.9 Declarations and statements

Statements

In SMALL a declaration is also considered to be a call of a routine value yielding a transition, where the parameter binding between formal and actual parameters is based on textual replacement , i.e., during the execution of the routine value the formal parameters denote the same value as the corresponding actual parameters, even if the value of the DEN function on the actual parameters changes, as is the case in the example of the assignment statement below.

When we write for instance in Pascal

```
i:=1;
```

the corresponding routine value is denoted by ':='. The actual parameters are the expressions 'i' and '1'. In the body of the routine value denoted by ':=', the formal parameters are textually replaced by the actual parameters 'i' and '1'. Thus

$$\text{DEN(i:=1)} = s$$

where s is a transition expressed by

$$\text{CONT.DEN.i} \leftarrow \text{DEN.1}$$

Hence in SMALL, the statement 'i:=1' is considered to be a compound expression denoting a call of the routine value denoted by ':=' (see also Section 8.3.4).

The following examples in Pascal illustrate this feature for various statements.

Example of assignment statement

```
var a:integer;
...
a:=5;
```

The value diagram just before the end of the execution of the assignment is shown in Figure 6.15. The transition s is expressed by

$$\text{CONT.DEN.a} \leftarrow \text{DEN.5}$$

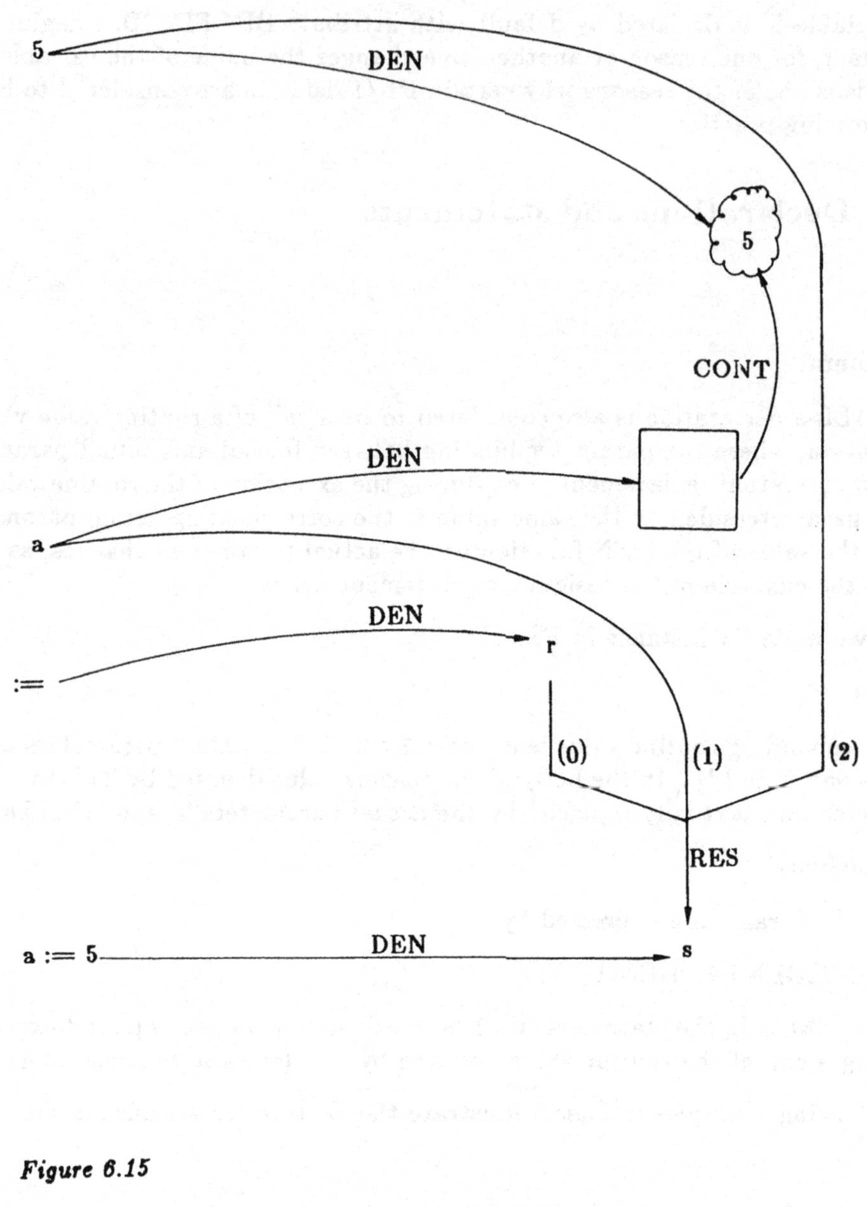

Figure 6.15

Example of repeat statement in Pascal

```
var a:integer;
...
a:=9;
repeat a:=a-2 until a<=0;
```

The routine value is denoted by '**repeat until**' and the actual parameters are the expressions 'a:=a-2' and 'a<=0'. Note that DEN(a<=0) changes during the execution of the repeat statement. At the beginning of the execution it might be DEN.false, but on termination it must be DEN.true.

The value diagram just before the end of the execution of the repeat statement is shown in Figure 6.16. The transition s, is expressed by

CONT.DEN.a $\leftarrow$ DEN(-1)

Example of compound statement in Pascal

```
var a:integer;
...
begin
    a:=5;
    repeat a:= a-2 until a ≤ 0
end;
```

The routine value is denoted by '**begin end**' and the actual parameters are the expressions 'a:=5' and '**repeat** a:=a-2 **until** a<=0'.

The value diagram just before the end of the execution of the compound statement is shown in Figure 6.17.

Declarations

In SMALL, a declaration is also considered to be a call of a routine value yielding a transition. The parameter binding is again based on textual replacement.

When in Pascal we write for instance

var i:integer;

the corresponding routine value is denoted by '**var:**'. It has two parameters, 'i' and 'integer' respectively. The latter denotes a type, which we discuss later in Chapter 9. The result of this call is a transition that is partly described by

AL $\leftarrow$ AL $\cup$ α

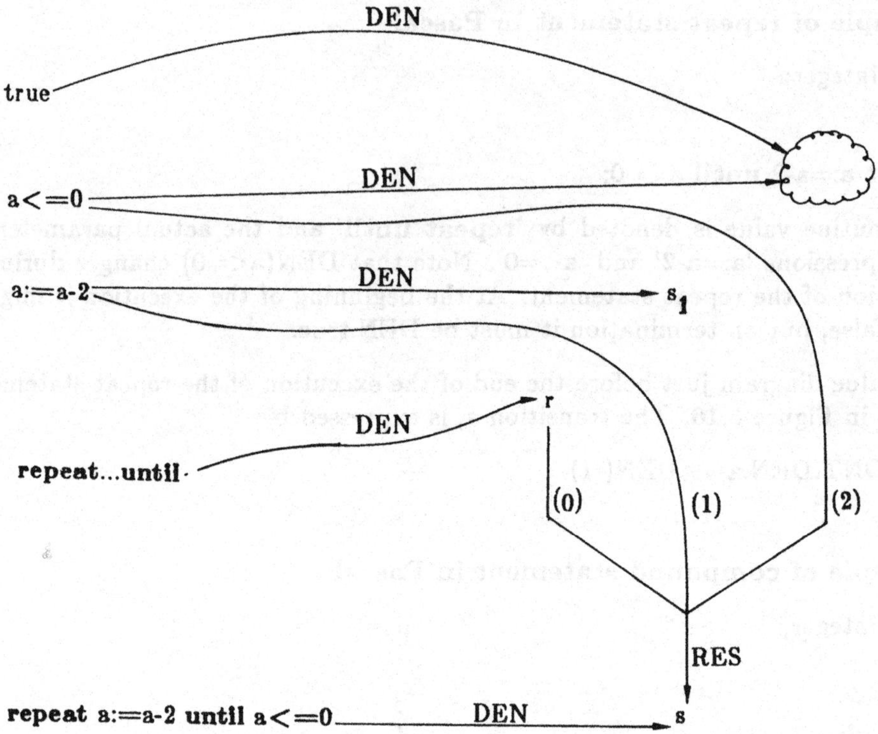
DEN
true
DEN
a<=0
a:=a-2
DEN
s1
r
DEN
repeat...until
(0)
(1)
(2)
RES
repeat a:=a-2 until a<=0
DEN
s

Figure 6.16

which indicates that a new location is created. The transition also indicates that 'i' is a name for α and that DEN.integer is its type. This will be explained in detail later.

As another example, consider the Pascal declaration

var v:**array** [1..2] **of** real;

The corresponding transition is partly described by

$$\begin{aligned}
&\text{CL} \leftarrow \text{CL} \cup \alpha \\
&\text{AL} \leftarrow \text{AL} \cup \beta \cup \gamma \\
&\text{SEL}(\alpha,\text{DEN.1}) \leftarrow \beta \\
&\text{SEL}(\alpha,\text{DEN.2}) \leftarrow \gamma
\end{aligned}$$

§6.10 Configurations

The set of routines R and the function RES are clearly components of the configurations. Hence, we add them to the definition of a configuration, so that, for the time being, a configuration is an 8-tuple (AD,AL,CD,CL,R,CONT,SEL,RES). Those routine values that are language defined (such as statements and declarations) are contained in the initial configuration. The declarations of functions or procedures that are program defined create new routine values, which are added to R. They are deleted from R by leaving the scope of the routine values.

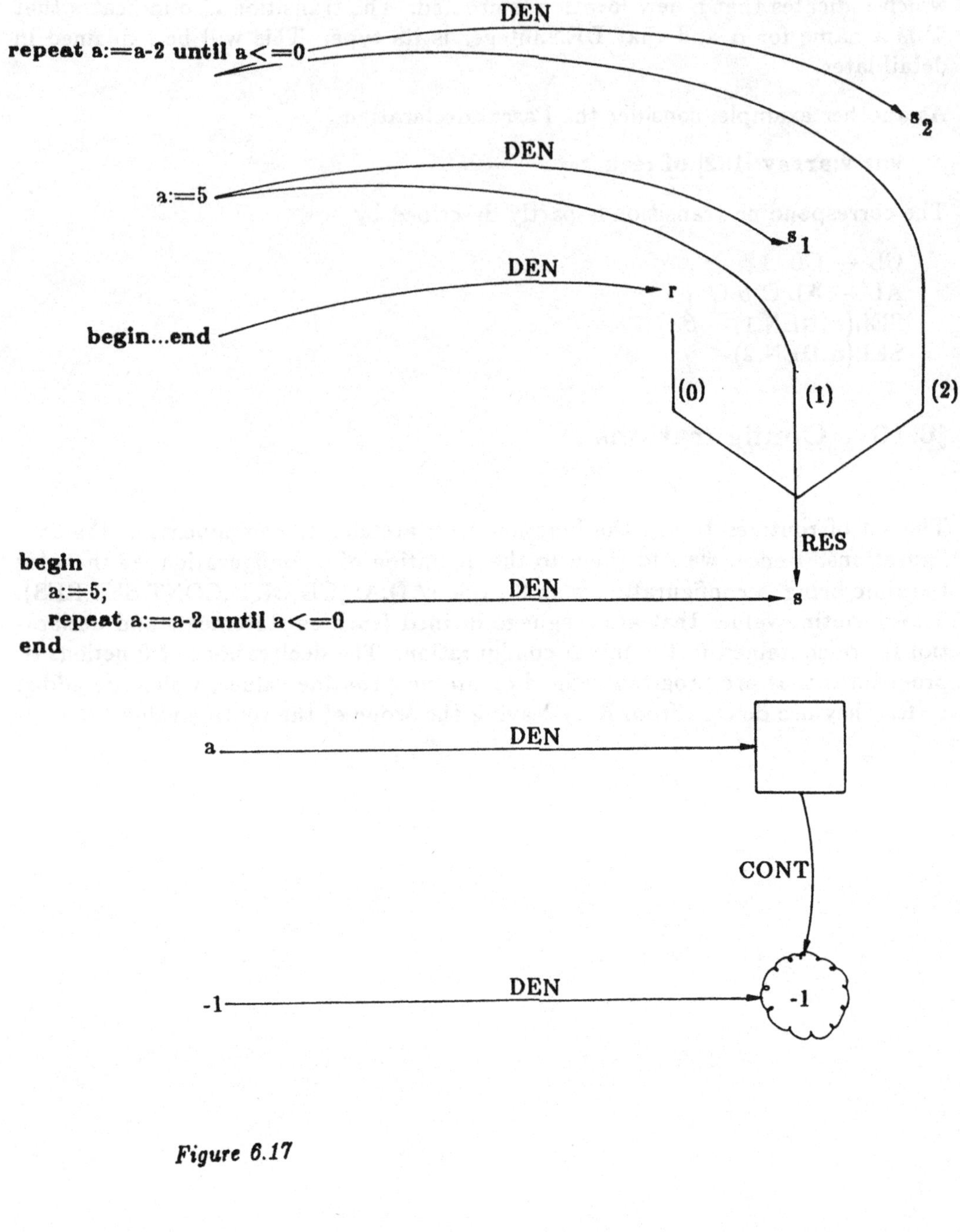
DEN
repeat a:=a-2 until a<=0
s2
DEN
a:=5
s1
DEN
r
begin...end
(0)
(1)
(2)
RES
begin
a:=5;
repeat a:=a-2 until a<=0
end
DEN
s
a
DEN
CONT
-1
DEN
-1

Figure 6.17

Chapter 7

CONTENTS FUNCTION

§7.1 Concept

The contents function is only defined on locations (L). It specifies for each location the value it contains. In SMALL, the contents of an atomic location can be any value except a composite datum, whereas the contents of a composite location can only be a composite datum. The motivation for these restrictions is explained in the present chapter.

The contents function CONT has up to now been defined (see Chapters 3 and 5) as a function of the form

$$\text{CONT} : \text{L} \rightarrow \text{V}$$

Since there are two classes of locations and six classes of values (see Figure 1.1), there are in theory twelve possible combinations.

Four combinations are conceptually excluded :

- The contents of a composite location is an atomic datum
- The contents of a composite location is an atomic location
- The contents of a composite location is a transition
- The contents of a composite location is a routine value.

Three other combinations do not exist in most programming languages and are not covered by SMALL:

- The contents of an atomic location is a composite datum
- The contents of an atomic location is a transition
- The contents of a composite location is a composite location.

They are perfectly legal from a conceptual point of view. Although they have interesting properties, we have decided not to include them in SMALL in the interests of keeping the model simple. In particular, the type functions described in Chapter 9 would have become considerably more complex if we had taken these three combinations into account.

Hence the following five combinations are considered. They will be discussed in the subsequent sections of this chapter.

(1) The contents of an atomic location is an atomic datum (Section 7.2)
(2) The contents of an atomic location is an atomic location (Section 7.3)
(3) The contents of an atomic location is a composite location (Section 7.4)
(4) The contents of an atomic location is a routine value (Section 7.5)
(5) The contents of a composite location is a composite datum (Section 7.6).

Each of these cases will be illustrated where possible by means of an example in Pascal, Algol 68, PL/1 and Ada. The types occurring in these examples are discussed in Chapter 9.

Recall that the contents of an atomic location can be neither a composite datum nor a transition, and that the contents of a composite location can only be a composite datum. The contents function is therefore of the form

$$\begin{aligned} \text{CONT}: \quad & \text{AL} \rightarrow \text{V - CD - TR} \\ & \text{CL} \rightarrow \text{CD} \end{aligned}$$

§7.2 Contents of an atomic location is an atomic datum

Example in Pacal

```
var x:integer;
begin
    x:=4;
    ...
end
```

Example in Algol 68

```
int x:=4;
...
```

Example in PL/1

```
DECLARE x BIN FIXED INIT(4);
...
```

Example in Ada

```
x:integer:=4;
...
```

In each of these examples, an atomic location, say α, is created statically.

The name 'x' is associated with α, so that DEN.x = α. The contents of α is DEN.4, so that CONT.α = DEN.4.

The corresponding value diagram is shown in Figure 7.1.

§7.3 Contents of an atomic location is an atomic location

Example in Pascal

```
var ptr:↑integer;
begin
    new(ptr);
    ptr↑:=4;
    ...
end
```

Example in Algol 68

```
ref int ptr:=heap int:=4;
```

Example in PL/1

```
DECLARE ptr POINTER;
DECLARE integer BIN FIXED BASED;
ALLOCATE integer SET (ptr);
ptr→integer=4;
```

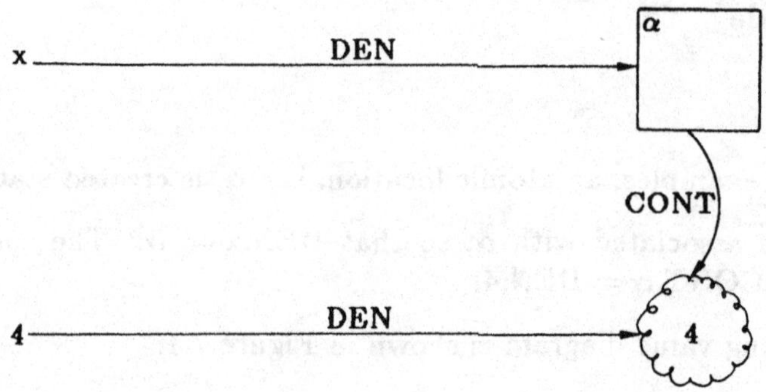

Figure 7.1.

Example in Ada

```
type pointer is access integer;
ptr:pointer;
begin
    ptr:=new integer'(4);
    ...
end
```

In each of these examples, two atomic locations are created. One location, say α, is created statically and another location, say β, is created dynamically.

The name 'ptr' is associated with α, so that DEN.ptr $= \alpha$. Furthermore, the contents of α is β and the contents of β is DEN.4, so that

CONT.$\alpha = \beta$ and CONT.$\beta =$ DEN.4.

The corresponding value diagram is shown in Figure 7.2. We recall that certain expressions are preceded by the names of the languages to which they refer. If it is not preceded by any language name, then an expression refers to all four languages.

§7.4 Contents of an atomic location is a composite location

Example in Pascal

```
type pack=
        record
            first:integer;
            second:real
        end;
    refpack=↑pack;
var ptr:refpack;
begin
    new(ptr);
    ...
end
```

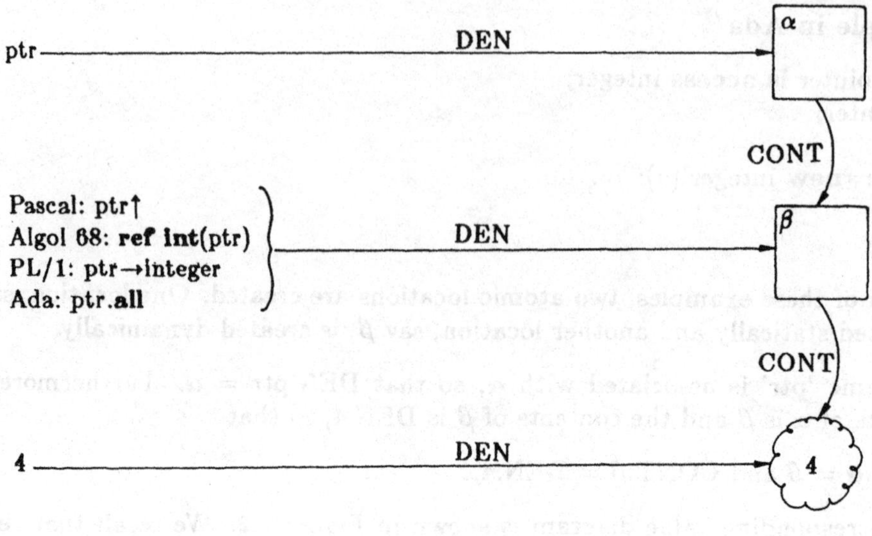
ptr
DEN
α
CONT
Pascal: ptr↑
Algol 68: ref int(ptr)
PL/1: ptr→integer
Ada: ptr.all
DEN
β
CONT
4
DEN
4

Figure 7.2.

Example in Algol 68

```
mode
    pack=struct(int first, real second),
    refpack=ref pack;
refpack ptr:=heap pack;
...
```

Example in PL/1

```
DECLARE
        1 refpack BASED,
            2 first BIN FIXED,
            2 second BIN FLOAT;
DECLARE ptr POINTER;
ALLOCATE refpack SET(ptr);
...
```

Example in Ada

```
type pack is
        record
            first:integer;
            second:float;
        end record;
type refpack is access pack;
ptr:refpack;
begin
    ptr:=new pack;
    ...
end
```

In each of these examples, two locations are created. An atomic location, say α, is created statically and a composite location, say β, is created dynamically. The sublocations of β are γ and δ with

SEL(β,DEN.first)=γ
SEL(β,DEN.second)=δ

Furthermore, α is denoted by 'ptr', so that DEN.ptr = α.

The contents of α is β, so that CONT.$\alpha = \beta$.

An important point is that we cannot select within the location α, since it is atomic. To select γ or δ, we must first take the contents of α. In Pascal, we have the contents operator '↑' in postfix notation, in Algol 68 we have '**refpack**' in prefix notation and in PL/1 we have 'ptr →', also in prefix notation, whereas in Ada the contents can only be specified by implicit dereferencing.

The corresponding value diagram is shown in Figure 7.3.

§7.5 Contents of an atomic location is a routine value

Example in Algol 68

```
proc(ref int,ref real)bool p;
proc(ref int,ref real)bool q=
    (ref int x,ref real y)bool: begin...end;
...
p:=q;
...
```

Example in PL/1

```
DECLARE p ENTRY(BIN FIXED,BIN FLOAT)
            RETURNS(BIT(1));

q : PROCEDURE(x,y) RETURNS(BIT(1));
      DECLARE
          x BIN FIXED,
          y BIN FLOAT;
          ...
    END q;
...
p=q;
...
```

This case does not exist in Pascal and Ada.

In the Algol 68 and PL/1 examples, a location, say α, is created statically and a routine value r is stored in it.
Notice that in PL/1 we can only write routine denotations in procedure and function declarations.

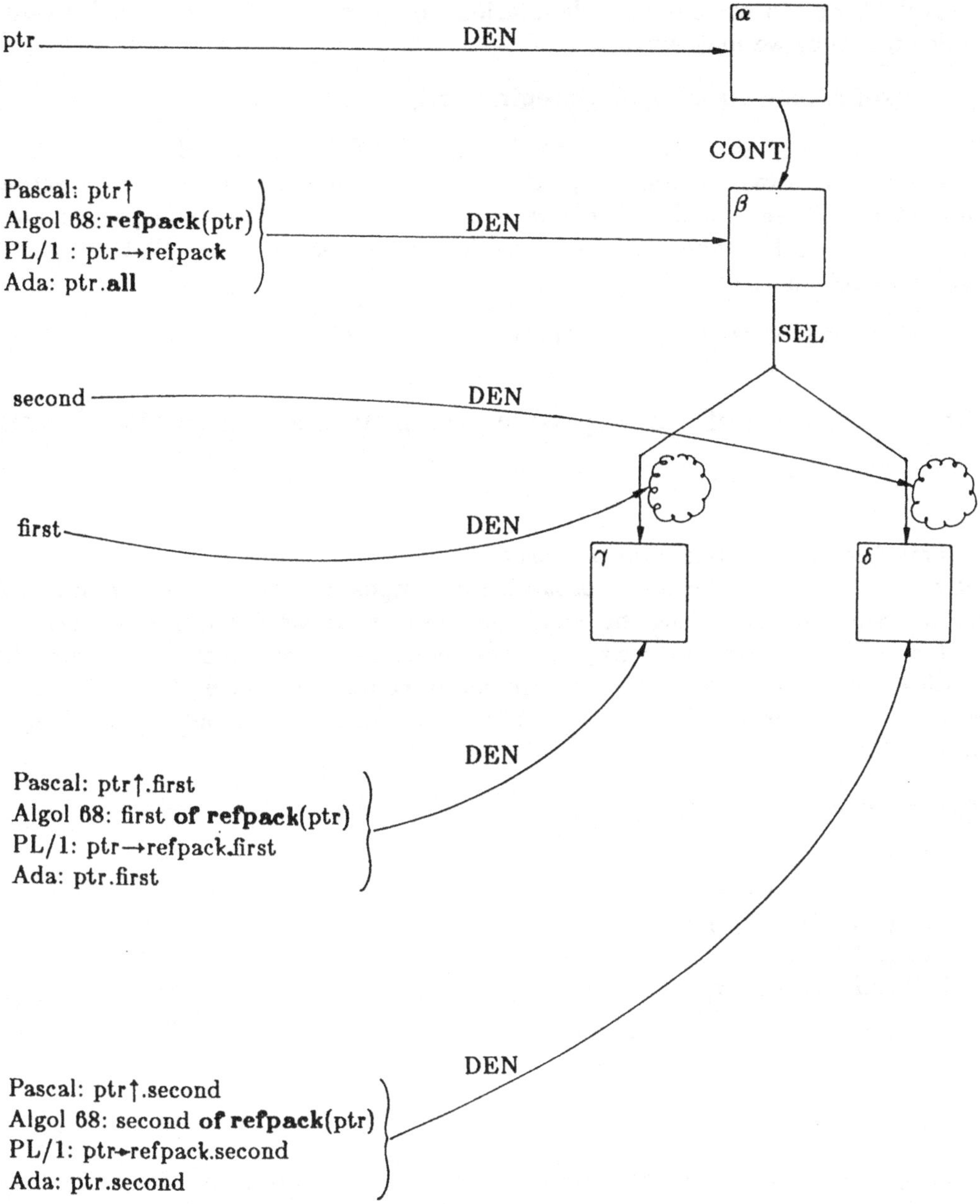
ptr
DEN
α
CONT
Pascal: ptr↑
Algol 68: refpack(ptr)
PL/1 : ptr→refpack
Ada: ptr.all
DEN
β
SEL
second
DEN
first
DEN
γ
δ
DEN
Pascal: ptr↑.first
Algol 68: first of refpack(ptr)
PL/1: ptr→refpack.first
Ada: ptr.first
DEN
Pascal: ptr↑.second
Algol 68: second of refpack(ptr)
PL/1: ptr→refpack.second
Ada: ptr.second

Figure 7.8

In Algol 68, we can write routine denotations in any context where a routine value is allowed. Thus we may write

p:=(**ref int** x,**ref real** y)**bool**:**begin**...**end**;

The routine denotation '(**ref int** x,**ref real** y)**bool**:**begin** ...**end**' specifies that there are two formal parameters, 'x' and 'y', which must be bound to actual parameters. These actual parameters must be locations holding respectively an integer and a real number. The routine denotation also specifies that the result will be a boolean value.

The corresponding value diagram is shown in Figure 7.4.

§7.6 Contents of a composite location is a composite datum

We first discuss a fundamental property.
Let α be a composite location containing a composite datum v. The number of components of α and v must be equal. Also, the selection function in α and in v must be defined in the same way, i.e., the selectors of components of α must be identical to the selectors of the corresponding components of v. There is also a strong relationship between the types of the components of α and v (see Chapter 9).

Suppose we have

$$\begin{aligned}
&\text{CONT}.\alpha = v\\
&\text{SEL}(\alpha,\text{DEN.a}) = \beta\\
&\text{SEL}(\alpha,\text{DEN.b}) = \gamma\\
&\text{SEL}(v,\text{DEN.a}) = v_1\\
&\text{SEL}(v,\text{DEN.b}) = v_2
\end{aligned}$$

Then it follows that

$$\begin{aligned}
&\text{CONT}.\beta = v_1\\
&\text{CONT}.\gamma = v_2
\end{aligned}$$

The above property can be rephrased in the following statement : for every composite location α containing a composite datum, and for every selector s of α, it is the case that

$$\text{CONT.SEL}(\alpha,s) = \text{SEL}(\text{CONT}.\alpha,s)$$

This is illustrated in Figure 7.5.

The reader is invited to verify this statement in the simple illustrations below.

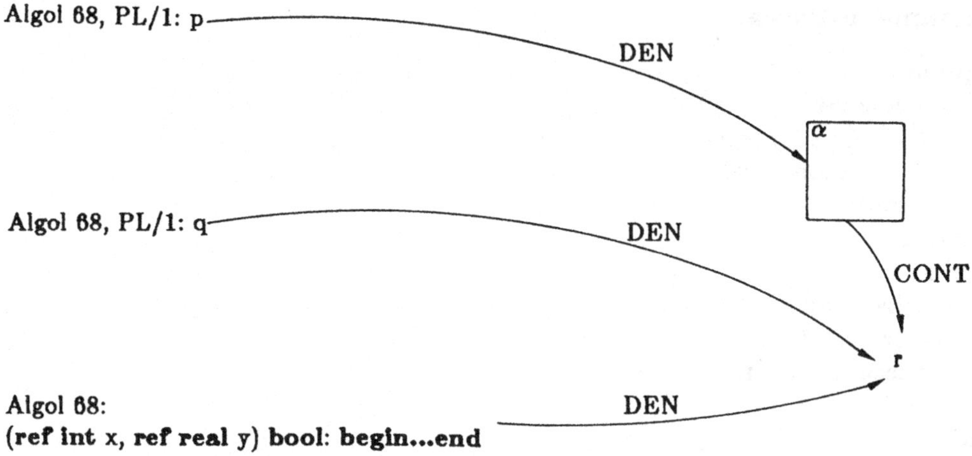
Algol 68, PL/1: p
DEN
α
Algol 68, PL/1: q
DEN
CONT
r
Algol 68:
(**ref int** x, **ref real** y) **bool**: **begin**...**end**
DEN

Figure 7.4

Example in Pascal

```
type m=
        record
            first:↑integer;
            second:real
        end;
var rec:m;
begin
    new(rec.first);
    rec.first↑:=3;
    rec.second:=3.14;
    ...
end
```

Example in Algol 68

```
mode m=struct(ref int first, real second);
m rec;
first of rec := heap int;
ref int(first of rec):=3;
second of rec:=3.14;
...
```

Example in PL/1

```
DECLARE
    integer BIN FIXED BASED,
    1 rec,
        2 first POINTER,
        2 second BIN FLOAT;
ALLOCATE integer SET(rec.first);
rec.first→integer=3;
rec.second=3.14;
...
```

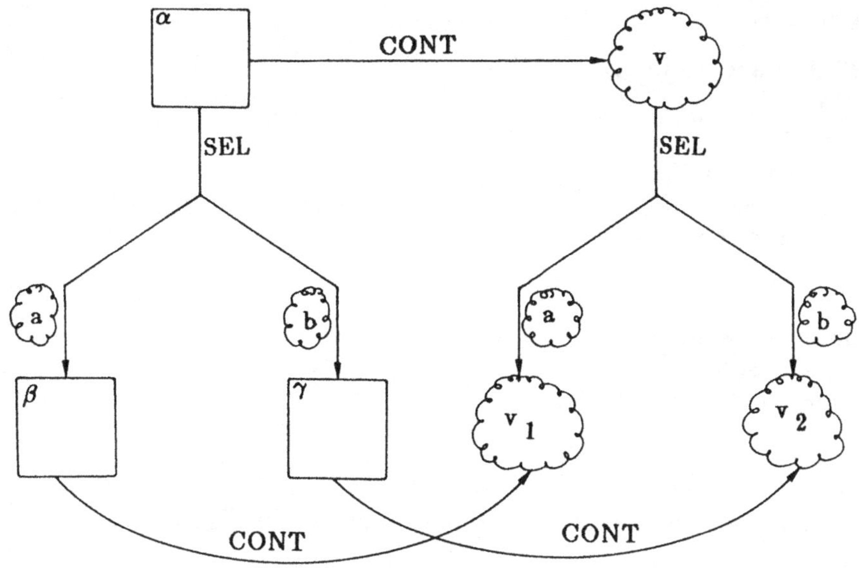

Figure 7.5

Example in Ada

```
type refint is access integer;
type m is
        record
            first:refint;
            second:float;
        end record;
rec:m;
begin
    rec.first:=new integer;
    rec.first.all:=3;
    rec.second:=3.14;
    ...
end
```

The value diagram for the above examples is shown in Figure 7.6.

There now follows a slightly more complex illustration.

Example in Pascal

```
type packref=
        record
            first:↑integer;
            second:↑real
        end;
var ptr:packref;
begin
    new(ptr.first);
    new(ptr.second);
    ptr.first↑:=4;
    ptr.second↑:=3.14;
    ...
end
```

Example in Algol 68

```
mode packref=struct(ref int first, ref real second);
packref ptr;
first of ptr:=heap int;
second of ptr:=heap real;
ref int(first of ptr):=4;
ref real(second of ptr):=3.14;
...
```

Example in PL/1

```
DECLARE
    integer BIN FIXED BASED,
    real BIN FLOAT BASED;
DECLARE
    1 ptr,
        2 first POINTER,
        2 second POINTER;
ALLOCATE integer SET(ptr.first);
ALLOCATE real SET(ptr.second);
ptr.first→integer=4;
ptr.second→real=3.14;
...
```

Example in Ada

```
type refint is access integer;
type reffloat is access float;
type packref is
            record
                first:refint;
                second:reffloat;
            end record;
ptr:packref;
begin
    ptr.first:=new integer;
    ptr.second:=new float;
    ptr.first.all:=4;
    ptr.second.all:=3.14;
    ...
end
```

The value diagram for these examples is shown in Figure 7.7.

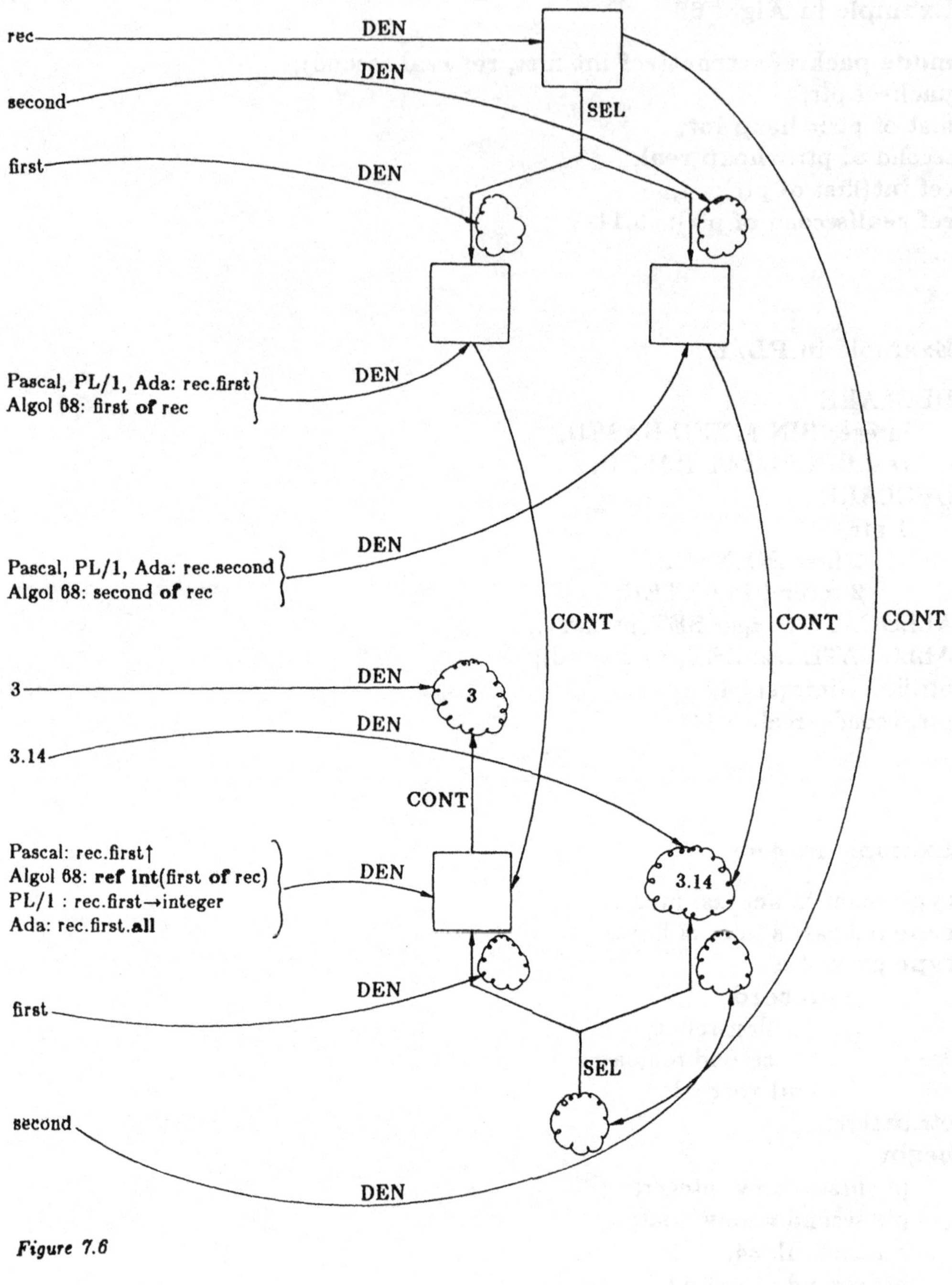
rec
second
first
DEN
DEN
SEL
DEN
Pascal, PL/1, Ada: rec.first
Algol 68: first of rec
DEN
Pascal, PL/1, Ada: rec.second
Algol 68: second of rec
DEN
CONT
CONT
CONT
3
DEN
3
3.14
DEN
CONT
Pascal: rec.first↑
Algol 68: ref int(first of rec)
PL/1 : rec.first→integer
Ada: rec.first.all
DEN
3.14
first
DEN
SEL
second
DEN

Figure 7.6

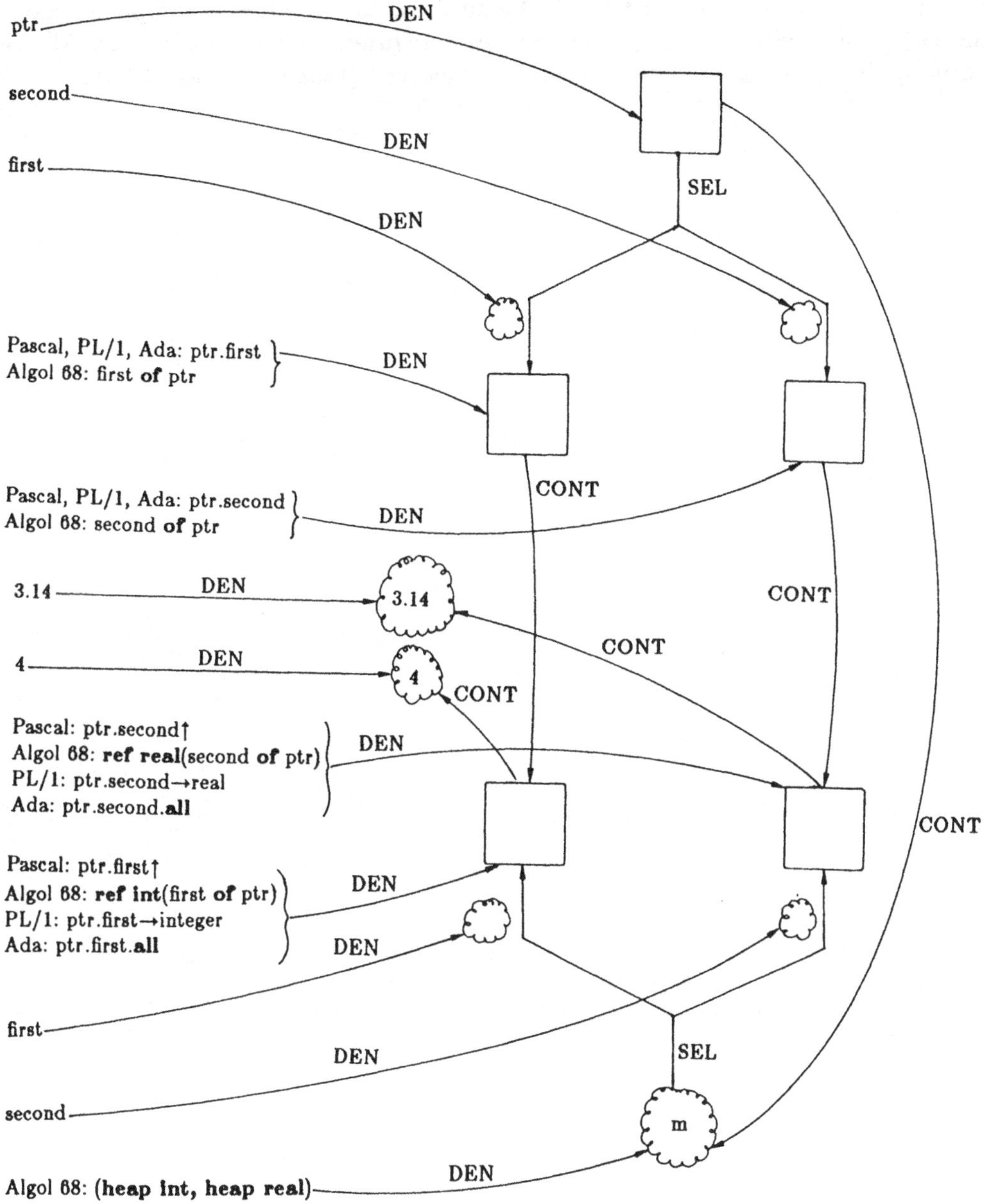
ptr
DEN
second
DEN
first
DEN
SEL
Pascal, PL/1, Ada: ptr.first
Algol 68: first of ptr
DEN
CONT
Pascal, PL/1, Ada: ptr.second
Algol 68: second of ptr
DEN
3.14
DEN
3.14
CONT
CONT
4
DEN
4
CONT
Pascal: ptr.second↑
Algol 68: ref real(second of ptr)
PL/1: ptr.second→real
Ada: ptr.second.all
DEN
CONT
Pascal: ptr.first↑
Algol 68: ref int(first of ptr)
PL/1: ptr.first→integer
Ada: ptr.first.all
DEN
DEN
first
DEN
SEL
second
m
Algol 68: (heap int, heap real)
DEN

Figure 7.7

Notice that in Pascal, Algol 68, PL/1 and Ada, 'm' denotes a composite datum and not a composite location, since the contents function is not defined on DEN.m. Actually, 'm' denotes a composite value whose components are locations.

Chapter 8

EXPRESSIONS

§8.1 Concept

Values are internal (abstract) objects for which we need notations called expressions. The set of expressions (E) is the set of all syntactically correct program constructions which may denote values. E is partitioned into two classes : the set of *names* (N) and the set of *compound expressions* (CE) (see Figure 8.1).
A *name* is a sequence of characters which is either language defined or program defined and which is not composed of other names or expressions. Examples of names are numbers, identifiers and operators. A *compound expression* is built up from names by a mechanism that is part of the syntax of the programming language. The syntax of the programming language defines for each expression its syntactic structure.

As we have seen, the relationship between expressions (E) and values (V) is described by the function DEN:E → V.

§8.2 Names

In contrast to the evaluation of the DEN function on compound expressions (see Section 8.3), the evaluation of the DEN function on names does not involve any of the basic functions SEL, CONT or RES.

Names can be either *program defined* or *language defined.* Program defined names are for instance constant identifiers, variables and identifiers for program defined functions or procedures. Examples of language defined names are numbers and identifiers and operators for language defined procedures or functions.

Names may be implicit, i.e., they may be represented by the context. A typical example is the use of the contents operator. It is common practice to write 'x:=x+1' instead of something of the form 'x:={contents(x)}+1'. Clearly, the left operand of the operation '+' is not 'x', since DEN.x is a location and we cannot add DEN.1 to a location. Implicit operators often constitute a source of programming errors and frequently cause a misunderstanding of language concepts. In SMALL, we will always make implicit operators explicit, so that there will be no confusion about the objects we are talking about.

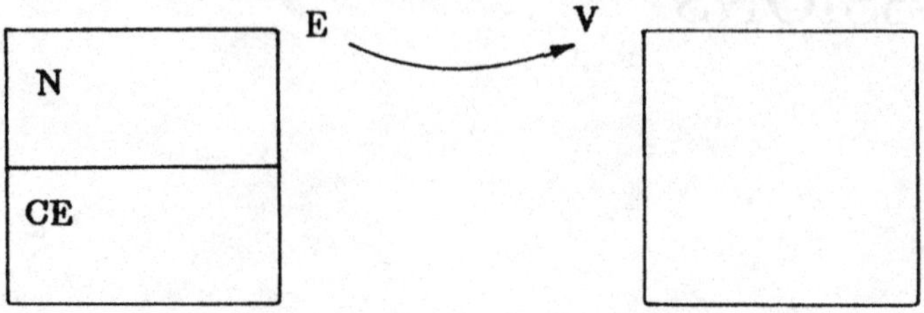

Figure 8.1

8.2.1 Names in Pascal

Names in Pascal are illustrated by means of the following example :

Example

```
const a=3;
type
    vectype=array[1..2] of integer;
    rectype=
        record
            first:integer;
            second:real
        end;
    ptrtype=↑integer;
var i:integer;
    vec:vectype;
    rec:rectype;
    ptr:ptrtype;
function f(var x:integer):boolean;
    <declarations>;
    begin
        <statements>
    end;
begin
    i:=a+1;
    new(ptr);
    ...
end
```

The value diagram is shown in Figure 8.2.

The names 'a', 'i', 'vec', 'rec', 'ptr' and 'f' are program defined, whereas the names '3' and '+' are language defined.

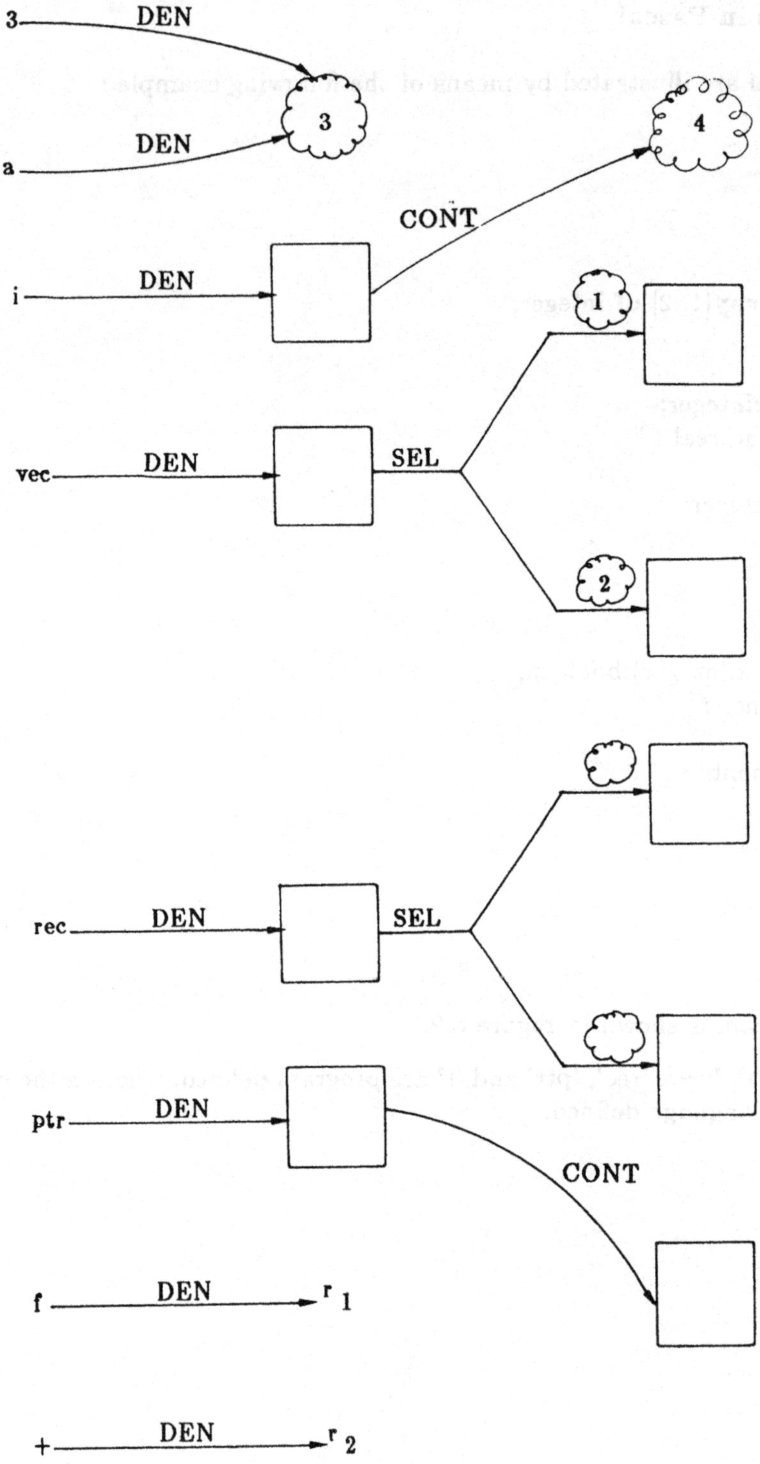
3
DEN
3
DEN
a
4
CONT
i
DEN
1
vec
DEN
SEL
2
rec
DEN
SEL
ptr
DEN
CONT
f
DEN
r 1
+
DEN
r 2

Figure 8.2

8.2.2 Names in Algol 68

Example

```
int a=3;
mode
    vectype=[1:2]int;
    rectype=struct(int first, real second);
    ptrtype=ref int;
int i;
vectype vec;
rectype rec;
ptrtype ptr;
proc(ref int)bool f=(ref int x)bool:
    begin
        <declarations and statements>;
        <boolean expression>
    end;
i:=a+1;
ptr:=heap int;
...
```

The value diagram is similar to that of Figure 8.2.

8.2.3 Names in PL/1

Example

```
DECLARE
    i BIN FIXED,
    vec(1:2)BIN FIXED,
    1 rec,
        2 first BIN FIXED,
        2 second BIN FLOAT,
    ptr POINTER,
    integer BIN FIXED BASED;
```

```
f : PROCEDURE(x) RETURNS(BIT(1));
        DECLARE x BIN FIXED;
        <declarations>
        <statements>
    END f;
i=a+1;
ALLOCATE integer SET(ptr);
...
```

The value diagram is similar to that of Figure 8.2.

8.2.4 Names in Ada

Example

```
type vectype is array(1..2) of integer;
type rectype is
    record
        first:integer;
        second:float;
    end record;
type refint is access integer;
a:constant integer:=3;
i:integer:=1;
vec:vectype;
rec:rectype;
ptr:refint;
function f(x:in integer) return boolean is
    <declarations>
    begin
        <statements>
    end f;
begin
    i:=a+1;
    ptr:=new integer;
    ...
end
```

The value diagram is similar to that of Figure 8.2.

§8.3 Compound expressions

Compound expressions are built up from names according to the syntax of the programming language being used. Suppose e is a compound expression. Then the evaluation of DEN.e involves at least one of the basic functions SEL, CONT and RES. In the subsequent sections, the DEN evaluation mechanism for each of the basic functions is discussed and illustrated by examples in each of the languages Pascal, Algol 68, PL/1 and Ada.

8.3.1 The DEN evaluation mechanism for the selection function

Let e be an expression denoting a composite value v with n components. Let s_i be the name of the selector of the ith component. The function SEL involves a syntactic operator M_{SEL} with two parameters, e and s_i. Its value is the expression that denotes the ith component of v. Hence we have

$$\text{DEN}.M_{SEL}(e,s_i) = \text{SEL}(\text{DEN}.e,\text{DEN}.s_i) \qquad (*)$$

This is illustrated by Figure 8.3.

Obviously, the representation of the operator M_{SEL} is language dependent.

Example of Pascal array locations

type vectype=**array**[1..n] **of** integer;
var vec:vectype;

'vec' is a name denoting a composite location. 'vec[1]',...,'vec[n]' are compound expressions each denoting an atomic location.

For each selector DEN.i ($1 \leq i \leq n$), we have

$$\text{DEN.vec[i]} = \text{SEL(DEN.vec,DEN.i)} \qquad \text{(cf.(*))}$$

Hence, M_{SEL}(vec,i) is equivalent to the compound expression 'vec[i]' in Pascal, in the sense that they both denote the same object. In the sequel we will express such an equivalence by writing

$$M_{SEL}(\text{vec,i}) \equiv \text{vec[i]}$$

The value diagram for this example is shown in Figure 8.4.

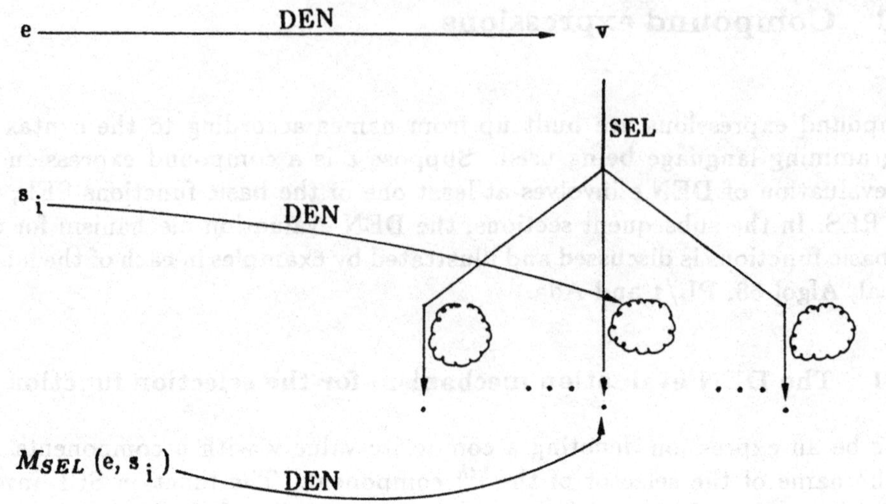

Figure 8.3

Example of Pascal record locations

type rectype=
    record
        s_1:μ_1;
        ...
        s_i:μ_i;
        ...
        s_n:μ_n
    end;{s_i stands for a field selector and μ_i stands for a type}
var rec:rectype;

For each selector DEN.s_i ($1 \leq i \leq n$), we have

DEN(rec.s_i) = SEL(DEN.rec,DEN.s_i) (cf.(*))

Hence, M_{SEL}(rec,s_i) $\equiv$ rec.s_i.

The value diagram is shown in Figure 8.5.

Example of Algol 68 array locations

mode vectype=[1:n]**int**;
vectype vec;

For each selector DEN.i (1≤i≤n), we have

DEN.vec[i] = SEL(DEN.vec,DEN.i) (cf.(*))

Hence, M_{SEL}(vec,i) $\equiv$ vec[i].

The value diagram is given in Figure 8.4.

Example of Algol 68 record locations

mode rectype=struct($\mu_1 s_1, ..., \mu_i s_i, ..., \mu_n s_n$);
    co s_i stands for a field selector, whereas μ_i stands for a mode **co**
rectype rec;

For each selector DEN.s_i ($1 \leq i \leq n$), we have

DEN(s_i **of** rec) = SEL(DEN.rec,DEN.s_i) (cf.(*))

Hence, M_{SEL}(rec,s_i) $\equiv$ s_i **of** rec.

The value diagram is similar to that of Figure 8.5.

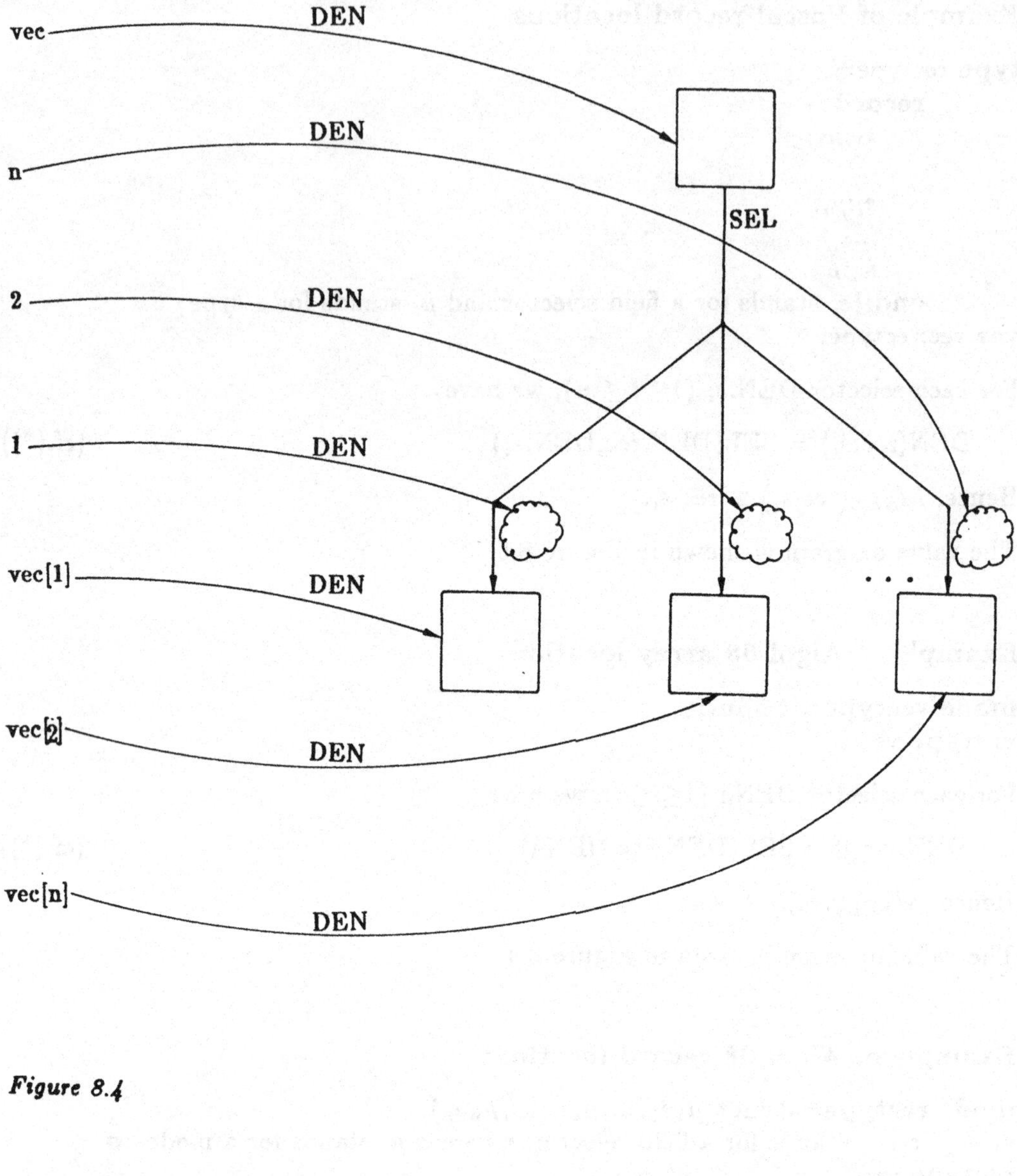

Figure 8.4

Example of PL/1 array locations

DECLARE vec(1:n) BIN FIXED;

For each selector DEN.i (1≤i≤n), we have

DEN.vec(i) = SEL(DEN.vec,DEN.i) (cf.(*))

Hence, M_{SEL}(vec,i) ≡ vec(i) .

The value diagram is similar to that of Figure 8.4.

Example of PL/1 record locations

```
DECLARE
    1 rec,
        2 s1μ1,
        ...
        2 siμi,
        ...
        2 snμn;
        /* si represents a field selector and μi represents a type
        description of the field */
```

For each selector DEN.s_i (1≤ $i \leq n$), we have

DEN(rec.s_i) = SEL(DEN.rec,DEN.s_i) (cf. (*))

Hence, M_{SEL}(rec,s_i) ≡ rec.s_i .

The value diagram is given in Figure 8.5.

Example of Ada array locations

type vectype **is** **array**(1..n) **of** integer;
vec:vectype;

For each selector DEN.i (1≤i≤n) we have

DEN.vec(i) = SEL(DEN.vec,DEN.i) (cf.(*))

Hence, M_{SEL}(vec,i) ≡ vec(i) .

The value diagram is similar to that of Figure 8.4.

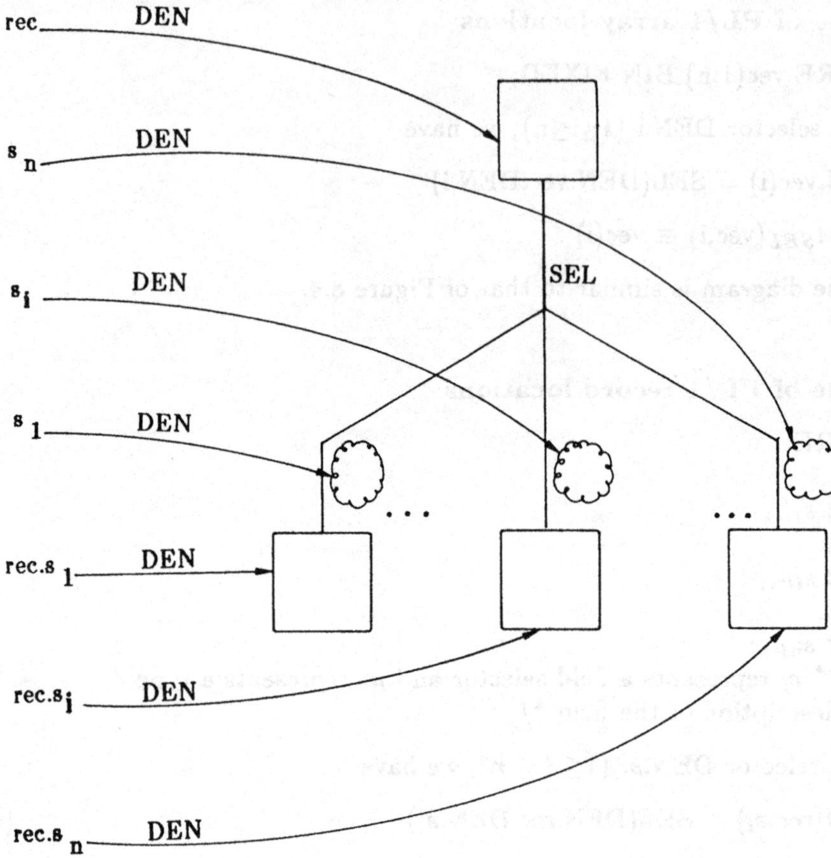

Figure 8.5

Example of Ada record locations

```
type rectype is
        record
            s1 : μ1;
            ...
            si : μi;
            ...
            sn : μn;
        end record;
rec:rectype;
```

For each selector DEN.s_i ($1\leq i \leq n$), we have

$$\text{DEN(rec.}s_i\text{)} = \text{SEL(DEN.rec,DEN.}s_i\text{)} \qquad \text{(cf.(*))}$$

Hence, $M_{SEL}(\text{rec},s_i) \equiv \text{rec.}s_i$.

The value diagram is similar to that of Figure 8.5.

8.3.2 The DEN evaluation mechanism for the contents function

Let e be an expression denoting a location α that contains the value v. The function CONT involves a syntactic operator M_{CONT} with one parameter, namely, the expression e. We have

$$\text{DEN.}M_{CONT}(e) = \text{CONT.DEN.}e \qquad (**)$$

This is illustrated by Figure 8.6.

The representation of the operator M_{CONT} is language dependent. As we have already mentioned, this operator is often defined by the context.

Example of Pascal atomic locations containing atomic data

```
var x:integer;
begin
    x:=3;
    ...
end
```

We have

DEN.{contents(x)} = CONT.DEN.x (cf.(**))

Hence, M_{CONT}(x) ≡ {contents(x)}.

As we have already seen in the examples, the contents operator is often implicit (context defined). For instance, in the statement 'x:=x+1', the second occurrence of 'x' must be read {contents(x)} .

The value diagram for this example is given in Figure 8.7.

Example of Pascal atomic locations containing atomic locations

```
var ptr:↑integer;
begin
    new(ptr);
    ptr↑:=3;
    ...
end
```

'ptr' is a name and 'ptr↑' is a compound expression, with

DEN.ptr↑ = CONT.DEN.ptr (cf.(**))

and

DEN.{contents(ptr↑)} = CONT.DEN.ptr↑ cf.(**))

Hence, M_{CONT}(ptr) ≡ ptr↑, and M_{CONT}(ptr↑) ≡ {contents(prt↑)} .

The contents operator in Pascal is represented by the postfix operator '↑'.

The value diagram is given in Figure 8.8.

Example of Pascal atomic locations containing composite locations

```
type rectype=
        record
            first:integer;
            second:↑real
        end;
var ptr:↑rectype;
begin
    new(ptr);
```

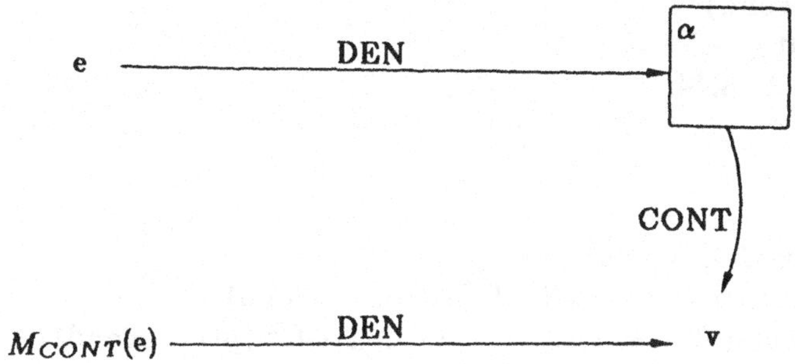

Figure 8.6

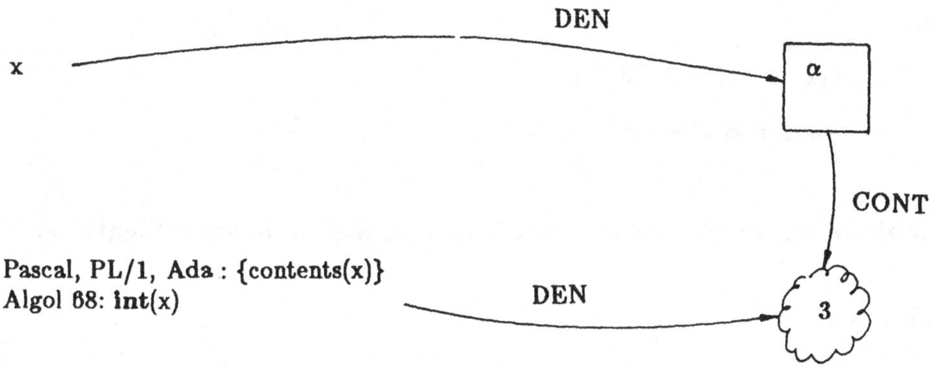

Figure 8.7

```
    new(ptr↑.second);
    ptr↑.first:=0;
    ptr↑.second↑:=3.14;
end
```

We have

DEN.ptr↑ = CONT.DEN.ptr
DEN(ptr↑.second↑) = CONT.DEN(ptr↑.second)
DEN.{contents(ptr↑.second↑)} = CONT.DEN(ptr↑.second↑) (cf.(**))

The value diagram is given in Figure 8.9.

Example of Algol 68 atomic locations containing atomic data

```
int x;
x:=3;
...
```

We have

DEN.int(x) = CONT.DEN.x (cf.(**))

The value diagram is given in Figure 8.7.

Example of Algol 68 atomic locations containing atomic locations

```
ref int ptr;
ptr:=loc int;
ref int(ptr):=3;
...
```

We have

DEN.**ref int**(ptr) = CONT.DEN.ptr
DEN.**int**(ptr) = CONT.DEN.**ref int**(ptr) (cf.(**))

The value diagram is given in Figure 8.8.

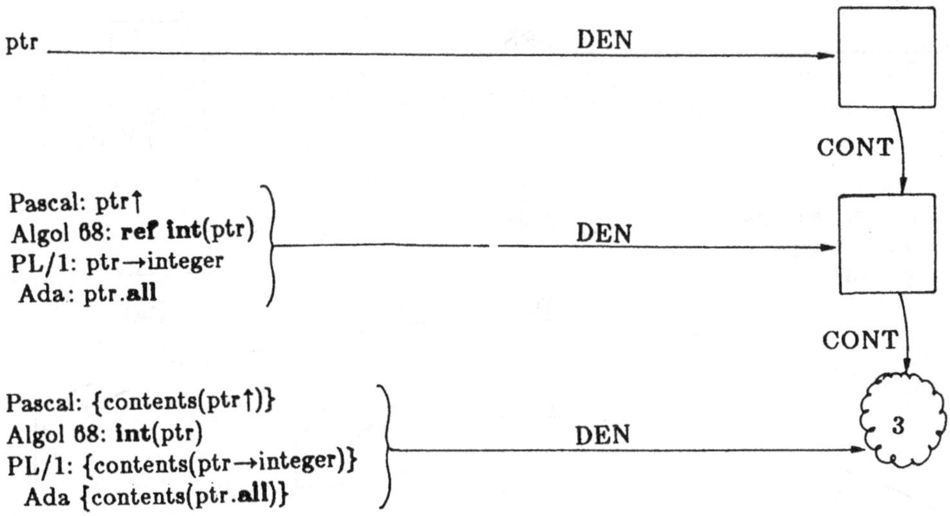
ptr
DEN
CONT
Pascal: ptr↑
Algol 68: **ref int**(ptr)
PL/1: ptr→integer
Ada: ptr.**all**
DEN
CONT
Pascal: {contents(ptr↑)}
Algol 68: **int**(ptr)
PL/1: {contents(ptr→integer)}
Ada {contents(ptr.**all**)}
DEN
3

Figure 8.8

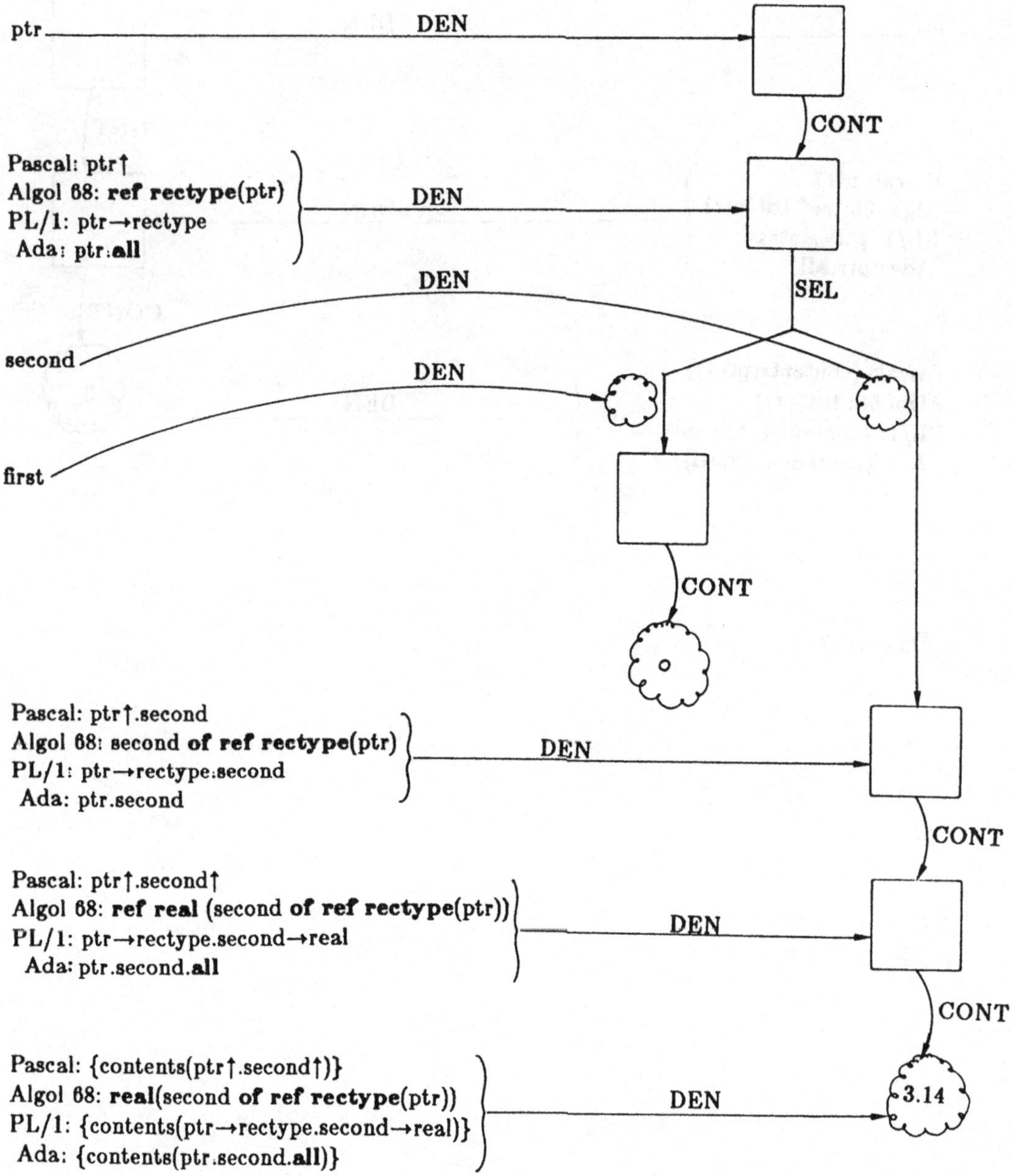
ptr
DEN
CONT
Pascal: ptr↑
Algol 68: **ref rectype**(ptr)
PL/1: ptr→rectype
Ada: ptr.**all**
DEN
SEL
DEN
second
DEN
first
CONT
0
Pascal: ptr↑.second
Algol 68: second **of ref rectype**(ptr)
PL/1: ptr→rectype.second
Ada: ptr.second
DEN
CONT
Pascal: ptr↑.second↑
Algol 68: **ref real** (second **of ref rectype**(ptr))
PL/1: ptr→rectype.second→real
Ada: ptr.second.**all**
DEN
CONT
Pascal: {contents(ptr↑.second↑)}
Algol 68: **real**(second **of ref rectype**(ptr))
PL/1: {contents(ptr→rectype.second→real)}
Ada: {contents(ptr.second.**all**)}
DEN
3.14

Figure 8.9

Example of Algol 68 atomic locations containing composite locations

mode rectype=**struct**(**int** first, **ref real** second);
ref rectype ptr;
ptr:=**loc rectype**;
second **of ref rectype**(ptr):=**loc real**;
first **of ref rectype**(ptr):=0;
ref real(second **of ref rectype**(ptr)):=3.14;
...

We have

DEN.**ref rectype**(ptr) = CONT.DEN.ptr
DEN.**ref real**(second **of ref rectype**(ptr)) =
CONT.DEN.second **of ref rectype**(ptr)
DEN.**real**(second **of ref rectype**(ptr)) =
CONT.DEN.**ref real**(second **of ref rectype**(ptr)) (cf.(**))

The value diagram is given in Figure 8.9.

Example of PL/1 atomic locations containing atomic data

DECLARE x BIN FIXED;
x=3;
...

We have

DEN.{contents(x)} = CONT.DEN.x (cf.(**))

The value diagram is given in Figure 8.7.

Example of PL/1 atomic locations containing atomic locations

```
DECLARE
    ptr POINTER,
    integer BIN FIXED BASED;
ALLOCATE integer SET(ptr);
ptr→ integer=3;
...
```

We have

DEN(ptr→integer) = CONT.DEN.ptr
DEN.{contents(ptr→integer)} = CONT.DEN(ptr→integer) (cf.(**))

The value diagram is given in Figure 8.8.

Example of PL/1 atomic locations containing composite locations

```
DECLARE
    1 rectype BASED,
        2 first BIN FIXED,
        2 second POINTER,
    real BIN FLOAT BASED,
    ptr POINTER;
ALLOCATE rectype SET(ptr);
ALLOCATE real SET(ptr→rectype.second);
ptr→rectype.first=0;
ptr→rectype.second→real=3.14;
...
```

We have

DEN(ptr→rectype) = CONT.DEN.ptr
DEN(ptr→rectype.second→real) =
    CONT.DEN(ptr→rectype.second)
DEN.{contents(ptr→rectype.second→real)} =
    CONT.DEN(ptr→rectype.second→real) (cf.(**))

The value diagram is given in Figure 8.9.

Example of Ada atomic locations containing atomic data

```
x:integer:=3;
...
```

We have

DEN.{contents(x)} = CONT.DEN.x (cf.(**))

The value diagram is given in Figure 8.7.

Example of Ada atomic locations containing atomic locations

```
type refint is access integer;
ptr:refint;
begin
    ptr:=new integer;
    ptr.all:=3;
```

```
    - - the last two statements can be replaced by
    - - ptr:=new integer' (3)

    ...
end
```

We have

$$\text{DEN}(\text{ptr.all}) = \text{CONT.DEN.ptr}$$
$$\text{DEN.}\{\text{contents}(\text{ptr.all})\} = \text{CONT.DEN}(\text{ptr.all}) \qquad (\text{cf.}(^{**}))$$

The value diagram is given in Figure 8.8.

Example of Ada atomic locations containing composite locations

```
type reffloat is access float;
type rectype is
        record
            first:integer;
            second:reffloat;
        end record;
type refrec is access rectype;
ptr:refrec;
ptr:=new rectype;
ptr.second:=new float'(3.14);
ptr.first:=0;
```

We have

$$\text{DEN}(\text{ptr.all}) = \text{CONT.DEN.ptr}$$
$$\text{DEN}(\text{ptr.second.all}) = \text{CONT.DEN}(\text{ptr.second})$$
$$\text{DEN.}\{\text{contents}(\text{ptr.second.all})\} = \text{CONT.DEN}(\text{ptr.second.all}) \qquad (\text{cf.}(^{**}))$$

The value diagram is given in Figure 8.9.

8.3.3 The DEN evaluation mechanism for the result function

Let e be an expression denoting a routine value, and let $a_1,...,a_n$ be the actual parameters of a call of that routine value. The function RES involves a syntactic operator M_{RES} with n+1 parameters, namely $e,a_1,...,a_n$. $M_{RES}(e,a_1,...,a_n)$ is an expression which denotes the value resulting from the execution of the routine value after the appropriate binding of the actual parameters to the corresponding formal parameters of the routine value.

Hence we have

$$\text{DEN}.M_{RES}(e,a_1,...,a_n) = \text{RES}(\text{DEN}.e,a_1,...,a_n) \qquad (***)$$

This is illustrated by Figure 8.10.

Example of Pascal functions

```
var a:integer;
    b:real;
    c:boolean;
function f(var x:integer;y:real):boolean;
    <declarations>;
    begin
        <statements>;
        f:=true
    end;
begin
    b:=0.0;
    c:=f(a,b);
    ...
end
```

We have

$$\text{DEN.f(a,b)} = \text{RES(DEN.f,a,\{contents(b)\})} \qquad \text{(Cf.(***))}$$

Hence, $M_{RES}(\text{f,a,b}) \equiv \text{f(a,b)}$

The value diagram just before the end of the execution of the call 'f(a,b)' is given in Figure 8.11. We assume that the routine value does not yield any transition.

Example of Algol 68 functions

```
int a;
real b;
bool c;
proc(ref int,real)bool f=
    (ref int x,real y)bool:
        begin
            <declarations and statements>;
            true
        end;
b:=0.0;
c:=f(a,b);co stands for 'c:=f(a,real(b))'co
...
```

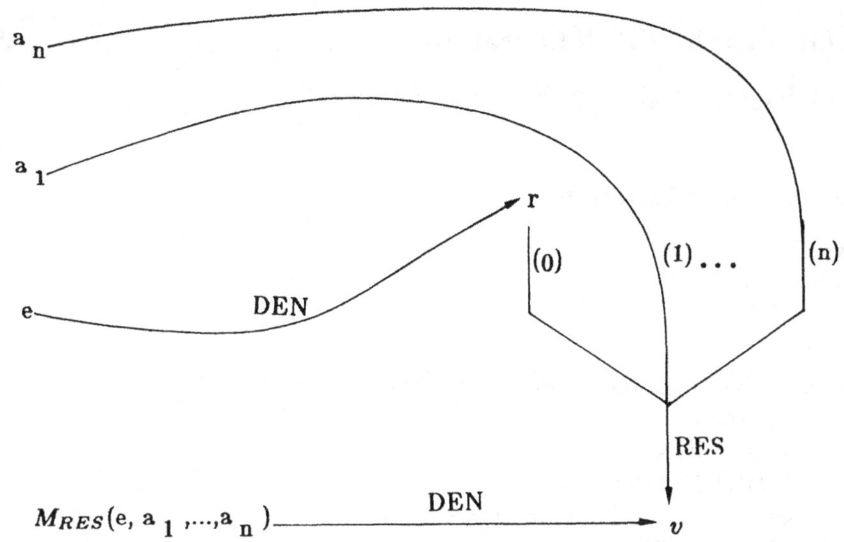

Figure 8.10

We have

DEN.f(a,b) = RES(DEN.f,a,**real**(b)) (cf.(***))

The value diagram is given in Figure 8.11.

Example of PL/1 functions

```
DECLARE
    a BIN FIXED,
    b BIN FLOAT,
    c BIT(1);
f : PROCEDURE(x,y) RETURNS(BIT(1));
        DECLARE
            x BIN FIXED,
            y BIN FLOAT;
        <declarations and statements>
        RETURN('1'B);
    END f;
b=0.0;
c=f(a,(b));
```

We have

DEN.f(a,(b)) = RES(DEN.f,a,{contents(b)}) (cf.(***))

The value diagram is given in Figure 8.11.

Example of Ada functions

```
b:float;
c:boolean;
function f(y:in float) return boolean is
    <declarations>
    begin
        <statements>
        return true;
    end f;
begin
    b:=0.0;
    c:=f(b);
end
```

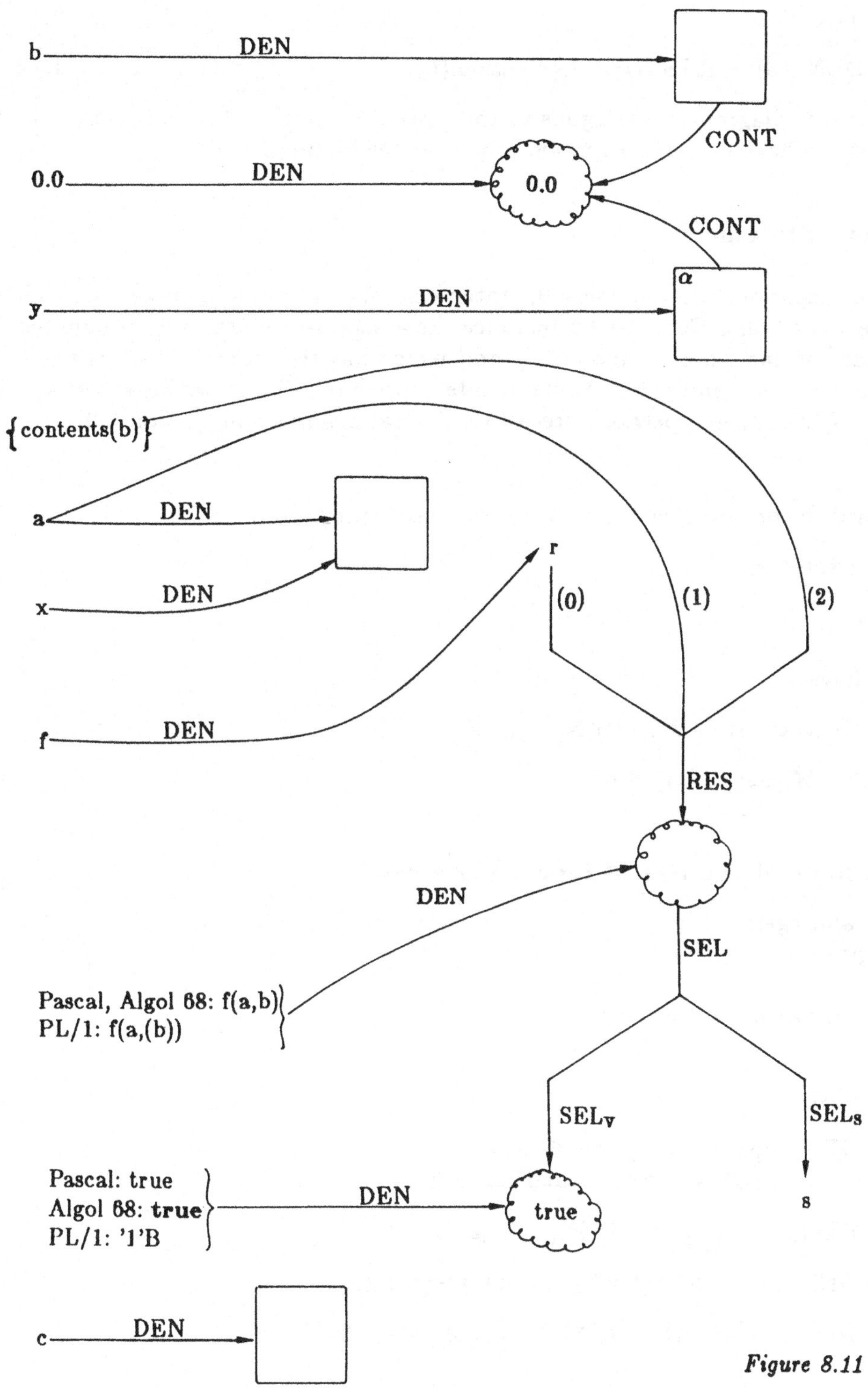
b
DEN
CONT
0.0
DEN
0.0
CONT
α
y
DEN
{contents(b)}
a
DEN
x
DEN
r
(0)
(1)
(2)
f
DEN
RES
DEN
SEL
Pascal, Algol 68: f(a,b)
PL/1: f(a,(b))
SELv
SELs
Pascal: true
Algol 68: **true**
PL/1: '1'B
DEN
true
s
c
DEN

Figure 8.11

We have

DEN.f(b) = RES (DEN.f,{contents(b)}) (cf.(***))

The value diagram is analogous to that given in Figure 8.11. Notice that, in Ada, functions have only the **in** mode of parameter binding.

8.3.4 Statements

As we mentioned in Section 6.9, statements are compound expressions which denote transitions. Consider for instance the assignment statement. It denotes a call of the routine whose name is ':=' and which has two parameters : the left hand side expression and the right hand side expression. Hence we have here a special case of the M_{RES} operator. Recall the Pascal examples in Section 6.9.

Example of the Pascal assignment statement

```
var a:integer;
...
a:=5;
```

We have

DEN(a:=5) = RES(DEN(:=),a,5)

Hence, M_{RES}(:=,a,5) $\equiv a := 5$.

Example of the Pascal repeat statement

```
var a:integer;
begin
   ...
   repeat a:=a-2 until a<0;
end
```

We have

DEN(**repeat** a:=a-2 **until** a<0) =
  RES(DEN(**repeat until**),a:=a-2,a<0)

DEN(a:=a-2)=RES(DEN(:=),a,a-2)

DEN(a-2) = RES(DEN(-),{contents(a)},2)

DEN(a<0) = RES(DEN(<),{contents(a)},0)

M_{RES}(-,{contents(a)},2) ≡ a-2

M_{RES}(:=,a,a-2) ≡ a:=a-2

M_{RES}(**repeat until**,a:=a-2,a<0) ≡ **repeat** a:=a-2 **until** a<0.

Example of the Pascal compound statement

var a:integer;
begin
    a:=5;
    repeat a:=a-2 **until** a<0
end

We have

DEN(**begin...end**) =
    RES(DEN(**begin...end**),a:=5,**repeat** a:=a-2 **until** a<0)

and

M_{RES}(**begin...end**, a:=5,**repeat** a:=a-2 **until** a<0) ≡
    begin a:=5; **repeat** a:=a-2 **until** a<0 **end**

§8.4 Configurations

In this chapter the set of names, the set of compound expressions and the function DEN were introduced. The set of names and the function DEN defined on it are both components of the configurations. Language defined names are initially added to N, and the function DEN is appropriately defined at the corresponding points.
Program defined names are added to N when the program execution enters their scope and are deleted from N when it leaves their scope. The function DEN is defined appropriately.

The set of compound expressions CE is not a component of the configurations. This is because it does not contain any new information as to the actual state of the program. Every time we need a compound expression we build it up from names using the various operators as we explained earlier in this chapter. Hence only the set N and the function DEN are added to the configurations, so that, for the time being, a configuration is a 10-tuple

(AD,AL,CD,CL,R,CONT,SEL,RES,N,DEN)

Chapter 9

TYPES

§9.1 Concept

In strongly typed languages (such as Pascal, Algol 68, PL/1 and Ada) each expression is given a number of properties, defining a set of values and the operations applicable to them. The collection of properties that define such a set of values is called a *type*.

The *type function* TYP associates with every expression (name or compound expression) a unique type. It has the form

$$\text{TYP} : \text{E} \rightarrow \text{T}$$

where T is the set of all types. Types are abstract objects that are denoted by expressions, in the same way as values are. Therefore the denotation function DEN discussed in Chapter 8 is extended as follows :

$$\text{DEN} : \text{E} \rightarrow \text{V} \cup \text{T}$$

A type can be associated with a *name* in two ways :

- by the language itself. For instance, in Pascal the type of the name '36' is the type denoted by the name 'integer', so that

  TYP.36 = DEN.integer

- by a declaration in the program. For instance, in Algol 68 the declarations

mode vectype=[1:3] **int**;
ref vectype vec=**loc vectype**;

create a location denoted by the name 'vec'. Furthermore, the type denoted by '**ref vectype**' is associated with the name 'vec'. Figure 9.1 illustrates the effect of this declaration. In the value diagrams, types are represented by points. The type of a compound expression is derived from the types of its subexpressions, which are described in SMALL by means of the functions M_{SEL}, M_{CONT} and M_{RES}, as explained in Chapter 8. Consider again the name 'vec' denoting a composite location. The compound expression 'vec[2]' has the type denoted by '**ref int**', which is derived from '**ref** [ ] **int**' (the type of 'vec') and '**int**' (the type of '2'). One of the main objects of Section 9.6 is to explain precisely how the type of compound expressions is derived from the types of their subexpressions.

Examples of type expressions

Pascal

integer
boolean
(red,blue,yellow)
↑integer
1..100
array[1..10,1..100] **of** integer

record
    first:integer;
    second:real
end

Algol 68

int
bool
ref int
[1:10,1:100] **int**
struct (**int** first,**real** second)
proc (**ref int**,**ref real**) **bool**

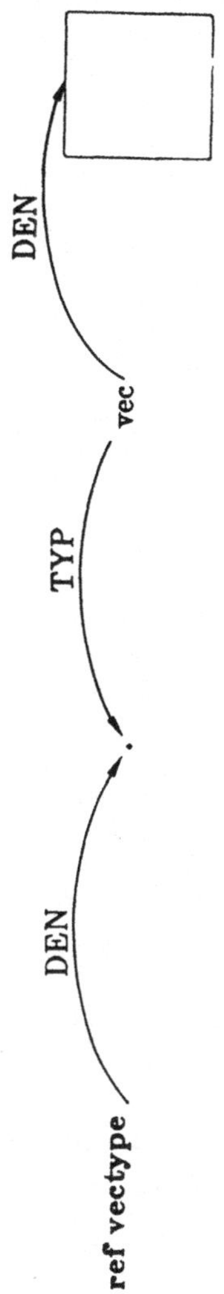

Figure 9.1.

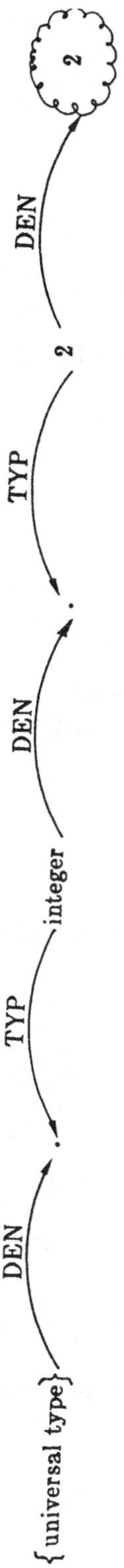

Figure 9.2.

PL/1

```
BIN FIXED
BIT(1)
POINTER
(1:10,1:100) BIN FIXED

1,
    2 first BIN FIXED,
    2 second BIN FLOAT

ENTRY(BIN FIXED,BIN FLOAT) RETURNS (BIT(1))
```

Ada

```
integer
boolean
(red,blue,yellow)
integer range 1..100
access integer
array (1..10,1..100) of integer
array(integer range <>,integer range <>) of integer

record
    first:integer;
    second:float;
end record
```

Four basic functions and two additional functions are defined on the set of types.

The basic functions are :

- the **reference function** REF (Section 9.2)
- the **structure function** STRUCT (Section 9.3)
- the **type of selector function** TOS (Section 9.3)
- the **routine function** ROUT (Section 9.4).

The additional type functions are :

- the **union function** UNION (Section 9.7)
- the **constraint function** CONSTR (Section 9.7).

Other type functions could be added.

There is a strong analogy between the functions CONT, SEL and RES (defining the structure of values) and the functions REF, STRUCT and ROUT (defining the structure of types). This analogy will be clear from the value diagrams.

Types in programming languages allow the compiler to check that each expression is used in a consistent way. Suppose e is an expression of type μ. The type μ defines the set of all those values that can be denoted by e, and at the same time defines the set of operations of which DEN.e can be an operand.

Note that an expression e which denotes a type μ has itself a type TYP.e. In Pascal, for instance, we have

TYP.2 = DEN.integer
TYP.integer = DEN.{universal type}

(The name 'universal type' does not exist in Pascal.) This is illustrated in Figure 9.2.

§9.2 The reference function REF

There exists a relationship between the type of an expression e_v denoting a value v and the type of an expression e_l denoting an atomic location α containing v. This relationship is described by the *reference function*, abbreviated REF. If a value v is contained in the location α denoted by the expression e_l, then v is denoted by an expression e_v with

$$\text{TYP}.e_l = \text{REF}.\text{TYP}.e_v$$

Hence REF is a function of the form

$$\text{REF} : \text{T} \rightarrow \text{T}$$

Formally, the above relationschip can be expressed as :

$$\begin{aligned}&\text{if CONT.DEN}.e_l = v\\&\quad\text{then } \exists\ e_v \text{ with DEN}.e_v = v \text{ and TYP}.e_l = \text{REF}.\text{TYP}.e_v\end{aligned}$$

This is illustrated in Figure 9.3. As we will see later, this definition does not exclude the possibility that v is denoted by expressions of different types.

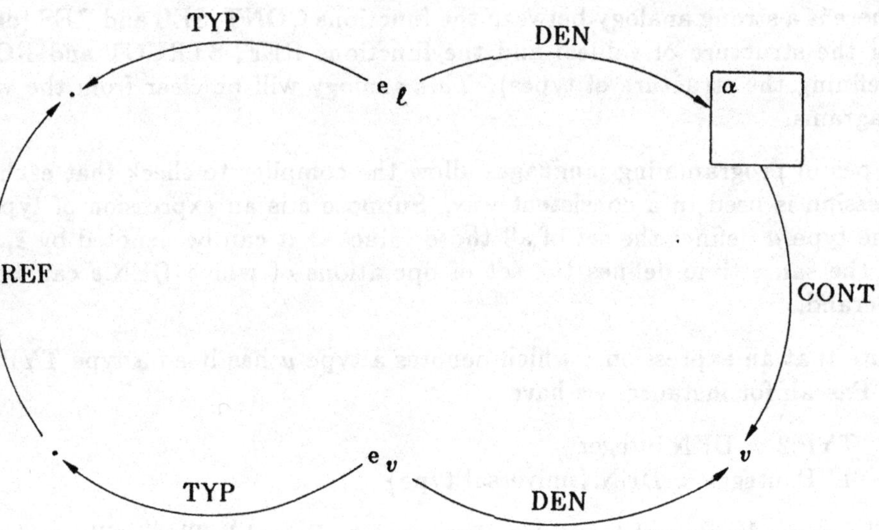

Figure 9.3.

In Pascal, PL/1 and Ada, there are a number of cases for which the language does not have suitable type expressions. In the value diagrams, type expressions which do not belong to the language concerned are written between { and }.

Examples using a single REF function

Consider the following four equivalent examples. Their value diagram is given in Figure 9.4, where the relevant type information has now been included.

Pascal

```
var x:integer;
begin
    x:=4;
    ...
end
```

Note that the type of '4' is denoted by 'integer'. The type of 'x' cannot be explicitly written in Pascal and is denoted here by {reference(integer)}. The declaration '**var** x:integer' stands for "create an atomic location with name 'x'. The contents of this location can only be an integer".

Algol 68

```
ref int x=loc int;
x:=4;

co this can be replaced by 'int x:=4' co;

...
```

PL/1

```
DECLARE x BIN FIXED;
x=4;

/* this can be replaced by
    DECLARE x BIN FIXED INIT(4) */;
...
```

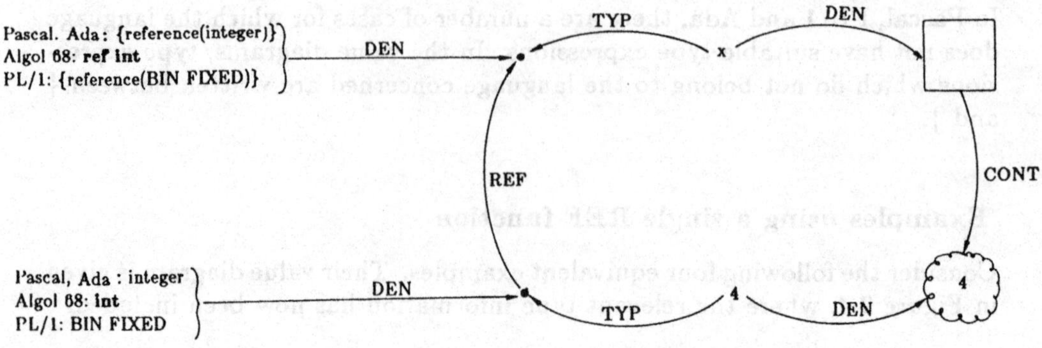
Pascal. Ada: {reference(integer)}
Algol 68: ref int
PL/1: {reference(BIN FIXED)}
DEN
TYP
x
DEN
REF
CONT
Pascal, Ada : integer
Algol 68: int
PL/1: BIN FIXED
DEN
4
TYP
DEN
4

Figure 9.4.

Ada

```
x:integer;
begin
    x:=4;

    - - this can be replaced by 'x:integer:=4;'
    ...
end
```

Examples using a double REF function

The following equivalent examples use the reference function twice. Their value diagram is shown in Figure 9.5.

Pascal

```
type refint=↑integer;
var ptr:refint;
begin
    new(ptr);
    ptr↑:=4;
    ...
end
```

Algol 68

```
mode refint=ref int;
ref refint ptr=loc refint;
ptr:=heap int:=4;

    co The last two lines can be replaced by 'refint ptr:= heap int:=4' co;

...
```

PL/1

```
DECLARE
    ptr POINTER,
    integer BIN FIXED BASED;
ALLOCATE integer SET(ptr);
ptr→integer=4;
...
```

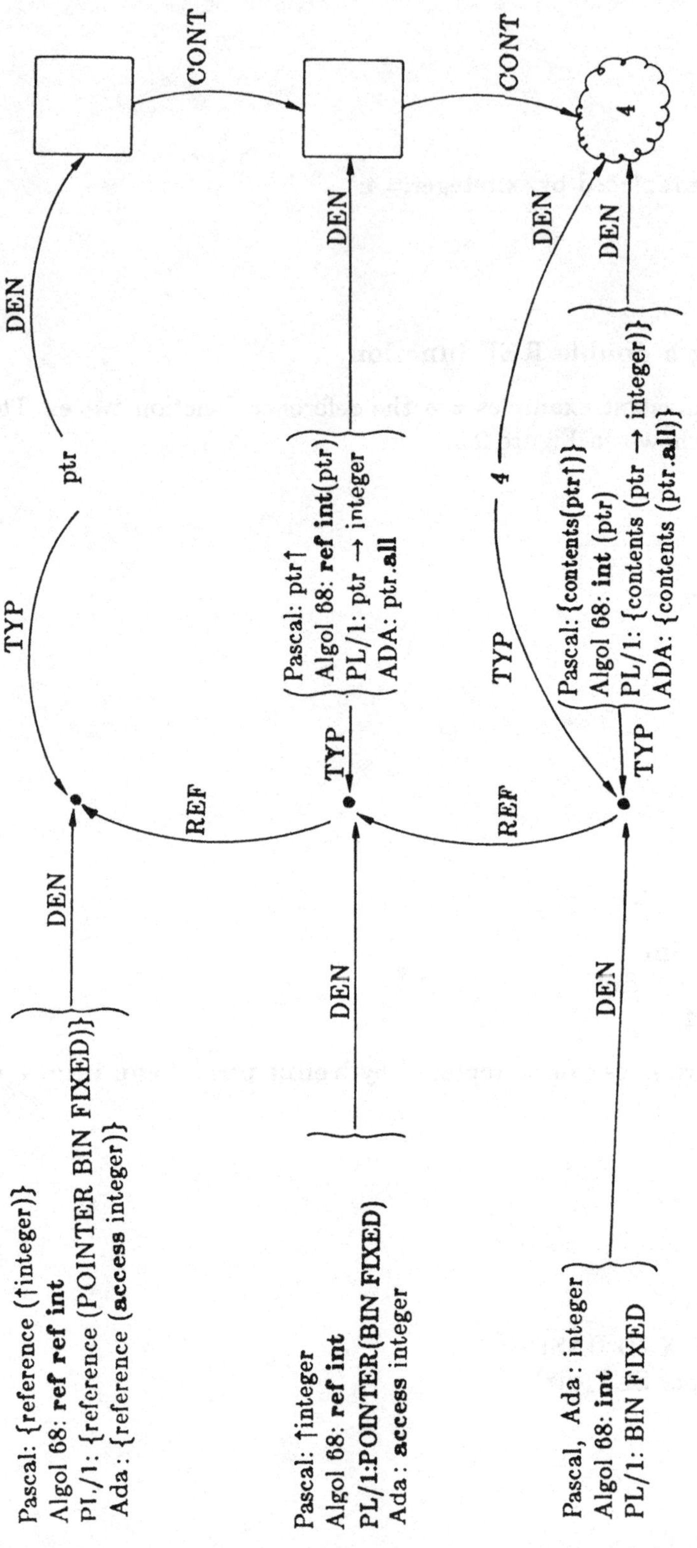

Pascal: {reference (↑integer)}
Algol 68: ref ref int
PL/1: {reference (POINTER BIN FIXED)}
Ada: {reference (access integer)}
DEN
REF
TYP
ptr
DEN
CONT
Pascal: ↑integer
Algol 68: ref int
PL/1:POINTER(BIN FIXED)
Ada: access integer
DEN
TYP
Pascal: ptr↑
Algol 68: ref int(ptr)
PL/1: ptr → integer
ADA: ptr.all
DEN
REF
CONT
Pascal, Ada: integer
Algol 68: int
PL/1: BIN FIXED
DEN
TYP
4
DEN
Pascal: {contents(ptr↑)}
Algol 68: int (ptr)
PL/1: {contents (ptr → integer)}
ADA: {contents (ptr.all)}
DEN
4

Figure 9.5.

Ada

```
type refint is access integer;
ptr:refint;
begin
    ptr:=new integer'(4);

    - - the declaration of 'ptr' and the allocation statement can be
    - - replaced by 'prt:refint:=new integer'(4);'

    ...
end
```

Examples using simple record locations

In the following four equivalent examples, a record location is declared. The value diagram for these examples is given in Figure 9.6.

Pascal

```
type m=
        record
            first:↑integer;
            second:real
        end;
var rec:m;
begin
    new(rec.first);
    rec.first↑:=3;
    rec.second:=3.14;
    ...
end
```

Algol 68

```
mode m=struct(ref int first,real second);
ref m rec=loc m;
first of rec:=heap int;
ref int(first of rec):=3;
second of rec:=3.14;
```

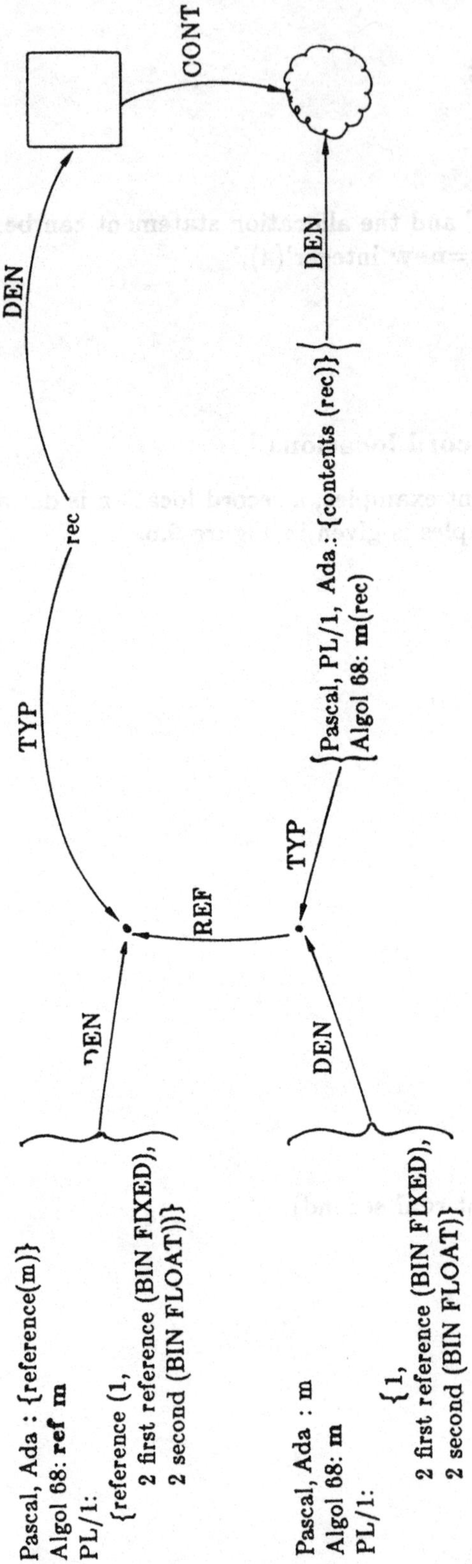
Pascal, Ada : {reference(m)}
Algol 68: ref m
PL/1:
{reference (1,
2 first reference (BIN FIXED),
2 second (BIN FLOAT))}
Pascal, Ada : m
Algol 68: m
PL/1:
{1,
2 first reference (BIN FIXED),
2 second (BIN FLOAT)}
DEN
DEN
REF
TYP
TYP
rec
DEN
CONT
DEN
Pascal, PL/1, Ada :{contents (rec)}
Algol 68: m(rec)

Figure 9.6.

```
    co The last four statements can be replaced by
    'm rec:=(heap int:=3,3.14)' co;

...
```

PL/1

```
DECLARE
    integer BIN FIXED BASED,
    1 rec,
        2 first POINTER,
        2 second BIN FLOAT;
ALLOCATE integer SET(rec.first);
rec.first→integer=3;
rec.second=3.14;
...
```

Ada

```
type refint is access integer;
type m is
    record
        first:refint;
        second:float;
    end record;
rec:m;
begin
    rec.first:=new integer;
    rec.first.all:=3;

    - - The last two statements can be replaced by
    - - 'rec.first:=new integer'(3);'

    rec.second:=3.14;
    ...
end
```

Examples using more complex record locations

Another set of four equivalent examples is given below. Their value diagram is shown in Figure 9.7, in which only the expressions for Algol 68 are indicated. The reader is invited to fill in the expressions for the other languages.

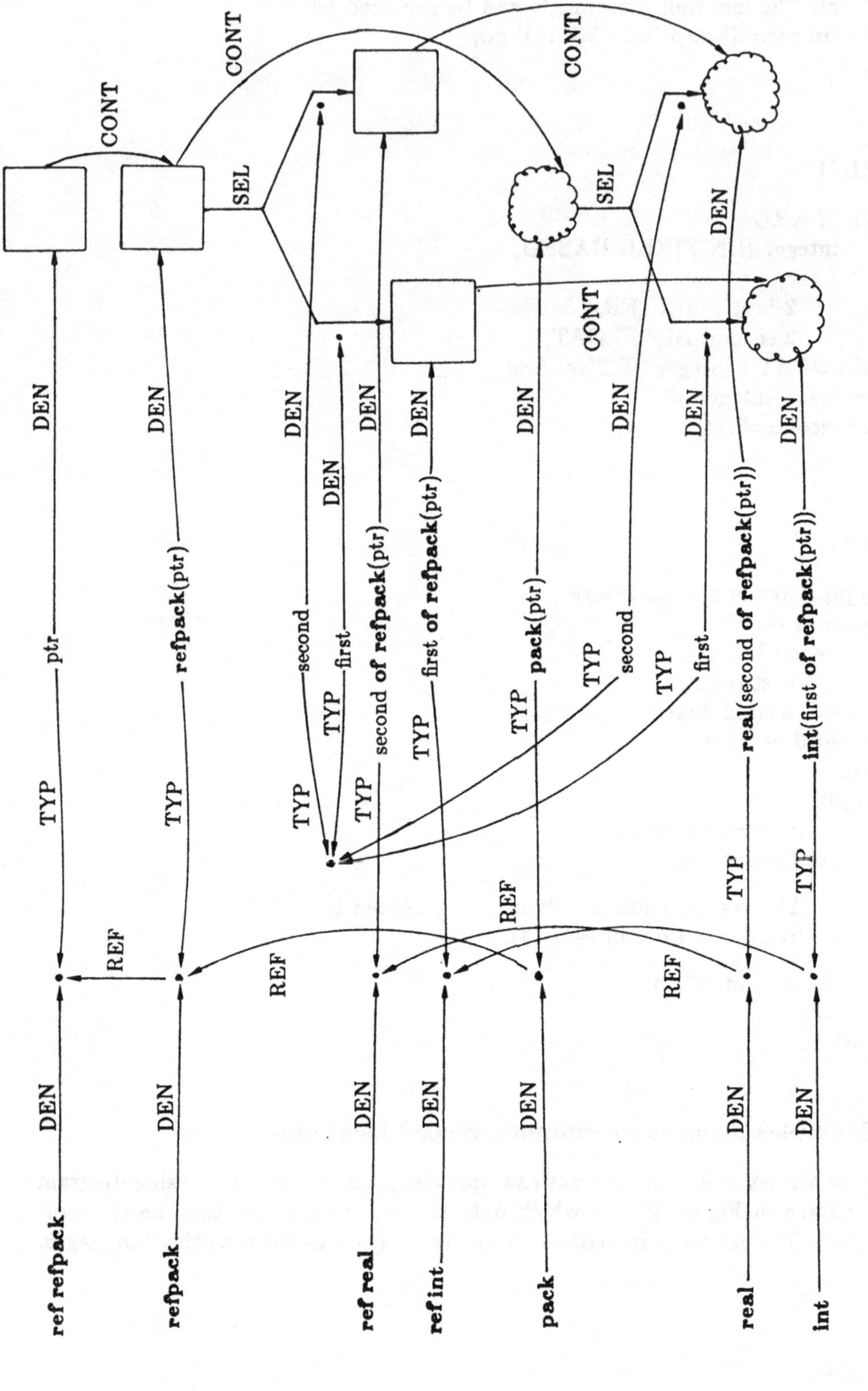
ref refpack
refpack
ref real
ref int
pack
real
int
DEN
REF
TYP
CONT
SEL
ptr
refpack(ptr)
second
first
second of refpack(ptr)
first of refpack(ptr)
pack(ptr)
real(second of refpack(ptr))
int(first of refpack(ptr))

Figure 9.7.

Pascal

```
type pack=
        record
            first:integer;
            second:real
        end;
    refpack=↑pack;
var ptr:refpack;
begin
    new(ptr);
    ptr↑.first:=4;
    ptr↑.second:=3.14;
    ...
end
```

Algol 68

```
mode
    pack=struct(int first,real second),
    refpack=ref pack;
ref refpack ptr=loc refpack;
ptr:=heap pack;
first of refpack(ptr):=4;
second of refpack(ptr):=3.14;

co The last four lines of code can be replaced by
    'refpack ptr:=heap pack:=(4,3.14)' co;
```

PL/1

```
DECLARE
    1 refpack BASED,
        2 first BIN FIXED,
        2 second BIN FLOAT,
    ptr POINTER;
ALLOCATE pack SET(ptr);
ptr→pack.first=4;
ptr→pack.second=3.14;
...
```

Ada

```
type pack is
        record
            first:integer;
            second:float;
        end record;
type refpack is access pack;
ptr:refpack;
begin
    ptr:=new pack;
    ptr.first:=4;
    ptr.second:=3.14;

    - - The last three statements can be replaced by
    - - 'ptr:=new pack'(4,3.14);'
    ...
end
```

Examples using two names denoting the same location

Compare the following four examples.

Pascal

```
var a,b:↑integer;
begin
    new(a); new(b);
    a↑:=1;
    b:=a;
    ...
end
```

Algol 68

```
ref ref int a=loc ref int, b=loc ref int,
...
a:=heap int;
b:=heap int;
ref int(a):=1;
b:=a;
...
```

PL/1

```
DECLARE (a,b) POINTER;
DECLARE integer BIN FIXED BASED;
...
ALLOCATE integer SET (a);
ALLOCATE integer SET (b);
a→integer=1;
b=a;
...
```

Ada

```
type pointer is access integer;
a,b:pointer;
begin
    a:=new integer;
    b:=new integer;
    a.all:=1;
    b:=a;
    ...
end
```

These examples are illustrated in Figure 9.8, in which only the Pascal expressions are given.

Examples using routine values as the contents of locations

Finally in this section, we give examples in Algol 68 and PL/1 of the use of a routine value as the contents of a location. This feature is not available in Pascal or Ada. The value diagram is given in Figure 9.9.

Algol 68

```
proc(ref int,ref real) bool p;
proc(ref int,ref real) bool q=
    (ref int x,ref real y) bool:begin ... end;
...
p:=q;
...
```

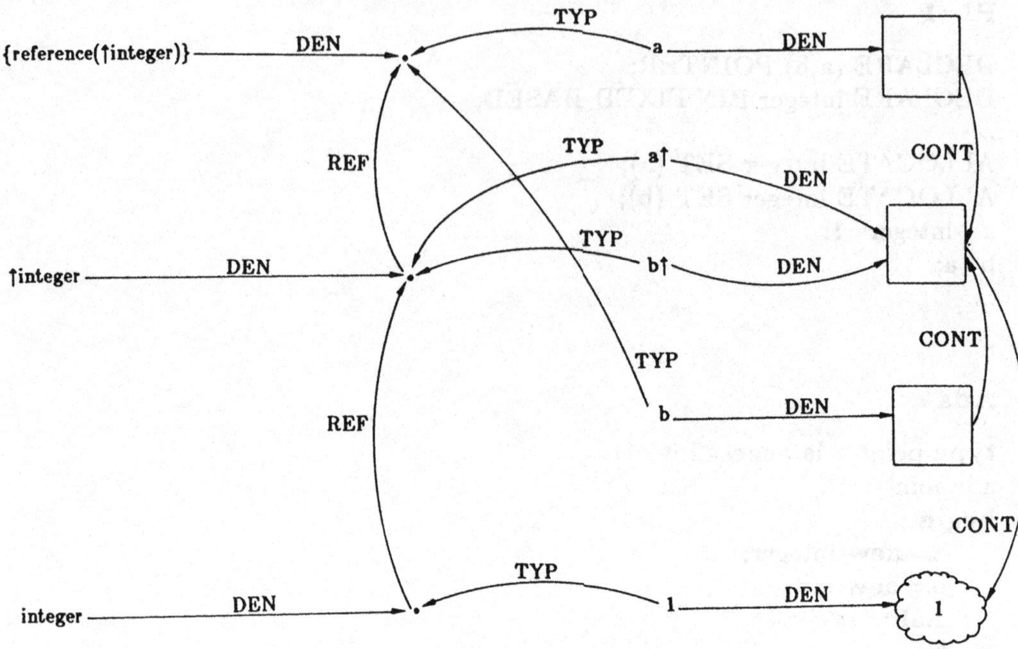

{reference(↑integer)}
DEN
TYP
a
DEN
REF
TYP
a↑
CONT
DEN
TYP
↑integer
DEN
b↑
DEN
CONT
TYP
REF
b
DEN
CONT
TYP
integer
DEN
1
DEN
1

Figure 9.8.

PL/1

```
DECLARE p ENTRY(BIN FIXED,BIN FLOAT) RETURNS (BIT (1));
q : PROCEDURE (x,y) RETURNS (BIT(1));
        DECLARE
            x BIN FIXED,
            y BIN FLOAT;
    ...
    END q; ...
p=q;
...
```

§9.3 The structure function STRUCT

There is a relationship between

(1) the type of an expression denoting a composite value,
(2) the types of expressions denoting the components of that composite value, and
(3) the selectors of that composite value.

This relationship is described by the *structure function*, abbreviated STRUCT. This is a function whose argument is a set of pairs $\{ (\sigma_1,\mu_1),\ldots,(\sigma_i,\mu_i),\ldots,(\sigma_n,\mu_n)\}$ with $n \geq 1$. The first element of each pair is a selector, whereas the second element is a type.

The function associates with this argument the type of the expressions denoting a composite value where the ith component is denoted by an expression of type μ_i and whose i^{th} selector is σ_i = DEN.s_i, for some s_i.

More precisely, if e is an expression of type μ = TYP.e, where e denotes a composite value v = DEN.e, then there exists an expression e_i for every component v_i of DEN.e such that

$$\text{TYP}.e = \text{STRUCT}.\{(\text{DEN}.s_1,\text{TYP}.e_1),\ldots,(\text{DEN}.s_n,\text{TYP}.e_n)\}$$

Hence STRUCT is a function of the form

$$\text{STRUCT} : \mathcal{P}(\text{AD x T}) \rightarrow \text{T}$$

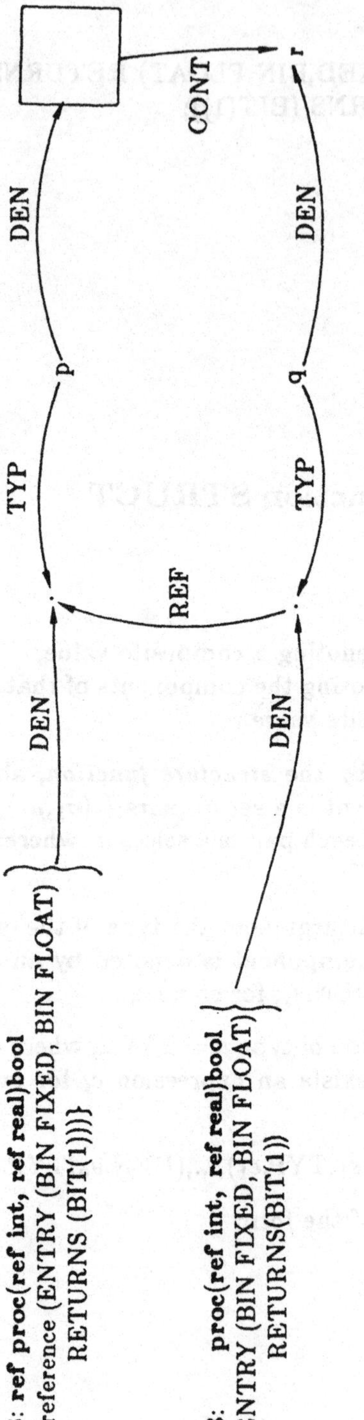
Algol 68: ref proc(ref int, ref real)bool
PL/1: {reference (ENTRY (BIN FIXED, BIN FLOAT) RETURNS (BIT(1)))}
Algol 68: proc(ref int, ref real)bool
PL/1: ENTRY (BIN FIXED, BIN FLOAT) RETURNS(BIT(1))
DEN
DEN
REF
TYP
TYP
p
q
DEN
DEN
CONT
r

Figure 9.9.

We thus have the following relationschip :

if SEL(DEN.e,DEN.s_i) = v_i, for all i, $1 \leq i \leq n$
    then $\exists e_1,\ldots,e_n$ with
        DEN.e_i = v_i and
        TYP.e = STRUCT.{(DEN.s_1,TYP.e_1),...,(DEN.s_n,TYP.e_n)}

This is illustrated by the diagram of Figure 9.10.

Furthermore, all the selectors of composite values denoted by expressions of the same type must have expressions (names) of one unique type. More precisely, if σ is a selector of DEN.e and σ' is a selector of DEN.e', and if TYP.e = TYP.e', then σ is denoted by some expression s and σ' by s' with TYP.s = TYP.s'.

More formally, we may state :

if SEL(DEN.e,σ) and SEL(DEN.e',σ') are defined
and if TYP.e = TYP.e'
    then $\exists s$, s' with
        DEN.s = σ,
        DEN.s' = σ' and
        TYP.s = TYP.s'

Moreover, the type TYP.s depends uniquely on the type TYP.e. This means that, with each type TYP.e of an expression which denotes a composite value, a unique type TYP.s of expressions denoting the selectors of the composite value is associated.
This association is described by the *type of selectors function*, TOS, which has the form

TOS : T $\rightarrow$ T

We thus have the following relationship :

if SEL(DEN.e,σ) is defined
    then $\exists s$ with
        DEN.s = σ and
        TYP.s = TOS.TYP.e

This is illustrated by the diagram of Figure 9.11.

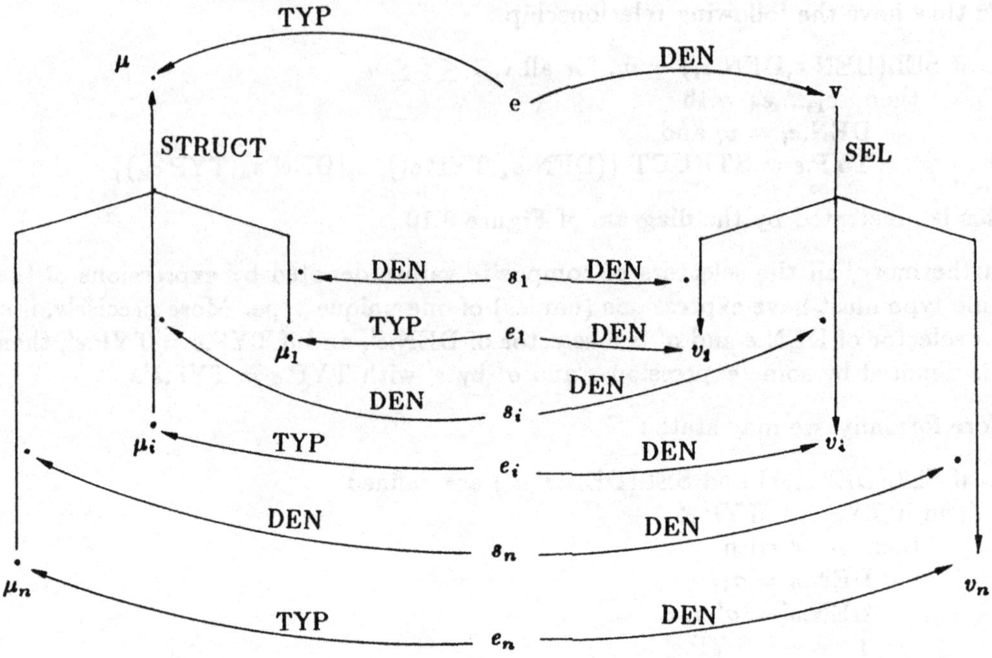
TYP
DEN
μ
e
v
STRUCT
SEL
DEN
s1
DEN
TYP
e1
DEN
μ1
v1
DEN
si
DEN
μi
TYP
vi
ei
DEN
DEN
DEN
sn
μn
vn
TYP
DEN
en

Figure 9.10.

Examples using records

In the four equivalent examples given below, a record location is declared and initialized. Conceptually, the type of the selectors of the record datum denoted by {contents(rec)} can be denoted as an enumeration type {(first,second)} . The expression 'first' in 'rec.first' is then of this enumeration type.
Notice that the type of selectors of record values is not explicit in any of the languages considered.

Pascal

```
type rectype=
    record
        first:integer;
        second:real
    end;
var rec:rectype;
begin
    rec.first:=2;
    rec.second:=3.14;
    ...
end
```

Algol 68

```
mode rectype=struct(int first,real second);
ref rectype rec=loc rectype;
first of rec:=2;
second of rec:=3.14;
...
```

PL/1

```
DECLARE
    1 rec,
        2 first BIN FIXED,
        2 second BIN FLOAT;
...
rec.first=2;
rec.second=3.14;
...
```

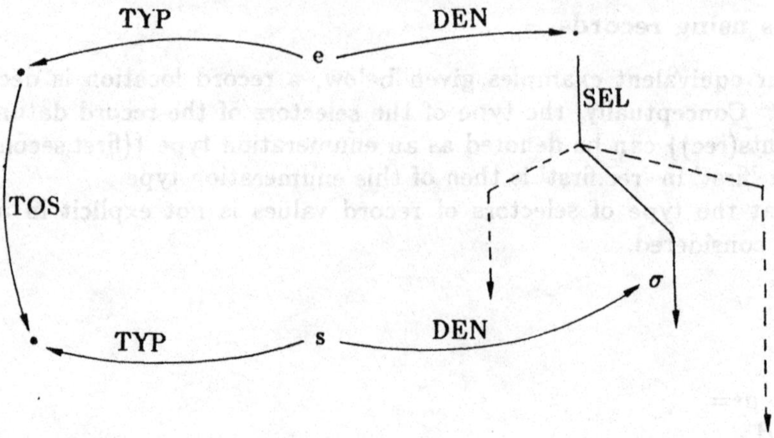

Figure 9.11.

Ada

```
type rectype is
    record
        first:integer;
        second:float;
    end record;
rec:rectype;
begin
    rec.first:=2;
    rec.second:=3.14;
    ...
end
```

Part of the value diagram is shown in Figure 9.12.

Examples using arrays

In the following four equivalent examples, an array location is declared and initialized. The type of the selectors of the array datum denoted by { contents(vector)} is denoted '1..3' and is called an index type in Pascal. The expression '1' in 'vector [1]' stands for {1..3(1)} , which is of type '1..3'. Informally, {1..3(1)} should be read "DEN.1 in the context of the type '1..3' ", in contrast to '1' which means "DEN.1 in the context of an integer". This is explained in more detail in Section 9.7.2.

Pascal

```
var vector:array[1..3] of integer;
begin
    vector[1]:=10;
    vector[2]:=20;
    vector[3]:=30;
    ...
end
```

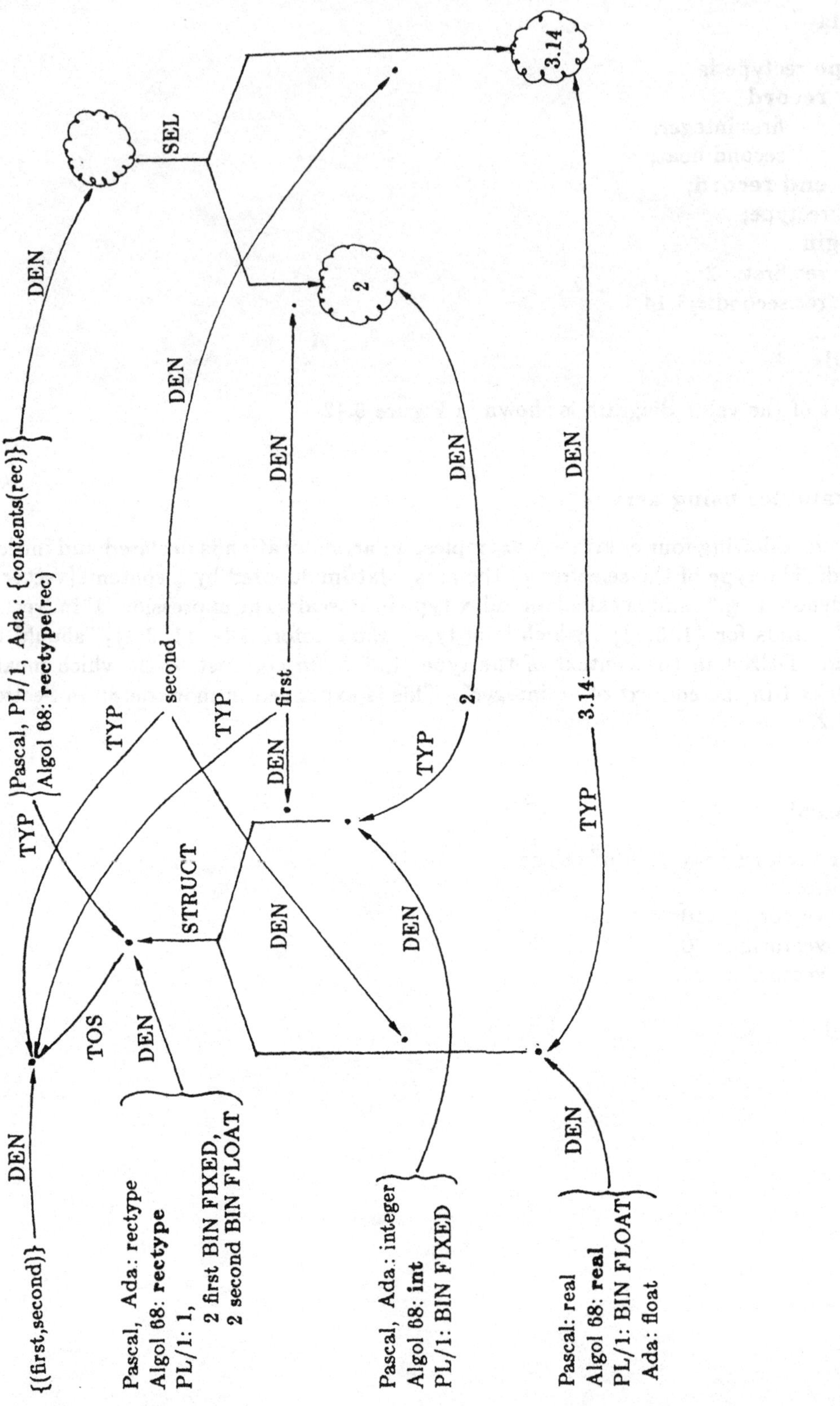
{(first,second)}
DEN
TOS
TYP
Pascal, Ada: rectype
Algol 68: **rectype**
PL/1: 1,
2 first BIN FIXED,
2 second BIN FLOAT
DEN
STRUCT
Pascal, PL/1, Ada : {contents(rec)}
Algol 68: **rectype**(rec)
DEN
SEL
second
first
TYP
DEN
Pascal, Ada: integer
Algol 68: **int**
PL/1: BIN FIXED
2
3.14
Pascal: real
Algol 68: **real**
PL/1: BIN FLOAT
Ada: float

Figure 9.12.

Algol 68

```
[1:3] int vector:=(10,20,30);
...
```

PL/1

```
DECLARE vector(1:3) BIN FIXED INIT (10,20,30);
...
```

Ada

```
vector:array(1..3) of integer:=(10,20,30);
...
```

Part of the value diagram is shown in Figure 9.13.

Examples using a combination of STRUCT and REF

The following four equivalent examples illustrate the use of a combination of STRUCT and REF.

Pascal

```
type rectype =
    record
        a:integer;
        b:real
    end;
var x:rectype;
begin
    x.a:=3;
    x.b:=3.14;
    ...
end
```

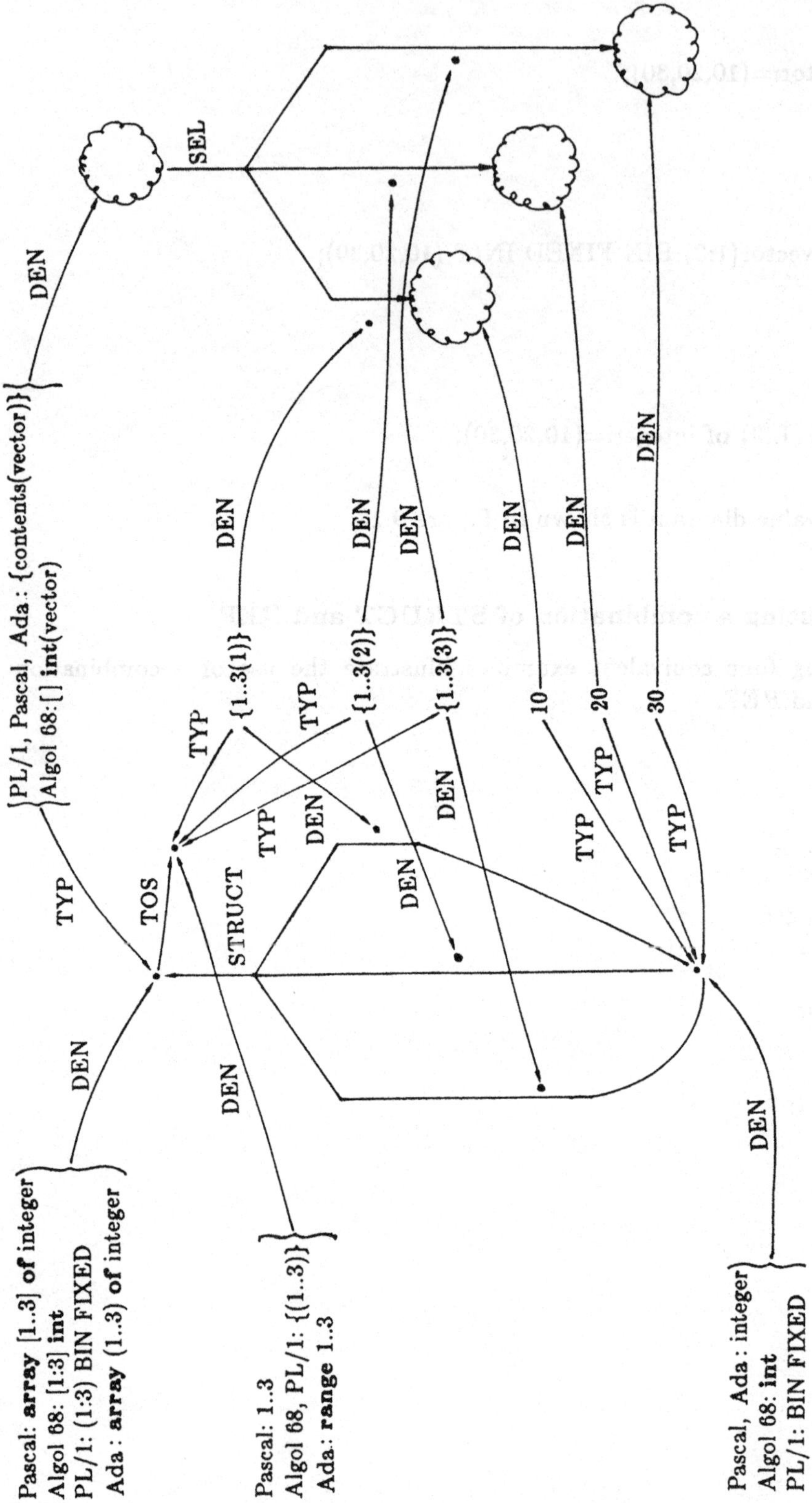
Pascal: array [1..3] of integer
Algol 68: [1:3] int
PL/1: (1:3) BIN FIXED
Ada : array (1..3) of integer
Pascal: 1..3
Algol 68, PL/1: {(1..3)}
Ada: range 1..3
Pascal, Ada : integer
Algol 68: int
PL/1: BIN FIXED
PL/1, Pascal, Ada : {contents(vector)}
Algol 68:[] int(vector)
{1..3(1)}
{1..3(2)}
{1..3(3)}
10
20
30
DEN
TYP
TOS
STRUCT
SEL

Figure 9.13.

Algol 68

```
mode rectype=struct(int a,real b);
rectype x:=(3,3.14);
...
```

PL/1

```
DECLARE
    1 x,
        2 a BIN FIXED INIT (3),
        2 b BIN FLOAT INIT (3.14);
```

Ada

```
type rectype is
    record
        a:integer;
        b:float;
    end record;
x:rectype:=(3,3.14);
```

These examples are illustrated in Figure 9.14, in which only the Pascal expressions are given.

Coexistence property

Note that in the previous Pascal example we have

$$\text{STRUCT.}\{(\text{DEN.a,REF.DEN.integer}),(\text{DEN.b,REF.DEN.real})\} = \text{REF.STRUCT.}\{(\text{DEN.a,DEN.integer}),(\text{DEN.b,DEN.real})\}$$

We call this property the *coexistence property* between REF and STRUCT. Its general form is

$$\text{STRUCT.}\{\ldots(\sigma_i,\text{REF.}\mu_i)\ldots\} = \text{REF.STRUCT.}\{\ldots(\sigma_i,\mu_i)\ldots\}$$

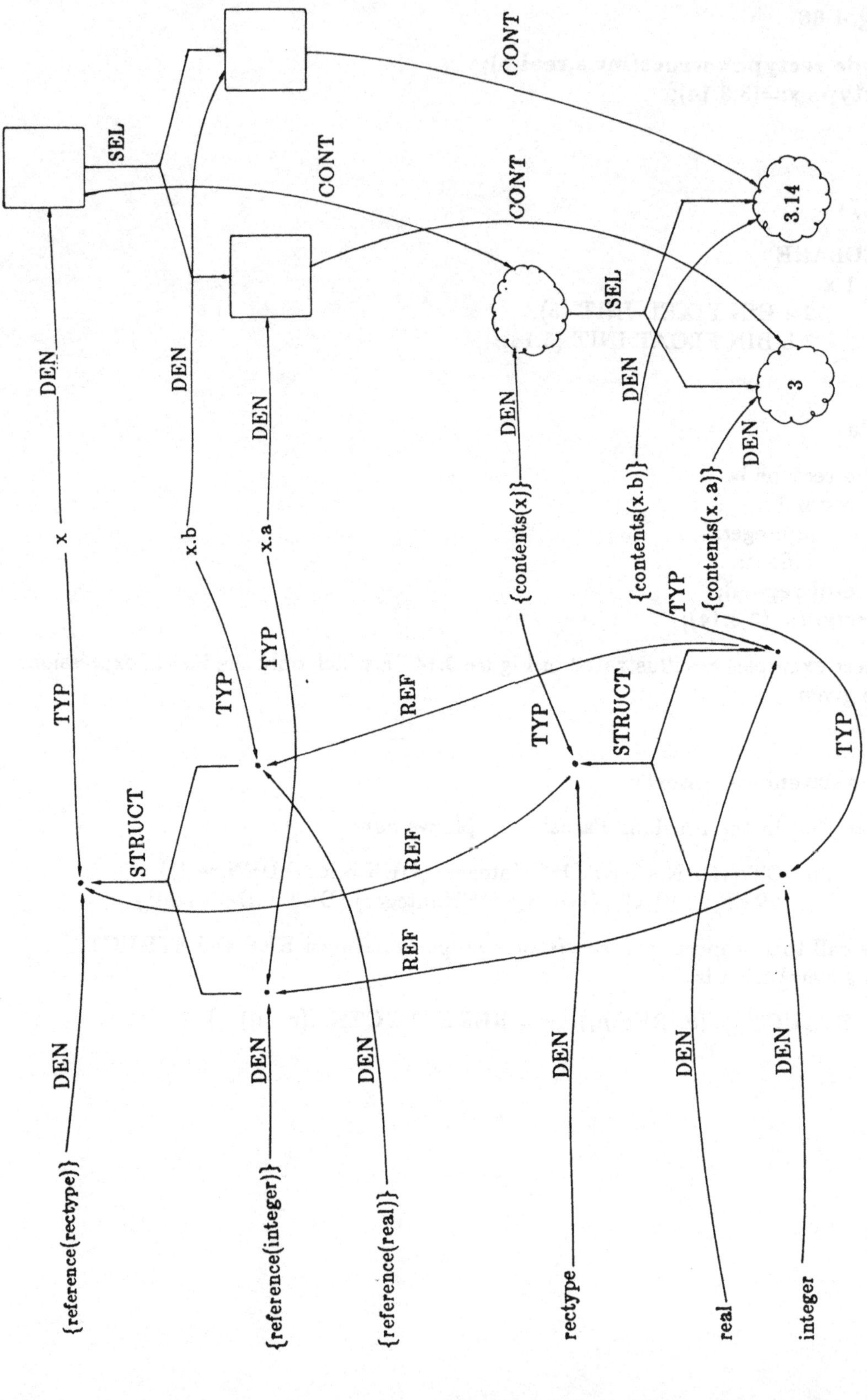
{reference(rectype)}
{reference(integer)}
{reference(real)}
rectype
real
integer
x
x.b
x.a
{contents(x)}
{contents(x.b)}
{contents(x.a)}
3.14
3
DEN
TYP
REF
STRUCT
SEL
CONT

Figure 9.14.

Examples illustrating the coexistence property

Pascal

```
type rectype=
    record
        b,c:integer
    end;
var ptr:↑rectype;
begin
    new(ptr);
    ptr↑.b:=1;
    ptr↑.c:=2;
    ...
end
```

Algol 68

```
mode rectype=struct(int b,c);
ref rectype ptr:=heap rectype:=(1,2);
...
```

PL/1

```
DECLARE
    1 rectype BASED,
        2 b BIN FIXED,
        2 c BIN FIXED,
    ptr POINTER;
...
allocate rectype SET(ptr);
ptr→rectype.b=1;
ptr→rectype.c=2;
...
```

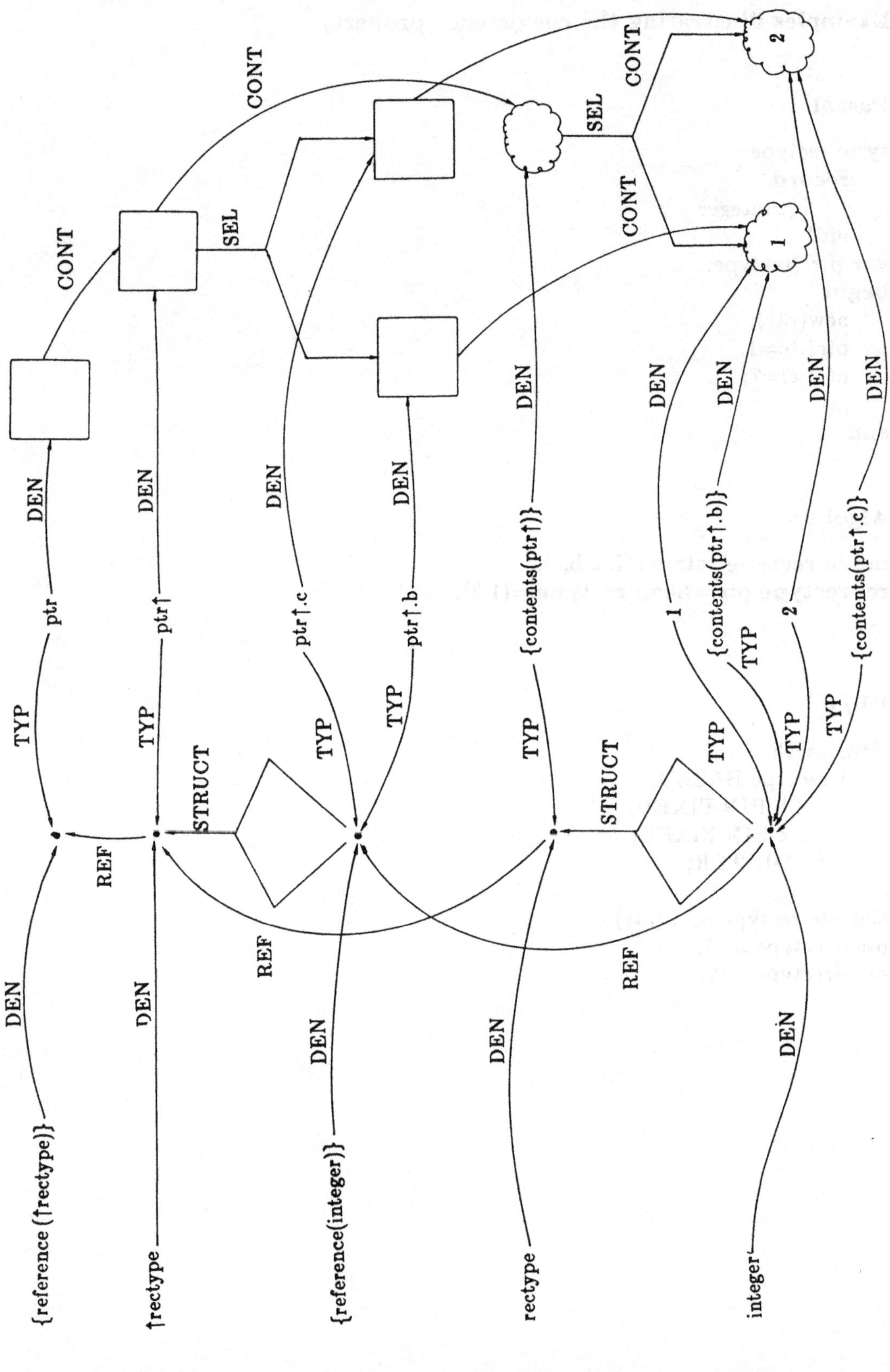
{reference (↑rectype)}
↑rectype
{reference(integer)}
rectype
integer
ptr
ptr↑
ptr↑.c
ptr↑.b
{contents(ptr↑)}
1
{contents(ptr↑.b)}
2
{contents(ptr↑.c)}
1
2
DEN
TYP
REF
STRUCT
SEL
CONT

Figure 9.15.

Ada

```
type rectype is
    record
        a,b:integer;
    end record;
type ptrtype is access rectype;
ptr:ptrtype:=new rectype(1,2);
...
```

Figure 9.15 illustrates these examples. Once again, only the Pascal expressions are given.

In the Pascal example below, the coexistence property between REF and STRUCT does not hold, since {contents(rec)} is not a location (it has no contents). In Pascal, there is no type μ with REF.μ = TYP.{contents(rec)} . This example is illustrated in Figure 9.16. The reader is asked to write equivalent Algol 68, PL/1 and Ada programs.

Pascal

```
type rectype=
    record
        b,c:↑integer
    end;
var rec:rectype;
begin
    new(rec.b);
    new(rec.c);
    rec.b↑:=1;
    rec.c↑:=2;
    ...
end
```

We now return to the Pascal example illustrated in Figure 6.4 of Chapter 6(see below). Note that there is a transition due to the call by variable of x. There is no Pascal notation for the selectors SEL_v and SEL_s, nor for the transition, nor for the type of 'f(z)'. Figure 6.4 is updated in Figure 9.17.

```
var z:integer;
function f(var x:integer):boolean;
    <declarations>;
```

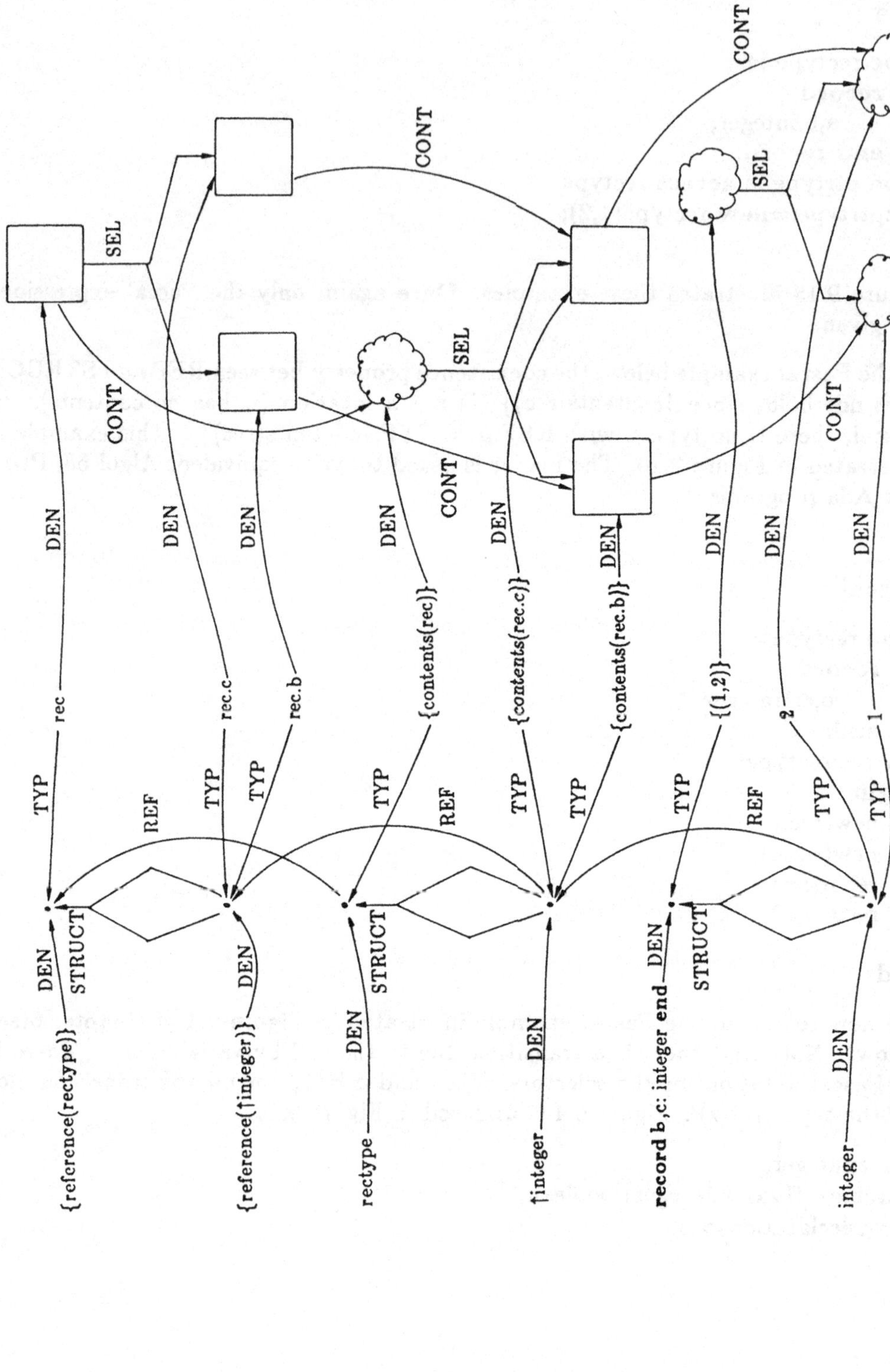

{reference(rectype)}
{reference(↑integer)}
rectype
↑integer
record b,c: integer end
integer
rec
rec.c
rec.b
{contents(rec)}
{contents(rec.c)}
{contents(rec.b)}
{(1,2)}
2
1
DEN
STRUCT
TYP
REF
SEL
CONT

Figure 9.16.

```
    begin
        <statements>;
        f:=true
    end;
begin
    z:=3;
    ... f(z) ...;
    ...
end
```

§9.4 The routine function ROUT

There is a relationship between the types of

(1) an expression denoting a routine value,
(2) the actual parameters of that routine value, and
(3) an expression denoting the result of the execution of that routine value.

This relationship is described by the *routine function*, abbreviated ROUT. ROUT is a function whose arguments are n+1 types $\mu_0,...,\mu_n$, where n is the number of actual parameters of the routine value. The function associates with these arguments the type of expressions denoting a routine value whose *ith* actual parameter is of type μ_i $(1 \leq i \leq n)$, and whose result is denoted by an expression of type μ_0.

More precisely, if e is an expression of type TYP.e, and if e denotes a routine value, whose actual parameters are $e_1, ..., e_n$, then there is an expression e_0 for the result RES(DEN.e,e_1,...,e_n) such that

$$\text{TYP.}e = \text{ROUT}(\text{TYP.}e_0,\text{TYP.}e_1,...,\text{TYP.}e_n)$$

Hence ROUT is a function of the form

$$\text{ROUT} : \text{T x T x ... x T} \rightarrow \text{T}$$

We thus have the following relationship :

if RES(DEN.e,e_1,...,e_n) $= v_0$
    then $\exists$ e_0 with
        DEN.e_0 $= v_0$ and
        TYP.e = ROUT(TYP.e_0,TYP.e_1,...,TYP.e_n)

This is illustrated by the diagram of Figure 9.18. Recall that routine values also include operations (such as +, -, * and /) and statements (see Chapter 6).

We first illustrate these concepts by four examples.

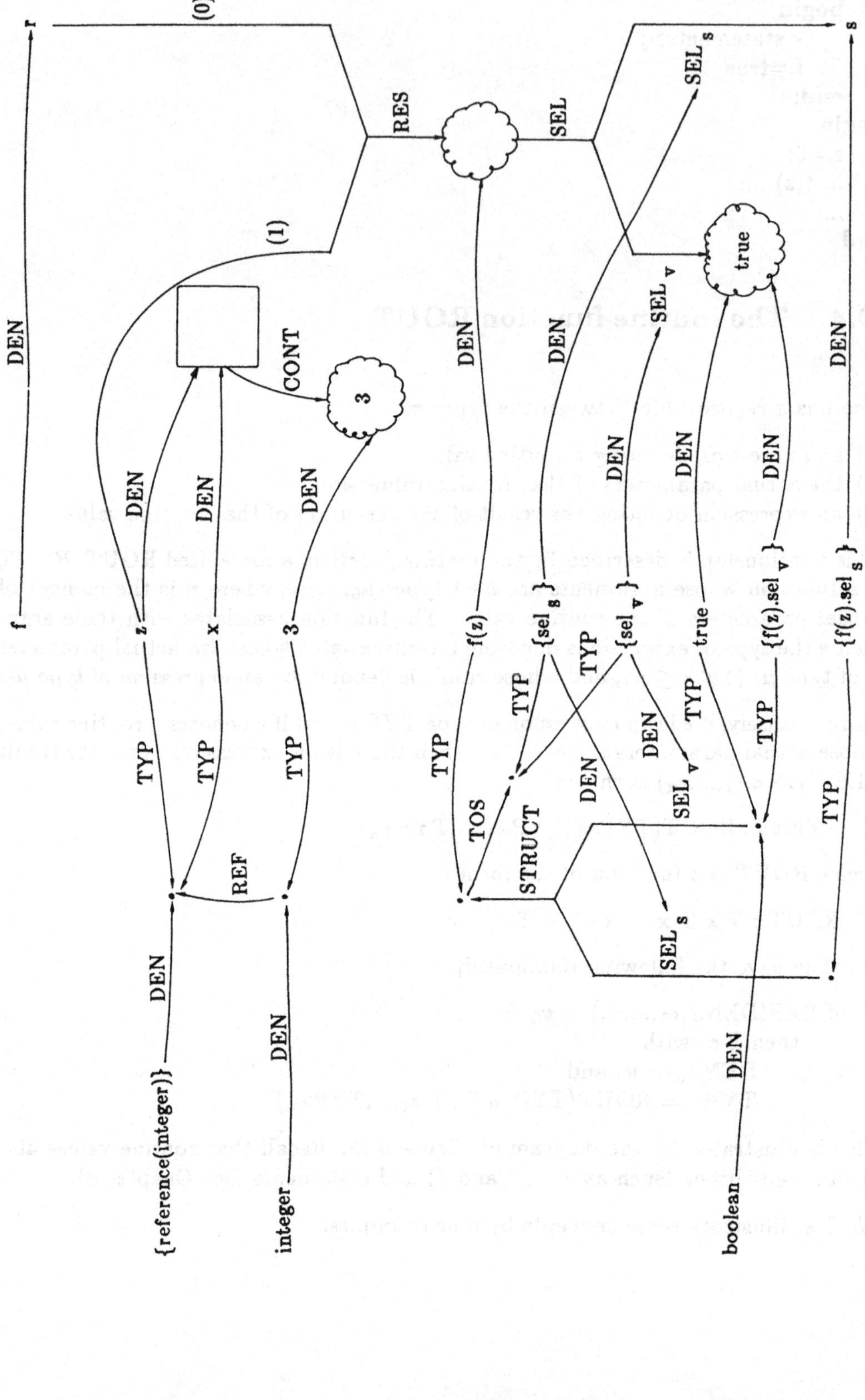

f
r
DEN
z
x
3
f(z)
{sel s}
{sel v}
true
{f(z).sel v}
{f(z).sel s}
s
{reference(integer)}
integer
boolean
TYP
REF
CONT
RES
SEL
SEL s
SEL v
TOS
STRUCT
(0)
(1)

Figure 9.17.

Pascal

```
function f(x:integer):integer;
    begin
        f:=x+1
    end;
begin
    ...f(5)...;
end
```

The value diagram just before the end of the execution of the function call 'f(5)' is shown in Figure 9.19.

Algol 68

```
proc(int)int f= (int x) int:
    begin
        x+1
    end;
...f(5)...;
...
```

The value diagram just before the end of the execution of the function call 'f(5)' is shown in Figure 9.20.

PL/1

```
f : PROCEDURE (x) RETURNS (BIN FIXED);
        DECLARE x BIN FIXED;
        ...
        RETURNS (x+1);
    END f;
...
...f(5)...;
...
```

The value diagram just before the end of the execution of the function call 'f(5)' is shown in Figure 9.19.

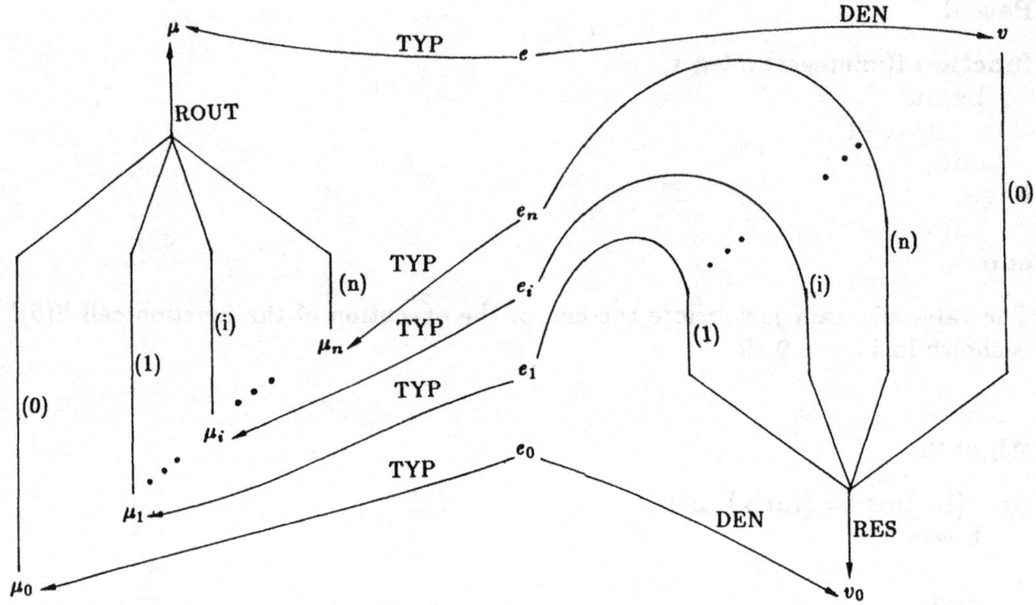

Figure 9.18.

Ada

```
function f(x:in integer) return integer is
    begin
        ...
        return x+1;
    end f;
begin
    ...f(5)...;
    ...
end
```

The value diagram just before the end of the execution of the function call 'f(5)' is shown in Figure 9.20.

In the following four examples, a function 'f' and a procedure 'p' are declared, and 'p' is executed with actual parameter 'f'.

Pascal

```
function f(x:real):boolean;
    <declarations>;
    begin
        <statements>;
        f:=true
    end;
procedure p(function g(y:real):boolean);
    <declarations>;
    begin
        <statements>;
        ...g(3.14)...
    end;
begin
    p(f);
    ...
end
```

The value diagram just before the end of the execution of the procedure call 'p(f)' is shown in Figure 9.21.

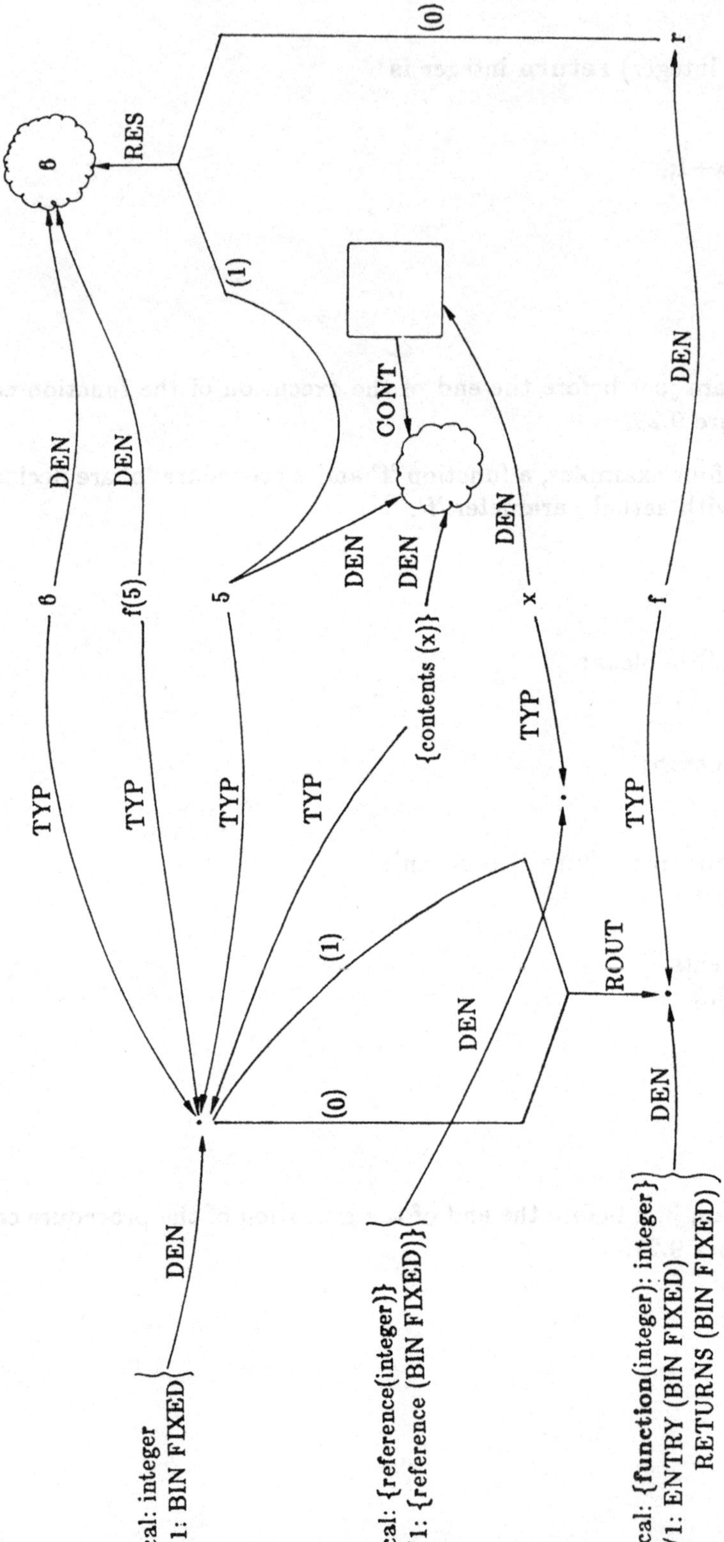
Pascal: integer
PL/1: BIN FIXED
Pascal: {reference(integer)}
PL/1: {reference (BIN FIXED)}
Pascal: {function(integer): integer}
PL/1: ENTRY (BIN FIXED)
RETURNS (BIN FIXED)
DEN
TYP
6
f(5)
5
{contents (x)}
x
f
r
RES
ROUT
CONT
(0)
(1)

Figure 9.19.

Algol 68

```
proc(real) bool f = (real x) bool :
    begin
        <declarations and statements>;
        true
    end;
proc(proc(real) bool) void p = (proc(real) bool g) void :
    begin
        <declarations and statements>;
        ... g(3.14) ...
    end
p(f);
```

The value diagram just before the end of the execution of the procedure call 'p(f)' is shown in Figure 9.22.

PL/1

```
f : PROCEDURE (x) RETURNS (BIT(1));
        DECLARE x BIN FLOAT;
        <declarations and statements>
        RETURN ('1'B);
    END f;
p : PROCEDURE (g);
        DECLARE g ENTRY (BIN FLOAT) RETURNS (BIT(1));
        <declarations and statements>
        ... g(3.14) ...;
    END p;
...
CALL p(f);
...
```

The value diagram just before the end of the execution of the procedure call 'CALL p(f)' is shown in Figure 9.21.

The parameterization of subprograms in Ada is only possible through the concept of generic subprograms see (Section 6.5.4). The Pascal, Algol 68 and PL/1 examples above can be simulated by the generic subprogram 'p-generic' and its instantiation '*p*' as follows.

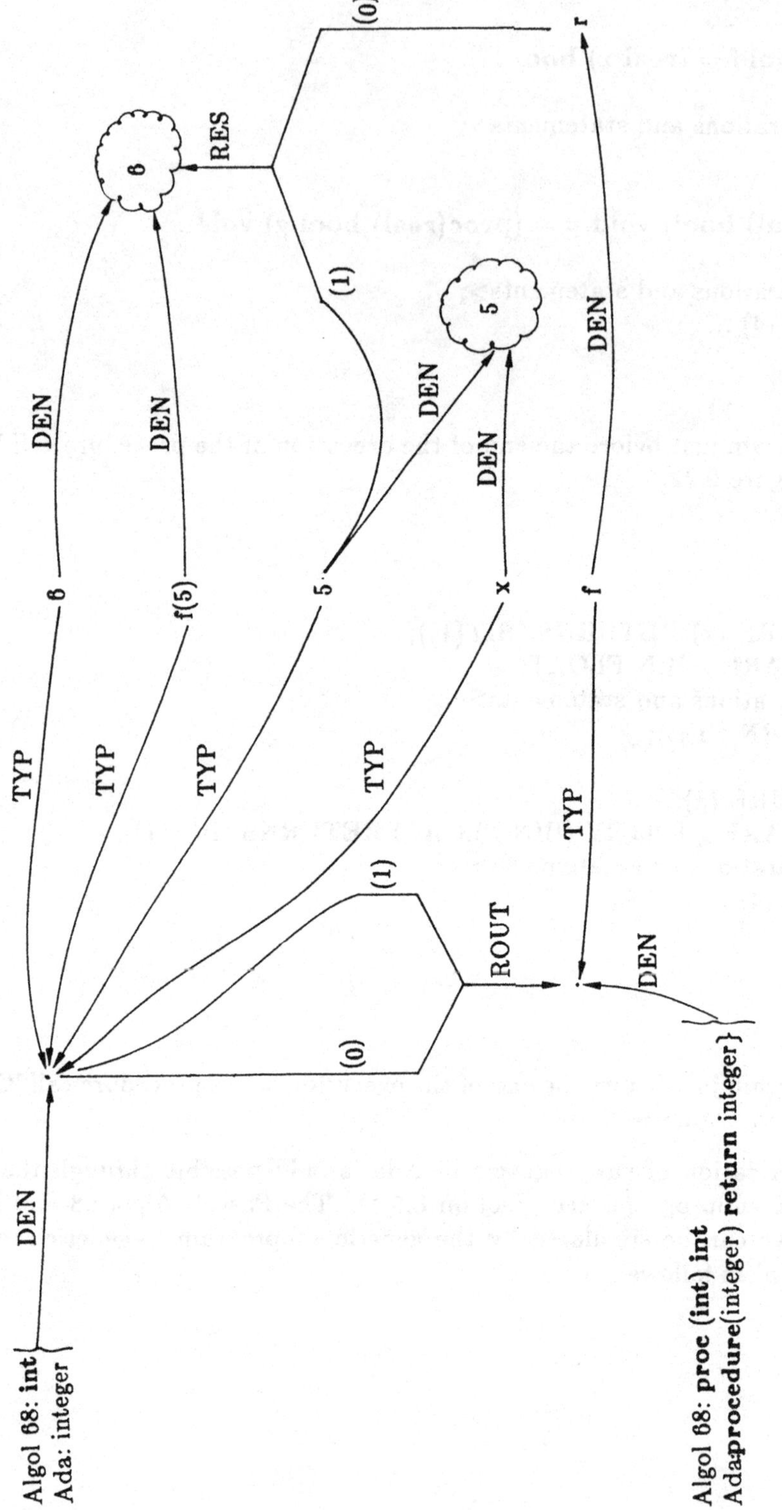
Algol 68: int
Ada: integer
DEN
TYP
TYP
TYP
TYP
TYP
6
f(5)
5
x
f
DEN
DEN
DEN
DEN
DEN
6
5
RES
(0)
(1)
r
(0)
(1)
ROUT
DEN
Algol 68: proc (int) int
Ada: procedure(integer) return integer

Figure 9.20.

Ada

```
function f(x:in float) return boolean is
    <declarations>
    begin
        <statements>
        return true;
    end f;

generic
    with function g(a:in float) return boolean;
procedure p_generic;
```

The body of the generic specification of 'p_generic' is

```
procedure p_generic is
    <declarations>
    begin
        <statements>
        ...g(3.14)...;
    end p_generic;
procedure p is new p_generic (f);
begin
    p;
    ...
end
```

The value diagram just before the end of the execution of the procedure call 'p' is shown in Figure 9.22.

Consider the following four equivalent programs which use two assignment statements and the sum function.

Pascal

```
var i,j:integer;
begin
    i:=5;
    j:=i+1;
    ...
end
```

Figure 9.21.

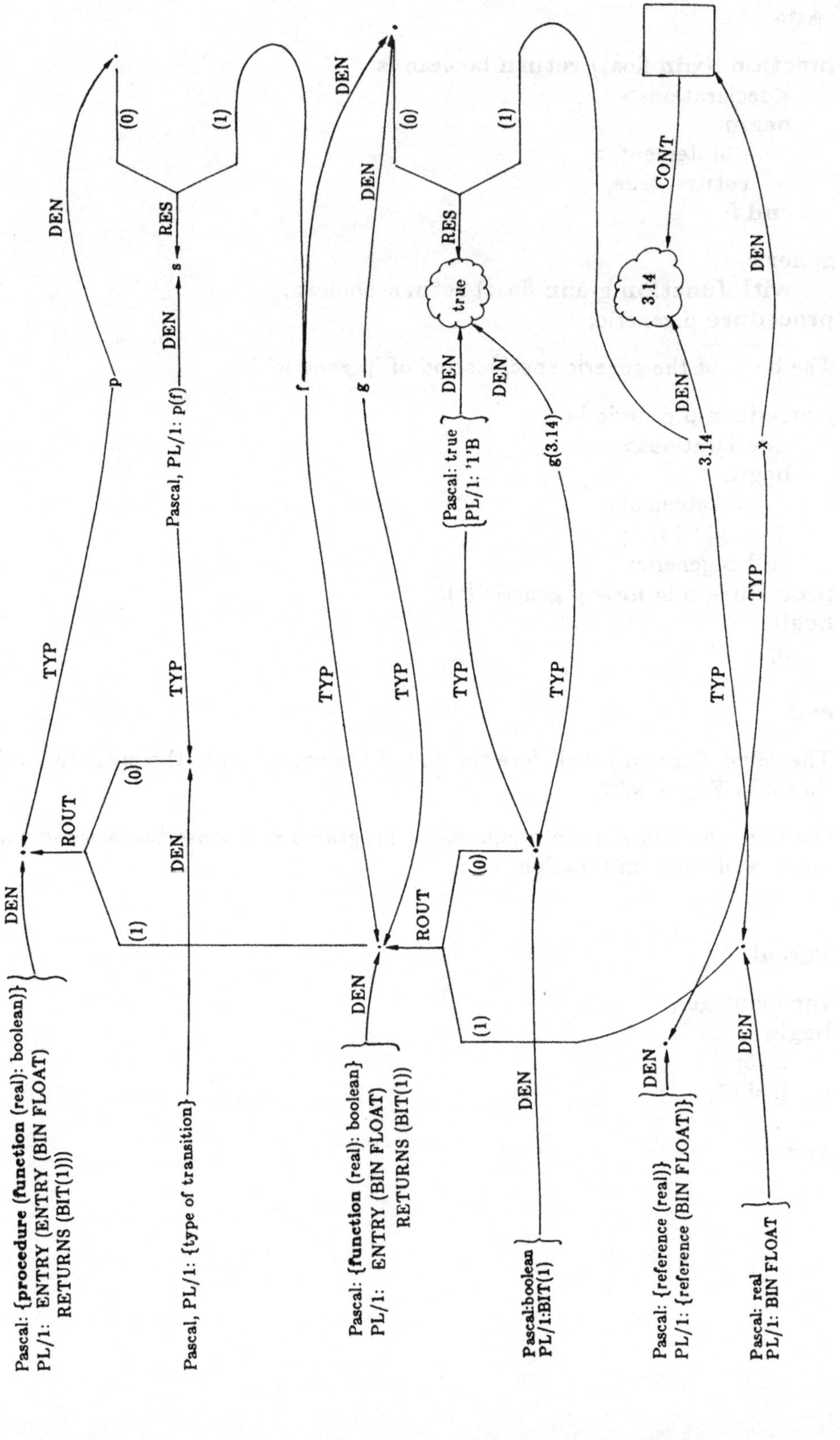
Pascal: {procedure (function (real): boolean)}
PL/1: ENTRY (ENTRY (BIN FLOAT) RETURNS (BIT(1)))
Pascal, PL/1: {type of transition}
Pascal: {function (real): boolean}
PL/1: ENTRY (BIN FLOAT) RETURNS (BIT(1))
Pascal:boolean
PL/1:BIT(1)
Pascal: {reference (real)}
PL/1: {reference (BIN FLOAT)}
Pascal: real
PL/1: BIN FLOAT
Pascal: true
PL/1: '1'B
Pascal, PL/1: p(f)
p
f
g
g(3.14)
3.14
x
s
true
DEN
TYP
ROUT
RES
CONT
(0)
(1)

Algol 68

```
begin
    int i,j;
    i:=5;
    j:=i+1;
    ...
end
```

PL/1

```
DECLARE (i,j) BIN FIXED;
i=5;
j=i+1;
...
```

Ada

```
i,j:integer;
begin
    i:=5;
    j:=i+1;
    ...
end
```

In the languages considered in this book, all transitions have the same type. This type has no notation in these languages, except for Algol 68, where it is denoted by **void**. Where there is no notation we use {type of transition}. The value diagram just before the end of the execution of the second assignment statement is shown in Figure 9.23, in which only the Pascal expressions are indicated.

The analogous example in Algol 68 is more complicated. In SMALL terminology, the execution of an assignment statement in Algol 68 results in a composite value with two components :

- the same transition as we considered for the other languages
- the location denoted by the left hand side of the assignment operator ':='.

The direct use of such a second component is illustrated by the following Algol 68 program fragment :

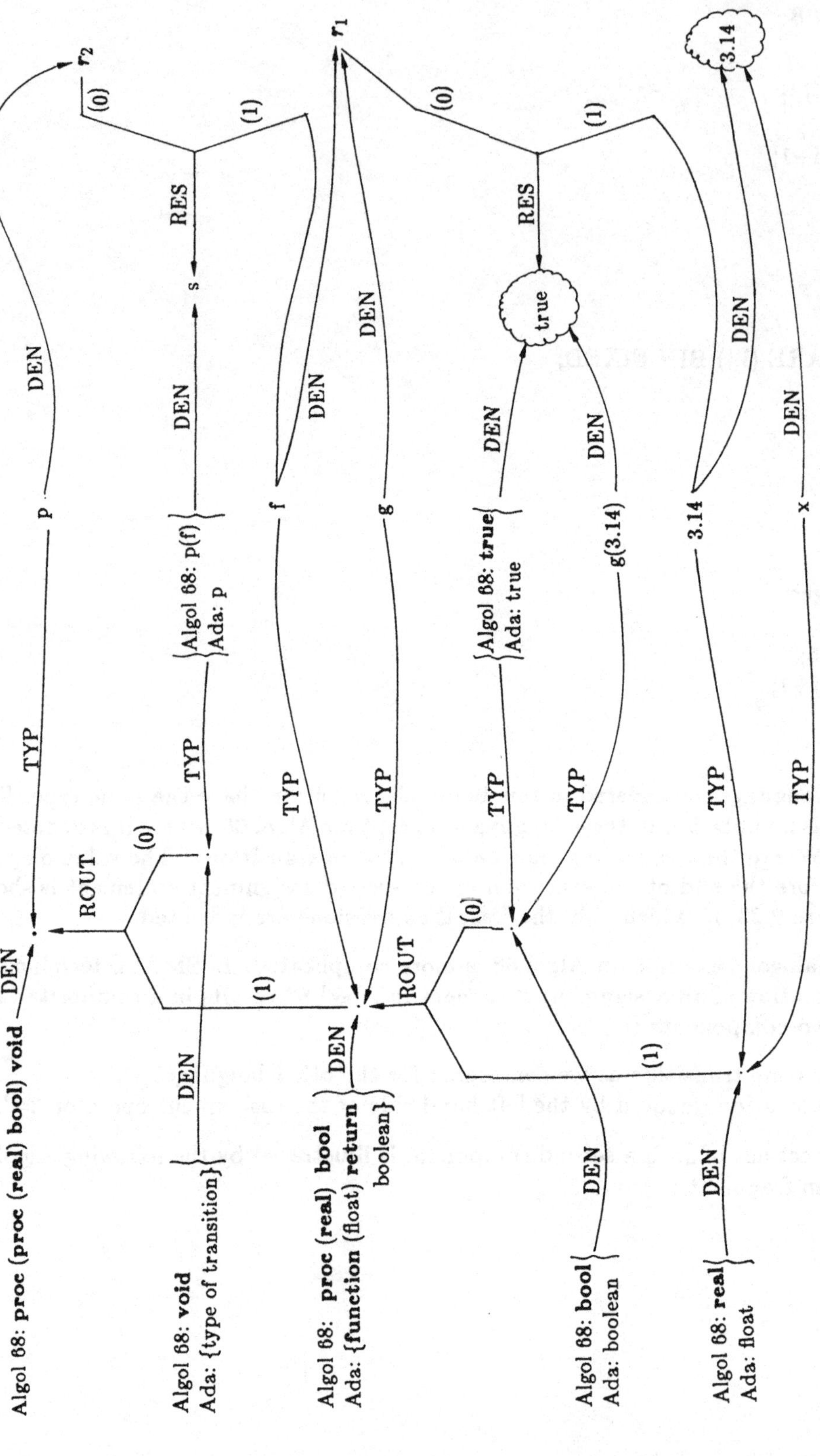
Algol 68: proc (proc (real) bool) void
Algol 68: void
Ada: {type of transition}
Algol 68: proc (real) bool
Ada: {function (float) return boolean}
Algol 68: bool
Ada: boolean
Algol 68: real
Ada: float
Algol 68: p(f)
Ada: p
Algol 68: true
Ada: true
p
f
g
g(3.14)
3.14
x
s
true
3.14
r_1
r_2
DEN
TYP
ROUT
RES
(0)
(1)

Figure 9.22.

```
...
ref real rr;
real r;
rr:=r:=0.0;
...
```

In Algol 68, the result of 'r:=0.0' consists of a transition and the value denoted by 'r', i.e., the location whose contents is DEN(0.0). The two selectors of the components of this composite value are defined by the context and are not explicitly written in Algol 68.

The Algol 68 example analogous to the above examples in Pascal, PL/1 and Ada is :

```
ref int i=loc int, j=loc int;
i:=5;
j:=i+1;
```

Part of the value diagram just before the end of the execution of the second statement is shown in Figure 9.24. This should be compared with Figure 9.23.

Finally, we recall the Pascal example illustrated in Figure 6.16, namely :

```
var a:integer;
begin
    a:=5;
    repeat a:=a-2 until a<=0;
end
```

Its value diagram just before the end of the execution of the repeat statement is shown in Figure 9.25.

§9.5 Configurations

As the final step in their definition, we add the set T of types, the function TYP, and the functions REF, STRUCT and ROUT to the configurations. When a new type is defined in a program, an infinite number of types is actually added to T : the given type itself, say t, and also REF.t, REF.REF.t, etc. Similarly, STRUCT and ROUT yield an infinite number of additional types. Hence the final definition of a

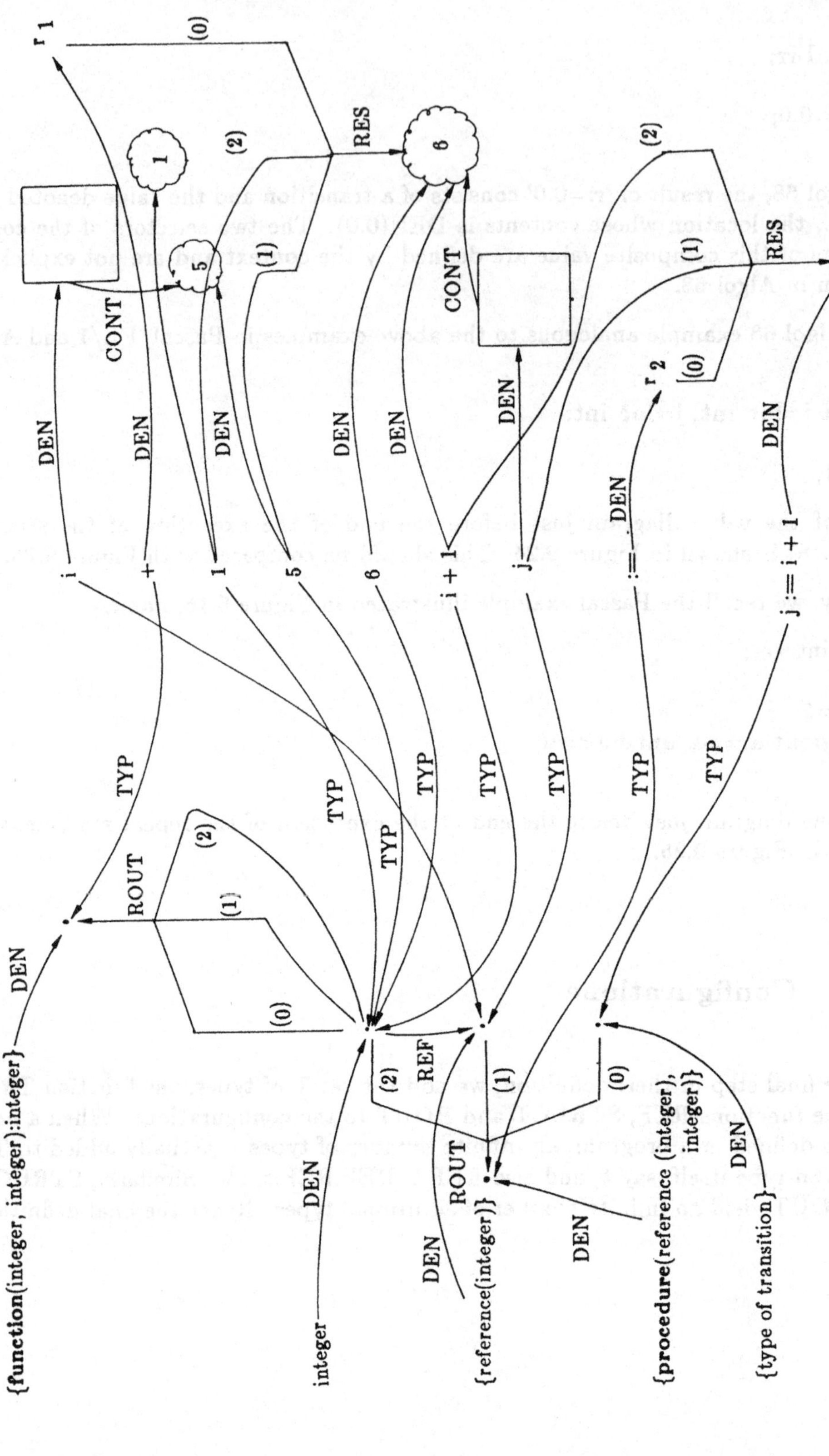
{function(integer, integer):integer}
integer
{reference(integer)}
{procedure(reference(integer), integer)}
{type of transition}
i
+
1
5
6
i + 1
j
:=
j := i + 1
r 1
r 2
s
DEN
ROUT
REF
TYP
CONT
RES

Figure 9.23.

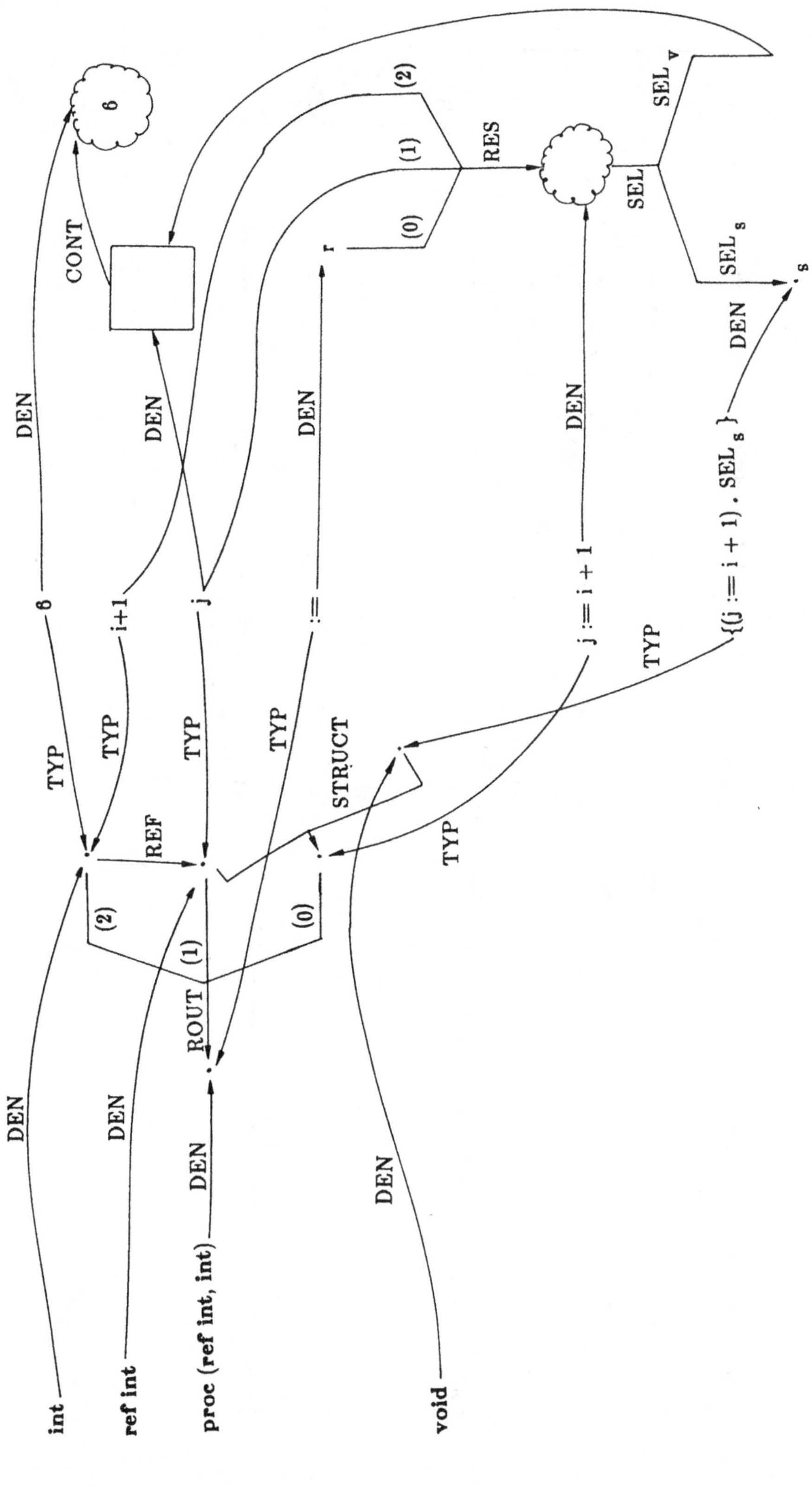

int
ref int
proc (ref int, int)
void
DEN
TYP
REF
ROUT
STRUCT
(0)
(1)
(2)
δ
i+1
j
:=
j := i + 1
{(j := i + 1) . SEL s}
CONT
RES
SEL
SEL v
SEL s
r
s

Figure 9.24.

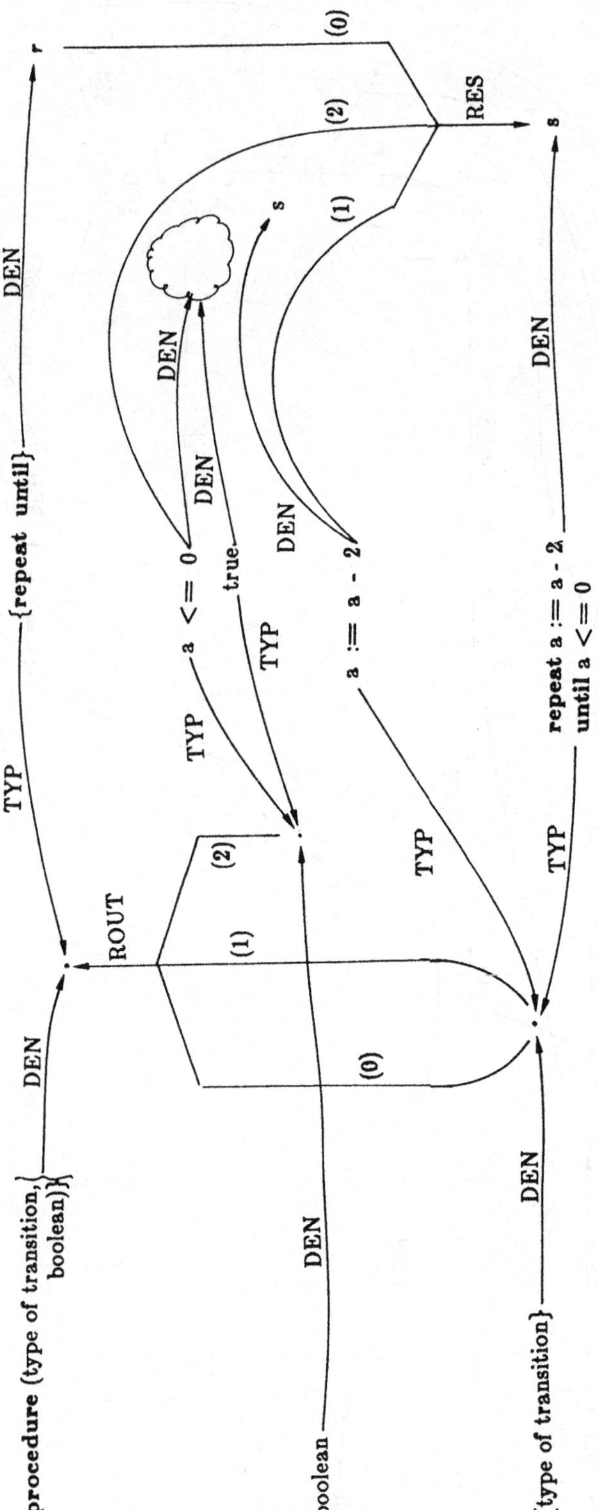
{procedure (type of transition, boolean)}
DEN
TYP
{repeat until}
DEN
r
ROUT
(0)
(1)
(2)
boolean
DEN
TYP
a <= 0
true
DEN
DEN
s
a := a - 2
TYP
DEN
(0)
(1)
(2)
RES
s
{type of transition}
DEN
TYP
repeat a := a - 2
until a <= 0
DEN

Figure 9.25.

configuration is a 15-tuple (AD,AL,CD,CL,R,CONT,SEL,RES,N,DEN,T,TYP, REF,STRUCT, ROUT). Such a configuration gives complete information about the actual state of a program. It also gives precisely the information which one needs in order to restart the given program at that particular moment.
Transitions are functions on the set CONF of configurations, as was explained in Section 6.2.

§9.6 Type expressions, declarations and programs

In Chapter 6 we studied routine values and stated that the actual parameters of routines are expressions that denote *values*. From now on we also allow them to denote *types*. Furthermore, we allow the result function RES to yield types as well as values, so that it is now of the form

$$\text{RES} : \text{R} \times \text{E} \times \ldots \times \text{E} \rightarrow \text{V} \bigcup \text{T}$$

The M_{RES} operator discussed in Section 8.3.3 constructs a compound expression for every routine call in the same way as before. This extension of RES is needed mainly for the description of declarations and of compound expressions which denote types.

Example in Pascal

var i:integer;

This declaration is a compound expression which denotes the call of a routine value denoted by '**var** :'. This routine value has two parameters :

- the name 'i' (the name itself is the parameter, since it is not yet associated with a location)
- the type REF.DEN.integer

The result of the routine call is a transition which

- creates an atomic location : AL $\leftarrow$ AL $\bigcup \alpha$
- makes DEN.i equal to that location : DEN.i $\leftarrow \alpha$
- makes TYP.i equal to REF.DEN.integer : TYP.i $\leftarrow$ REF.DEN.integer

Recalling Section 8.3.3, we have

DEN.M_{RES}(**var** :,i,integer)=RES(DEN.**var** :,i,{reference(integer)})

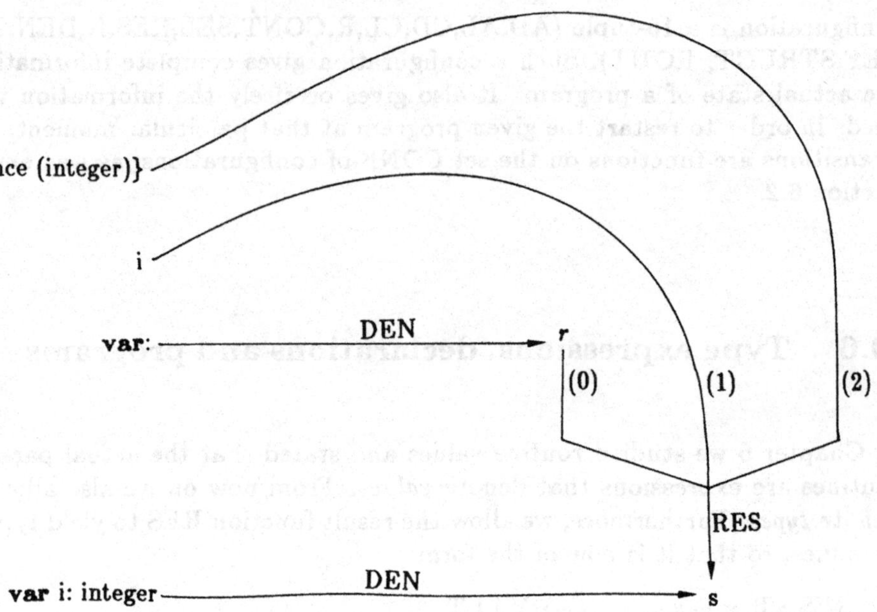

Figure 9.26.

Just before the end of the call of this routine, the situation is as illustrated in Figure 9.26. The situation after the call is illustrated in Figure 9.27.

Example in Pascal

type a=**array**[1..10] **of** real;

This declaration actually contains two routine calls. The first call is denoted by '**array**[1..10] **of** real', in which the routine value denoted by '**array**[..] **of**' is called with three parameters : '1', '10', and 'real', denoting respectively two atomic data and a type. The result of the call is a new type. The second call is the type declaration itself. The routine value denoted by '**type** = ' is called with two arguments : 'a' and '**array**[1..10] **of** real'. The only transition here involves the name 'a' being associated with the type by the DEN function.

This example is illustrated in Figure 9.28.

So far, we have described the DEN function for expressions, statements and declarations. Since a program simply consists of a number of declarations followed by a statement, we can also describe the transition that results from the execution of a whole program.

§9.7 Additional type functions

Some characteristics of Pascal, Algol 68, PL/1 and Ada cannot be described by the concepts of SMALL which we have introduced so far. In particular, sets of values which are denoted by expressions of two different types cannot be treated by set-theoretical operators such as inclusion, union, intersection and equality. In order to introduce this possibility, two additional type functions are added to SMALL.

This list of additional functions is in no way exhaustive. The study of other languages might introduce other additional type functions which we do not discuss in this book.

9.7.1 The union function

The *union function*, called UNION, is a function having as arguments a number of types $\mu_1,...,\mu_n$ $(n > 1)$. The function UNION associates with its arguments another type μ. Let e be an expression denoting the value v and having the type μ = UNION($\mu_1,...,\mu_n$). Then v belongs to one of the sets of values described by the types $\mu_1,...,\mu_n$. This means that there is an expression e_i for some i $(1 \leq i \leq n)$ such that e_i also denotes v and e_i has the type μ_i.

Figure 9.27.

We thus have the following relationship :

$$\text{if TYP}.e = \text{UNION}(\mu_1,...,\mu_n) \text{ and DEN}.e = v$$
$$\text{then } \exists i(1 \leq i \leq n)\ \exists e_i \text{ with TYP}.e_i = \mu_i \text{ and DEN}.e_i = v$$

This illustrated in Figure 9.29. The union function is one of the cases where two different expressions e and e_i denote the same value but have different types.

Among the languages Pascal, Algol 68, PL/1 and Ada, only Algol 68 treats the union concept in a general way.

The Deunion operator $M_{DEUNION}$

Given an expression e with TYP.e = UNION$(\mu_1,...,\mu_i,...,\mu_n)$, we might ask how DEN.$e$ can be used as a value of the type μ_i. In other words, how can we construct from e an expression e_i such that DEN.e_i = DEN.e and TYP.$e_i = \mu_i$? In SMALL, such an e_i is written as $M_{DEUNION}(e)$, where $M_{DEUNION}$ is called the *Deunion operator*.

We thus have, for some i,

$$\text{DEN}.M_{DEUNION}(e) = \text{DEN}.e$$
$$\text{TYP}.e = \text{UNION}(\mu_1,...,\mu_i,...,\mu_n)$$
$$\text{TYP}.M_{DEUNION}(e) = \mu_i$$

As we will see in Section 10.5, the evaluation of the operator $M_{DEUNION}$ should imply a *dynamic* type check for reasons of safety. In each of the programming languages considered, $M_{DEUNION}$ is written in a different way, and only Algol 68 and Ada provide for a dynamic type check. This means that Pascal and PL/1 are unsafe in this respect.

Example using a constant identifier of type union

Algol 68

```
union(int,real) const=
    if <boolean expression>
        then 3
        else 3.14
    fi;
```

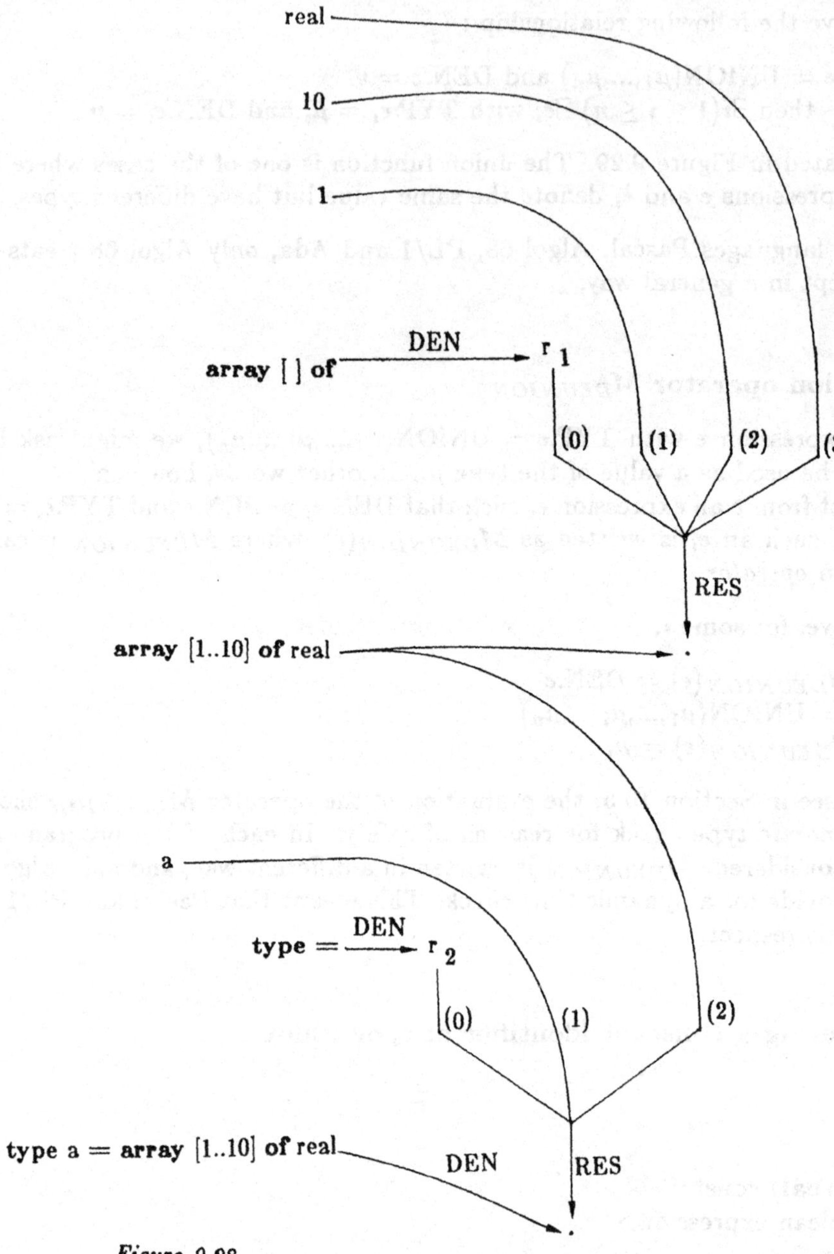
real
10
1
DEN
array [ ] of
r 1
(0)
(1)
(2)
(3)
RES
array [1..10] of real
a
DEN
type =
r 2
(0)
(1)
(2)
type a = array [1..10] of real
DEN
RES

Figure 9.28.

```
case const in
        (int i): ... i ...,
        (real j): ... j ...
esac;
...
```

For the sake of clarity, we will make all implicit (context defined) notations explicit in the following examples. In Algol 68, the context of the name '3' in the declaration of 'const' can be written explicitely as '**union(int,real)**(3)'. We then have

$M_{DEUNION}$(**union(int,real)**(3)) ≡ 3

where the equivalence relation is as defined in Section 8.3.1.
We also have

DEN.3 = DEN.**union(int,real)**(3)
TYP.**union(int,real)**(3) = **union**(DEN.**int**,DEN.**real**)
TYP.3 = DEN.**int**

Similar equalities hold for the expression '**union(int,real)**(3.14)' which replaces the name '3.14' in the declaration of 'const', except of course that TYP(3.14) = DEN.**real**. Notice that in Algol 68, the expression '**union(int,real)**(α)', where α is an integer or a real expression, is a legal construction; it is called a *cast*.

In Algol 68, the operator $M_{DEUNION}$ is expressed by means of a so-called *conformity clause*. If 'const' denotes an integer value, then we have in the conformity clause

DEN.i = DEN.const
TYP.const = UNION(DEN.**int**,DEN.**real**)
TYP.i = DEN.**int**

The conformity clause implies a dynamic type check. Since the conformity clause is the only way to express the operator $M_{DEUNION}$ in Algol 68, the union concept in Algol 68 is completely safe (see type checking for union types in Chapter 10). In other words, the conformity clause acts as a guard controlling the use of the values involved in the union type.

The example is illustrated in Figure 9.30, where we have assumed that DEN. <boolean expression> = DEN.**true**.

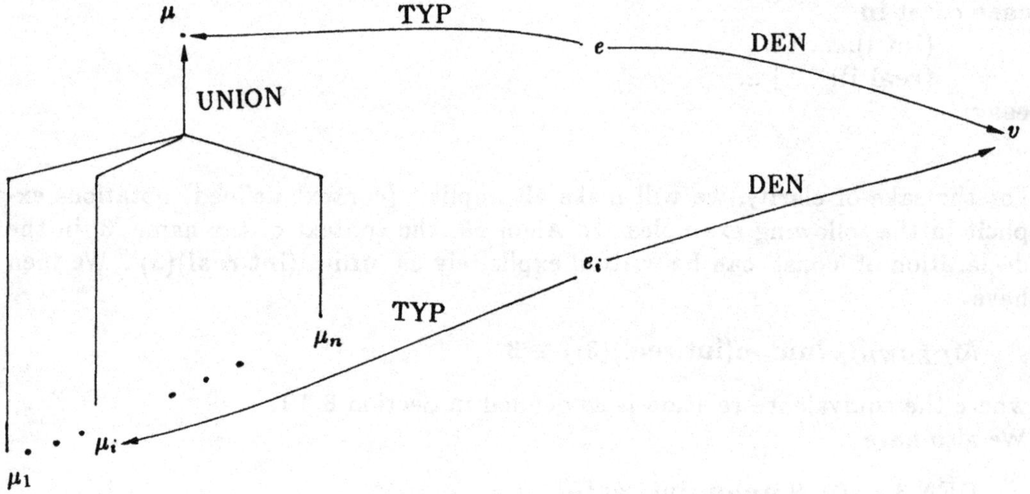

Figure 9.29.

Example using a variable of type union

Algol 68

```
union(int,real) u;
u:=3;
case u in
    (int i): ... i ...,
    (real r): ... r ...
esac;
```

The name 'u' denotes a location and is of type DEN(**ref union** (**int**,**real**)). The name '3' in the assignment 'u:=3' stands for '**union**(**int**,**real**)(3)'.

The name 'u' in the conformity clause stands for '**union**(**int**,**real**)(u)', which denotes the contents of DEN.u. Within the conformity clause, if '**union**(**int**,**real**)(u)' denotes an integer value, then CONT.DEN.u is denoted by 'i' and TYP.i = DEN.**int**. If '**union**(**int**,**real**)(u)' denotes a real value, then CONT.DEN.u is denoted by 'r' and TYP.r = DEN.**real**.

Figure 9.31 illustrates this example.

Example using a record type with a field of type union

Algol 68

```
mode variant=struct(bool c, union(int,real) ab);
variant x:=(true,3.14);
ab of x:=...;
case ab of x in
    (int i): ... i ...,
    (real r): ... r ...
esac;
```

The expression '3.14' in the declaration '**variant** x:=(**true**,3.14)' stands for '**union** (**int**,**real**)(3.14)'. The expression 'ab **of** x' in the conformity clause stands for 'ab **of variant**(x)'.

Figure 9.32 illustrates this example.

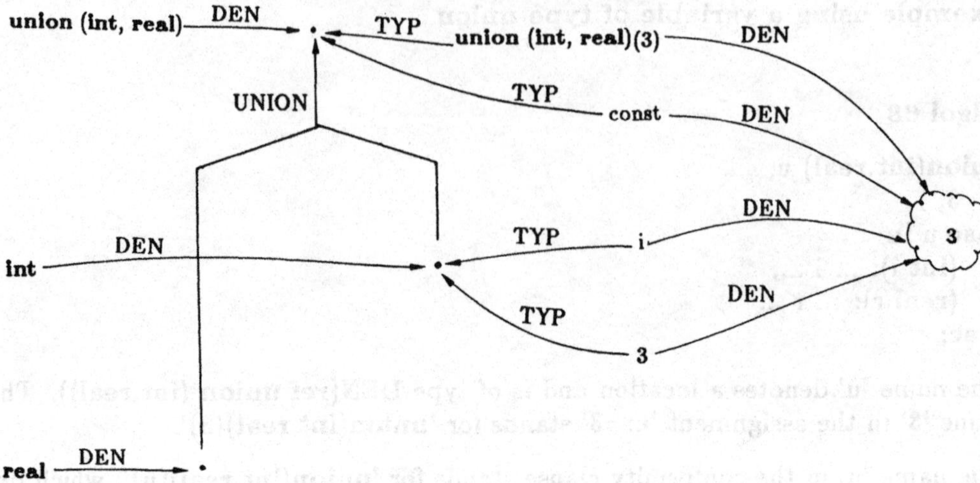
union (int, real)
DEN
TYP
union (int, real)(3)
DEN
UNION
TYP
const
DEN
DEN
TYP
i
3
int
DEN
DEN
TYP
3
real
DEN

Figure 9.30.

Example using a Pascal variant record

In Pascal, the variant part of a record can be described in terms of the union function. Consider the following example :

```
type
    tagtype=(ping,pong);
    variant=
        record
            c:boolean;
            case tag:tagtype of
                ping:(a:integer);
                pong:(b:real)
        end;
var x:variant;
begin
    x.c:=true;
    x.tag:=pong;
    x.b:=3.14;
    if x.tag=ping
        then ... x.a ...
        else ... x.b ...;
end
```

Conceptually, the composite datum denoted by {contents(x)} has 3 components, each component having a selector. Two of the selectors are DEN.c and DEN.tag. The third selector cannot be written in Pascal, so we shall denote it here by {s}. The type of SEL(CONT.DEN.x,DEN.{s}) is the union of two structured types, each having one component.
Note that the value denoted by the expression {contents(x.b)} is

SEL(SEL(CONT.DEN.x,DEN.{s}),DEN.b)

The safety aspect of the variant record in Pascal is discussed in Section 10.5. The value diagrams just after execution of the first three assignment statements are given in Figures 9.33 and 9.34 and 9.35.

Example using PL/1 pointers

The PL/1 pointer is being used to simulate UNION.

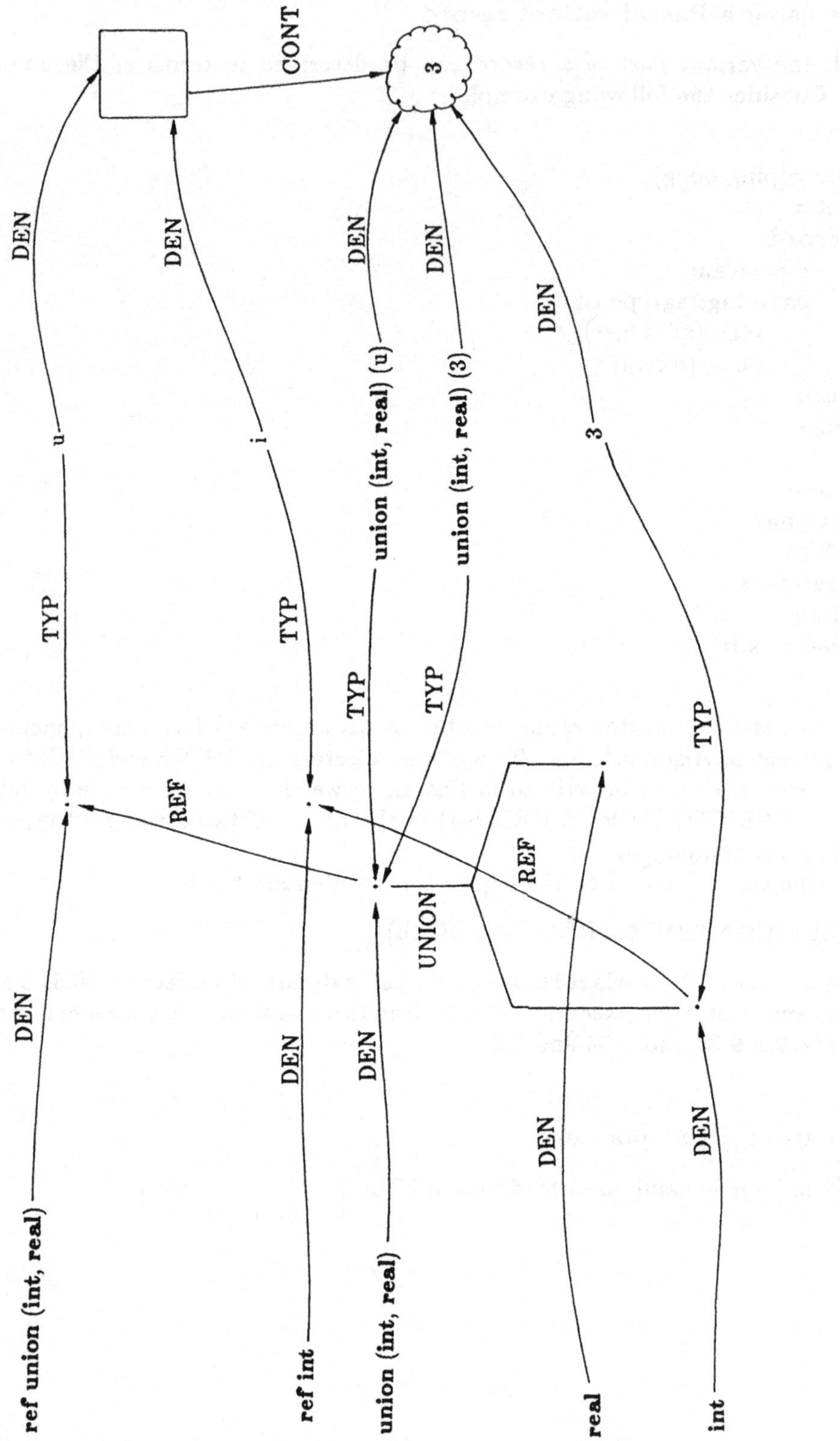
ref union (int, real)
ref int
union (int, real)
real
int
DEN
TYP
REF
UNION
CONT
u
i
3
union (int, real) (u)
union (int, real) (3)

Figure 9.31.

Figure 9.32.

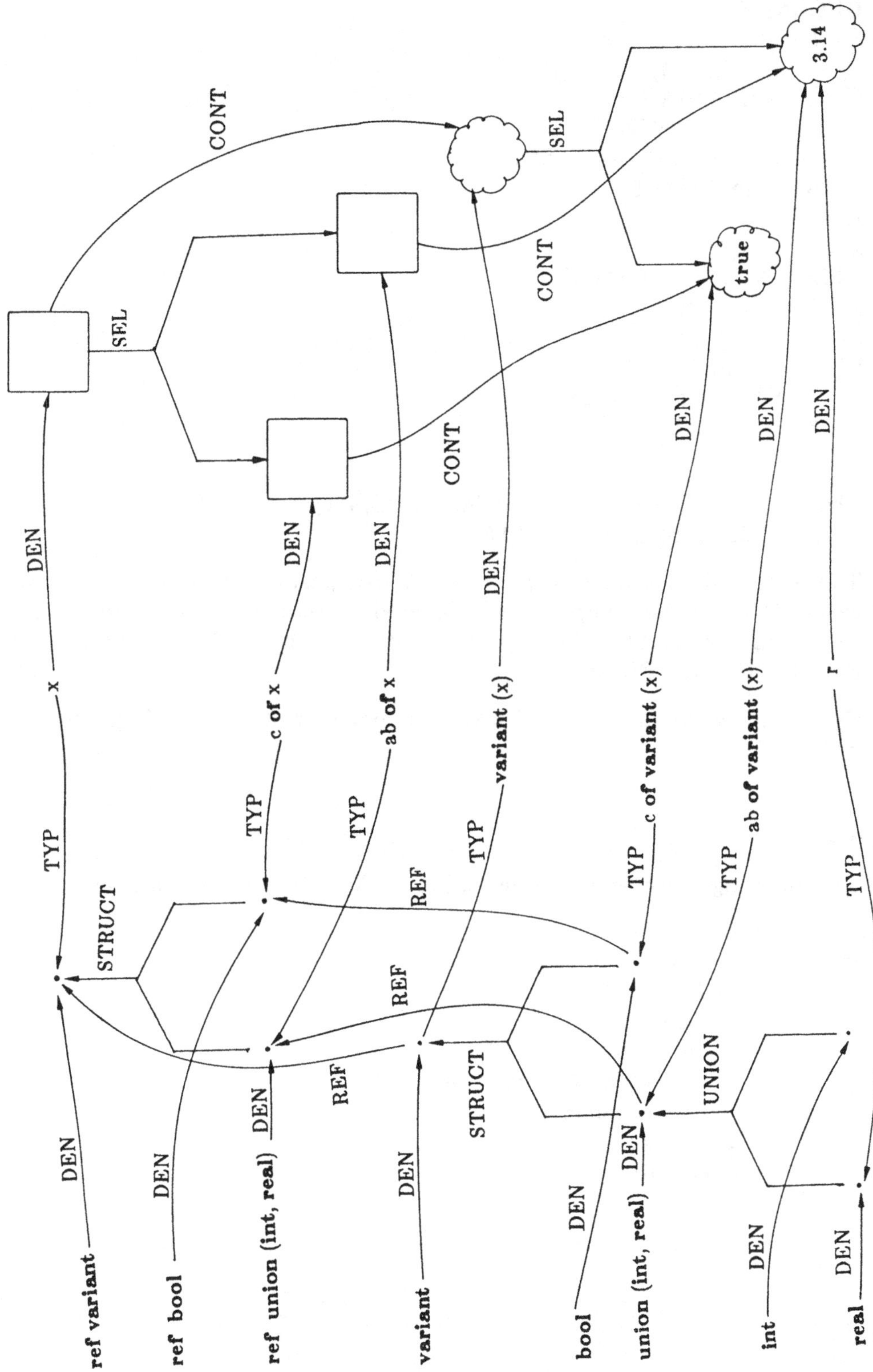
ref variant
ref bool
ref union (int, real)
variant
bool
union (int, real)
int
real
x
c of x
ab of x
variant (x)
c of variant (x)
ab of variant (x)
r
DEN
TYP
REF
STRUCT
UNION
SEL
CONT
true
3.14

```
DECLARE
    1 x,
        2 c BIT(1),
        2 tag CHAR(4),
        2 ab POINTER,
    integer BIN FIXED BASED,
    real BIN FLOAT BASED;
x.c='1'B;
x.tag='pong';
ALLOCATE real SET(x.ab);
x.ab→real=3.14;
...
IF x.tag='ping'
    THEN ... x.ab→integer ...;
    ELSE ... x.ab→real ...;
...
```

The union concept can be simulated in PL/1 by means of pointers. The safety aspect is discussed in Section 10.5.

The expression {contents(x)} denotes a composite datum with three components. One of these components is denoted by {contents(x.ab)}and is a location containing DEN(3.14). The type of {contents(x.ab)} is REF(UNION(DEN.BIN FIXED,DEN.BIN FLOAT)).

Part of the value diagram just after the first four statements is given in Figure 9.36.

Ada

The following example is an illustration of the union concept in Ada.

```
type tagtype is (ping,pong);
type variant (tag:tagtype:=pong) is
        record
            c:character;
            case tag is
                when ping ⇒ a:integer;
                when pong ⇒ b:float;
            end case;
        end record;
...
```

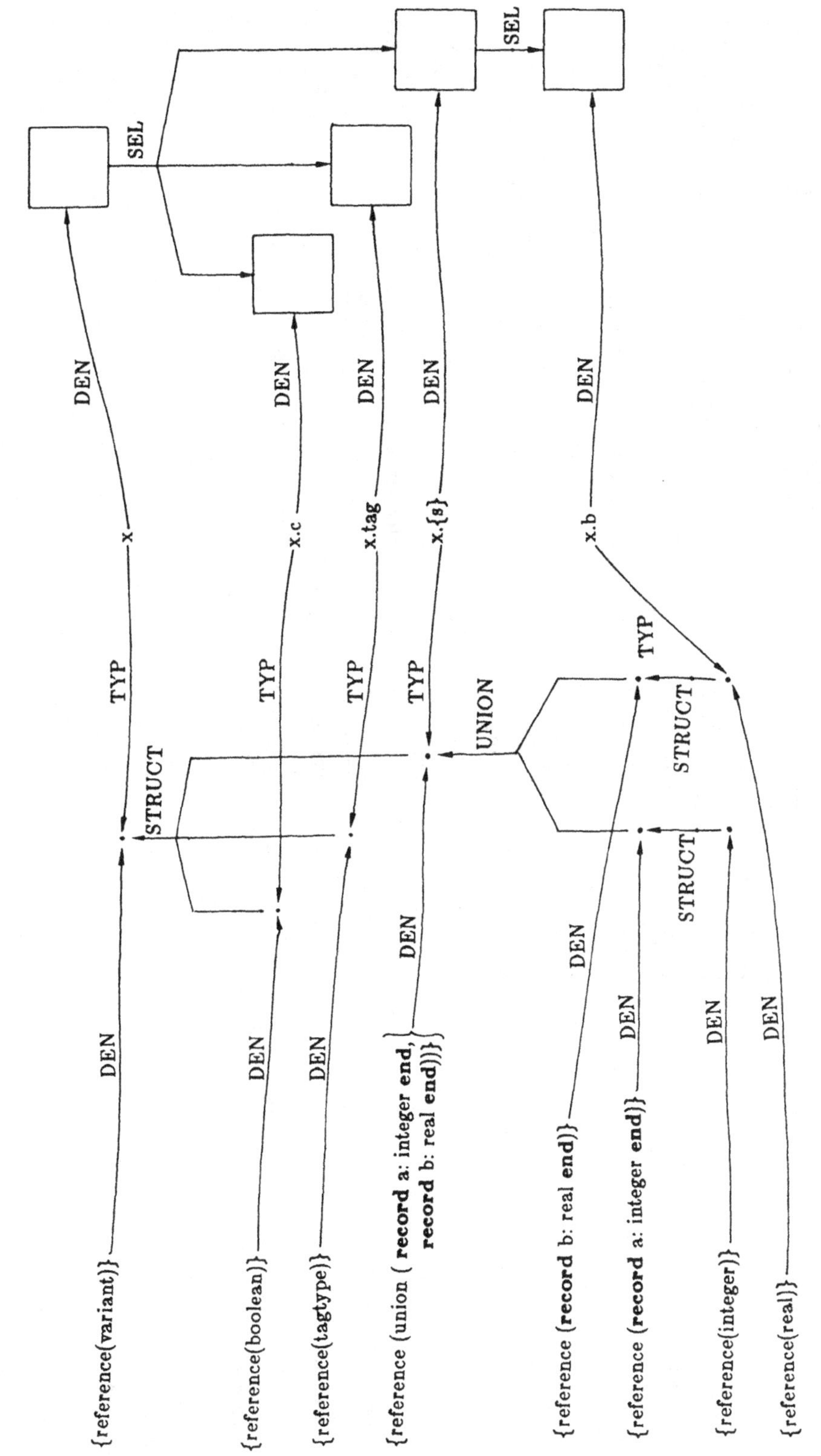
{reference(variant)}
{reference(boolean)}
{reference(tagtype)}
{reference (union (**record** a: integer **end**,
record b: real **end**))}
{reference (**record** b: real **end**)}
{reference (**record** a: integer **end**)}
{reference(integer)}
{reference(real)}
DEN
STRUCT
UNION
TYP
x
x.c
x.tag
x.{s}
x.b
SEL

Figure 9.33.

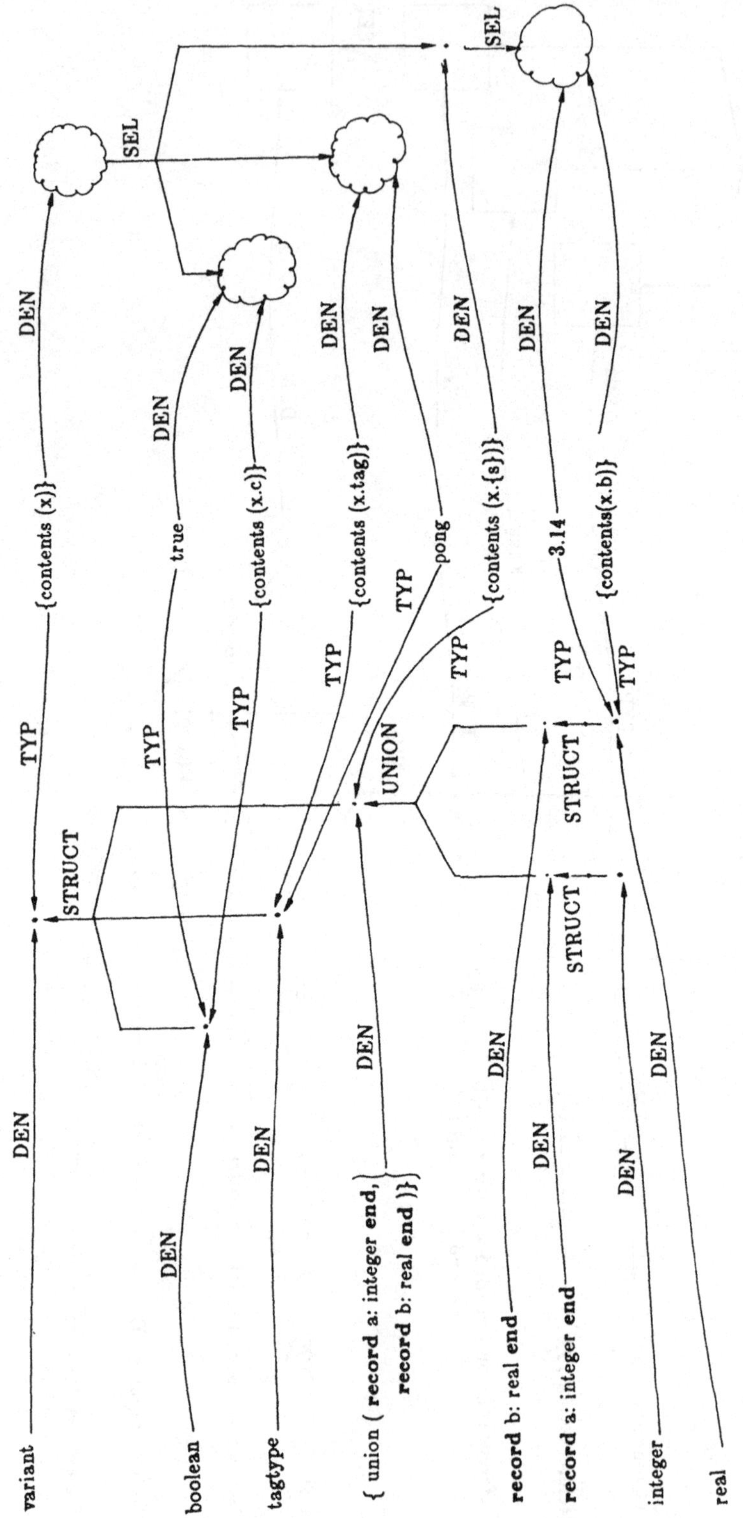
variant
boolean
tagtype
{ union (record a: integer end,
record b: real end)}
record b: real end
record a: integer end
integer
real
{contents (x)}
true
{contents (x.c)}
{contents (x.tag)}
pong
{contents (x.{s})}
3.14
{contents(x.b)}
DEN
TYP
STRUCT
UNION
SEL

Figure 9.34.

```
x:variant;
x.c:='a';
x.b:=3.14;
...
x:=(ping,'b',3);
y:variant(pong);
y.c:='a';
y.b:=3.14;
```

In Ada, the union concept has been implemented here by means of a variant part in record types. In contrast to Pascal, variant records in Ada are safe. The reason for this is that the discriminant of the record variable 'x' above (which is an unconstrained variable) can only be changed when a complete record value is assigned to 'x'. In constrained variables, such as 'y' above, the discriminant cannot be changed. This point is discussed further in Section 10.5.

9.7.2 The constraint function

A type μ associated with an expression e defines the set S of values that can be denoted by e and characterizes the set of operations applicable on DEN.e.

The *constraint function*, denoted CONSTR, takes as arguments a type μ and a number of constraints, and associates with its arguments a type μ' defining a subset of S. A constraint is a predicate on values, i.e., a function which assigns to each value either true or false. The type μ' defines the subset of those values of S for which all the given constraints are true.

More precisely, let e' be an expression of type

$$\mu' = \text{CONSTR}(\mu, c_1, \ldots, c_n)$$

where $c_1,\ldots,c_n$ represent constraints. This implies that there is another expression e denoting the same value as e' and having type μ. Furthermore, DEN.e satisfies all the constraints $c_1, \ldots, c_n$.

We thus have the following relationship :

$$\begin{array}{l} \text{if TYP.}e' = \text{CONSTR}(\mu, c_1, \ldots, c_n) \\ \quad \text{then } \exists e \text{ with} \\ \qquad \text{DEN.}e = \text{DEN.}e' \\ \qquad \text{TYP.}e = \mu \text{ and} \\ \qquad c_i(\text{DEN.}e) = \text{true for all } i (1 \le i \le n) \end{array}$$

This is illustrated in Figure 9.37.

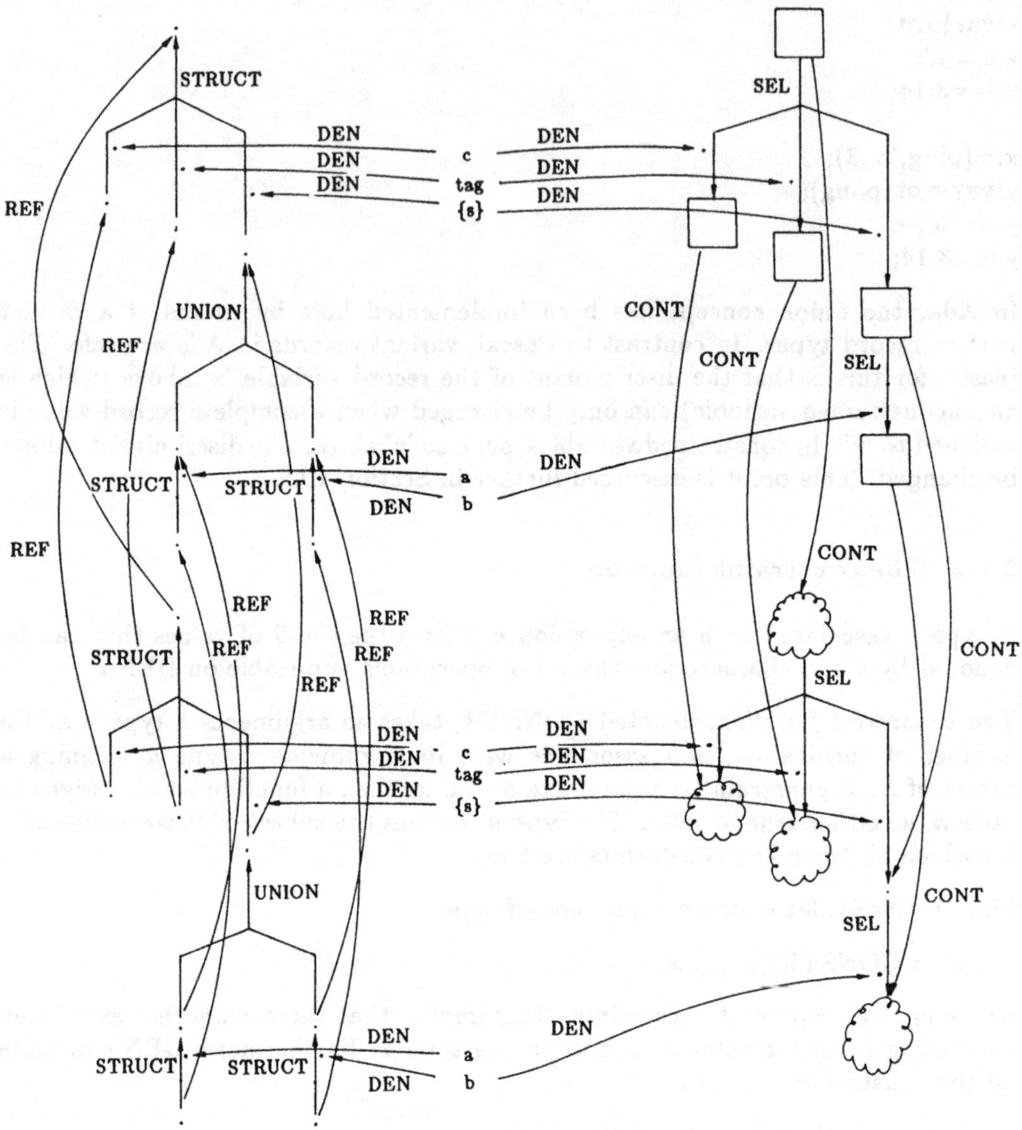
STRUCT
SEL
DEN
DEN
c
DEN
DEN
tag
DEN
DEN
{s}
REF
UNION
CONT
REF
CONT
SEL
DEN
DEN
a
STRUCT
STRUCT
DEN
b
REF
CONT
REF
REF
STRUCT
REF
REF
CONT
REF
SEL
DEN
DEN
c
DEN
DEN
tag
DEN
DEN
{s}
UNION
CONT
SEL
DEN
DEN
a
STRUCT
STRUCT
DEN
b

Figure 9.35.

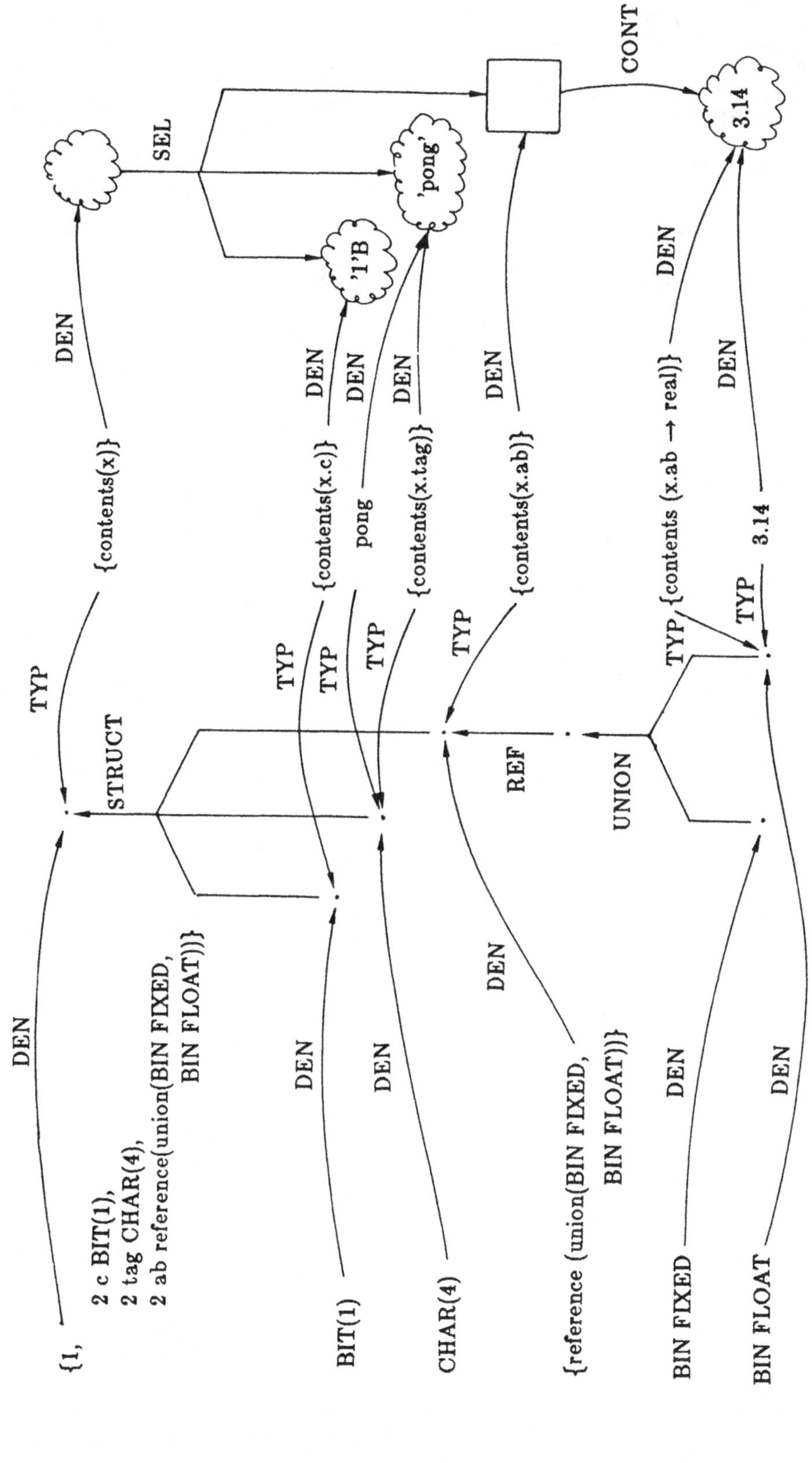

{1,
2 c BIT(1),
2 tag CHAR(4),
2 ab reference(union(BIN FIXED,
BIN FLOAT))}
BIT(1)
CHAR(4)
{reference (union(BIN FIXED,
BIN FLOAT))}
BIN FIXED
BIN FLOAT
DEN
TYP
STRUCT
REF
UNION
SEL
CONT
{contents(x)}
{contents(x.c)}
pong
{contents(x.tag)}
{contents(x.ab)}
{contents (x.ab → real)}
3.14
'1'B
'pong'

Figure 9.96.

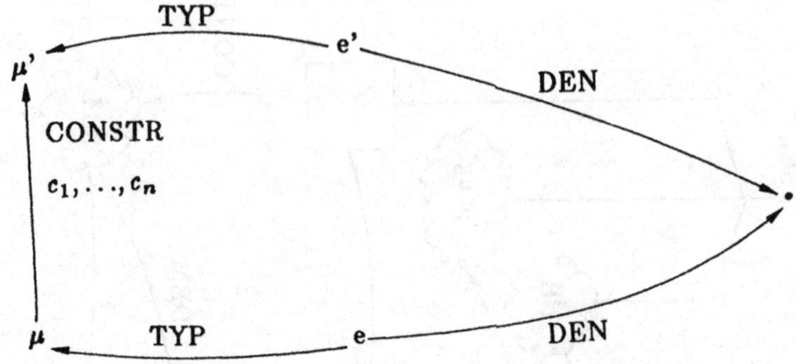

Figure 9.37.

The constraint operator M_{CONSTR}

Given an expression e with TYP.$e = \mu$, and n constraints $c_1,\ldots,c_n$, we might ask how DEN.e can be used as a value of type μ', where $\mu' = \text{CONSTR}(\mu, c_1, \ldots, c_n)$. In other words, how can we construct from e an expression e' such that DEN.$e' =$ DEN.e and TYP.$e' = \text{CONSTR}(\mu,c_1,\ldots,c_n)$? In SMALL, such an e' is written as $M_{CONSTR}(e,c_1,\ldots,c_n)$, where M_{CONSTR} is called the *constraint operator*.

We thus have

DEN.$M_{CONSTR}(e,c_1,\ldots,c_n) =$ DEN.e
DEN.e satisfies the constraints $c_1,\ldots,c_n$
TYP.$e = \mu$
TYP.$M_{CONSTR}(e,c_1,\ldots,c_n) = \text{CONSTR}(\mu,c_1,\ldots,c_n)$

In most programming languages, M_{CONSTR} is context defined and cannot be written explicitly. In this case, we will write $M_{CONSTR}(e,c_1,\ldots,c_n)$ as $\{c_1,\ldots,c_n(e)\}$.

For safety reasons, the elaboration of the operator M_{CONSTR} should involve a dynamic type check. Type checking for constrained types is discussed in Section 10.6.

Example in Pascal

In Pascal, one application of the constraint function is the subrange type, where the constraint specifies that a value belongs to a subrange of the range associated with a given scalar type.

```
var x:1..5;
    y:integer;
...
read (y);
x:=3;
x:=y;
y:=3;
```

Let us first again make all implicit (context defined) notations explicit. Thus, the occurrence of '3' in 'x:=3' actually stands for {1..5(3)}, where 1..5 is the constraint operator M_{CONSTR} in SMALL. DEN.{1..5(3)} should be read as "take the value DEN.3 and check that it satisfies the constraint 1..5".

We then have

DEN.{1..5(3)} = DEN.3
TYP.3 = integer
TYP.{1..5(3)} = 1..5

Analogously, the occurrence of 'y' in 'x:=y' stands for {1..5(contents(y))}. This example illustrates that a datum DEN.3 can be denoted by two different expressions, each of a different type.

Example in Ada

```
type integer1to5 is range 1..5;
x:integer1to5;
y:integer;
begin
    get(y);
    x:=3;
    x:=y;
    y:=3;
end
```

The first occurrence of '3' stands for 'integer1to5'(3)', which is a legal Ada expression. In Ada terminology, the name '3' is qualified with the subtype 'integer 1to5'.

We have

DEN.3 = DEN(integer1to5'(3))
check if DEN.3 satisfies the constraints 1..5
TYP.3 = integer
TYP.integer1to5'(3) = **range** 1..5

§9.8 A note on type equivalence

The definition of type equivalence is language dependent and it does not form part of the model SMALL. Some languages adopt name equivalence of types, while others adopt structural equivalence.

Name equivalence is described in [Welsh 1977] as follows : 'Two variables are considered to be of the same type only if they are declared together or if they are declared using the same type identifier'.

Pascal and Ada have adopted name equivalence of types. To illustrate this, consider the following Ada program. It describes the class of queues by means of the type 'queue_type' together with five primitive queue operations : put, get, empty, full and init. Queues are implemented by means of character vectors used as cyclic buffers. Elements are added to the tail of the buffer and removed from its head.

In this example, the types 'queue_type' and 'other_queue_ type' are not equivalent. As a consequence, the variables 'q' and 'otherq' are of different types and one may not write statements such as 'q:=otherq'.

This program can easily be transcribed into Pascal, for which the same discussion holds.

Example in Ada

```
declare
    limit:constant:=100;
    type queue_type is
        record
            queue:array(1..limit) of character;
            head,tail:integer range 1..limit;
            length:integer range 0..limit;
        end record;
    procedure put(q:in out queue_type; c:in character) is
        begin
            q.queue(q.tail):=c;
            q.tail:=q.tail mod limit+1;
            q.length:=q.length+1;
        end put;
    procedure get(q:in out queue_type; c:out character)is
        begin
            c:=q.queue(q.head);
            q.head:=q.head mod limit+1;
            q.length:=q.length-1;
        end get;
    function empty(q:in queue_type) return boolean is
        begin
            return q.length=0;
        end empty;
```

```
    function full(q:in queue_type)return boolean is
        begin
            return q.length=limit;
        end full;
    procedure init(q:in out queue_type) is
        begin
            q.head:=1;
            q.tail:=1;
            q.length:=0;
        end init;
    c:character;
    q:queue_type;
    type other_queue_type is
        record
            queue:array(1..limit) of character;
            head,tail:integer range 1..limit;
            length:integer range 0..limit;
        end record;
    otherq:other_queue_type;
begin
    init(q);
    ...
    if not full(q)
        then put(q,'c');
        else - - take some action
    end if;
    ...
    if not empty(q)
        then get(q,c);
        else - - take some action
    end if;
    ...
end
```

Structural equivalence is described in [Welsh 1977] as follows :"Two variables are considered to be of the same type whenever they have components of the same type structured in the same way".

Algol 68 and PL/1 have adopted structural equivalence of types. To illustrate this, consider the following Algol 68 program. Again, a class of queues is described by means of the type **queue**, together with five queue operations: put, get, empty, full and init.

In this example, the types **queue** and **other_queue** are equivalent. As a consequence, the variables 'q' and 'otherq' are of the same type and one may write, for example, 'q:=otherq'.

This program can easily be transcribed into PL/1, for which the same discussion holds.

Example in Algol 68

```
begin
    int limit=100;
    mode queue=struct(
                [1:limit] char queue,
                int head,tail,length);
    proc put=(ref queue q,char c) void:
        begin
            queue of q[tail of q]:=c;
            tail of q:=tail of q mod limit+1;
            length of q+:=1
        end co put co;
    proc get=(ref queue q,ref char c)void:
        begin
            c:=queue of q [head of q];
            head of q:=head of q mod limit+1;
            length of q-:=1
        end co get co;
    proc empty=(ref queue q) bool:
        begin
            length of q=0
        end co empty co;
    proc full=(ref queue q) bool:
        begin
            length of q=limit
        end co full co;
```

```
    proc init=(ref queue q) void:
        begin
            head of q:=1;
            tail of q:=1;
            length of q:=0;
        end co init co;
    char c;
    queue q;
    mode other_queue=struct(
                [1:limit] char queue,
                int head, tail, length);
    other_queue otherq;
    init (q);
    if not full(q)
        then put (q,"c")
    fi;
    if not empty(q)
        then get(q,c)
    fi
end
```

There has always been a controversy between the use of name equivalence and structural equivalence in programming languages. This controversy has to do with the notions of ***unauthorized access*** and ***impersonation***, as defined in [Jensen 1978].
Applying these notions to our queue example, unauthorized access means that the queue operations put, get, empty, full and init are not the only allowable actions on variables of type 'queue_type'. Impersonation means that these actions can be (unintentionally) applied to variables of other types such as 'other_queue_type'.

Actually, both name equivalence and structural equivalence of types fail to protect variables from unauthorized access and impersonation. We illustrate this in detail below.

In the Ada example, 'q' denotes a queue variable. Unauthorized access to the queue variable is possible by writing 'q.queue (99)'. It might seem that impersonation does not exist because we cannot write statements such as 'get(otherq,'z')'. However, impersonation can be obtained by first writing the following two procedures:

```
procedure assign_q_otherq (q:in out queue_type;
                           otherq:in other_queue_type) is
    begin
        for i in 1..otherq.length loop
            q.queue(i):=otherq.queue(i);
        end loop;
        q.head:=otherq.head;
        q.tail:=otherq.tail;
        q.length:=otherq.length;
    end;
procedure assign_otherq_q(otherq:in out other_queue_type;
                        q:in queue_type) is
    begin
        for i in 1..q.length loop
            otherq.queue(i):=q.queue(i);
        end loop;
        otherq.head:=q.head;
        otherq.tail:=q.tail;
        otherq.length:=q.length;
    end;
```

Recall that the assignment 'q:=otherq' is illegal. Finally, we can write

```
    assign_q_otherq(q,otherq);
    get(q,'z');
    assign_otherq_q(otherq,q);
```

The overall effect is as we had written 'get(otherq,'z'). The reason for this problem is that assignment is forbidden between the composite types 'queue_type' and 'other_queue_type', but not between their corresponding component types 'character' or 'integer'.

Note that in Ada, the component declarations of the record type definition for 'queue_type' may include expressions specifying default initial values. The record type definition 'queue_type' becomes :

```
type queue_type is
    record
        queue:array(1..limit) of character;
        head,tail:integer range 1..limit:=1;
        length:integer range 0..limit:=0;
    end record;
```

Any record variable 'q' declared as 'q:queue_type' has the components 'head' and 'tail' initialized to 1 and the component 'length' initialized to 0. The 'init' action becomes :

```
procedure init(q:in out queue_type) is
    begin
        null;
    end init;
```

In the Algol 68 example, we may write

```
(queue of q)[90]:="z";
get(otherq,c);
```

Thus both unauthorized access and impersonation exist here also.

Protection against unauthorized access and impersonation can be obtained via the concepts of abstract data and abstract data types [Wulf 1980]. Language constructs supporting these concepts are :

packages in Ada [Ada 1983]
classes in Smalltalk-80 [Goldberg 1983]
clusters in CLU [Liskov 1977]
forms in Alphard [Shaw 1981]
modules in Modula 2 [Wirth 1980]
classes in Concurrent Pascal [Brinch Hansen 1977]

Abstract data and abstract data types are outside the scope of this comparative study of programming languages.

Chapter 10

TYPE CHECKING

§10.1 Concept

The role of type checking is to verify that every expression and subexpression is used in a consistent way within the program. In SMALL, compound expressions are built up from subexpressions in the way explained in Chapters 8 and 9, using the operators M_{RES}, M_{CONT}, M_{SEL}, $M_{DEUNION}$ and M_{CONSTR}. The subexpressions which are the arguments of such an operator cannot have arbitrary types, but have to obey a number of laws. These type laws are verified by the *type checker*. Furthermore, the type checker derives the type of the compound expression from the types of its subexpressions.

We call a type check for a given operator *static* if it can always be performed at compile time, and *dynamic* if it *cannot* always be performed at compile time. We do not take into account the various possible optimizations, whereby for specific operands type checking could be transferred from run time to compile time. Obviously, static type checking is preferable to dynamic type checking. Indeed, static verification of programs signals the abscence of programming errors, whereas dynamic verification can only indicate their presence.

Type checking is an important aspect of *safety* in programming languages. It plays an important role in the *reliability* and the *maintenance* of programs.

In the following sections, type checking is explained in terms of SMALL and illustrated by examples in Pascal, Algol 68, PL/1 and Ada.

§10.2 The M_{CONT} operator

Let e_l be an expression denoting a location. Then $M_{CONT}(e_l)$ is the compound expression denoting the contents of DEN.e_l.

The type checker treats $M_{CONT}(e_l)$ by

(1) verifying whether there is a type μ with TYP.e_l = REF.μ.
(2) associating the type μ with $M_{CONT}(e_l)$, so that TYP. $M_{CONT}(e_l) = \mu$.

This type check is static.

Consider the following Pascal example :

```
var x:integer;
begin
    x:=x+1;
    ...
end
```

The expression 'x+1' stands for '{contents(x)}+1'. We have $M_{CONT}(\mathrm{x}) \equiv$ {contents(x)} .

The type checker treats {contents(x)} by

(1) verifying whether there is a type μ with TYP.x = REF.μ:
DEN.integer satisfies this condition.
(2) associating DEN.integer with {contents(x)} :
hence, TYP.{contents(x)} = DEN.integer.

The equivalent program in Algol 68 is :

```
int x;
x:=int(x)+1;
```

The latter statement may also be written as 'x:=x+1'. We have $M_{CONT}(\mathrm{x}) \equiv$ **int**(x).

The type checker treats '**int**(x)' by

(1) verifying whether there is a type μ with TYP.x = REF.μ:
DEN.**int** satisfies this condition.
(2) associating DEN.**int** with '**int**(x)' :
hence, TYP.**int**(x) = DEN.**int**.

Consider now the following, more complicated example in Pascal :

```
var p:↑integer;
begin
    p↑:=p↑+1;
    ...
end
```

The expression 'p↑+1' stands for {contents(p↑)+1}. We have that M_{CONT}(p) ≡ p↑.

The type checker treats 'p↑' by

(1) verifying whether there is a type μ with TYP.p = REF.μ :
DEN.{reference(integer)} satisfies this condition.
(2) associating DEN.{reference(integer)} with 'p↑' :
hence, TYP(p↑) = DEN.{reference(integer)}.

Furthermore, we have that M_{CONT}(p↑) ≡ {contents(p↑)}.

The type checker treats {contents(p↑)} by

(1) verifying whether there is a type μ with TYP.p↑ = REF.μ :
DEN.integer satisfies this condition.
(2) associating DEN.integer with {contents(p↑)} :
hence, TYP.{contents(p↑)} = DEN.integer.

Consider finally the following example in Pascal:

```
type vectype=array[1..2] of integer;
var v,w:vectype;
begin
    v:=w;
end
```

We have that M_{CONT}(w) ≡ {contents(w)}.

The type checker treats {contents(w)} by

(1) verifying whether there is a type μ with TYP.w = REF.μ:
DEN.vectype satisfies this condition.
(2) associating DEN.vectype with {contents(w)} :
hence, TYP.{contents(w)} = DEN.vectype.

§10.3 The M_{SEL} operator

Let e_c be an expression denoting a composite value, and let e_s be an expression denoting a selector. Then $M_{SEL}(e_c, e_s)$ denotes the component value selected by DEN.e_s of the composite value denoted by e_c.

The type checker treats $M_{SEL}(e_c, e_s)$ by

(1) verifying whether there is a type μ with
TYP.e_c = STRUCT.{...,(DEN.e_s, μ), ...}.
(2) verifying whether TYP.e_s = TOS.TYP.e_c.
(3) associating the type μ with $M_{SEL}(e_c, e_s)$, so that TYP.$M_{SEL}(e_c, e_s) = \mu$.

This type check is also static.

Consider first a Pascal example where a composite location is used :

```
var
    vec:array[1..2] of integer;
    i:integer;
...
vec[1]:=i;
```

We have M_{SEL}(vec,{1..2(1)}) ≡ vec[1].

The type checker treats 'vec[1]' by

(1) verifying whether there is a type μ with
TYP.vec = STRUCT.{...,(DEN.{1..2(1)},μ),...}:
REF.DEN.integer satisfies this condition.
(2) verifying whether TYP.{1..2(1)} = TOS.TYP.vec:
this condition holds.
(3) associating the type REF.DEN.integer with 'vec[1]':
hence, TYP.vec[1] = REF.DEN.integer.

Consider a more complicated example in Algol 68:

```
[1:2] int vec;
int i;
i:=int(vec[1]); co one may also write 'i:=([ ]int(vec))[1]'co
...
```

Consider the assignment statement 'i:=int(vec[1])'.

We have

M_{SEL}(vec,{1..2(1)}) ≡ vec[1]
M_{CONT}(vec[1]) ≡ **int**(vec[1])

When the type checker encounters '**int**(vec[1])', it interpretes this expression as M_{CONT}(M_{SEL}(vec,{1..2(1)})) by

(1) verifying whether there is a type μ_1 with
TYP.vec = STRUCT.{...,(DEN.{1..2(1)},μ_1)...}:
REF.DEN.**int** satisfies this condition.
(2) verifying whether TYP.{1..2(1)} = TOS.TYP.vec:
this condition holds.
(3) associating the type REF.DEN.**int** with 'vec[1]'.
(4) verifying whether there is a type μ_2 with
TYP.vec[1] = REF.μ_2:
DEN.**int** satisfies this condition.
(5) associating the type DEN.**int** with '**int**(vec[1])':
hence, TYP.**int**(vec[1])=DEN.**int**.

Consider the alternative assignment statement 'i:=([ ]**int**(vec))[1]'.

We have

M_{CONT}(vec) ≡ [ ]**int**(vec)
M_{SEL}([ ]**int**(vec),{1..2(1)}) ≡ ([ ]**int**(vec))[1]

When the type checker encounters '([ ]**int**(vec))[1]', it interpretes this expression as
M_{SEL}(M_{CONT}(vec),{1..2(1)}) by

(1) verifying whether there is a type μ_1 with TYP.vec = REF.μ_1:
STRUCT.{(DEN.**int**,DEN.{1..2(1)}),(DEN.**int**,DEN.{1..2(2)})}
satisfies this condition.
(2) associating this type with '[ ]**int** (vec)'.
(3) verifying whether there is a type μ_2 with
TYP.[ ]**int**(vec) = STRUCT.{...,(DEN.{1..2(1)},μ_2),...}:
DEN.**int** satisfies this condition.
(4) verifying whether TYP.{1..2(1)} = TOS.TYP.[ ]**int**(vec):
this condition holds.
(5) associating DEN.**int** with '([ ]**int**(vec)) [1]'.

Now follows the Pascal version of the preceding Algol 68 example:

```
var
    vec:array[1..2] of integer;
    i:integer;
begin
    i:=vec[1];
end
```

We have

$$M_{SEL}(\text{vec},\{1..2(1)\}) \equiv \text{vec}[1]$$
$$M_{CONT}(\text{vec}[1]) \equiv \{\text{contents}(\text{vec}[1])\}$$

When the type checker encounters 'vec[1]', it interprets this expression as $M_{CONT}(M_{SEL}(\text{vec},\{1..2(1)\})$ in a way which is analogous to the first assignment statement of the Algol 68 example.

Finally, we note a remarkable feature of Pascal. Consider the following example:

```
var x:array[1..2] of ↑integer;
begin
    new(x[1]);new(x[2]);
    read(x[1]↑);read(x[2]↑);
end
```

We have

$$M_{CONT}(M_{SEL}(\text{x},\{1..2(1)\})) \equiv \text{x}[1]\uparrow$$
$$M_{CONT}(M_{CONT}(M_{SEL}(\text{x},\{1..2(1)\}))) \equiv \{\text{contents}(\text{x}[1]\uparrow)\}$$
$$M_{SEL}(\text{x},\{1..2(2)\}) \equiv \text{x}[2]$$
$$M_{CONT}(M_{SEL}(\text{x},\{1..2(1)\})) \equiv \{\text{contents}(\text{x}[1])\}$$

Notice the difference between the first and fourth equivalences. $M_{CONT}(M_{SEL}(\text{x}, \{1..2(1)\}))$ is written in Pascal in two different ways:

(1) 'x[1]↑', to indicate that it is a location.
(2) {contents(x[1])}, to indicate that it is a value to be put into another location.

§10.4 The M_{RES} operator

Let e_r be an expression denoting a routine value, and let $a_1,...,a_n$ be expressions denoting actual parameters. Then $M_{RES}(e_r,a_1,...,a_n)$ denotes the result of the call of the routine value DEN.e_r with actual parameters $a_1,...,a_n$.

The type checker treats $M_{RES}(e_r,a_1,...,a_n)$ by

(1) verifying whether there is a type μ with
ROUT(μ,TYP.a_1,...,TYP.a_n) = TYP.e_r
(2) associating the type μ with $M_{RES}(e_r,a_1,...,a_n)$, so that
TYP.$M_{RES}(e_r,a_1,...,a_n) = \mu$
This type check is again static.

Consider as a first example the following call by value in Pascal:

```
function f(i:integer):boolean;
    begin
    ...
    end;
begin
    ... f(5) ...
end
```

We have M_{RES}(f,5) $\equiv$ f(5).

The type checker treats 'f(5)' by

(1) verifying whether there is a type μ with TYP.f = ROUT(μ,TYP.5):
DEN.boolean satisfies this condition, since
TYP.f = ROUT(DEN.boolean,DEN.integer).
(2) associating the type DEN.boolean with M_{RES}(f,5):
hence TYP.f(5) = DEN.boolean.

We now give an example of call by variable in Pascal:

```
var j:integer;
procedure p(var i:integer);
    begin
        ...
    end;
begin
    j:=5;
    p(j);
end
```

We have M_{RES}(p,j) $\equiv$ p(j).

The type checker treats 'p(j)' by

(1) verifying whether there is a type μ with
TYP.p = ROUT(μ,TYP.j) = ROUT(μ,REF.DEN.integer):
μ_s, the type of transitions in Pascal, satisfies this condition, since
TYP.p = ROUT(μ_s,REF.DEN.integer).
(2) associating the type μ_s with M_{RES}(p,j):
hence TYP.p(j) = μ_s.

Type checking for function and procedure calls in Algol 68, PL/1 and Ada is analogous to the above.

An operator and its operands are also checked for their types. The next example is common to the four languages we discuss in this book. Consider the expression 'i+1', where 'i' is a variable of type REF.DEN.integer.

The expression 'i+1' stands for M_{CONT}(i)+1.
We have M_{RES}(+,M_{CONT}(i),1) ≡ i+1.

The type checker treats 'i+1' by

(1) verifying whether there is a type μ with
TYP(+) = ROUT(μ,TYP.M_{CONT}(i),TYP.1).
Since TYP.M_{CONT}(i) = DEN.integer (which results from the type check on M_{CONT}(i)), and TYP.1 = DEN.integer, the question is whether there is a type μ with TYP(+) = ROUT(μ,DEN.integer,DEN.integer):
DEN.integer satisfies this condition.
(2) associating DEN.integer with M_{RES}(+,M_{CONT}(i),1):
hence TYP(i+1) = DEN.integer.

As we explained in earlier chapters, statements (such as assignment statements) are considered to be calls of routine values in SMALL.

Consider the following example in Pascal:

```
var r:real;
begin
    r:=0.0;
end
```

We have M_{RES}(:=,r,0.0) ≡ r:=0.0.

The type checker treats M_{RES}(:=,r,0.0) by

(1) verifying whether there is a type μ with
TYP(:=) = ROUT(μ,TYP.r,TYP(0.0)).
Since TYP.r = REF.DEN.real, and TYP(0.0) = DEN.real, the question is whether there is a type μ with
TYP(:=) = ROUT(μ,REF.DEN.real,DEN.real):
the type μ_s of transitions satisfies this condition.
(2) associating μ_s with r:=0.0:
hence TYP(r:=0.0) = μ_s.

Actually, the same name ':=' is used for an infinity of routine values each of a given type. As an example, let i be declared by

var i:integer;

Consider the assignment statement

i:=0;

Then TYP(:=) = ROUT(μ_s,REF.DEN.integer,DEN.integer).

Examples of other types for the name ':=' are

ROUT(μ_s,REF.DEN.real,DEN.real)
ROUT(μ_s,REF.DEN.boolean,DEN.boolean)

In programming languages, the name ':=' is said to be *generic*.

In Algol 68, the type of an assignment statement is more complicated. Indeed, the above assignment statement actually is the call of the routine value DEN(:=) with two actual parameters : the names '*i*' and '0'. The result of this call consists of two values : the transition where the value DEN.0 is stored in the location DEN.i, and the location DEN.i itself.

Consider the following Algol 68 example :

real r;
r:=0.0;

We have $M_{SEL}(M_{RES}$(:=,r,0.0),SEL_s) ≡ r:=0.0, where SEL_s is a name denoting the selector for the transition. In Algol 68, there is no explicit notation for SEL_s.

The type checker

(1) verifies whether there is a type μ with
TYP(:=) = ROUT(μ,TYP.r,TYP(0.0)):
since TYP.r = REF.DEN.**real**, and TYP(0.0) = DEN.**real**, the type
STRUCT.{(DEN.SEL_v,REF.DEN.**real**),(DEN.SEL_s,DEN.**void**)}
satisfies this condition. (The name SEL_v denotes the selector of the location DEN.r, and is implicit in Algol 68.)
(2) associates this type with M_{RES}(:=,0.0):
hence TYP.M_{RES}(:=,r,0.0) =
STRUCT.{(DEN.SEL_v,REF.DEN.**real**),(DEN.SEL_s,DEN.**void**)}.

Then, the type checker

(1) verifies whether there is a type μ' with
TYP.M_{RES}(:=,r,0.0) = STRUCT.{ ...,(DEN.SEL_s,μ'),...}:
clearly, DEN.**void** satisfies this condition.
(2) associates the type DEN.**void** with M_{SEL}(M_{RES}(:=,r,0.0),SEL_s):
hence TYP(r:=0.0) = DEN.**void**.

If we were to make all the notation explicit in the assignment statement 'r:=0.0', we would obtain something of the form { SEL_s **of** (r:=0.0)}, where ':=' is a dyadic operation resulting in a structure with two components, the location DEN.r and a transition:

TYP(r:=0.0) = STRUCT.({(DEN.SEL_v,REF.DEN.**real**),
(DEN.SEL_s.DEN.**void**)}
TYP.{SEL_s **of** (r:=0.0)} = DEN.**void**
TYP.SEL_s=TOS.STRUCT.{(DEN.SEL_v,REF.DEN.**real**),
(DEN.SEL_v,DEN**void**)}
= {(SEL_v,SEL_s)}

Consider now the following Algol 68 example:

ref real rr;
real r;
rr:=r:=0.0;

In SMALL, the assignment is written

$$M_{SEL}(M_{RES}(:=,rr,M_{SEL}(M_{RES}(:=,r,0.0)SEL_v)),SEL_s) \quad (1)$$

First, the type checker infers that the type of the leftmost assignment operator is

ROUT(STRUCT.{(DEN.SEL_v,REF.DEN.**real**),(DEN.SEL_s,
DEN.**void**)},REF.DEN.**real**,DEN.**real**)

It therefore sets

$$\begin{aligned}&\text{TYP}(M_{RES}(:=,\text{r},0.0)) = \\ &\quad \text{STRUCT.}\{(\text{DEN.}SEL_v,\text{REF.DEN.real}),(\text{DEN.}SEL_s,\text{DEN.}\mathbf{void})\}\end{aligned}$$

and thus

$$\text{TYP}(M_{SEL}(M_{RES}(:=,\text{r},0.0),SEL_v)) = \text{REF.DEN.}\mathbf{real}$$

Furthermore,

$$\begin{aligned}&\text{TYP}(M_{RES}(:=,\text{rr},M_{SEL}(M_{RES}(:=,\text{r},0.0),SEL_v))) = \\ &\quad \text{STRUCT.}\{(\text{DEN.}SEL_v,\text{REF.REF.DEN.}\mathbf{real}),(\text{DEN.}SEL_s,\text{DEN.}\mathbf{void})\}\end{aligned}$$

and finally the type checker associates with (1) the type DEN.**void**.

If we were to make all the notation explicit in the assignment 'rr:=r:=0.0', we would obtain something of the form

$\{SEL_s$ **of** (rr:=(SEL_v **of** (r:=0.0)))$\}$.

We have explained how the type checker handles assignment statements. It handles all statements in a similar way, starting from the basic ones, such as procedure calls and assignment statements, and proceeding bottom-up until it handles the compound statement of the entire program (or of a subprogram).

We consider a simple example of the Pascal for-statement, consisting of a single assignment:

```
var i,j:integer;
begin
    j:=0;
    for i:=1 to 3 do j:=j+1;
end
```

We have M_{RES}(**for to do**,i,1,3,j:=j+1) ≡ **for** i:=1 **to** 3 **do** j:=j+1.

The type checker treats this statement by

(1) verifying whether there is a type μ with
TYP(**for to do**) = ROUT(μ,TYP.i,TYP.1,TYP.3,TYP(j:=j+1)).
To do this, it first calculates
TYP.i, which is REF.DEN.integer
TYP.1, which is DEN.integer
TYP.3, which is DEN.integer
TYP(j:=j+1), which is μ_s, the type of transitions (this type is associated with 'j:=j+1' during the type check of this assignment statement).

Hence, the type checker determines a type μ such that
TYP(**for to do**) = ROUT(μ,REF.DEN.integer,DEN.integer,DEN.integer,μ_s):
μ_s, the type of transitions, satisfies this condition.

(2) associating μ_s with the for-statement:
hence, TYP(**for** i:=1 **to** 3 **do** j:=j+1) = μ_s.
This type can be used later in the checking of (say) the compound statement that contains this for-statement.

Note that, if we were to replace 3 by 3.0 in the preceding example, the type checker would search for a type μ such that

TYP(**for to do**) = ROUT(μ,REF.DEN.integer,DEN.integer,DEN.real,μ_s)

Such a type μ does not exist, and the type checker would therefore signal a type error.

§10.5 Type checking for union types

Type checking for union types (cf. Section 9.7.1) is partly static, partly dynamic. Let e be an expression of type UNION(μ_1,...,μ_i,...,μ_n). Suppose the evaluation of e results in a value v which belongs to the set of values described by μ_i. Then there exists an expression, say e_i, which denotes the value v, i.e., DEN.$e_i = v$. The type checker verifies that e will always be used in the context of UNION (μ_1,...,μ_i,...,μ_n) and that e_i will always be used in the context of μ_i. This type checking is static. However, the use of the expression e_i should always be combined with a check to see if the value denoted by e belongs to the set described by μ_i. This type checking is dynamic. If there is no such language-defined type checking, the programmer must implement the checks explicitly. This is the case with variant records in Pascal and pointers in PL/1, which are considered unsafe implementations of the union concept. The reliability of the Pascal and PL/1 union feature is based on the self discipline of the programmer. It is important to realize that the debugging of programs written in a language which does not have language defined dynamic type checking can be extremely difficult. This will be illustrated in the examples below.

Example in Algol 68

union (**int**,**real**) const=
    if <boolean expression>
        then 3 **co** stands for '**union** (**int**,**real**) (3)' **co**
        else 3.14 **co** stands for '**union** (**int**,**real**) (3.14)' **co**
    fi;
case const
    in
        (**int** i): ... i ... **co** 'i' denotes DEN.3 **co**
        (**real** j): ... j ... **co** 'j' denotes DEN(3.14) **co**
esac;
...

The following types are equal:

TYP.const
TYP(**union** (**int**,**real**) (3))
TYP(**union** (**int**,**real**) (3.14))
UNION(DEN.**int**,DEN.**real**)

Type checking of the declaration

During the elaboration of the declaration of 'const', the type checker interpretes '**if** <boolean expression> **then** 3 **else** 3.14 **fi**' as

M_{RES}(**if then else fi**, <boolean expression>, **union** (**int**,**real**) (3),
    union (**int**,**real**) (3.14))

The type checker associates with this expression the type DEN(**union** (**int**,**real**)). It also checks whether the expressions on the left and right hand sides of "=" in the declaration have the same type. This holds, since

TYP.const = TYP(**if** <boolean expression> **then** 3 **else** 3.14 **fi**) =
    DEN(**union** (**int**,**real**))

This part of the type checking is static.

Type checking of the confirmity clause

The deunion operator $M_{DEUNION}$, explained in Section 9.7.1, has the form of a conformity clause in Algol 68. In the above example, $M_{DEUNION}$(const) is of type DEN.int if 'const' denotes an integer value; it is of type DEN.real if 'const' denotes a real value. This implies a dynamic type check. We thus have:

if DEN.const is an integer value then
  DEN.$M_{DEUNION}$(const) = DEN.i and
  TYP.$M_{DEUNION}$(const) = TYP.i = DEN.int

if DEN.const is a real value then
  DEN.$M_{DEUNION}$(const) = DEN.j and
  TYP.$M_{DEUNION}$(const) = TYP.j = TYP.real

The type checks for 'i' and 'j' within the alternatives of the conformity clause are again static. Indeed,

TYP.i = DEN.int and TYP.j = DEN.real.

In Algol 68, one cannot use the value DEN.const outside a conformity clause for DEN.const. This makes the union concept in Algol 68 completely safe.

Example in Pascal

Recall the Pascal example of Figures 9.33, 9.34 and 9.35.

```
type
    tagtype=(ping,pong);
    variant=
        record
            c:boolean;
            case tag:tagtype of
                ping:(a:integer);
                pong:(b:real)
            end;
var x:variant;
begin
    x.c:=true;
    x.tag:=pong;
    x.b:=3.14;
    ...
```

```
    if x.tag=ping
        then ... x.a ...
        else ... x.b ...;
    ...
end
```

From the figures we deduce that

```
    TYP.x
        = STRUCT.{
            (DEN.c,REF.DEN.boolean),
            (DEN.tag,REF.DEN.tagtype),
            (DEN.{s},REF.UNION(STRUCT.{(DEN.a,DEN.integer)},
                STRUCT.{(DEN.b,DEN.real)}))
            }
        = REF.STRUCT.{
            (DEN.c,DEN.boolean),
            (DEN.tag,DEN.tagtype),
            (DEN.{s},UNION(STRUCT.{(DEN.a,DEN.integer)},
                STRUCT.{(DEN.b,DEN.real)}))
            }
```

The type checking of the first two statements is purely static and proceeds as explained in Section 10.1.

In Pascal, there is no dynamic type check involved when $M_{DEUNION}$ is evaluated. Unfortunately, we may therefore write

```
x.tag:=pong;
x.b:=3.14;
write(x.a);
```

In this case, the bit pattern (or part of it) of the real value DEN(3.14) is interpreted as an integer value.

The type checking of 'x.b' is expressed in SMALL as follows :

$M_{SEL}(M_{DEUNION}(M_{SEL}(\text{x},\{\text{s}\})),\text{b})$

(1) It is verified whether there is a type μ such that
TYP.x = STRUCT.{...,(DEN{s},μ),...}:
the type DEN.{reference(union(**record** a:integer **end**,**record** b:real **end**))} satisfies this condition.
This type is therefore associated with $M_{SEL}(\text{x},\{\text{s}\})$.

(2) $M_{DEUNION}(M_{SEL}(\text{x},\{\text{s}\}))$ is considered next.
The value of the tag field indicates that
TYP.$M_{DEUNION}(M_{SEL}(\text{x},\{\text{s}\}))$ = DEN.{reference(**record** b:real **end**)}.
(3) Finally $M_{SEL}(M_{DEUNION}(M_{SEL}(\text{x},\{\text{s}\})),\text{b})$ is considered.
It is verified whether there is a type μ such that
TYP.$M_{DEUNION}(M_{SEL}(\text{x},\{\text{s}\}))$ = STRUCT{...(DEN.b,μ)...}:
DEN.{reference(real)} satisfies this condition.
Hence DEN.{reference(real)} is associated with x.b.

The type checking of the assignment and conditional statements is analogous to the previous examples.

Another illustration of the unsafe nature of the variant record in Pascal is the so-called *wild store*:

```
program wildstore(input,output);
type wildrecord= record
        case b:boolean of
            true:(value:integer);
            false:(pointer:↑integer)
        end;
var
    wildvar:wildrecord;
    i:integer;
begin
    for i:=1 to 10000 do
        begin
            new(wildvar.pointer);
            wildvar.value:=i;
            wildvar.pointer↑:=0
        end
end
```

Example in PL/1

Recall the PL/1 example of Figure 9.36:

```
DECLARE
    1 x,
        2 c BIT(1),
        2 tag CHAR(4),
        2 ab POINTER,
    integer BIN FIXED BASED,
    real BIN FLOAT BASED;
x.c='1'B;
x.tag='pong';
ALLOCATE real SET(x.ab);
x.ab→real=3.14;
IF x.tag='ping'
    THEN ... x.ab→integer ...;
    ELSE ... x.ab→real ...;
```

We have

```
TYP.x
    = STRUCT.{
        (DEN.c,REF.DEN.BIT(1)),
        (DEN.tag,REF.DEN.CHAR(4)),
        (DEN.ab,REF.UNION(DEN(BIN FIXED),DEN(BIN FLOAT)))
        }
    = REF.STRUCT.{
        (DEN.c,DEN.BIT(1)),
        (DEN.tag,DEN.CHAR(4)),
        (DEN.ab,REF.UNION(DEN(BIN FIXED),DEN(BIN FLOAT)))
        }
```

The type checking of {contents(x.ab→real)} is expressed in SMALL as follows :

$M_{CONT}(M_{DEUNION}(M_{SEL}(\text{x,ab})))$

(1) It is verified whether there is a type μ such that
TYP.x = STRUCT.{...,(DEN.ab,μ),...}:
the type DEN.{reference(union(BIN FIXED,BIN FLOAT))} satisfies this condition.
This type is therefore associated with $M_{SEL}(\text{x,ab})$.

(2) $M_{DEUNION}(M_{SEL}(\text{x,ab}))$ is considered next.
The value of the tag field indicates that
TYP.$M_{DEUNION}(M_{SEL}(\text{x,ab}))$ = DEN.{reference(BIN FLOAT)}.

(3) Finally, $M_{CONT}(M_{DEUNION}(M_{SEL}(\text{x,ab})))$ is considered.
It is verified whether there is a type μ such that
TYP.$M_{DEUNION}$.M_{SEL}(x,ab)) = REF.μ:
DEN(BIN FIXED) satisfies this condition.
Hence DEN(BIN FIXED) is associated with {contents(x.ab→real)}.

The type checking of the assignment and conditional statements is as in the previous examples.

Dynamic type checking

In PL/1, there is no dynamic type checking involved in the elaboration of $M_{DEUNION}$, and the PL/1 union concept is therefore unsafe.
Indeed, one may write in PL/1

```
ALLOCATE real SET(x.ab);
x.ab→real=3.14;
... x.ab→integer ...;
```

As is the case with the variant record in PASCAL, the bit pattern of the real value is then interpreted as an integer value.

In PL/1, the type of a location does not specify the type of values that are contained in that location. Therefore, the amount of type checking is considerably less than in Pascal, Algol 68 and Ada. Pointer handling in PL/1 is, however, a very dangerous tool in the hands of inexperienced (and even experienced) programmers. We advise PL/1 programmers to use pointers in a disciplined way as if they were programming in Pascal, Algol 68 or Ada.

So, instead of the declaration

```
DECLARE x POINTER;
```

the programmer should write for example

```
DECLARE x POINTER; /* BIN FIXED */
```

In this way, program readability can be increased by appropriate type comments.

§10.6 Type checking for constrained types

The constraint function CONSTR (cf. Section 9.7.2) involves a type check

which is partly static and partly dynamic. This is illustrated by the following example:

Pascal

```
var
    x:1..5;
    y:integer;
begin
    read(y);
    x:=3;
    x:=y+1;
    ...
end
```

a. Type checking of 'read(y)'.

The only type check is a static one. It verifies whether 'y' has a type corresponding to the parameter of the read procedure.

b. Type checking of 'x:=3'.

'3' stands for {1..5(3)}. We thus have

x:=3 ≡ M_{RES}(:=,x,{1..5(3)})

b.1. Type checking of M_{RES}.

When the type checker encounters 'x:=3', it

(1) verifies whether there is a type μ with
TYP(:=) = ROUT(μ,TYP.x,TYP.{1..5(3)}):
since TYP.x = REF.DEN(1..5) and
TYP.{1..5(3)} = DEN(1..5),
μ_s, the type of transitions, satisfies this condition.

(2) associates with M_{RES}(:=,x,{1..5(3)}) the type μ_s:
hence TYP(x:=3) = μ_s.

b.2. Type checking of {1..5(3)}.

The type checking of {1..5(3)} is dynamic. It checks whether DEN.3 is included in the set described by DEN(1..5).

c. Type checking of 'x:=y+1'.

'y' stands for M_{CONT}(y) and 'y+1' stands for {1..5(M_{CONT}(y)+1)}. We thus have

'x:=y+1' ≡ M_{RES}(:=,x,{1..5(M_{RES}(+,M_{CONT}(y),1))})

c.1. Type checking of M_{CONT}(y).

This type check is static. When the type checker encounters M_{CONT}(y), it

(1) verifies whether there is a type μ with TYP.y = REF.μ:
DEN.integer satisfies this condition.
(2) associates the type μ with M_{CONT}(y):
hence TYP.M_{CONT}(y) = DEN.integer

c.2. Type checking of M_{RES}(+,M_{CONT}(y),1) ≡ y+1.

This is also a static type check. When the type checker encounters M_{RES}(+,M_{CONT}(y),1),it

(1) verifies whether there is a type μ with
TYP(+) = ROUT(μ,TYP.M_{CONT}(y),TYP.1):
since TYP.M_{CONT}(y) = TYP.1 = DEN.integer and
TYP(+) = ROUT(DEN.integer,DEN.integer,DEN.integer),
DEN.integer satisfies this condition.
(2) associates the type DEN.integer with M_{RES}(+,M_{CONT}(y),1):
hence TYP.M_{RES}(+,M_{CONT}(y),1) = DEN.integer.

c.3. Type checking of {1..5(M_{RES}(+,M_{CONT}(y),1))}.

This dynamic type check consists in verifying that the value DEN.M_{RES}(+,M_{CONT}(y),1) is described by the type DEN(1..5).

c.4. Type checking of M_{RES}(:=,x,{1..5(M_{RES} (+,M_{CONT} (y),1))}).

This is a static type check.
The type checker

(1) verifies whether there is a type μ with
TYP(:=) = ROUT(μ,TYP.x,TYP.{1..5(M_{RES}(+,M_{CONT}(y),1))}):
By c.2 and other obvious reasons μ_s satisfies this condition.
(2) associates the type μ_s with the statement 'x:=y+1':
hence TYP(x:=y+1) = μ_s.

We now give another example, again in Pascal:

```
var
    a:array[1..10] of boolean;
    i:integer;
begin
    a[i]:=true;
end
```

This statement is written in SMALL as

M_{RES}(:=,M_{SEL}(a,{1..10(M_{CONT}(i))}),true)

a) Type checking of M_{CONT}(i).

This is analogous to c.1 of the preceding example, and we obtain TYP.M_{CONT}(i) = DEN.integer.

b) Type checking of {1..10(M_{CONT}(i))}.

This is analogous to c.3 of the preceding example. It is a dynamic type check which consists in verifying whether the value DEN.M_{CONT}(i) belongs to the interval 1..10. We thus obtain
TYP.{1..10(M_{CONT}(i))} = DEN(1..10).

c) Type checking of M_{SEL}(a,{1..10(M_{CONT}(i))}).

When the type checker encounters M_{SEL}(a,{ 1..10(M_{CONT}(i))}) it

(1) verifies whether there is a type μ with
TYP.a = STRUCT.{...,(DEN.{1..10(M_{CONT}(i))},μ),...}:
REF.DEN.boolean satisfies this condition.
(2) verifies whether TYP.{1..10(M_{CONT}(i))} = TOS.TYP.a:
since both are equal to DEN(1..10), this condition is satisfied.
(3) associates the type REF.DEN.boolean with
M_{SEL}(a,{1..10(M_{CONT}(i))}):
hence, TYP.M_{SEL}(a,{1..10(M_{CONT}(i))}) = REF.DEN.boolean.

d) Type checking of M_{RES}(:=,M_{SEL}(a,{1..10(M_{CONT}(i))}),true).

This is analogous to c.4 of the preceding example.

§10.7 Type checking of a complete program

We are now in a position to describe the type checking of a complete program. Consider the following Pascal program:

```
program example(input,output);
type recordtype=
        record
            first:integer;
            second:↑real
        end;
var object:array[1..2] of recordtype;
begin
    object[1].first:=1;
    new(object[1].second);
    object[1].second↑:=3.14
end
```

This program (without the declarations) is written in SMALL as follows:

M_{RES}(
  begin...end,
  M_{RES}(
    :=,
    M_{SEL}(M_{SEL}(object,{1..2(1)}),first),
    1),
  M_{RES}(
    new,
    M_{SEL}(M_{SEL}(object,{1..2(1)}),second),
  M_{RES}(
    :=,
    M_{CONT}(M_{SEL}(M_{SEL}(object,{1..2(1)}),second)),
    3.14)
)

The type checking consists of 11 static checks and 3 dynamic checks. The reader is asked to elaborate the type checking of this example carefully.

APPENDIX

Syntax diagrams of Pascal, Algol 68, PL/1 and Ada

Syntax diagrams give an excellent overview of the (subset of) languages used in this book. The syntax diagrams only describe context-free features of the languages. Context-dependent features, such as visibility rules for declarations and coercion positions (soft, weak, firm and strong) in Algol 68, are not described by the diagrams.

Terminal symbols in the diagrams are indicated as follows : symbols which appear in programs (such as keywords and delimiters) are enclosed in circles, while other symbols whose definitions are not elaborated in the diagrams (such as 'identifier' and 'integer') are enclosed in rectangles with an additional bar at the bottom.

As mentioned earlier, the book only treats Pascal-like subsets of Algol 68, PL/1 and Ada. In the syntax diagrams, an effort is made to situate these subsets within the full languages. Therefore, the diagrams contain parts drawn with dotted lines, indicating that these parts do not belong to the given subset and that the nonterminal symbols occurring in them are not defined further. This device makes it possible for the user to consider the subset as an effective starting point for learning the complete language. As the programmer's needs grow, more and more features can be added to the infrastructure.

Another convention which enhances the readability of the syntax diagrams is the use of italic words within terminal and nonterminal symbols. These words act only as comments. As an example, '*entry*-expression' simply stands for the nonterminal symbol 'expression'.

It will surprise nobody that the most difficult language to be moulded into a context-free syntax diagram is PL/1. In order to obtain a useful result, we had to introduce a few restrictions. The first restriction is that for each BEGIN and PROCEDURE symbol there must be a corresponding END, i.e., the possibility of closing several blocks with a single END is excluded here. Actually, from a programming point of view, this seems to be a very useful restriction. A second restriction is that, where PL/1 permits an arbitrary order of elements in a program construct, we have imposed a unique order. The reason for this is to minimize the number of syntax rules. Examples are the attributes in a declaration and the WHILE and UNTIL clauses in a DO-statement.

Pascal

Start symbol is **program**

block

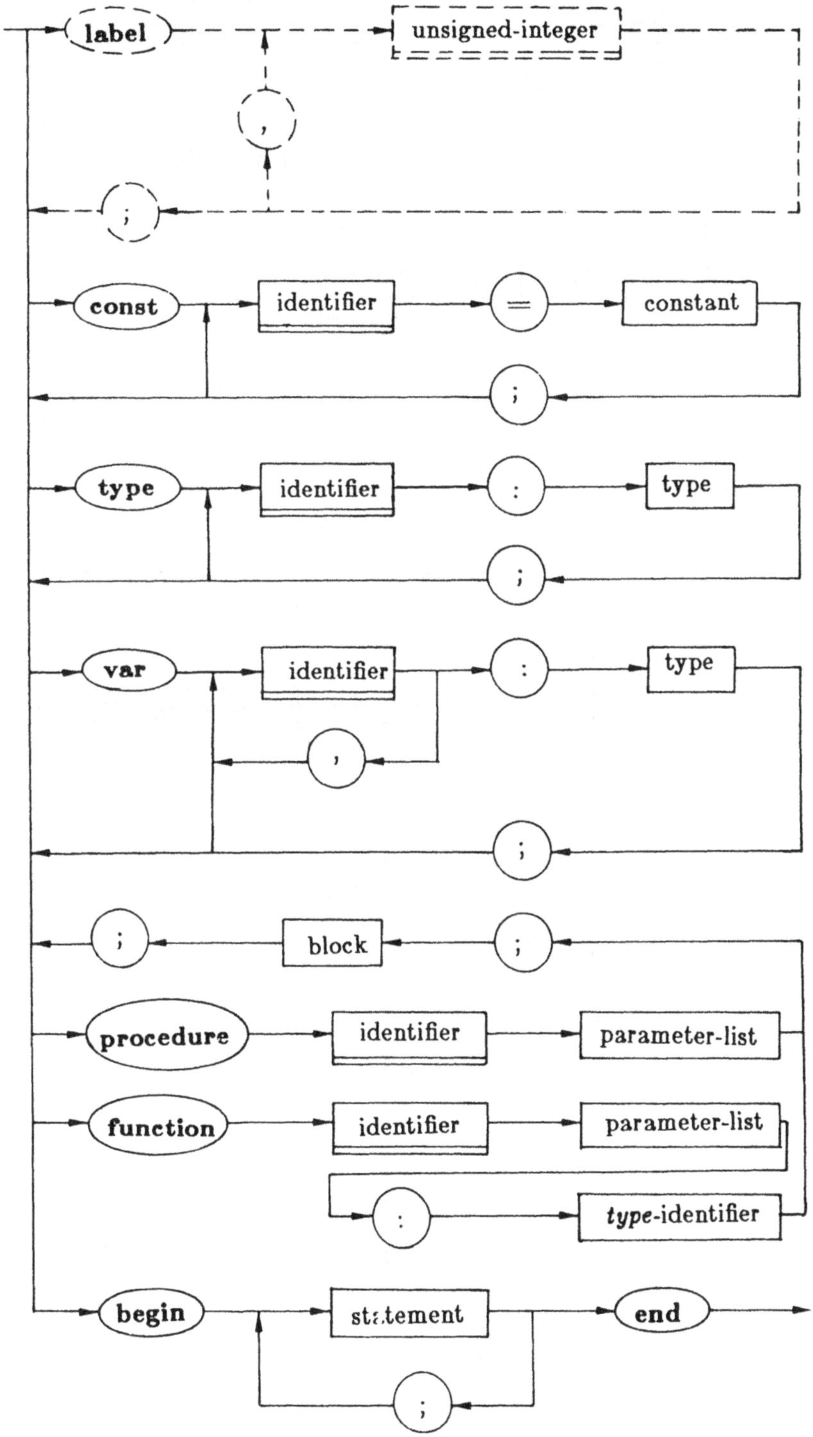
label
unsigned-integer
,
;
const
identifier
=
constant
;
type
identifier
:
type
;
var
identifier
:
type
,
;
;
block
;
procedure
identifier
parameter-list
function
identifier
parameter-list
:
type-identifier
begin
statement
end
;

constant

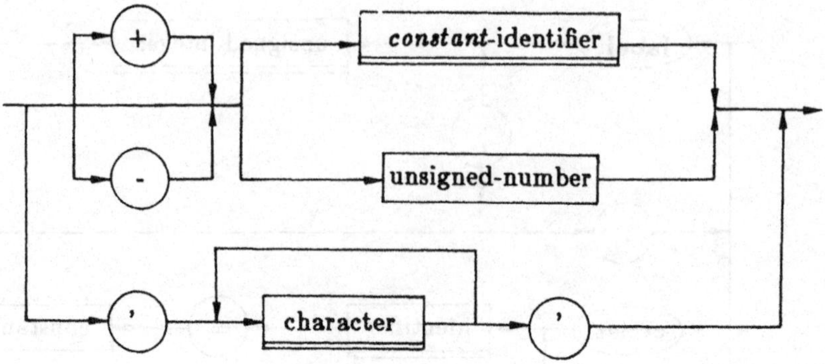

expression

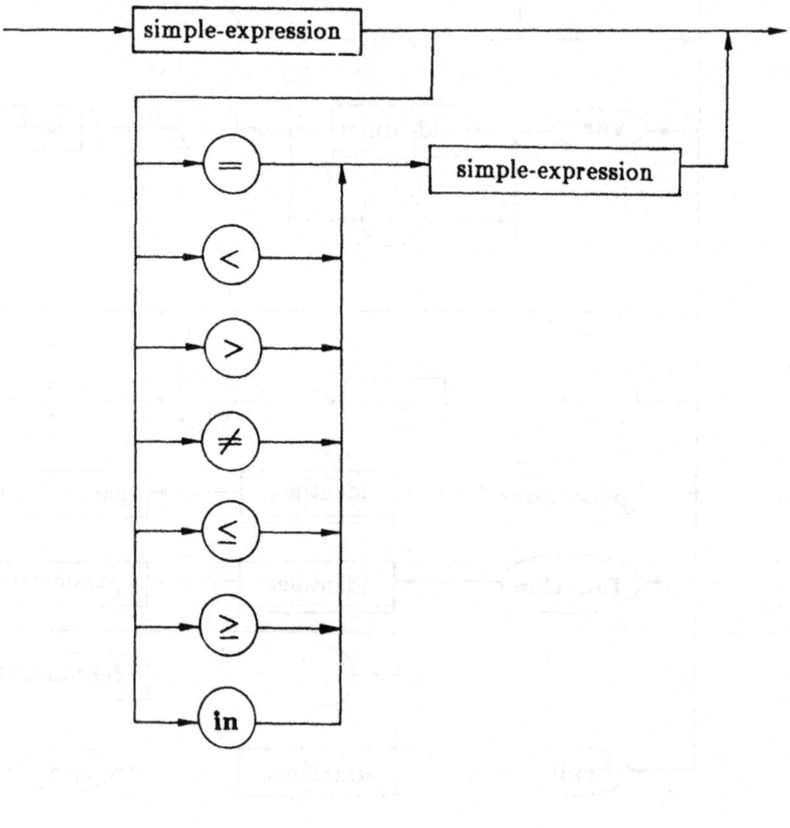

factor

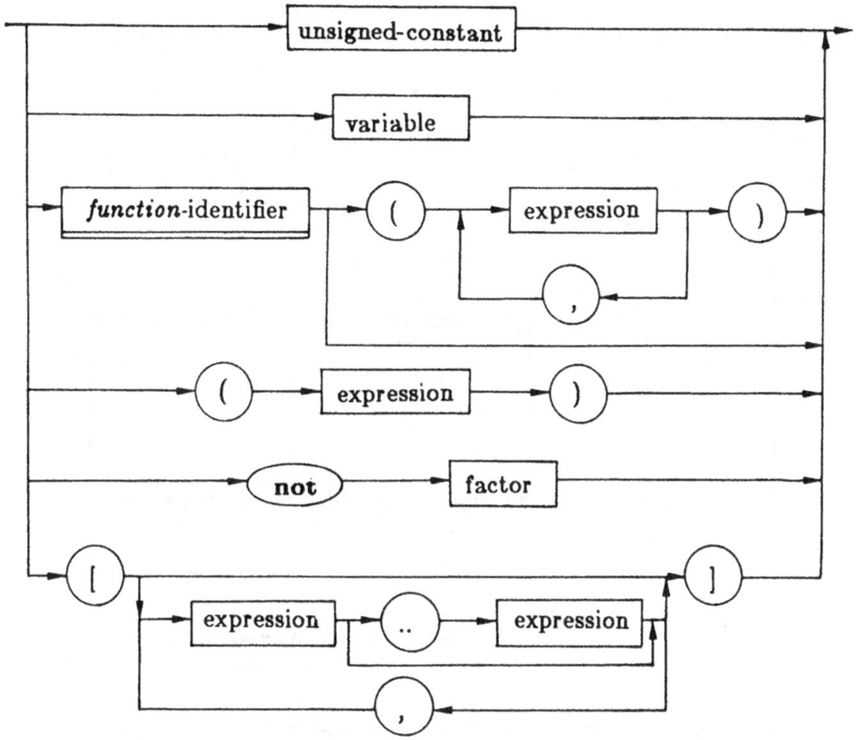

field-list

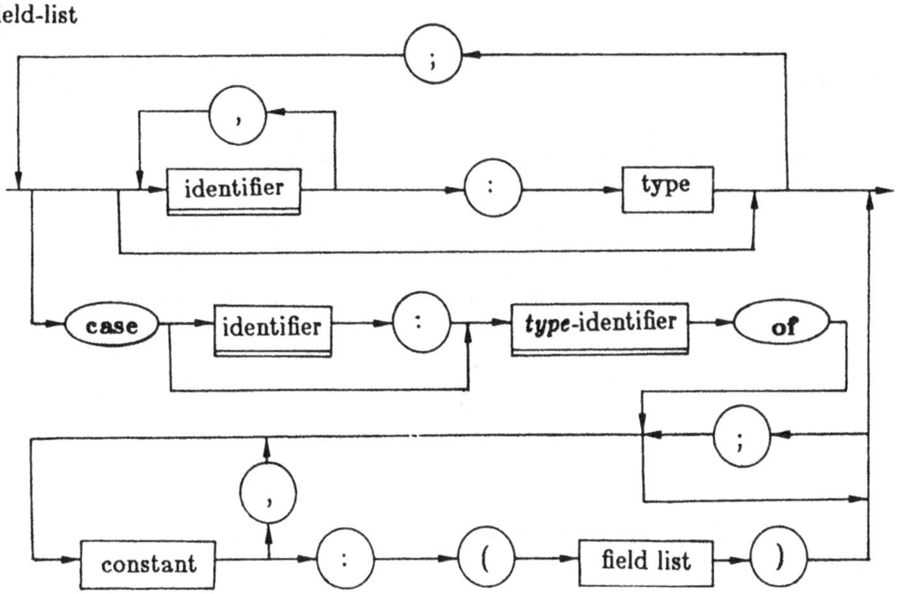

parameter-list

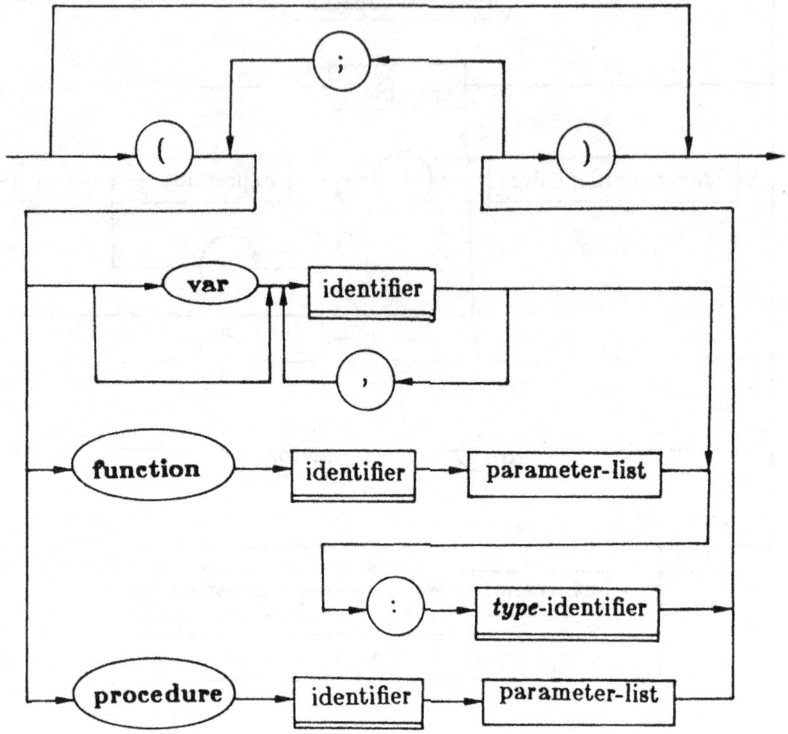

program

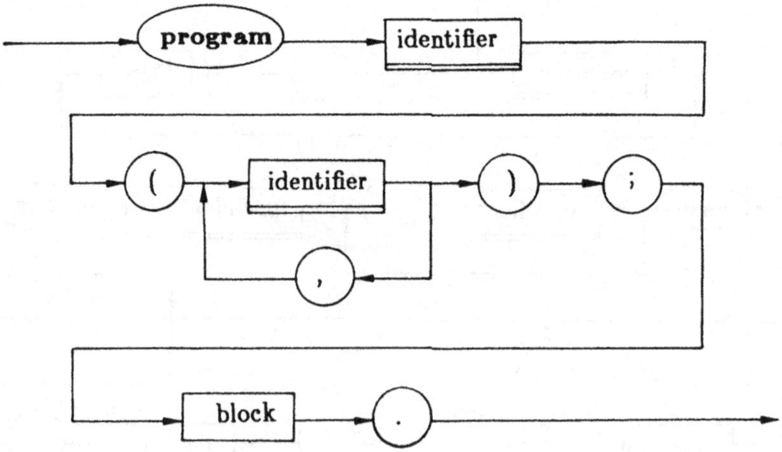

simple-expression

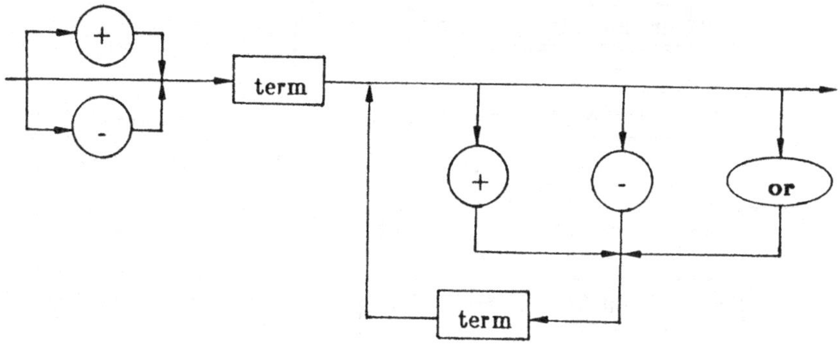

simple-type

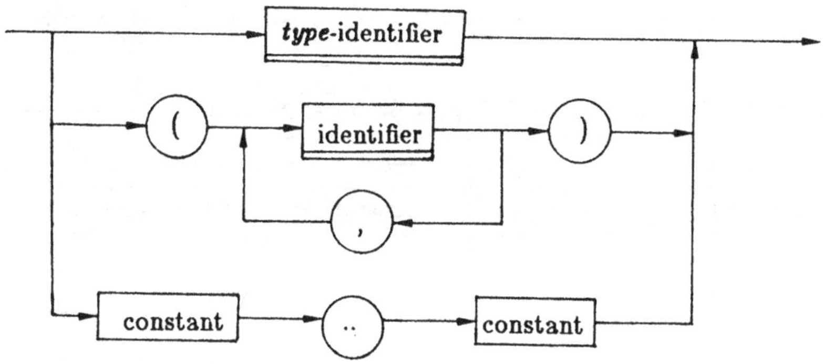

statement

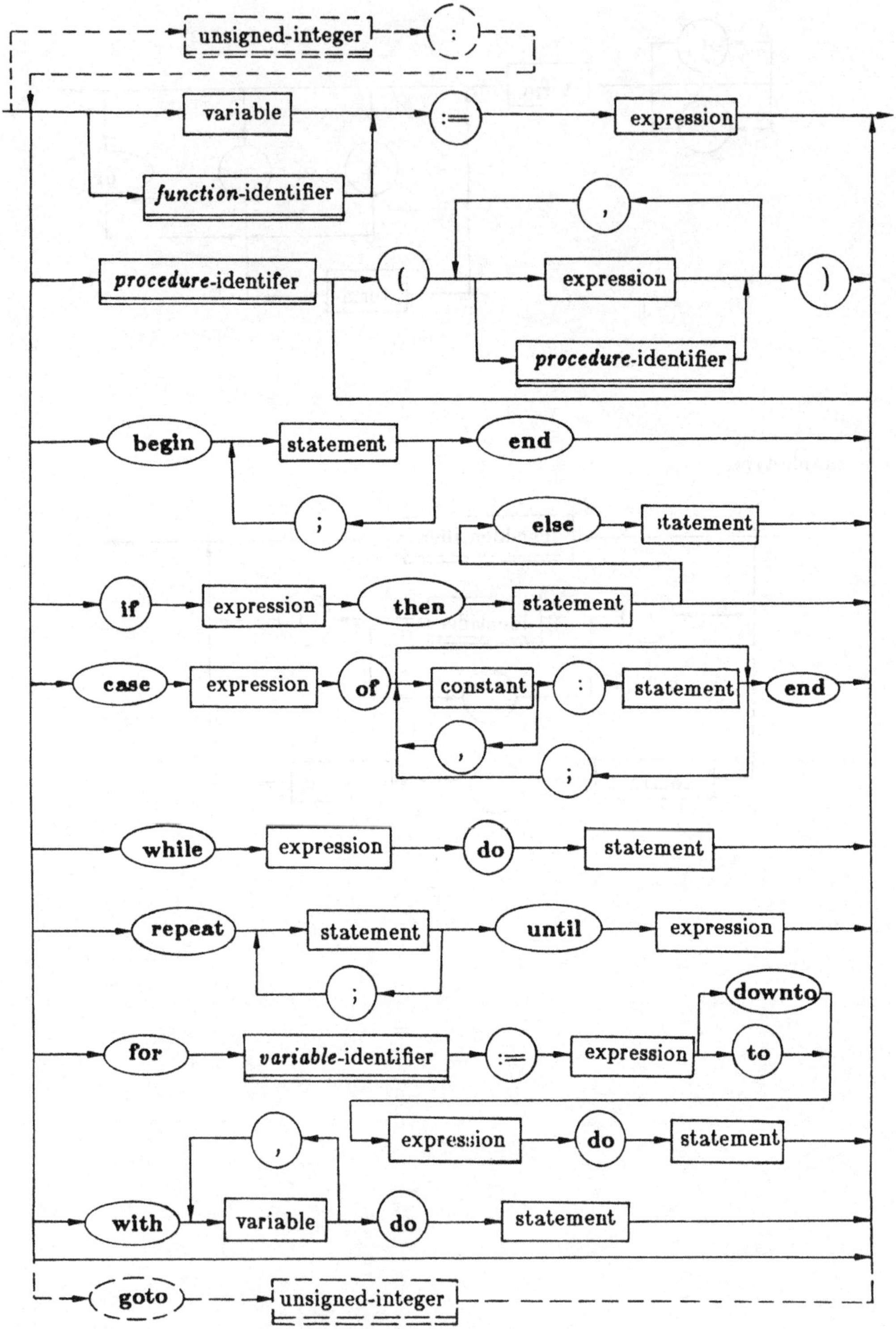
unsigned-integer
:
variable
:=
expression
function-identifier
,
procedure-identifer
(
expression
)
procedure-identifier
begin
statement
end
;
else
statement
if
expression
then
statement
case
expression
of
constant
:
statement
end
,
;
while
expression
do
statement
repeat
statement
until
expression
;
downto
for
variable-identifier
:=
expression
to
expression
do
statement
,
with
variable
do
statement
goto
unsigned-integer

term

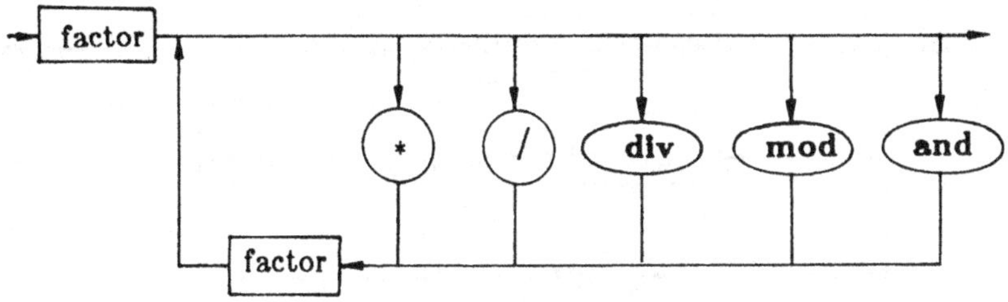
factor
*
/
div
mod
and
factor

type

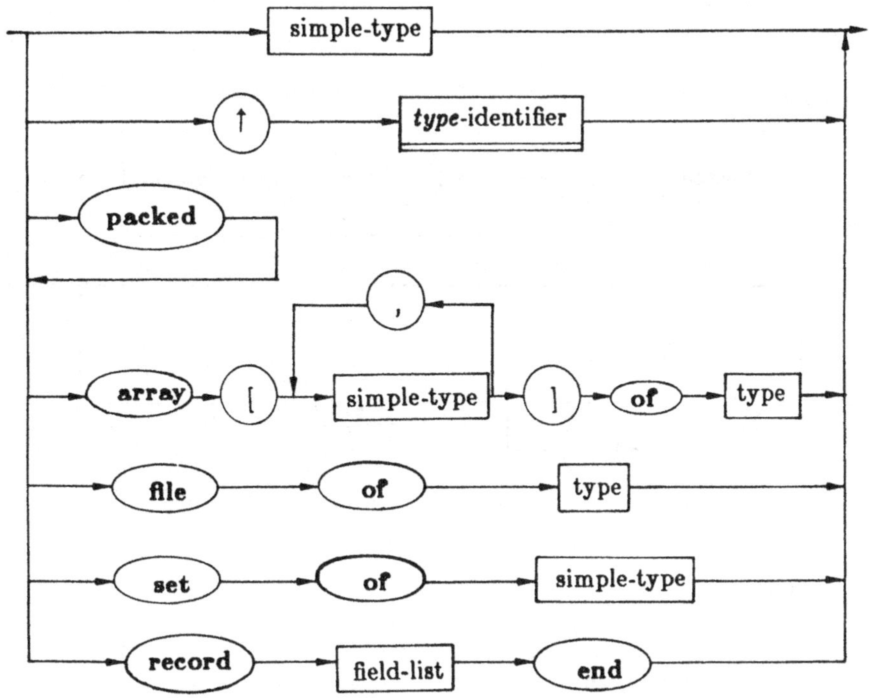
simple-type
↑
type-identifier
packed
,
array
[
simple-type
]
of
type
file
of
type
set
of
simple-type
record
field-list
end

unsigned-constant

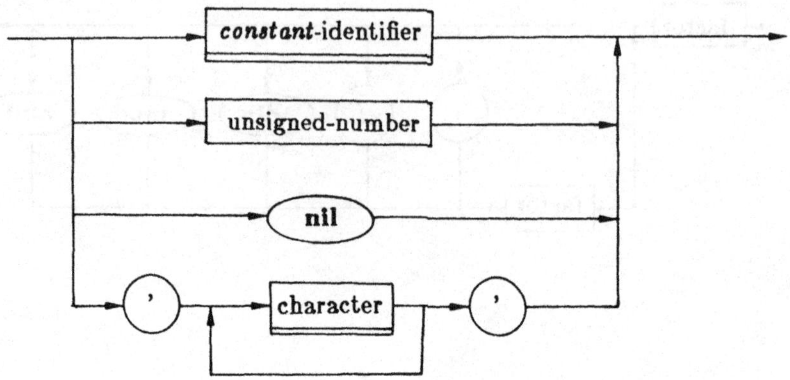

unsigned-number

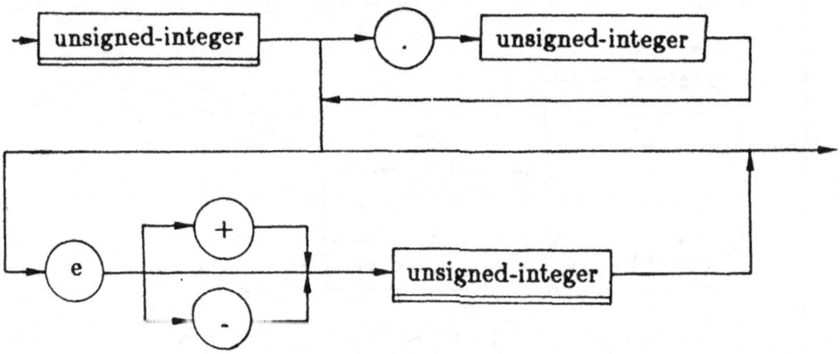

variable

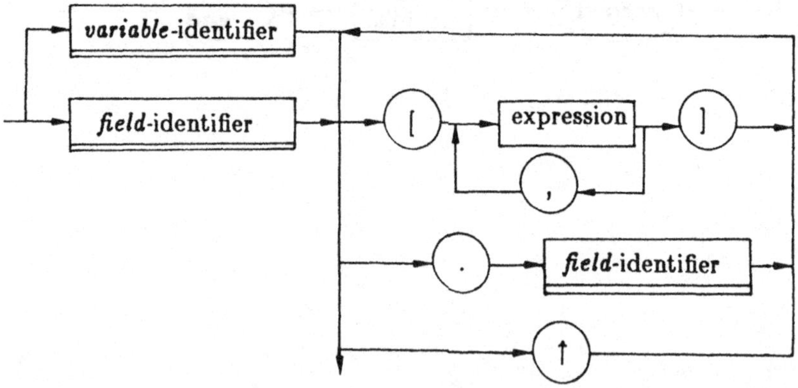

Algol 68

Start symbol is **particular-program**

actual-MODE-declarer

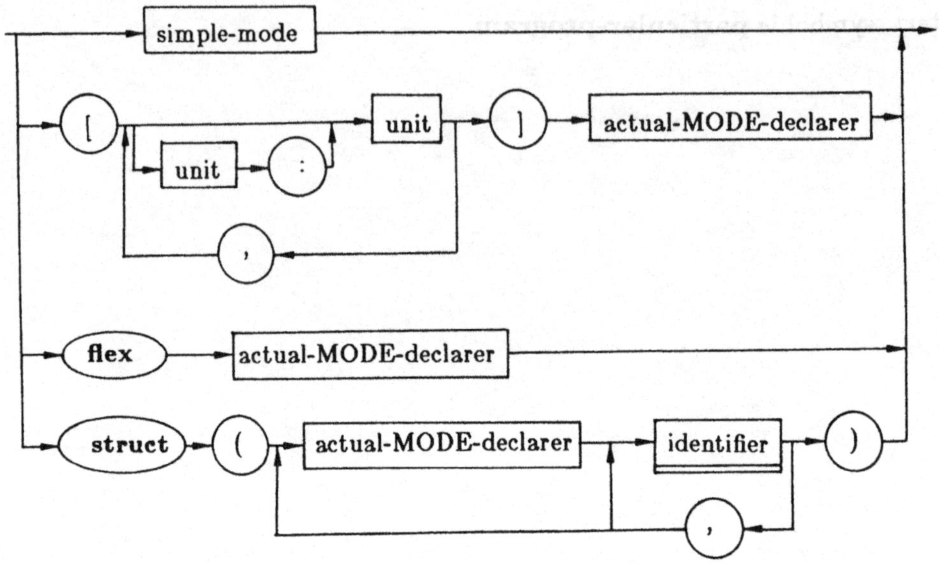

assignation

bits-denotation

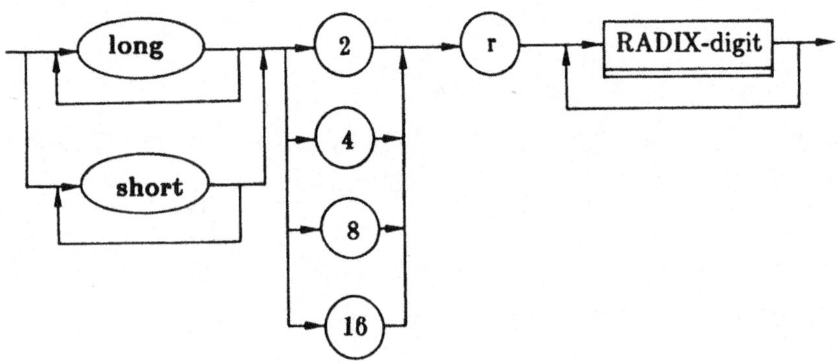

boolean-chooser

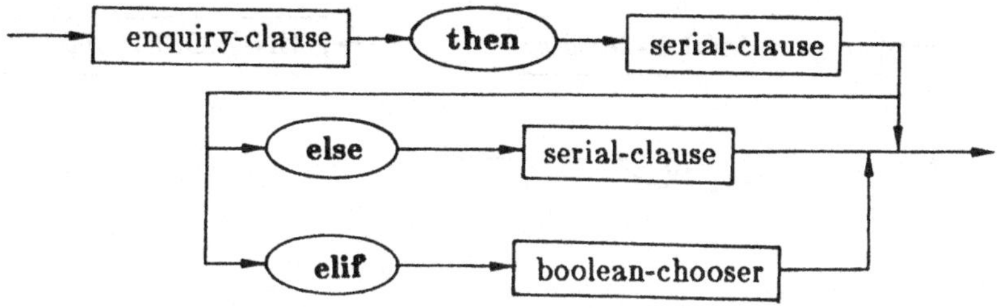

boolean-denotation

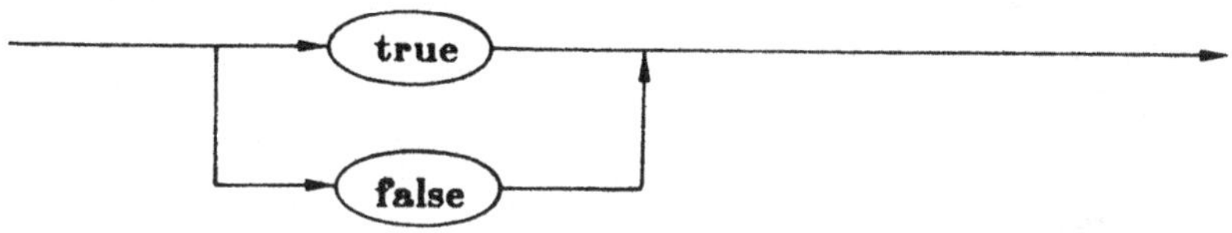

call

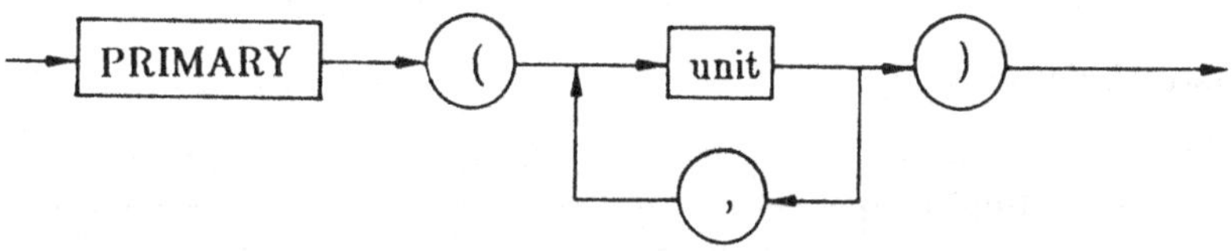

case-clause

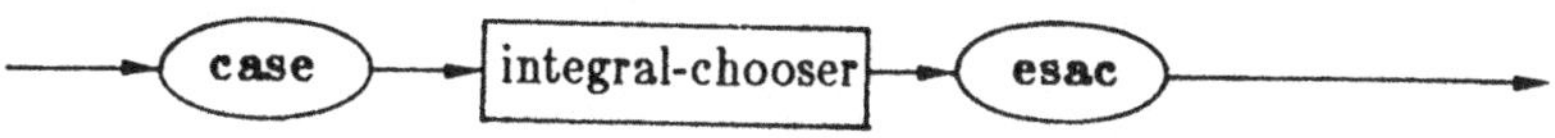

cast

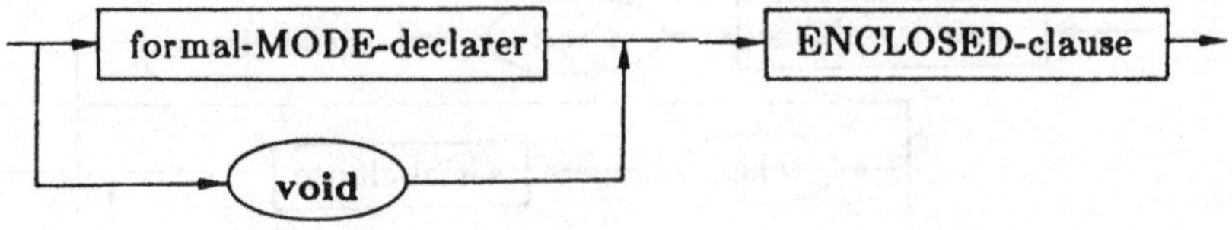

character-denotation

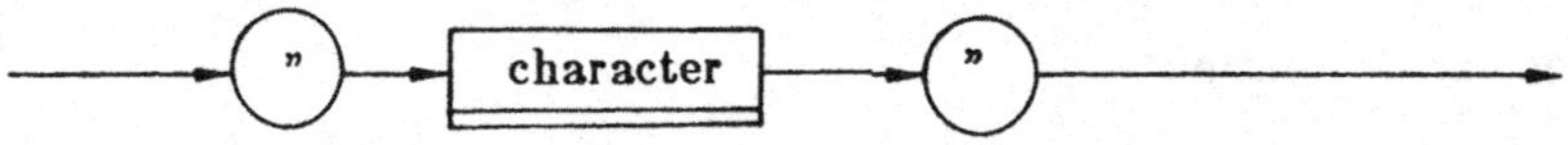

closed-clause

collateral-clause

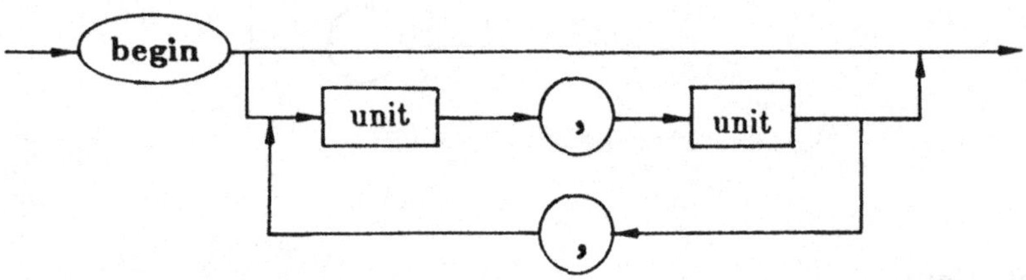

conditional-clause

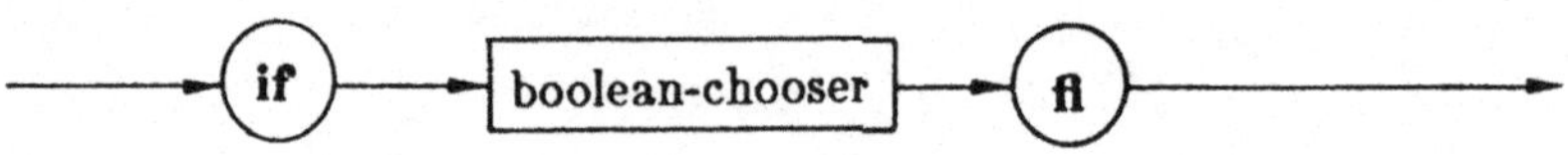

conformity-clause

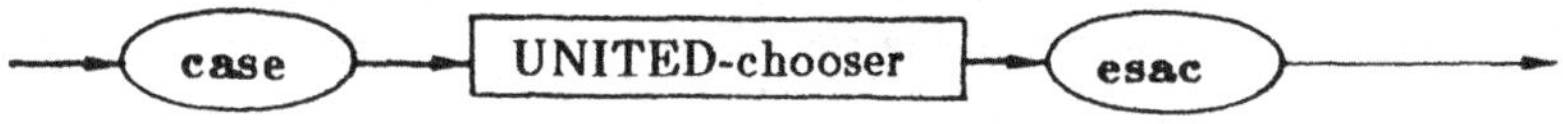

declaration

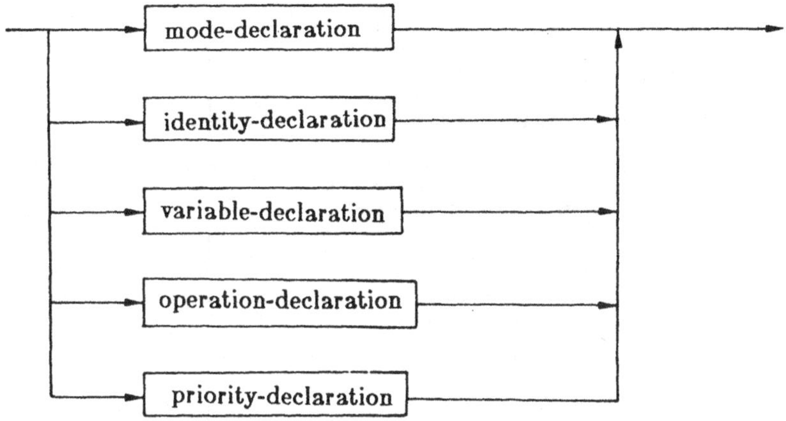

denotation

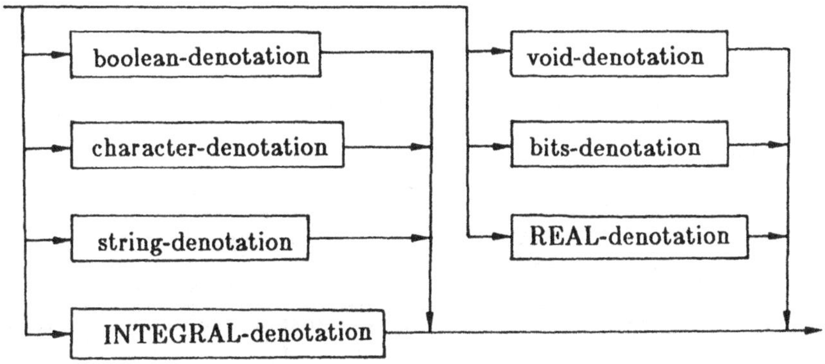

ENCLOSED-clause

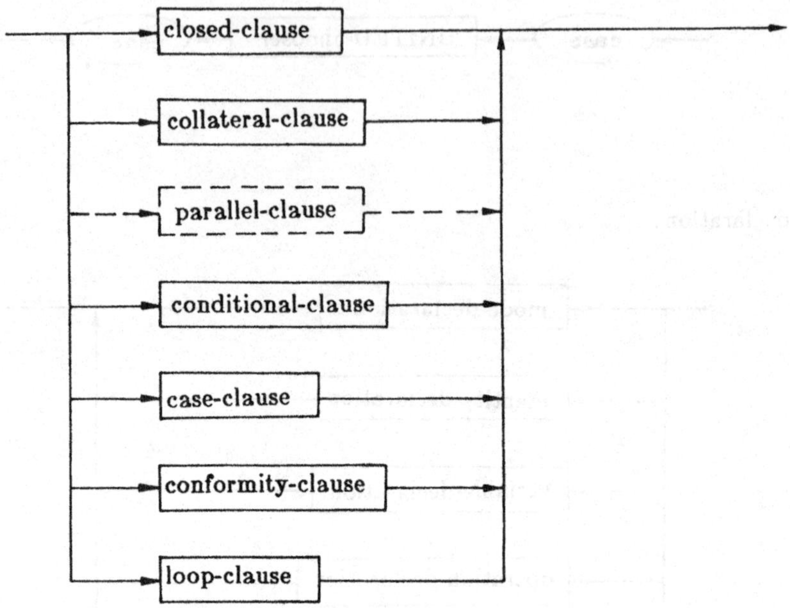

enquiry-clause

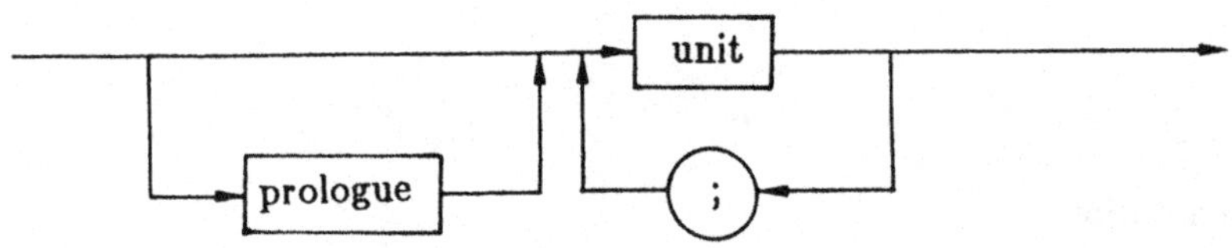

formula

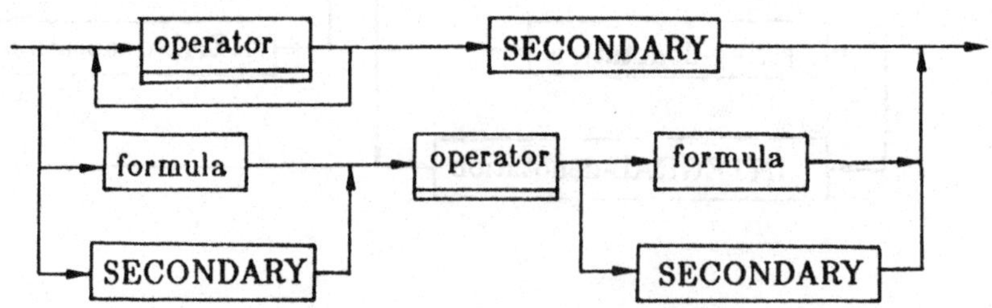

formal-MODE-declarer

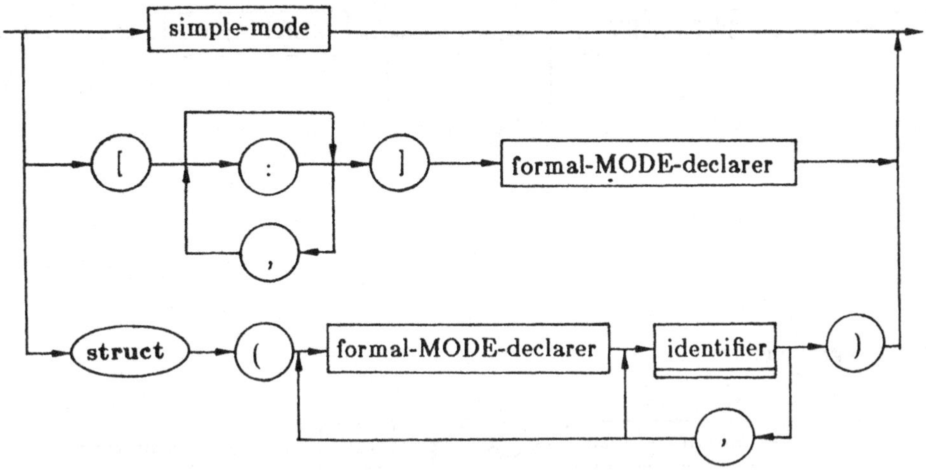

generator

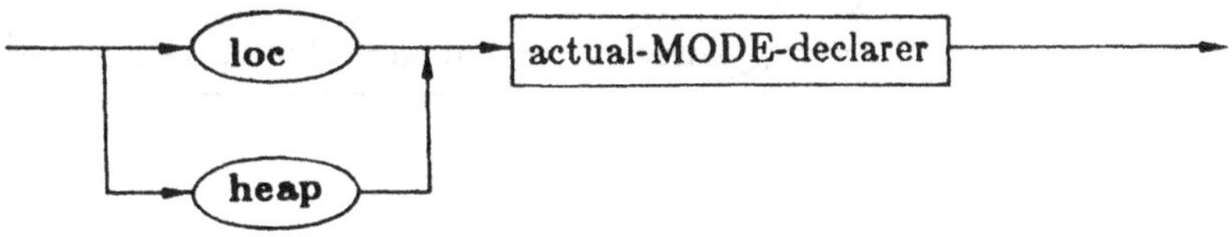

identity-declaration

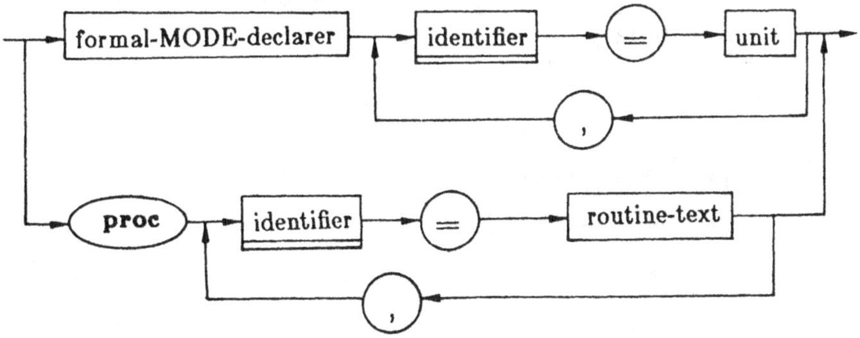

identity-relation

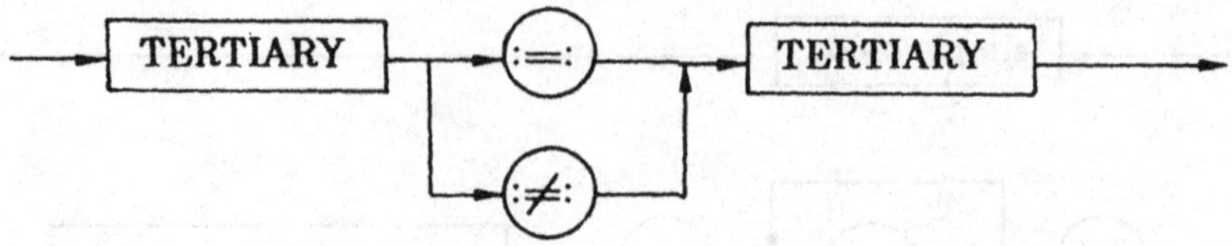

integral-chooser

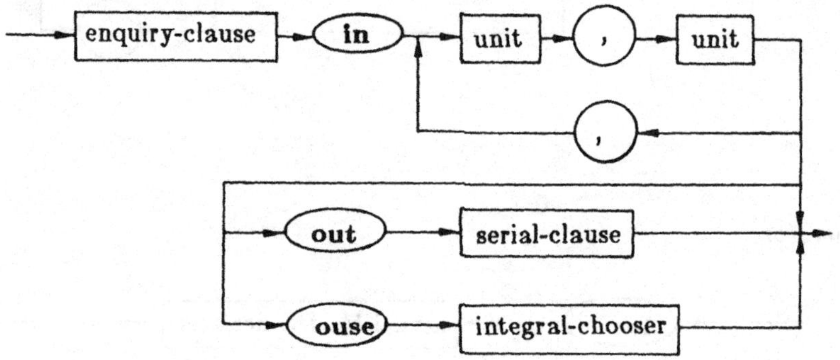

INTEGRAL-denotation

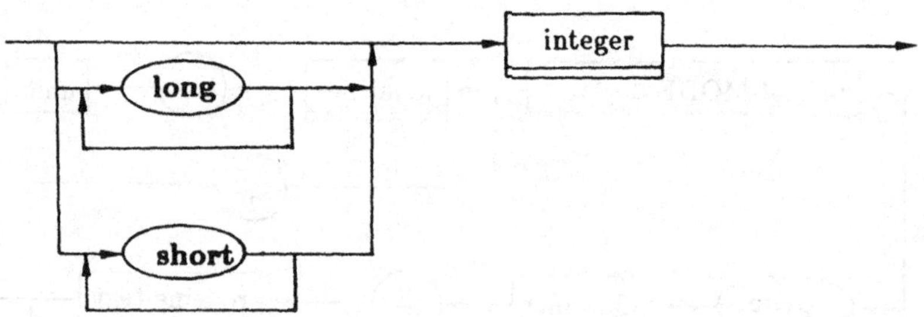

loop-clause

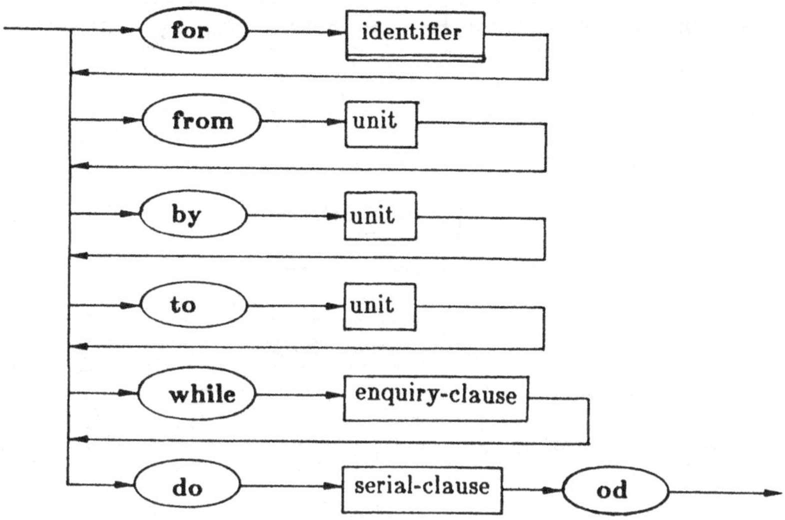

mode-declaration

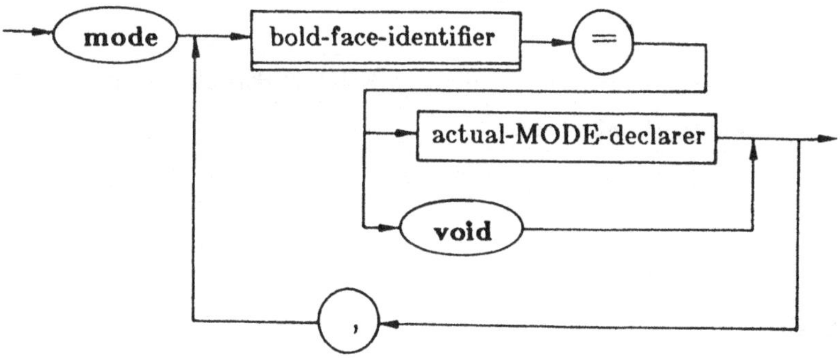

operator-declaration

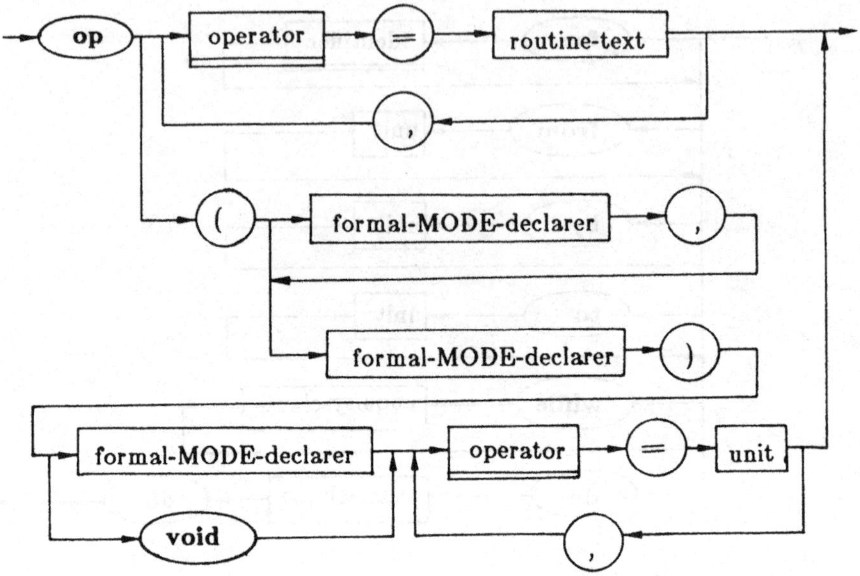

particular-program

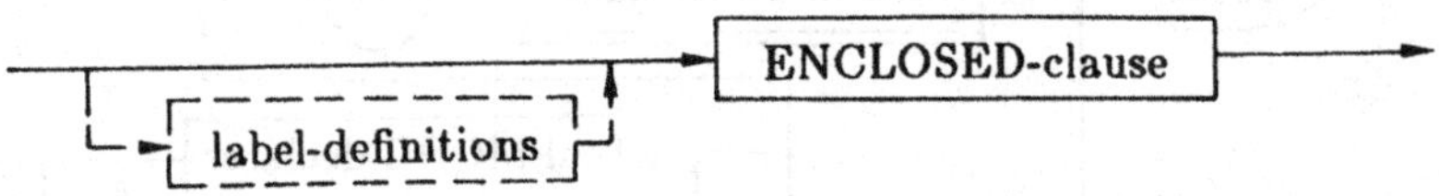

PRIMARY

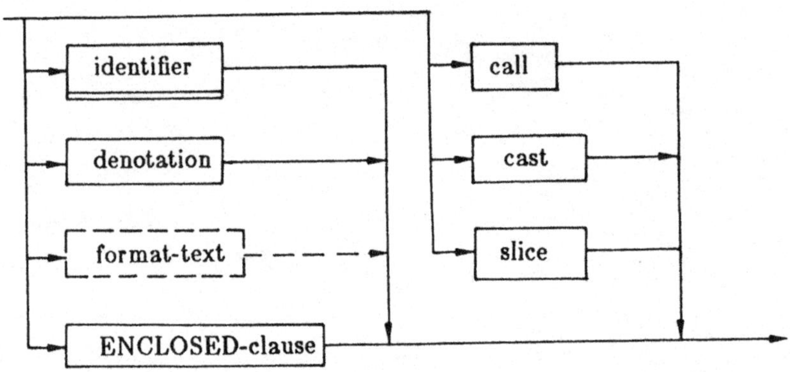

priority-declaration

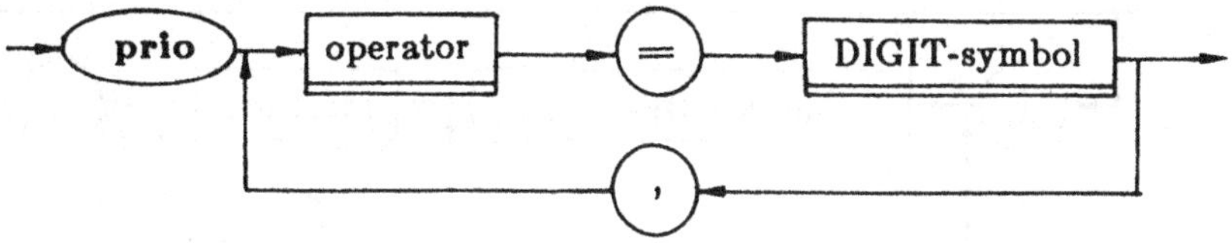

prologue

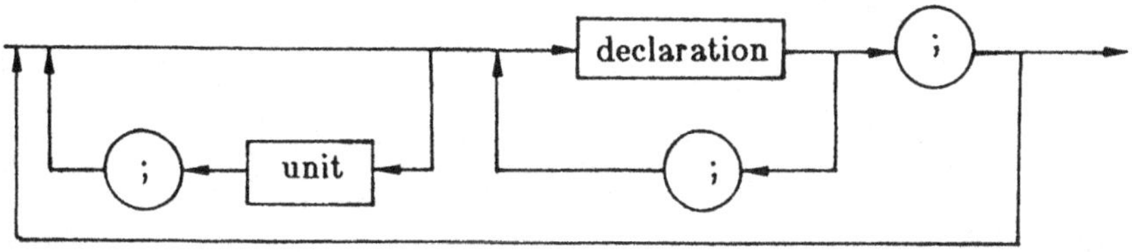

REAL-denotation

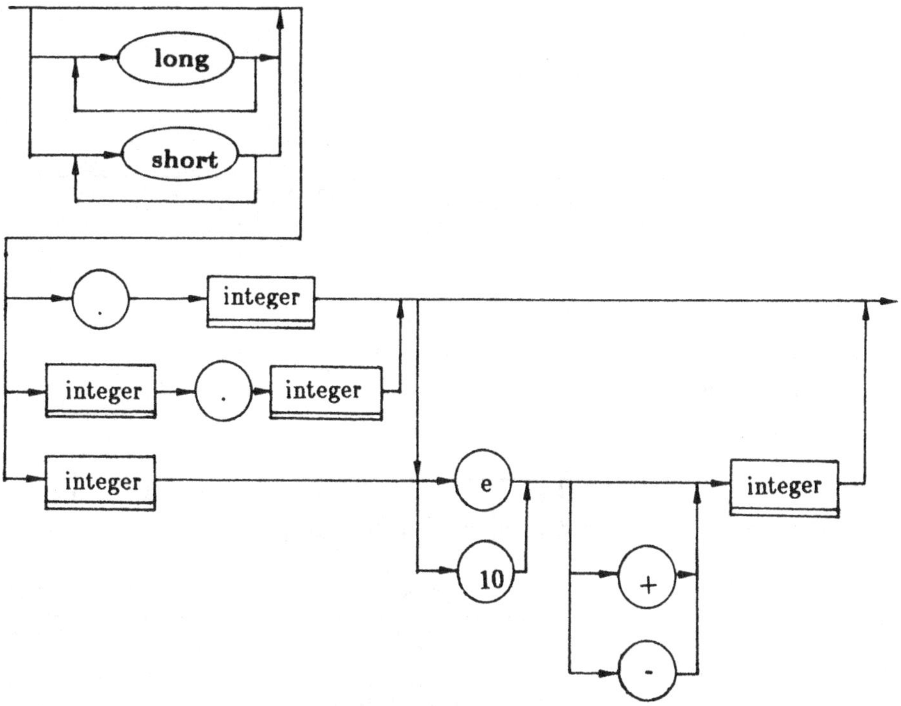

routine-text

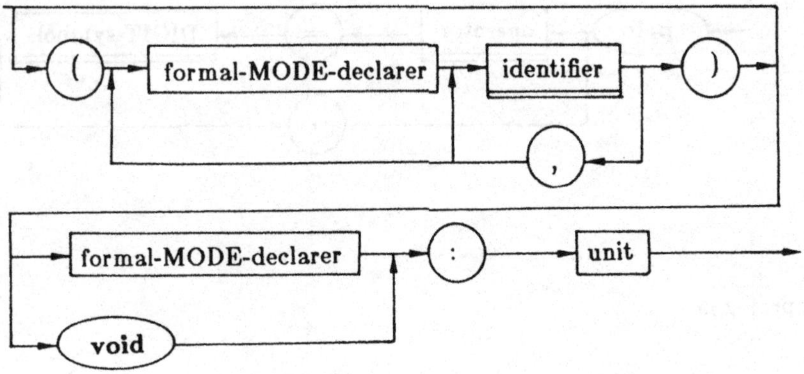

SECONDARY

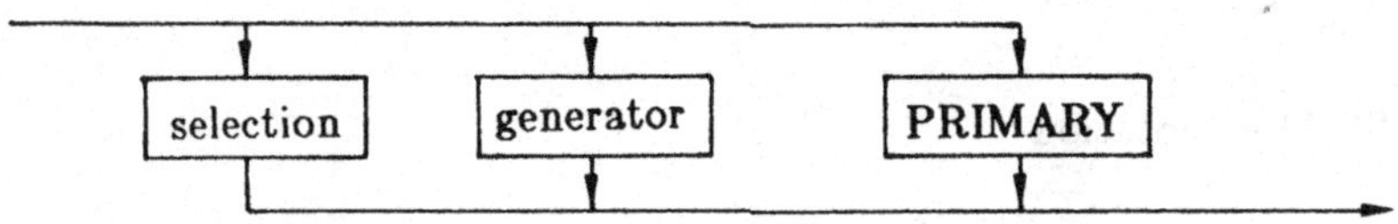

selection

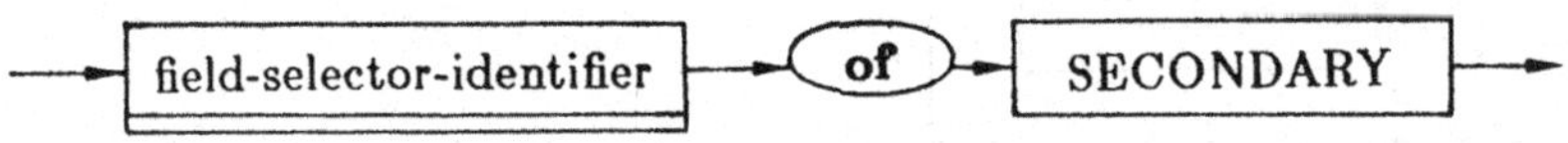

serial-clause

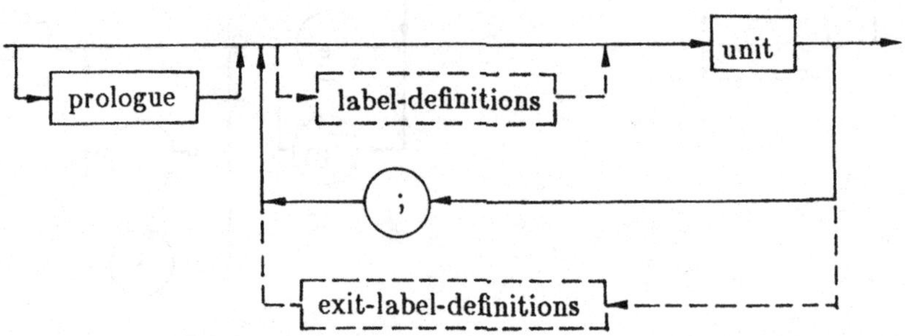

simple-mode

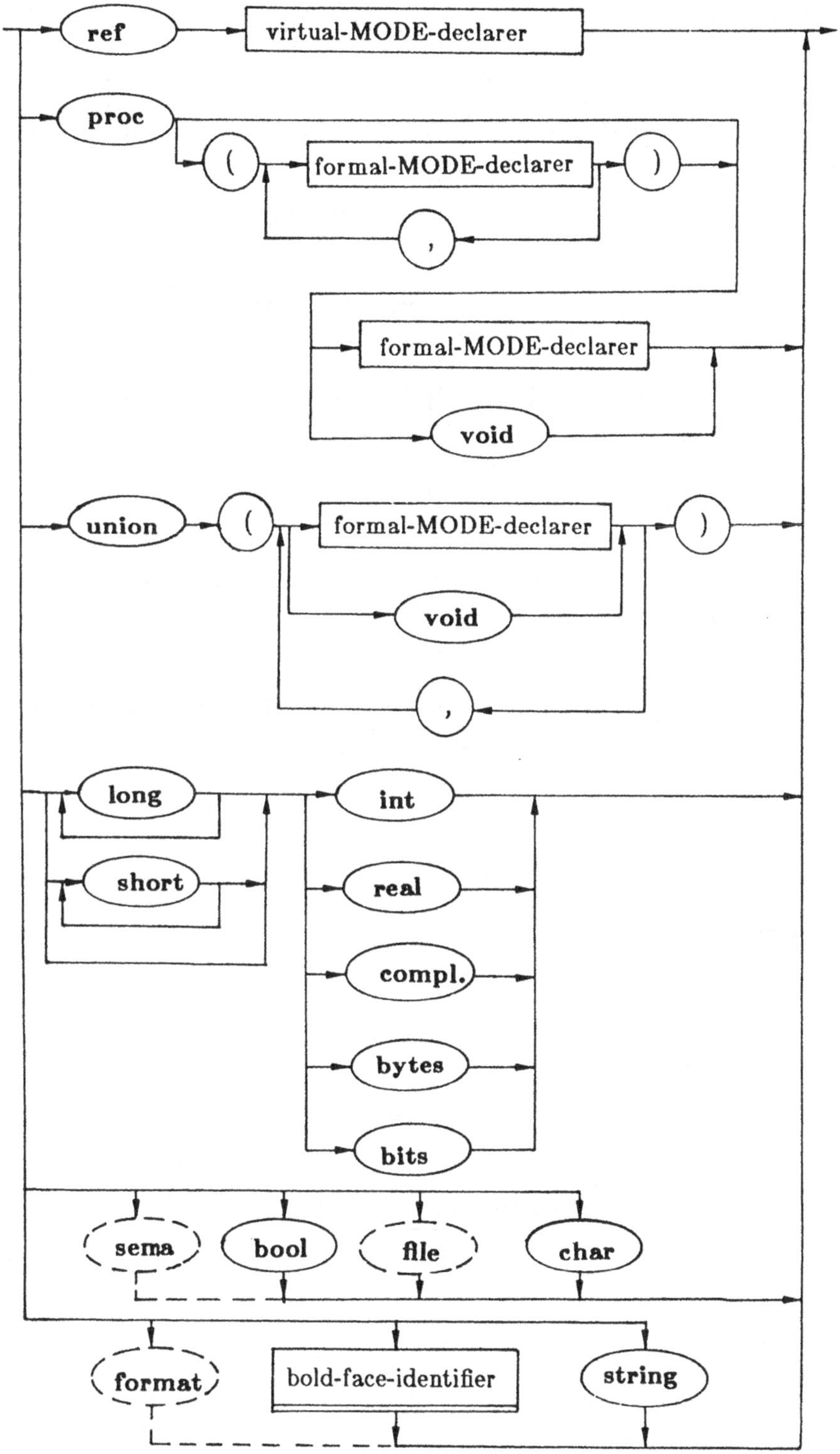
ref
virtual-MODE-declarer
proc
(
formal-MODE-declarer
)
,
formal-MODE-declarer
void
union
(
formal-MODE-declarer
)
void
,
long
short
int
real
compl.
bytes
bits
sema
bool
file
char
format
bold-face-identifier
string

slice

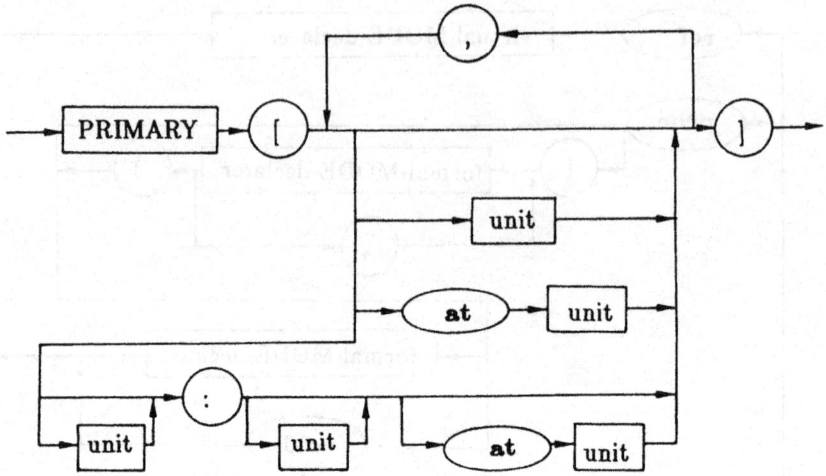

string-denotation

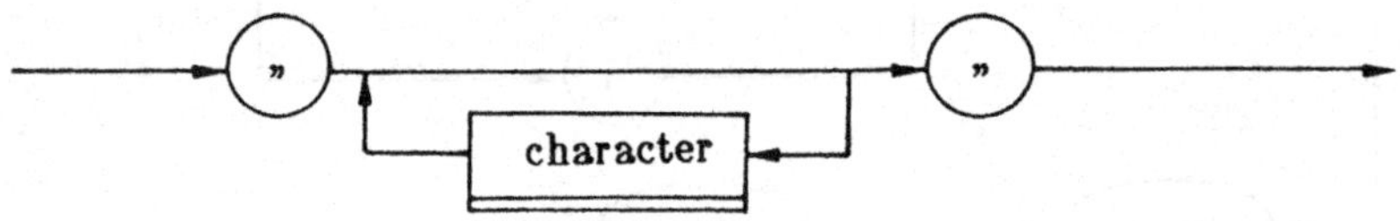

TERTIARY

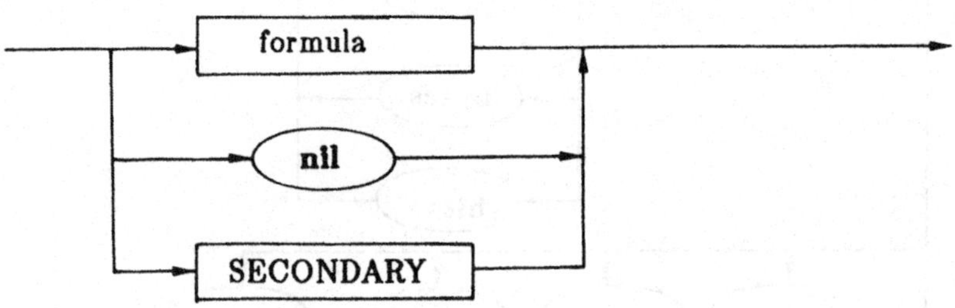

unit

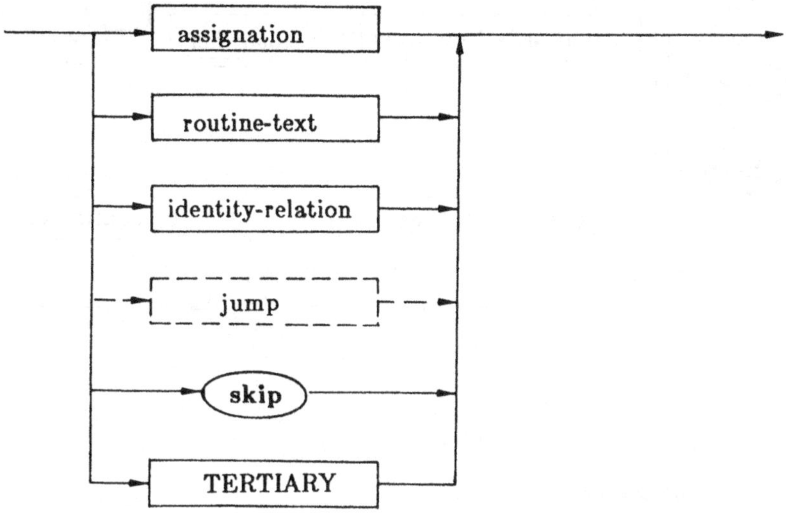

UNITED-chooser

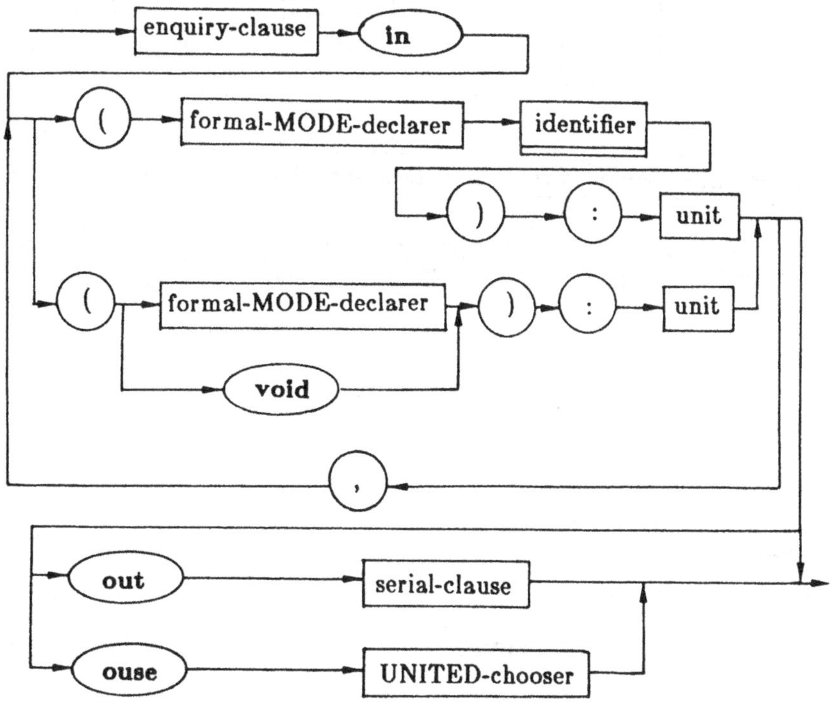

variable-declaration

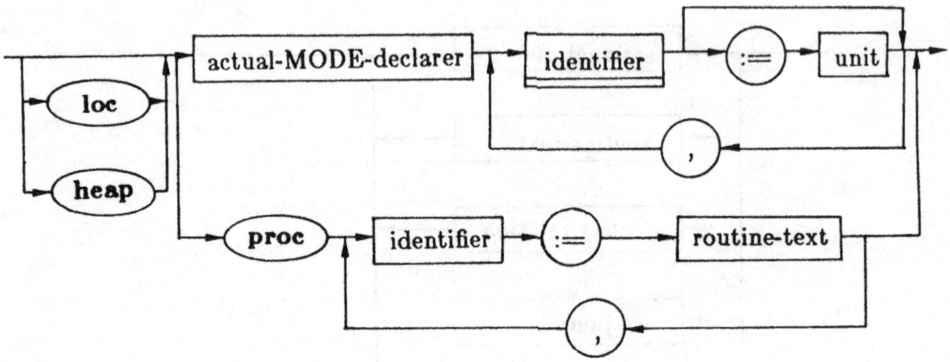

virtual-MODE-declarer

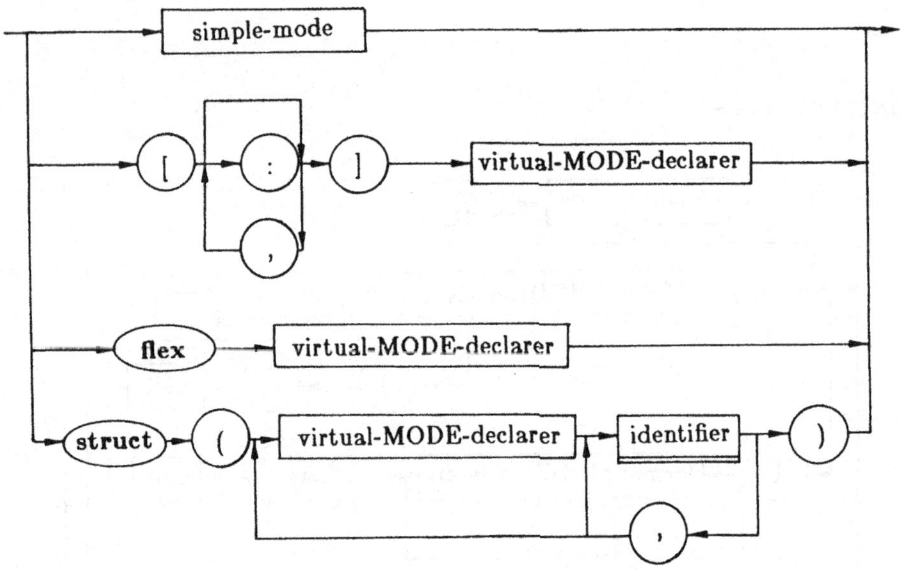

void-denotation

PL/1

Start symbol is **program**

allocate-statement

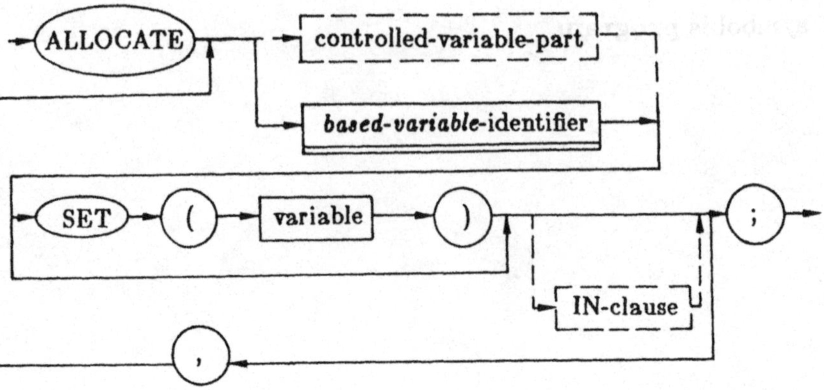

assignment-statement

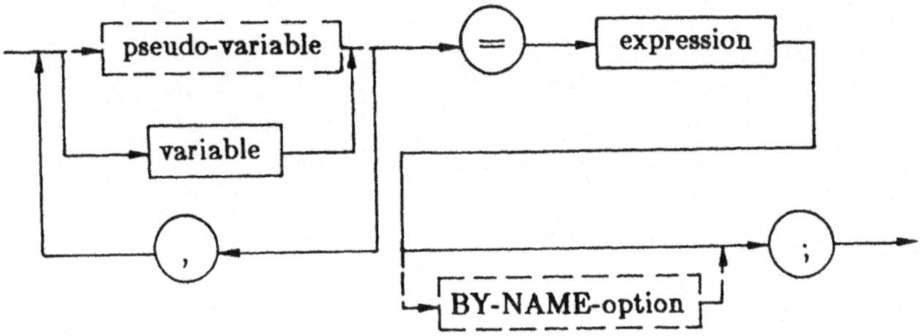

attribute

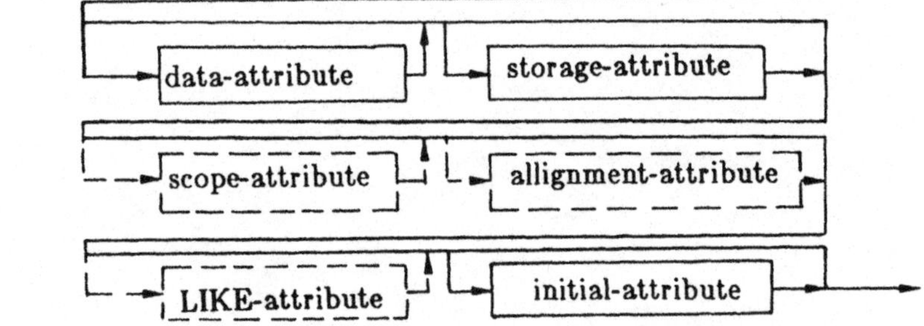

begin-block

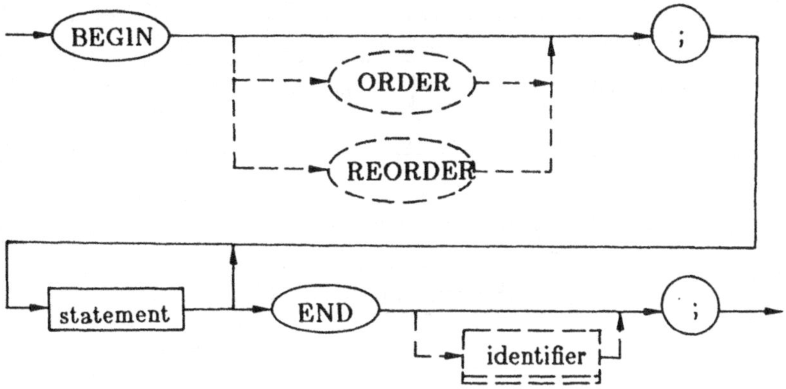

bit-string-constant

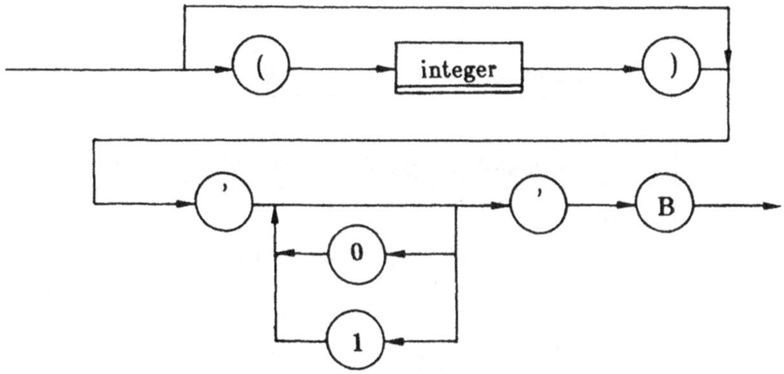

call-statement

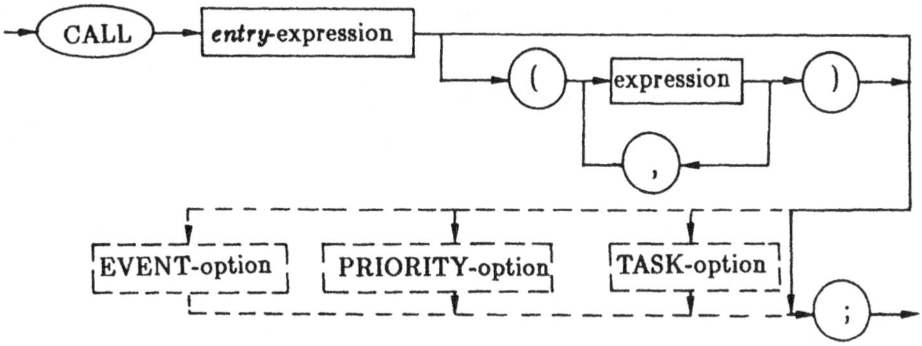

character-string-constant

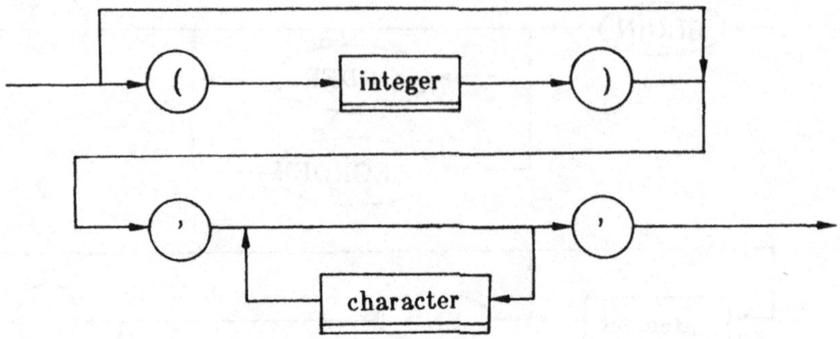

constant

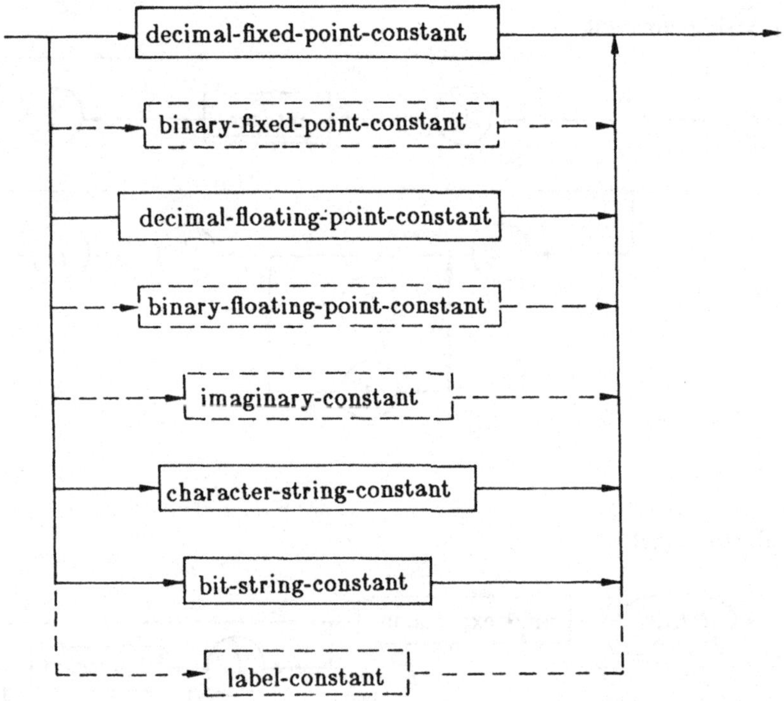

control-statement

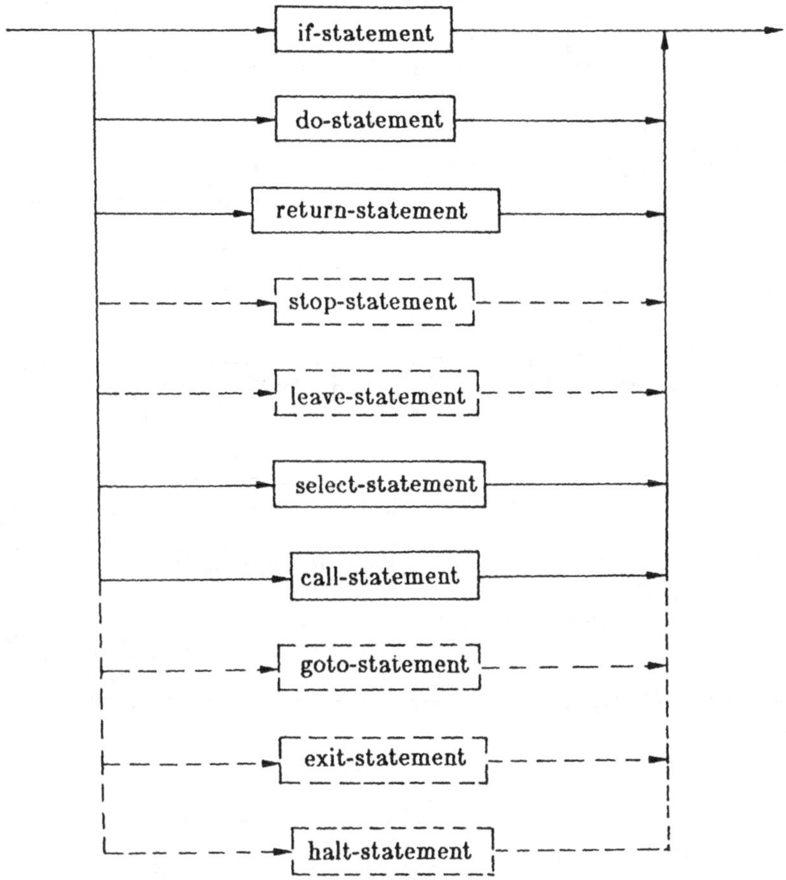

data-attribute

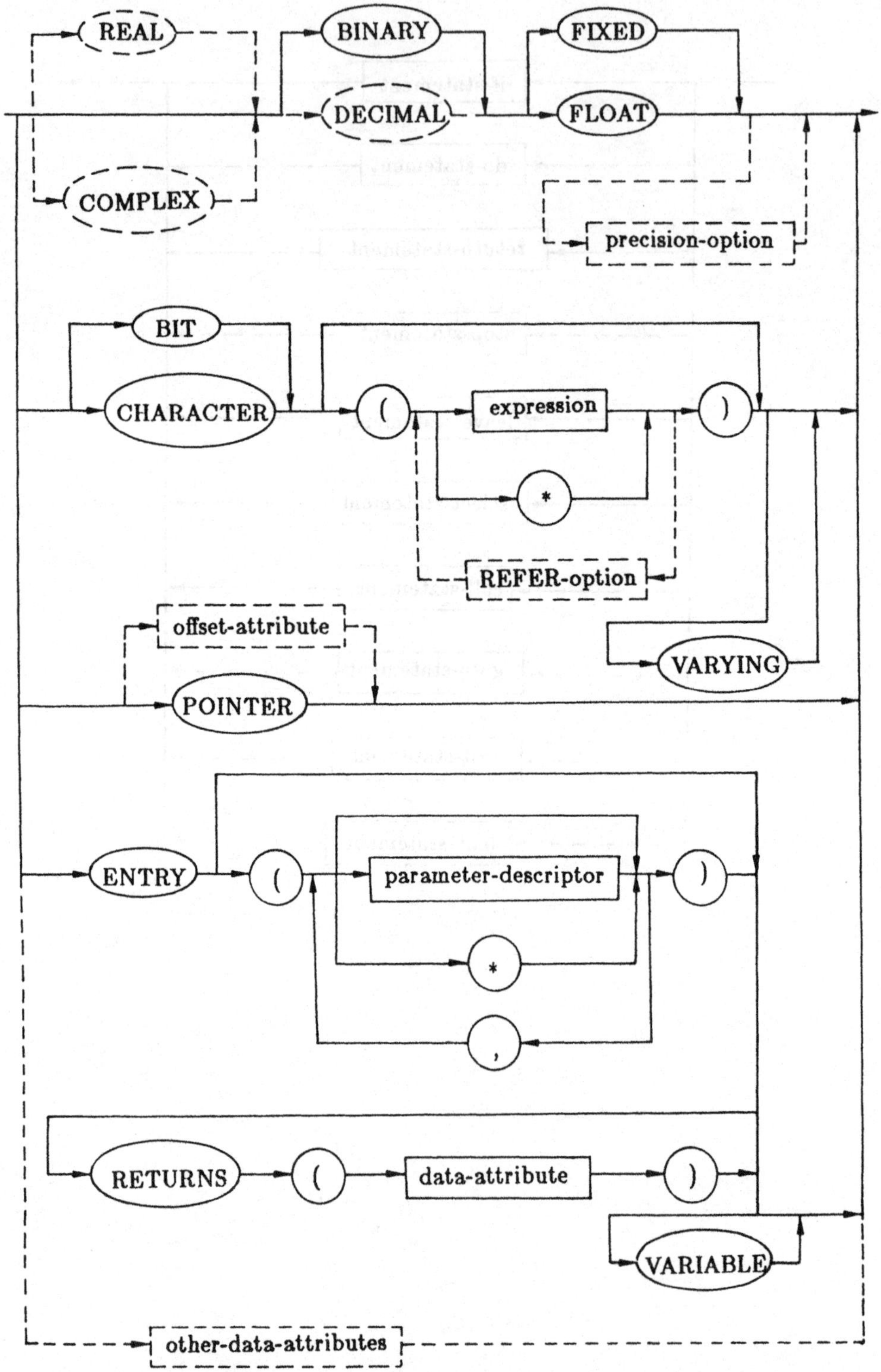

decimal-fixed-point-constant

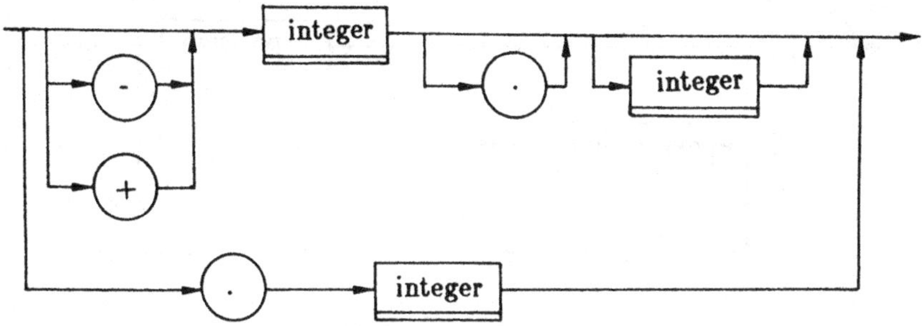

decimal-floating-point-constant

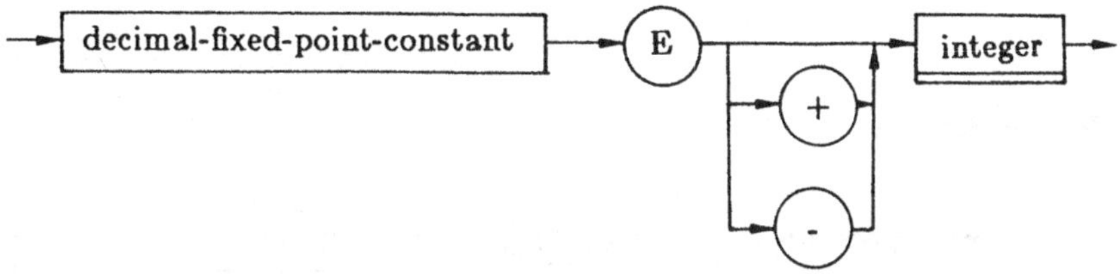

declare-statement

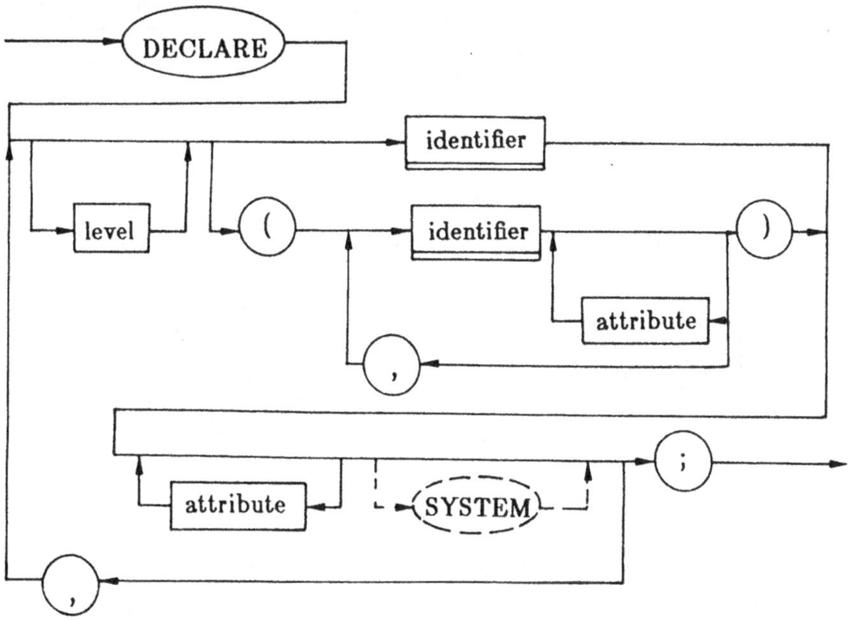

dimension-attribute

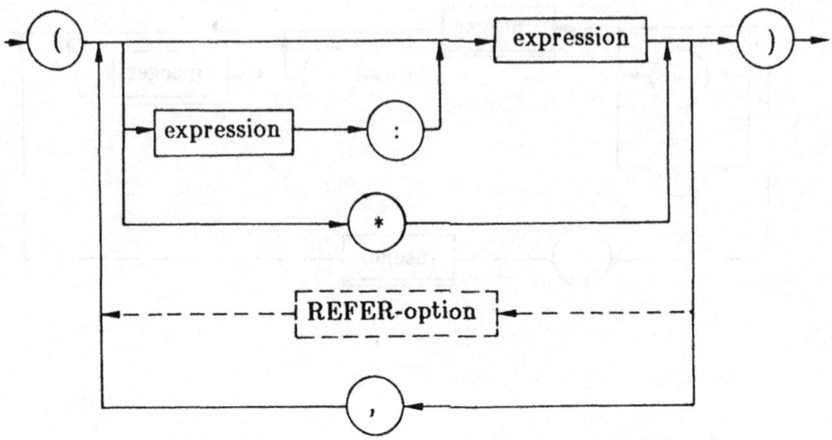

do-specification

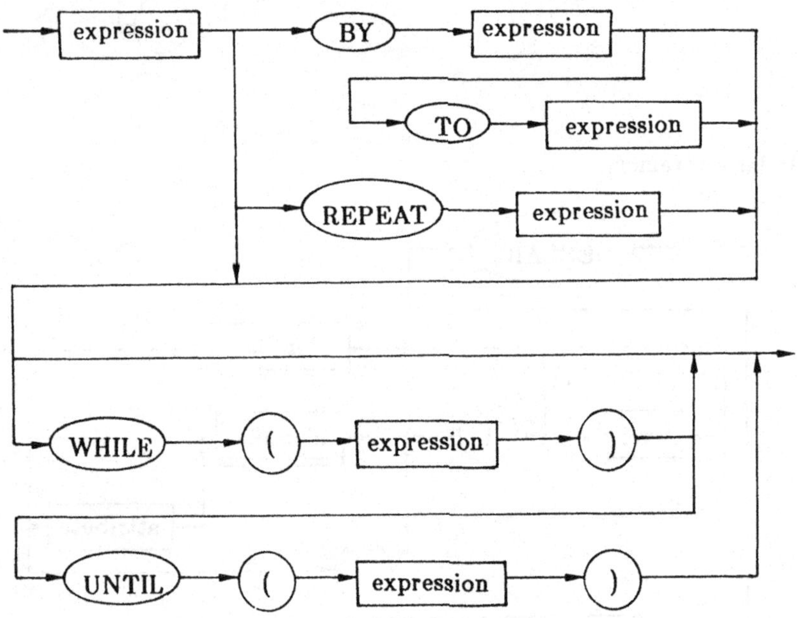

do-statement

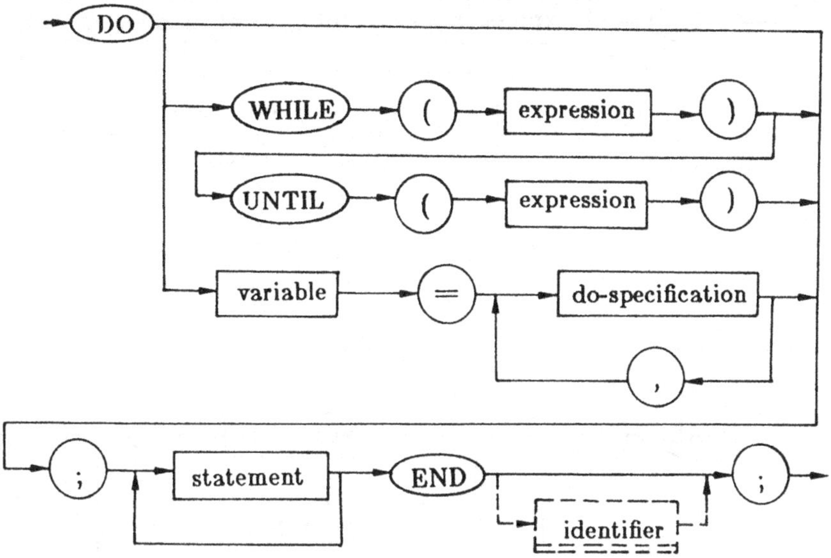

expression

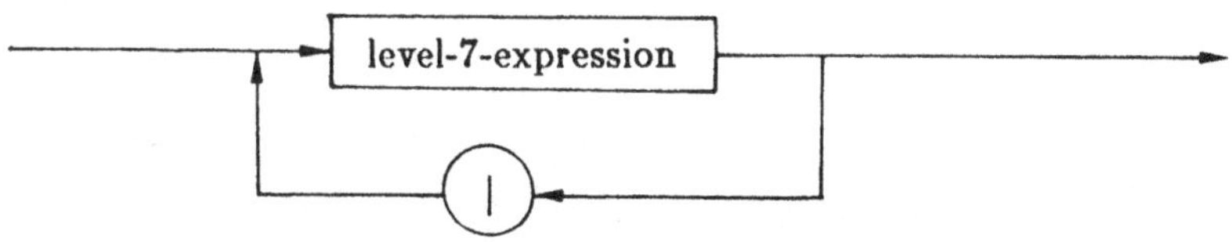

free-statement

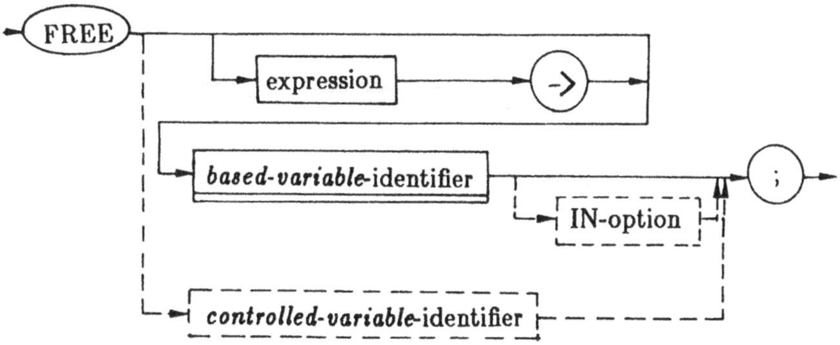

if-statement

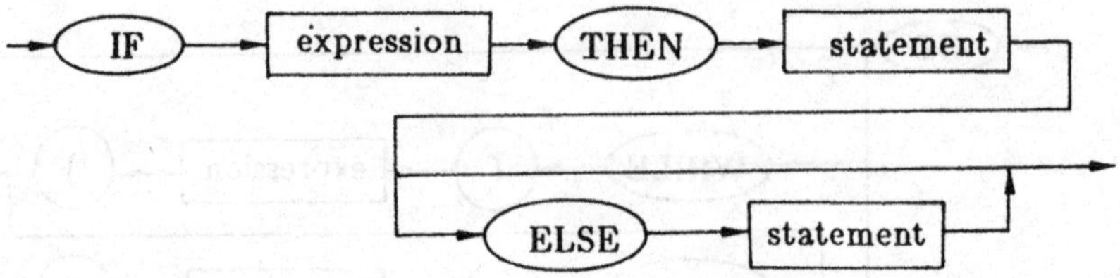

intial-attribute

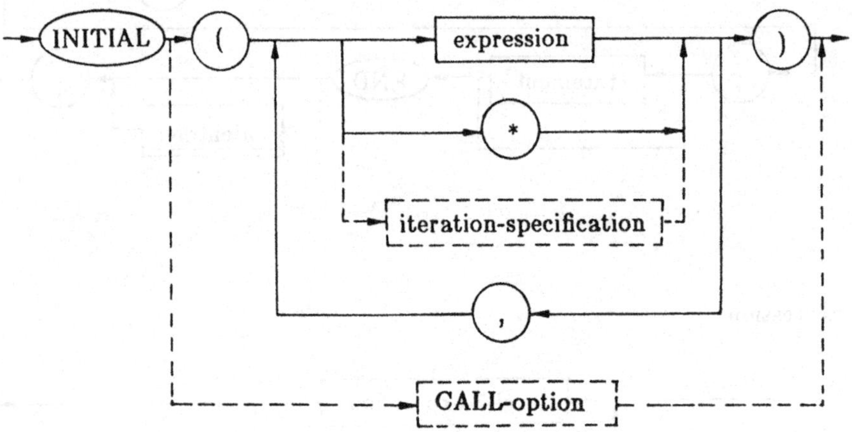

I/O-statement

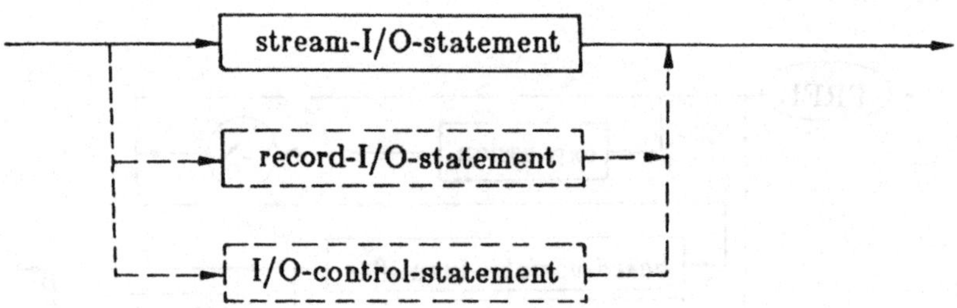

level

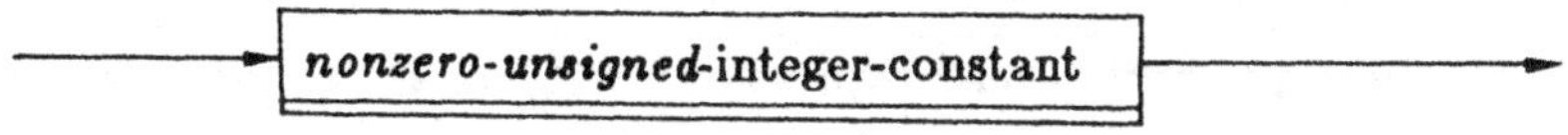

level-1-expression

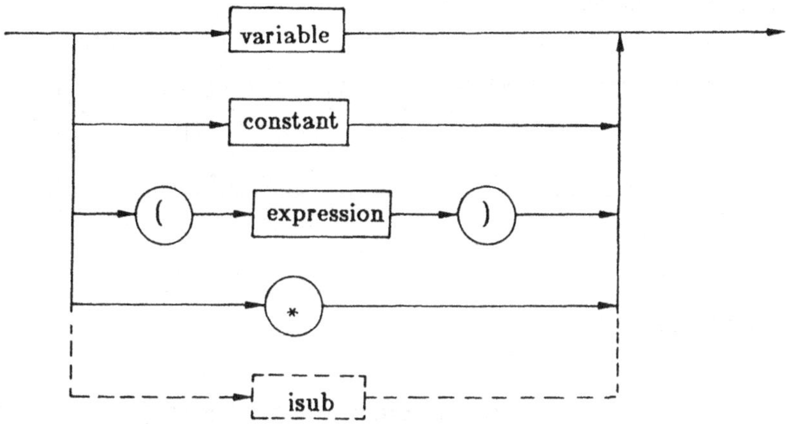

level-2-expression

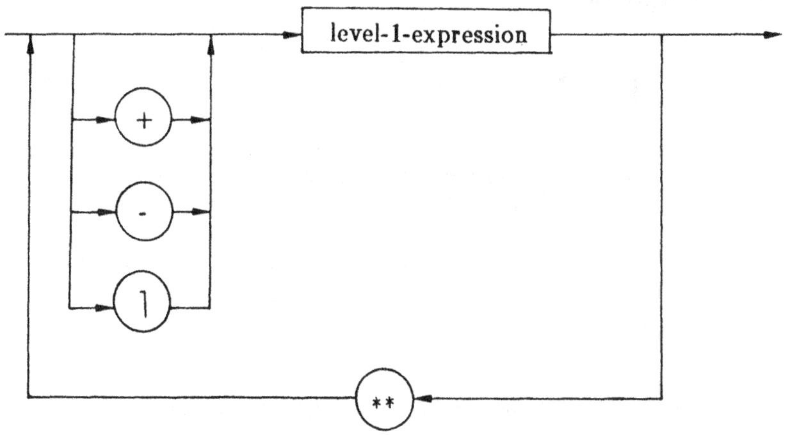

level-3-expression

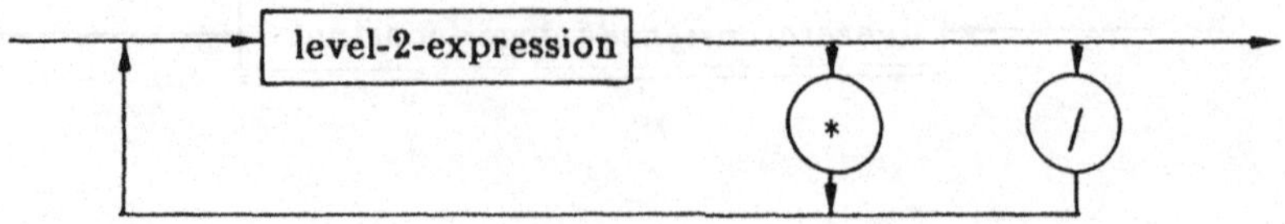

level-4-expression

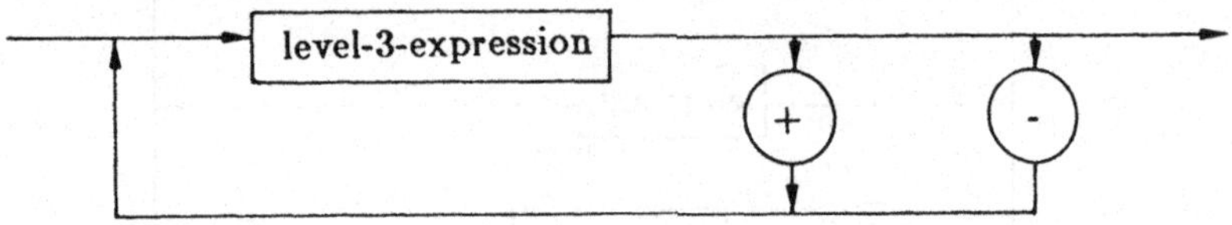

level-5-expression

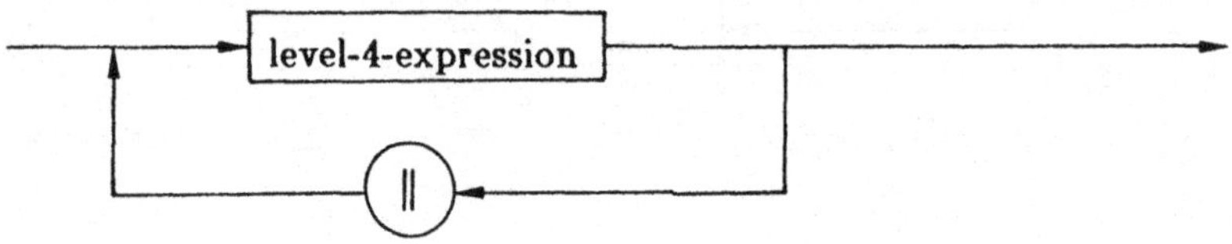

level-6-expression

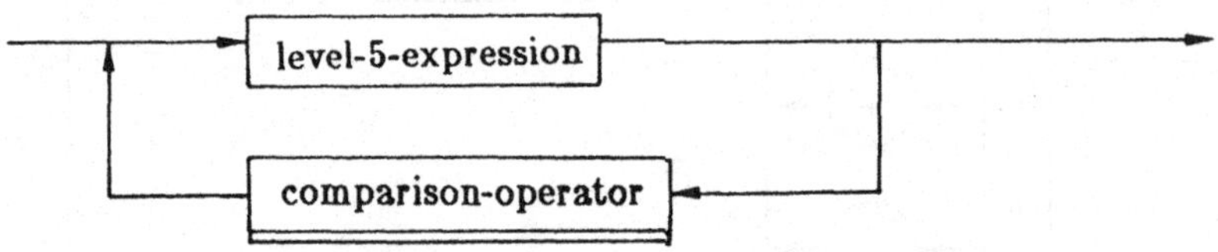

level-7-expression

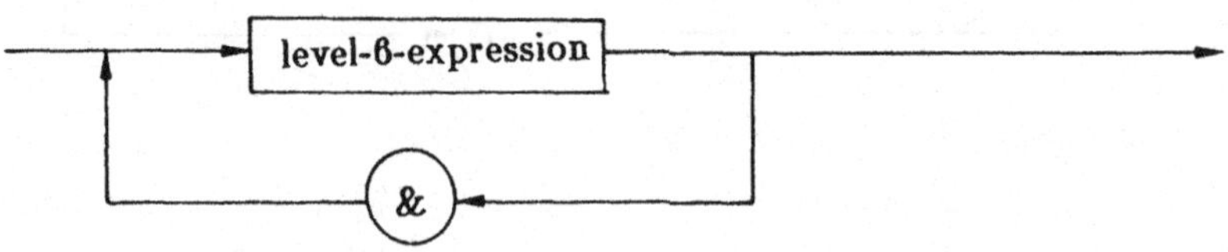

list-directed-transmission

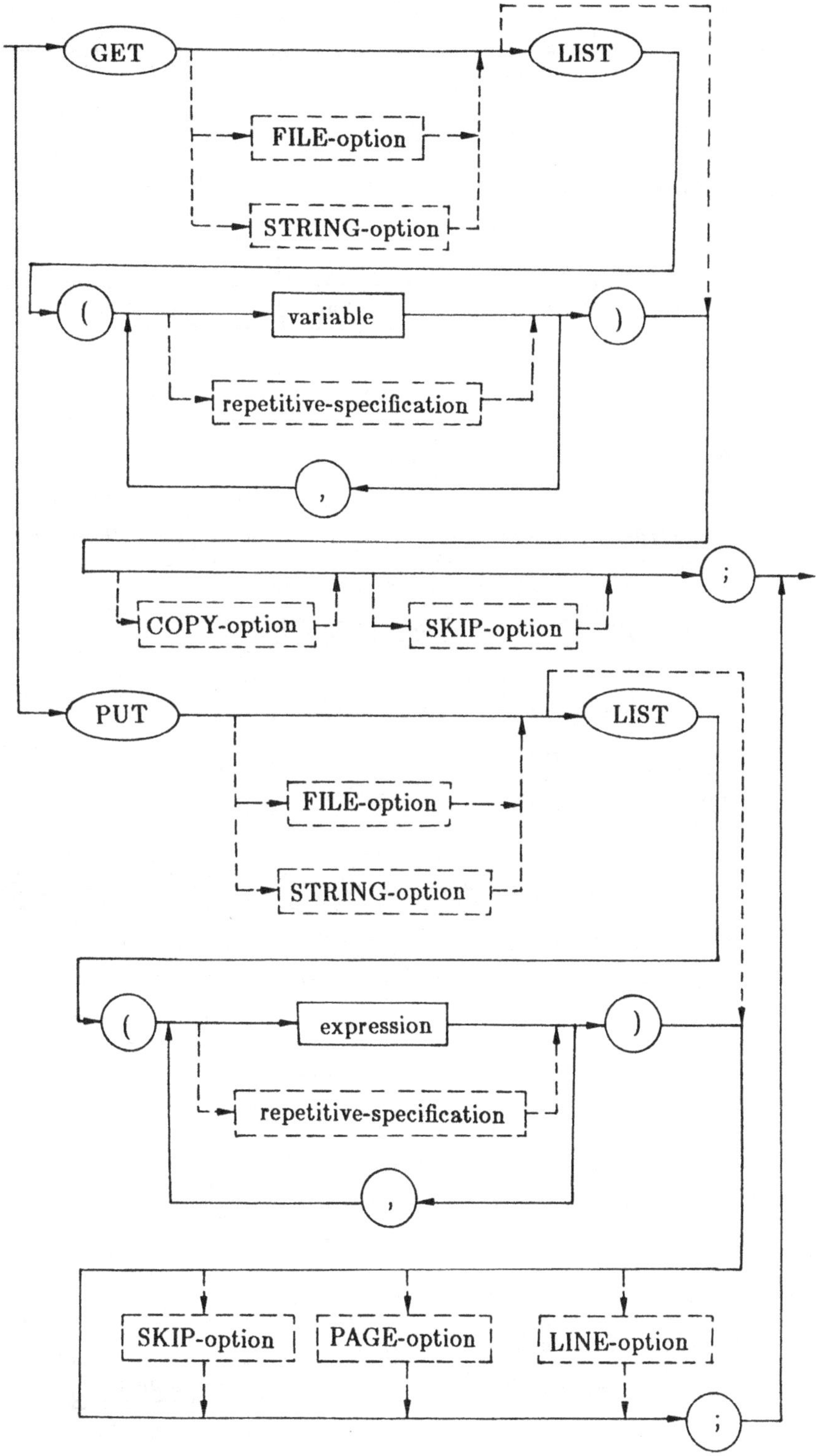

null-statement

parameter-descriptor

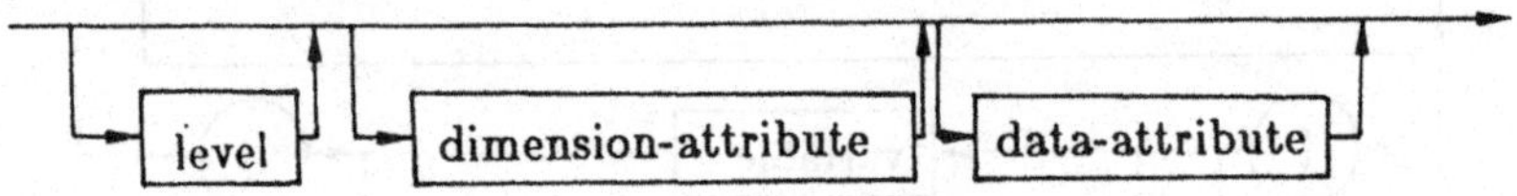

procedure-block

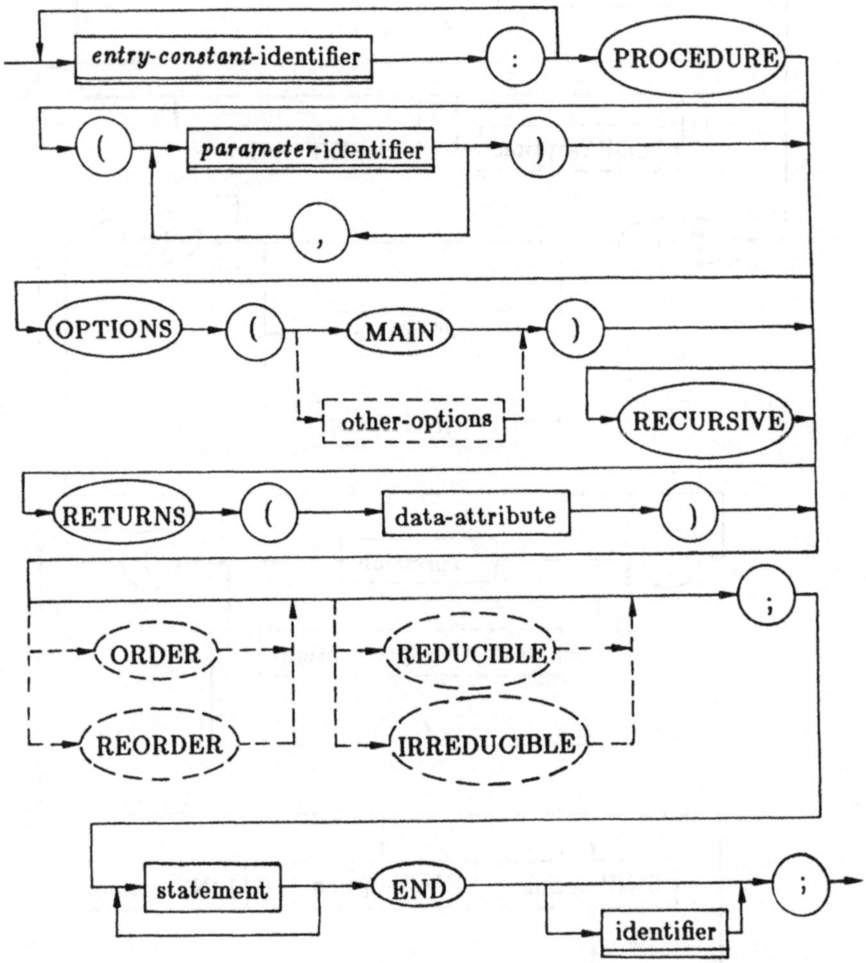

program

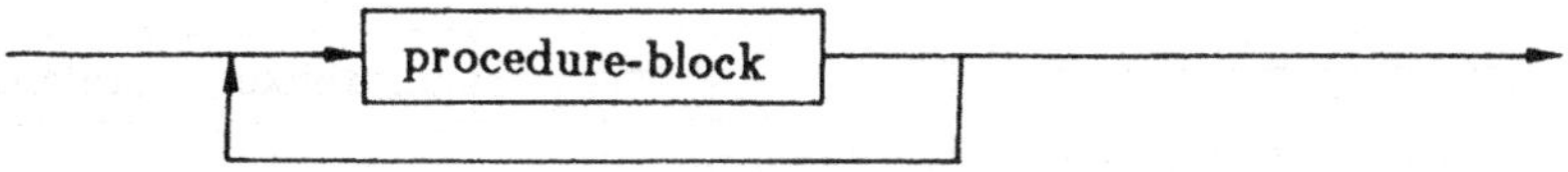

return-statement

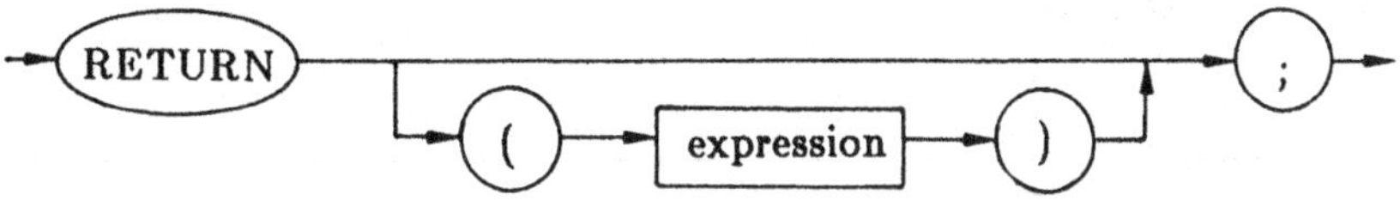

select-statement

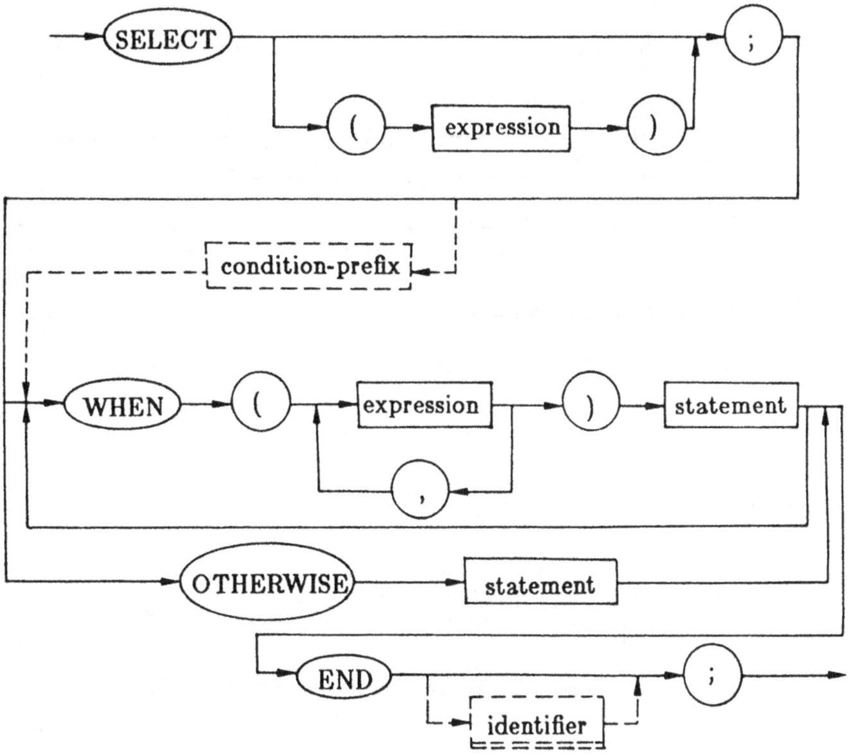

statement

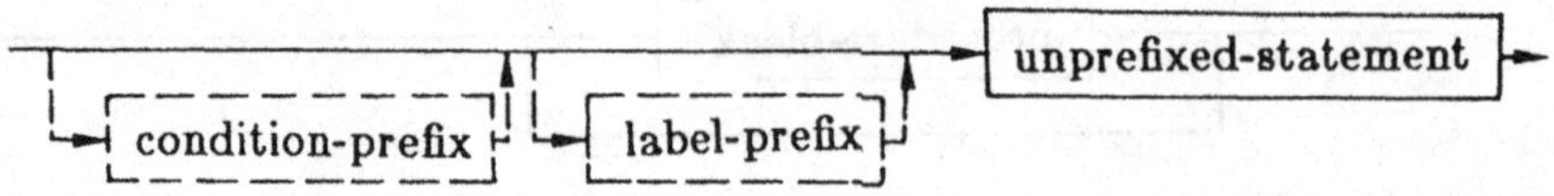

storage-attribute

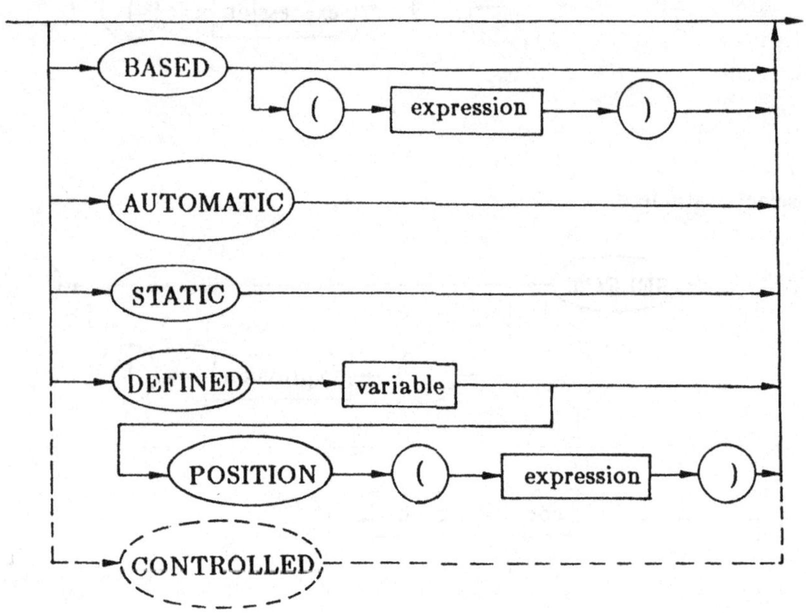

stream-I/O-statement

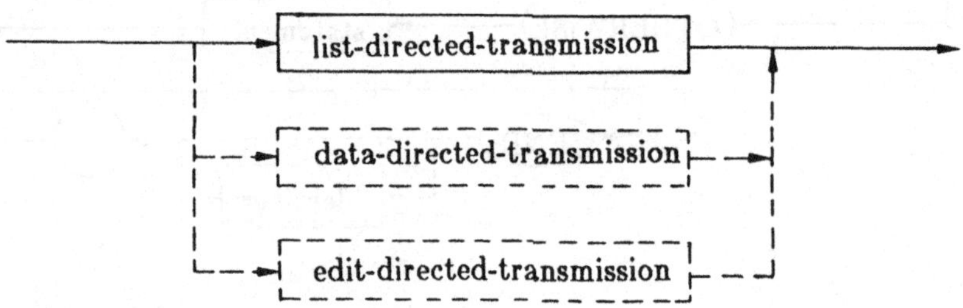

unprefixed-statement

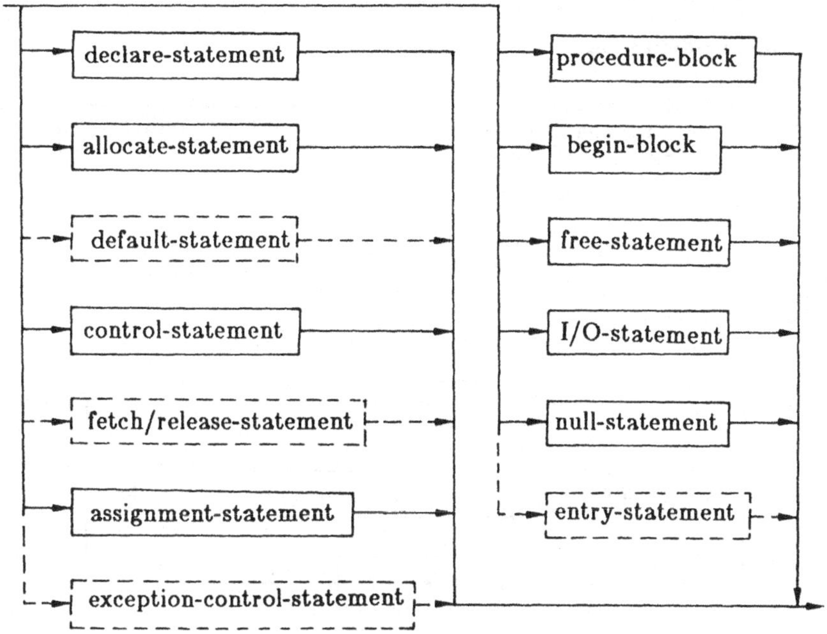

variable

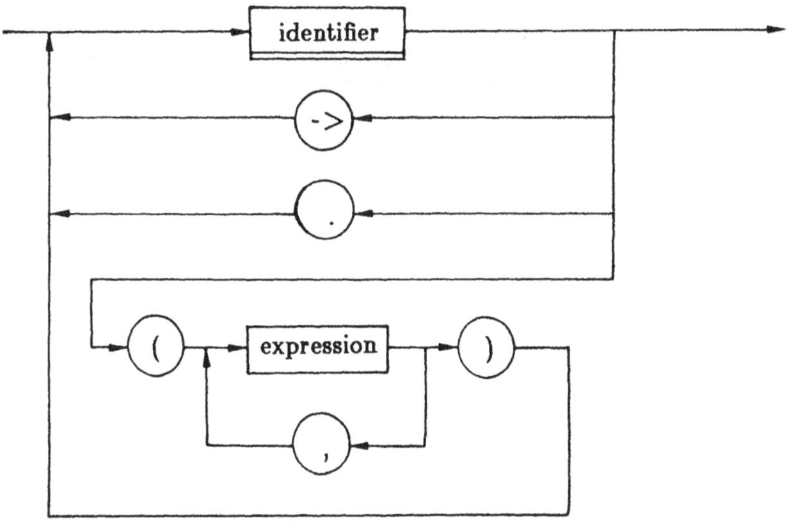

Ada

Start symbol is compilation

access-type-definition

actual-parameter

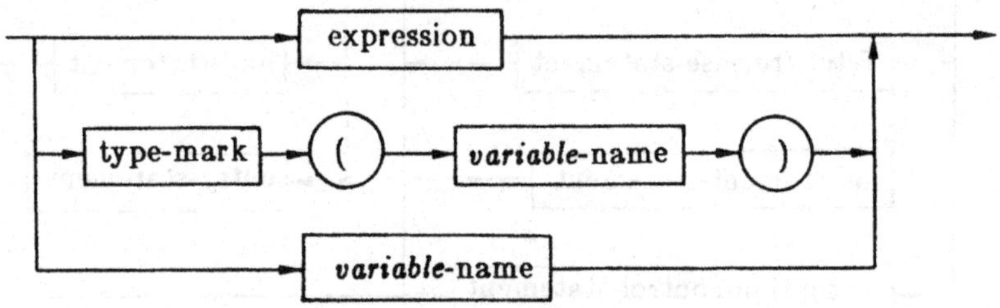

actual-parameter-part

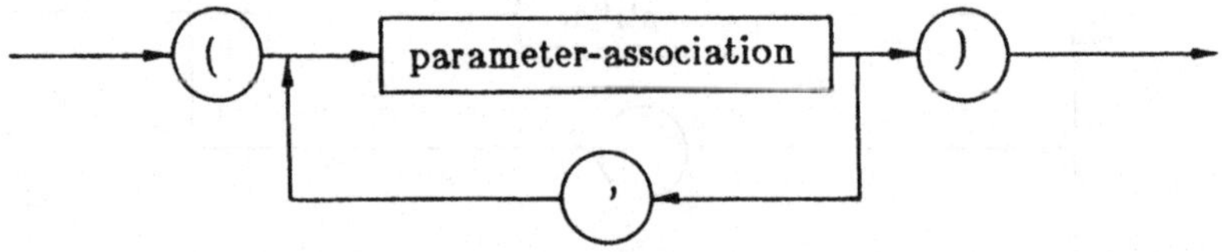

aggregate

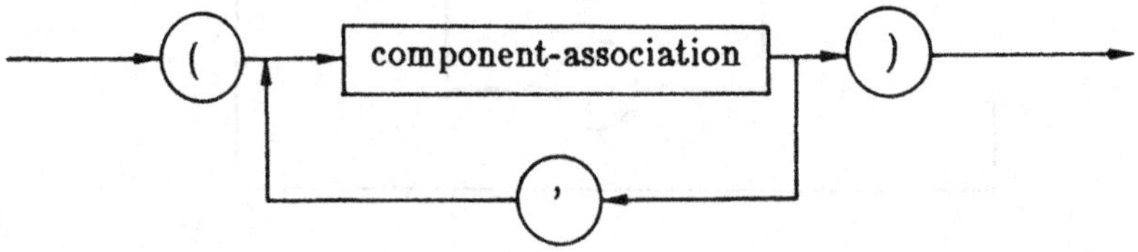

allocator

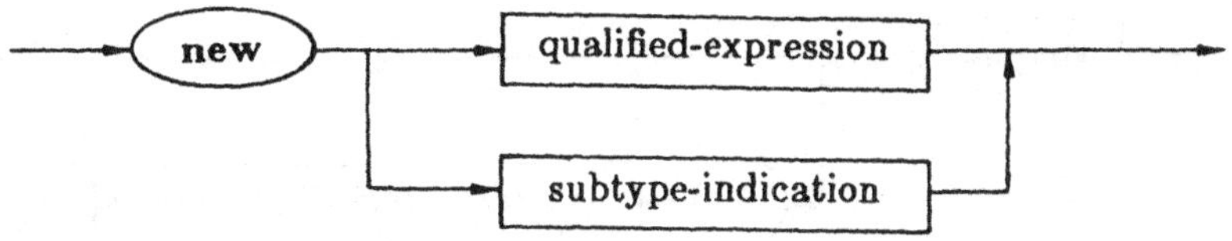

argument-association

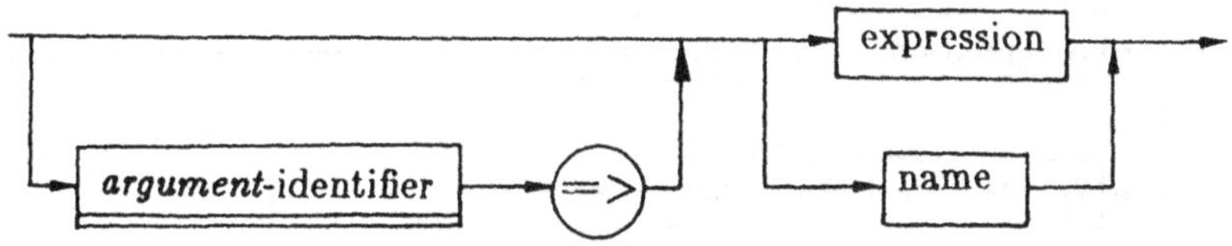

array-type-definition

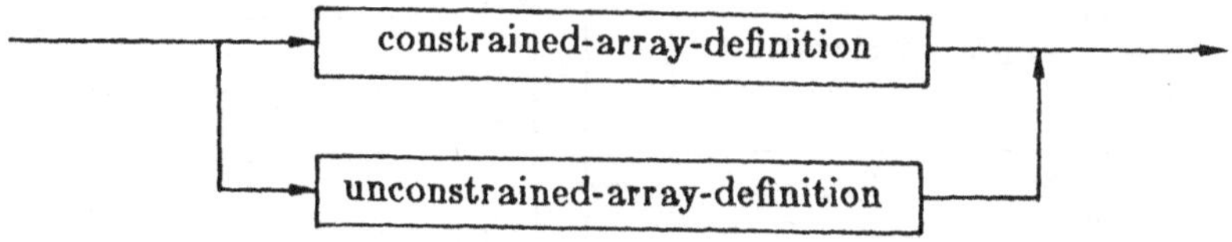

assignment-statement

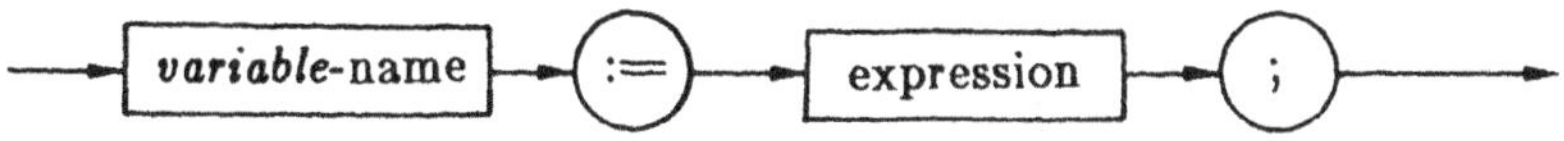

attribute

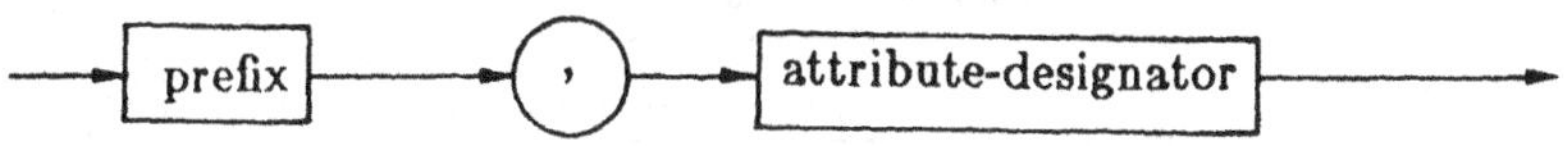

attribute-designator

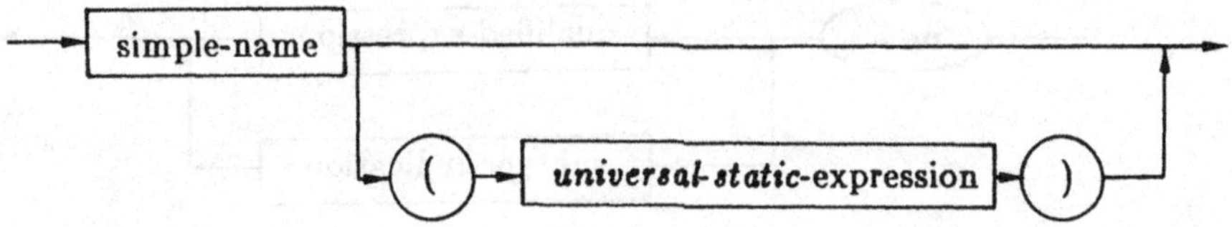

basic-declaration

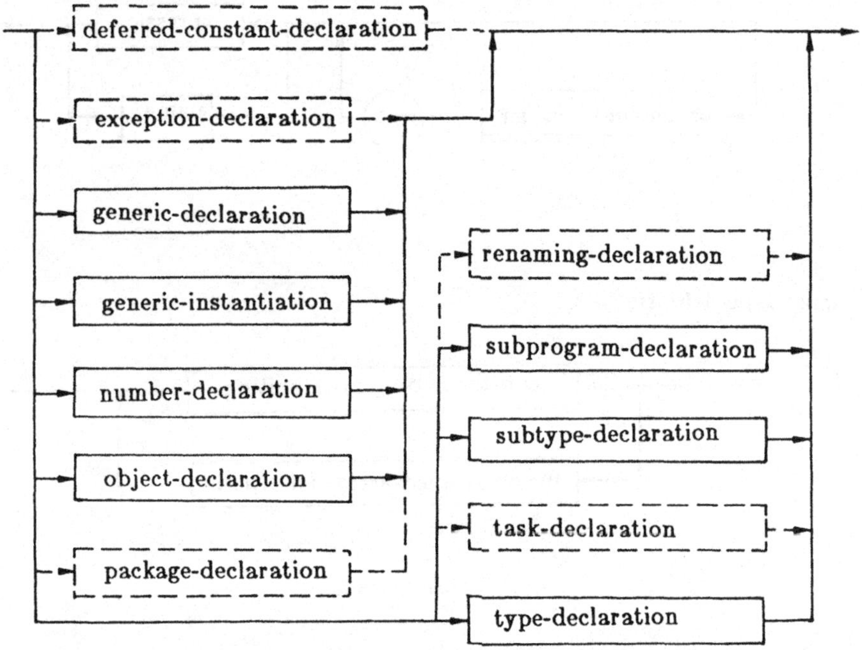

basic-declarative-item

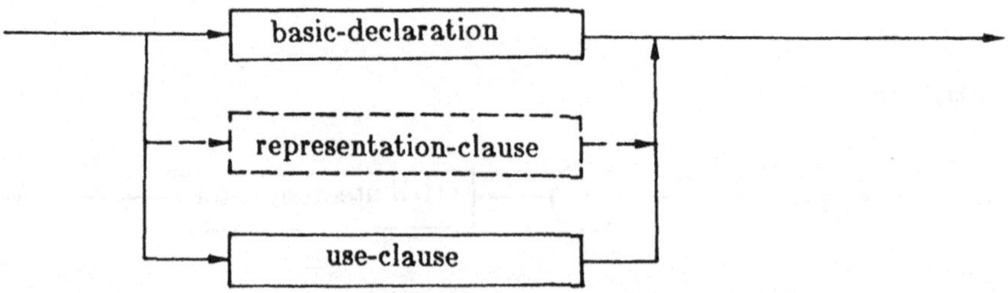

binary-adding-operator

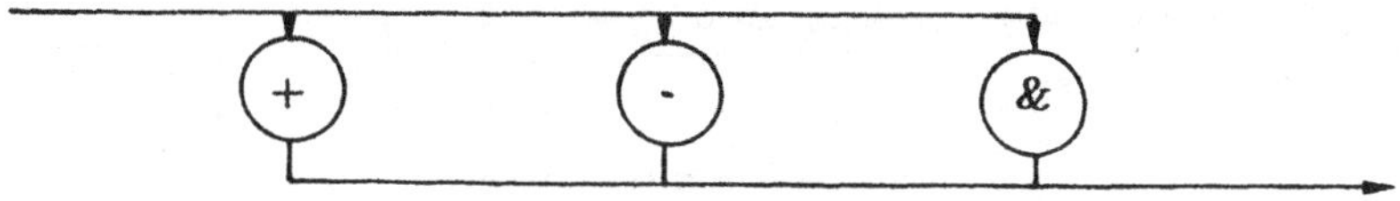

block-statement

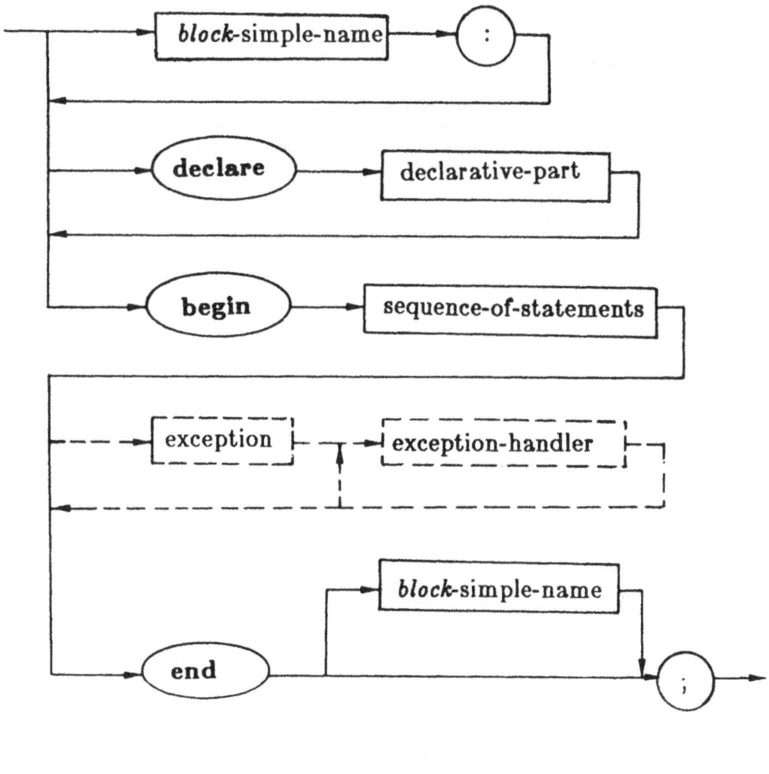

body

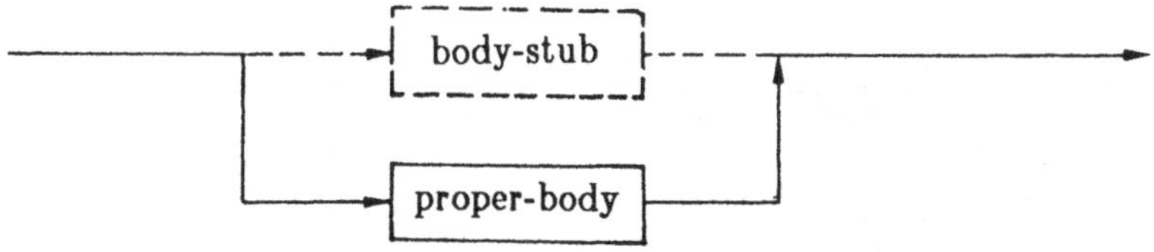

case-statement

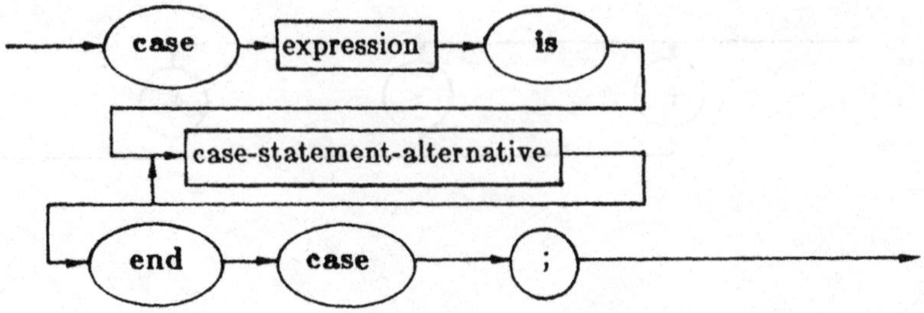

case-statement-alternative

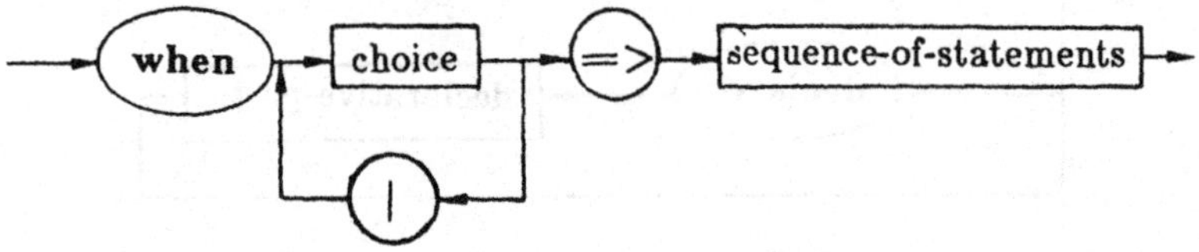

character-literal

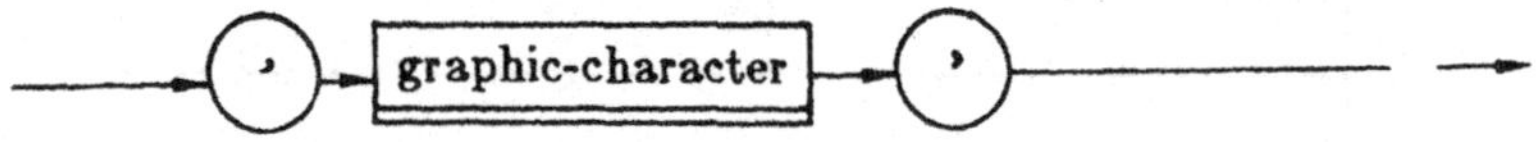

choice

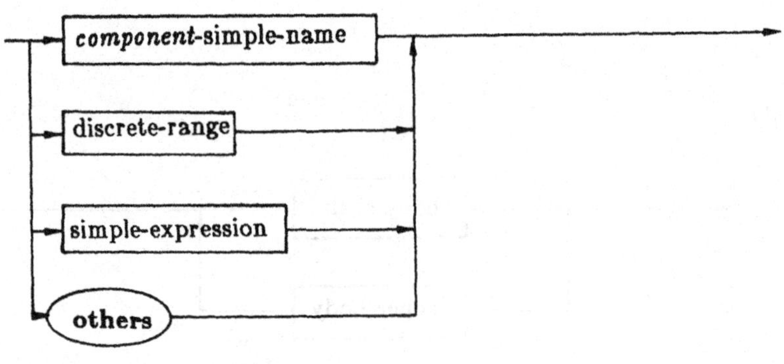

compilation

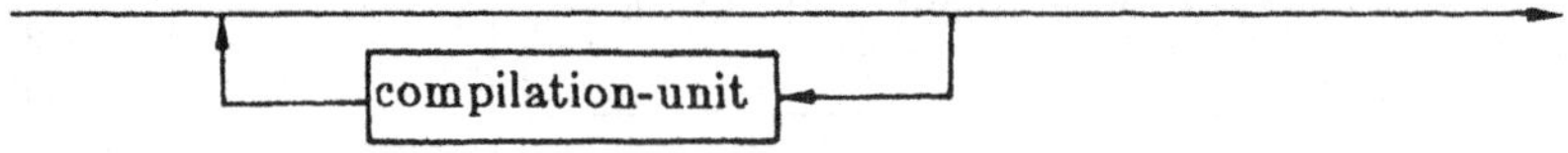

compilation-unit

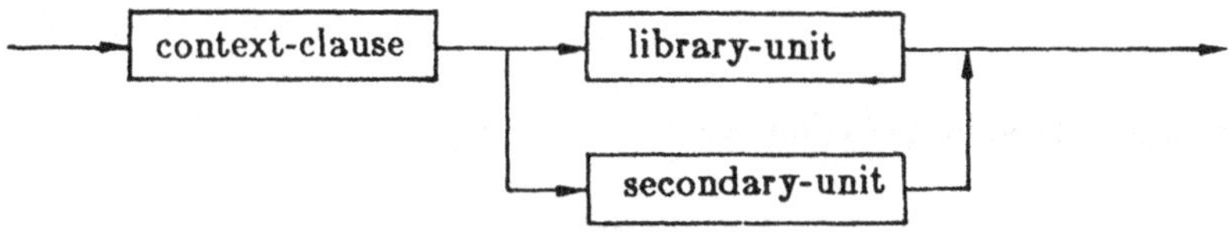

component-association

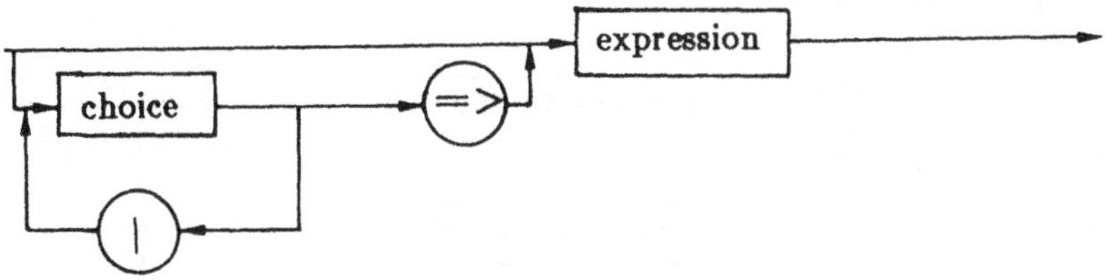

component-declaration

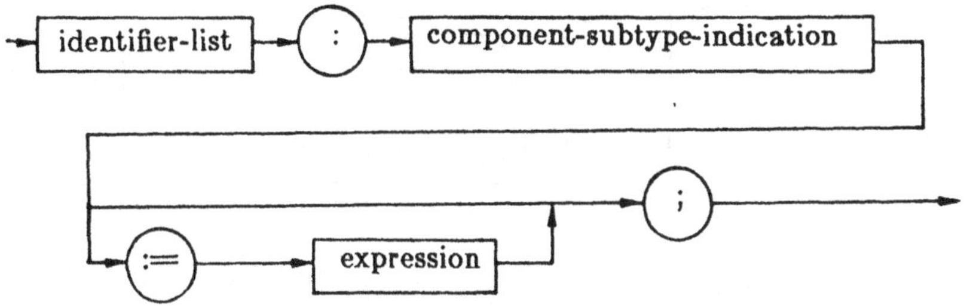

component-list

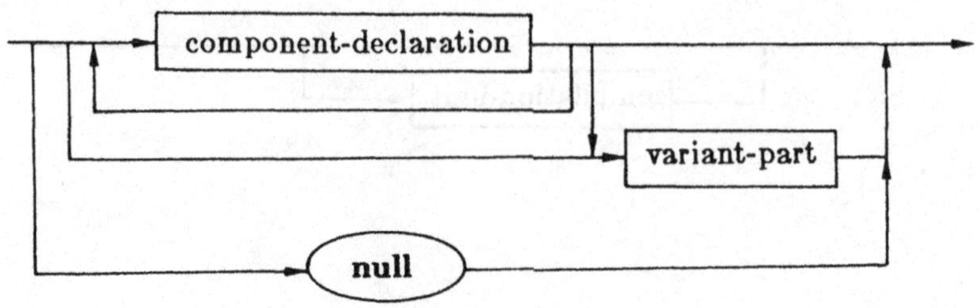

component-subtype-definition

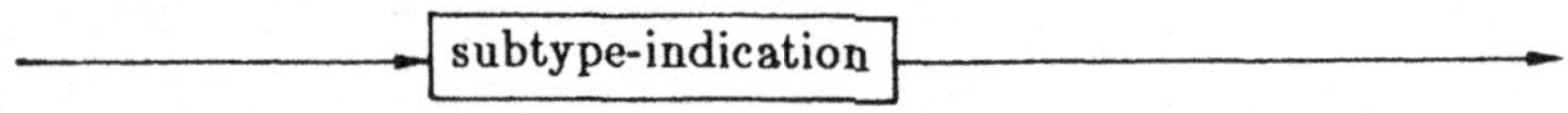

compound-statement

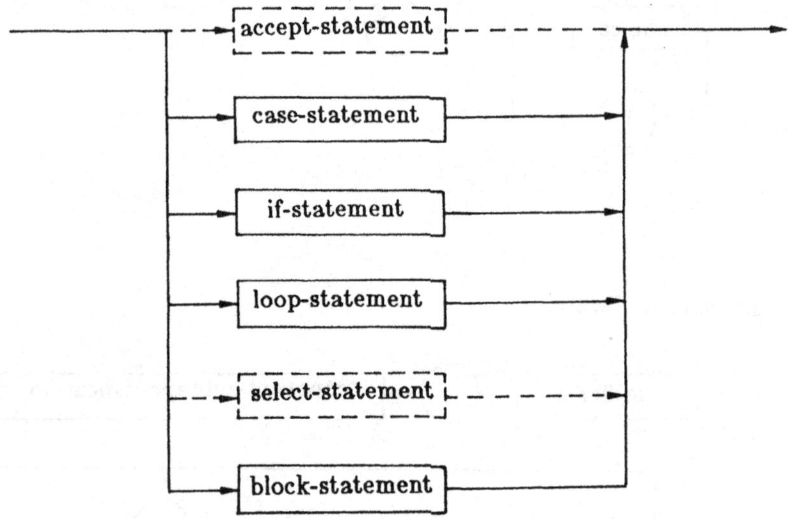

condition

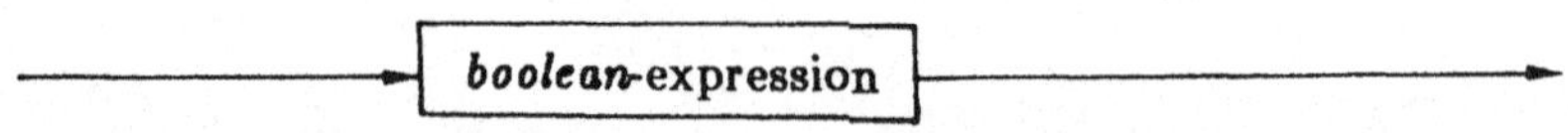

constrained-array-definition

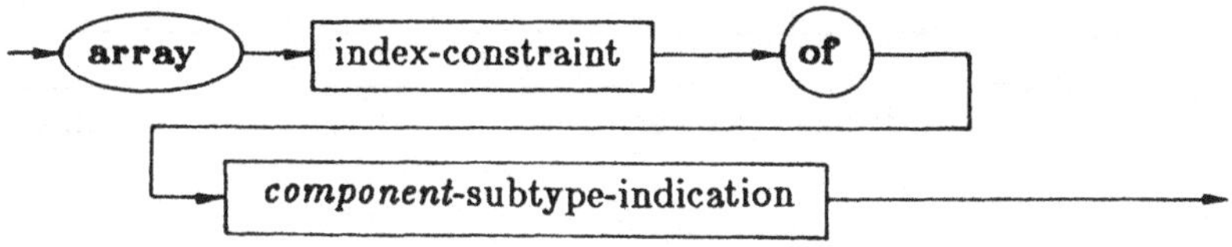

constraint

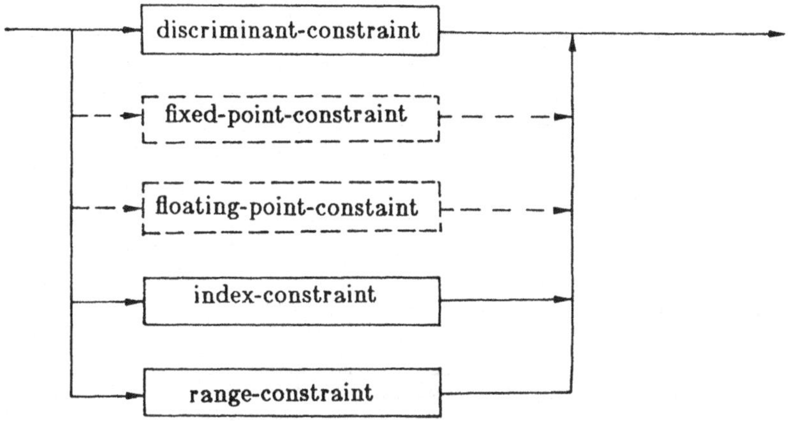

context-clause

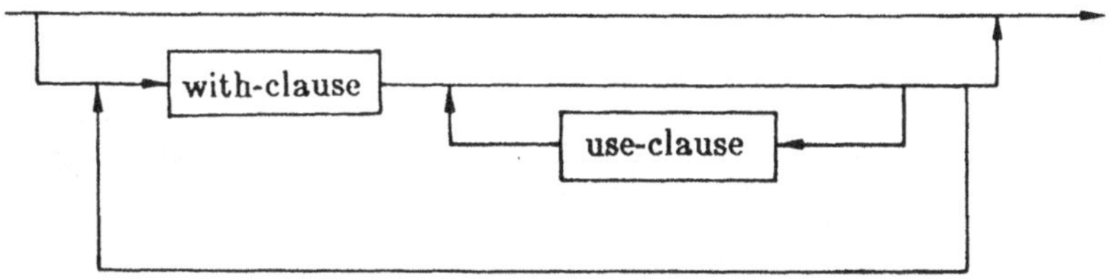

decimal-literal

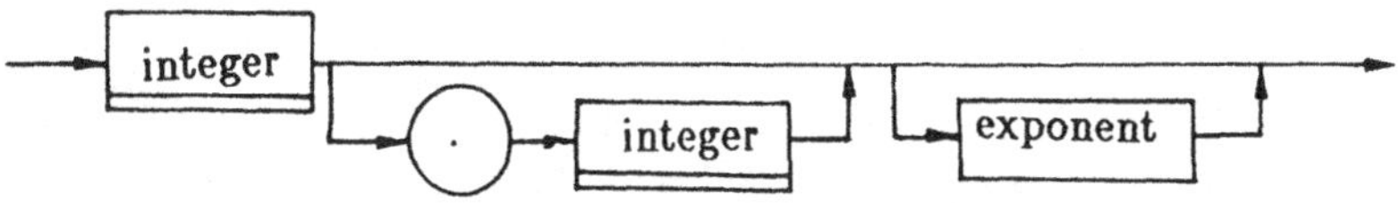

declarative-part

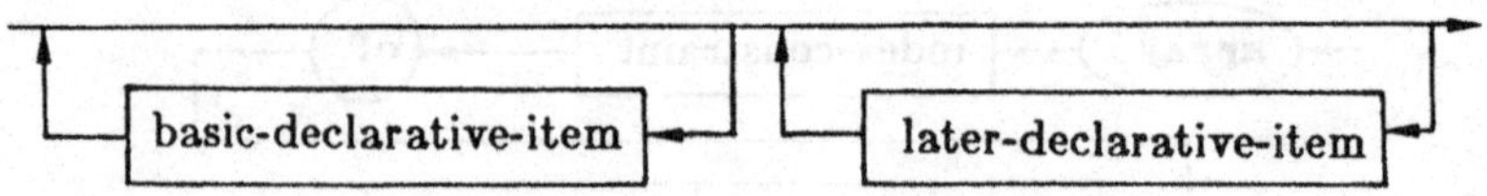

designator

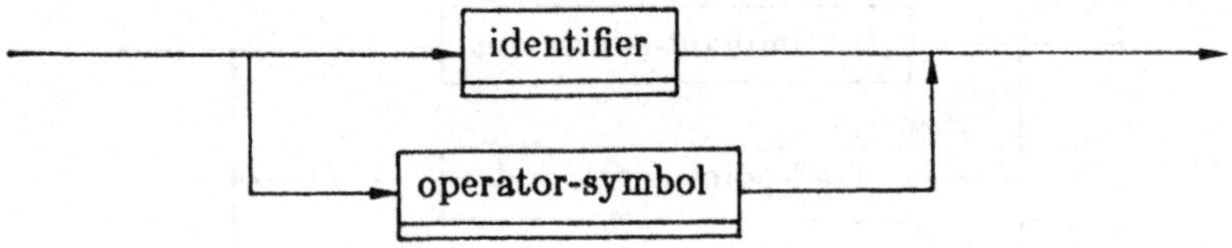

discrete-range

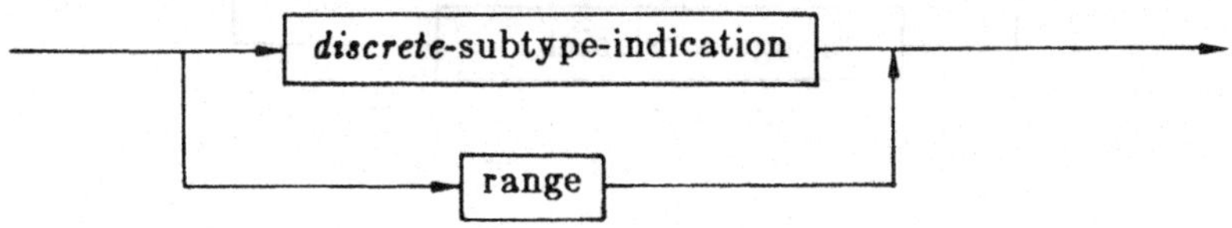

discriminant-association

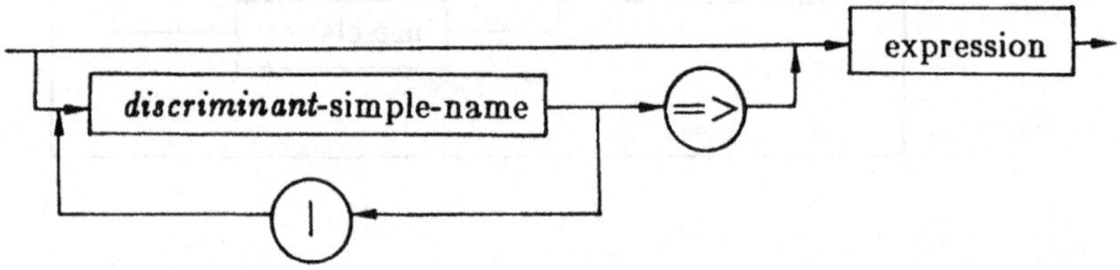

discriminant-constraint

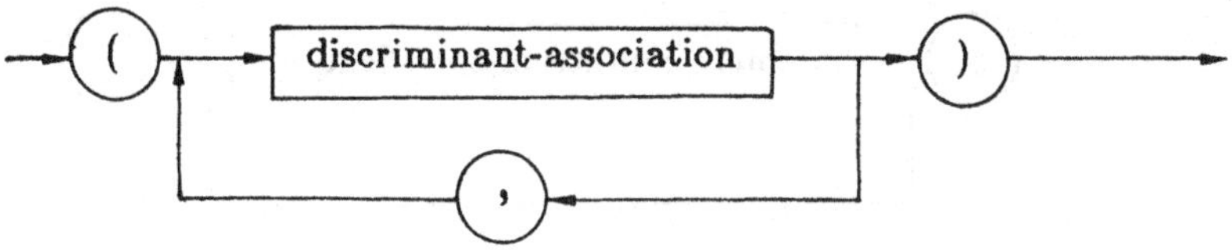

discriminant-specification

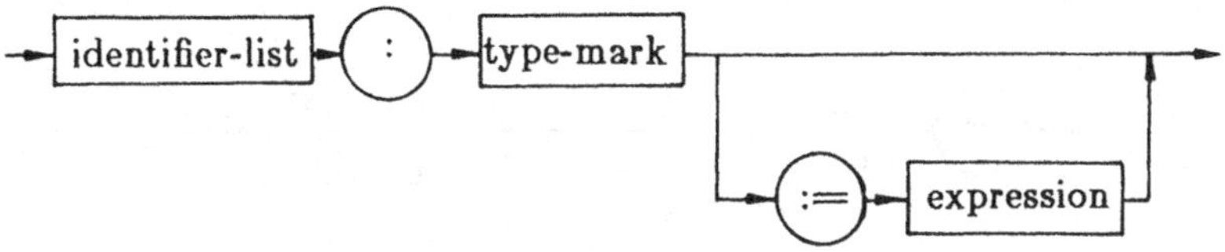

discriminant-part

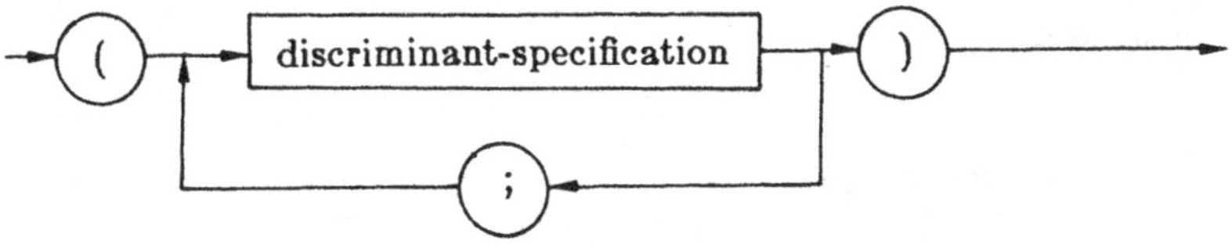

enumeration-literal

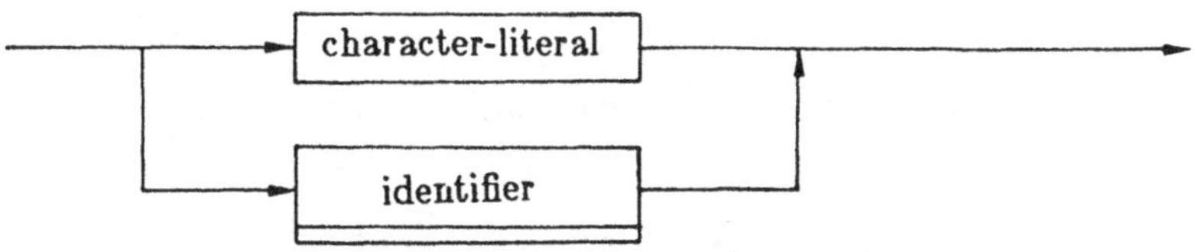

enumeration-literal-specification

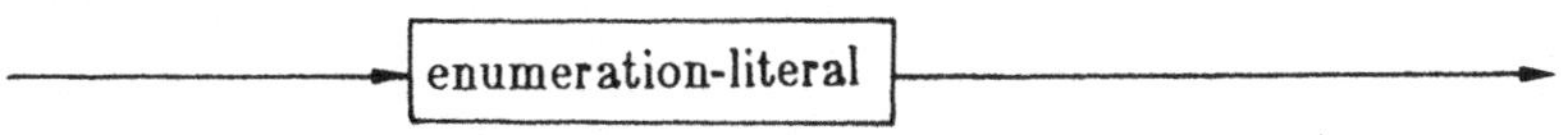

enumeration-type-definition

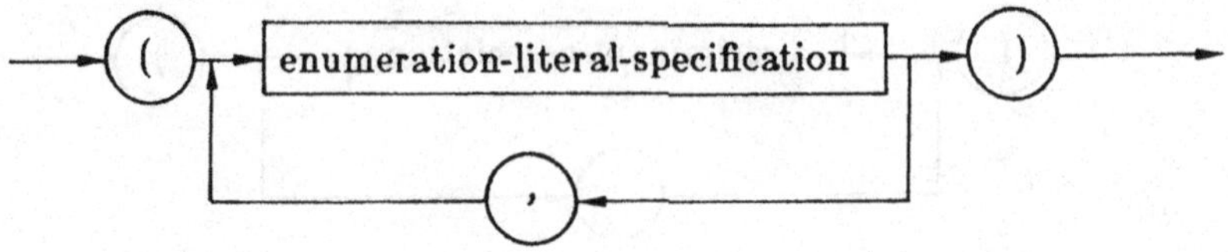

exponent

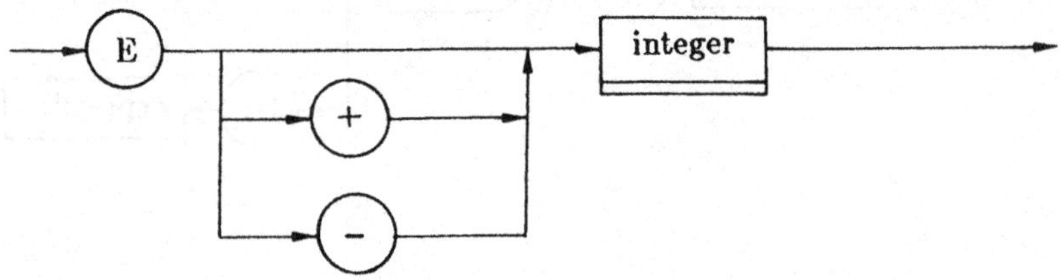

expression

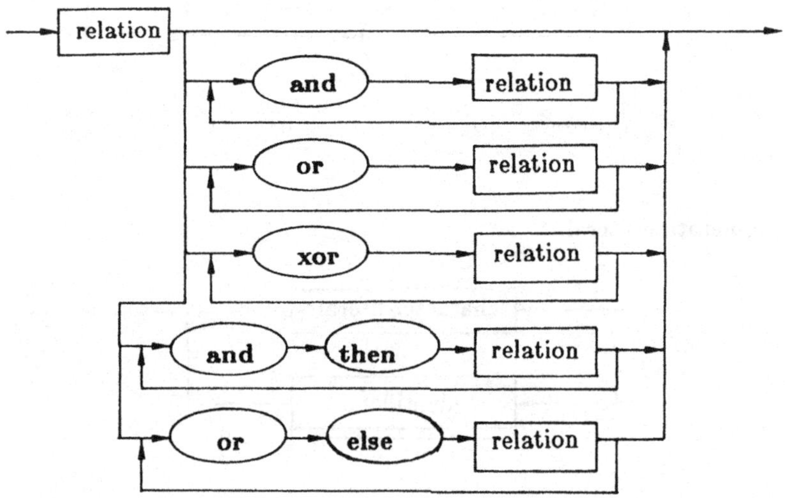

factor

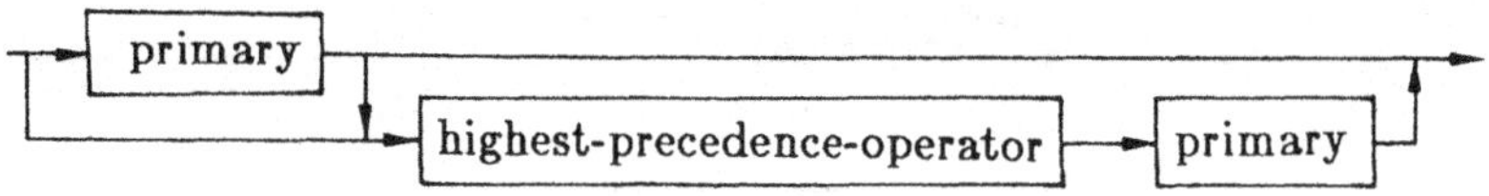

formal-parameter

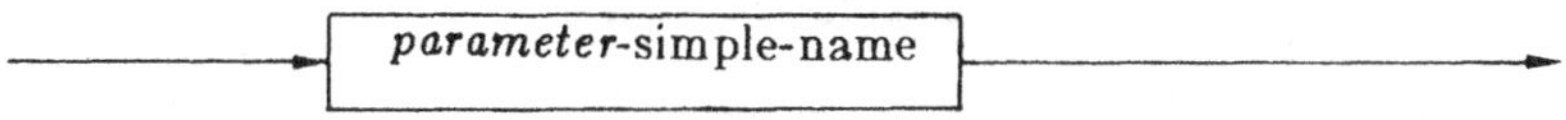

formal-part

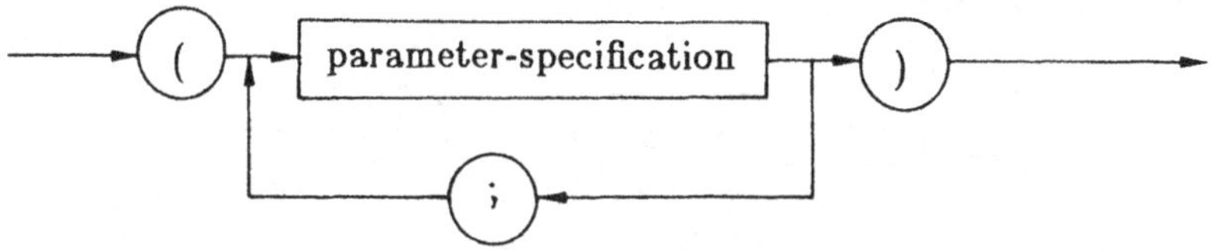

full-type-declaration

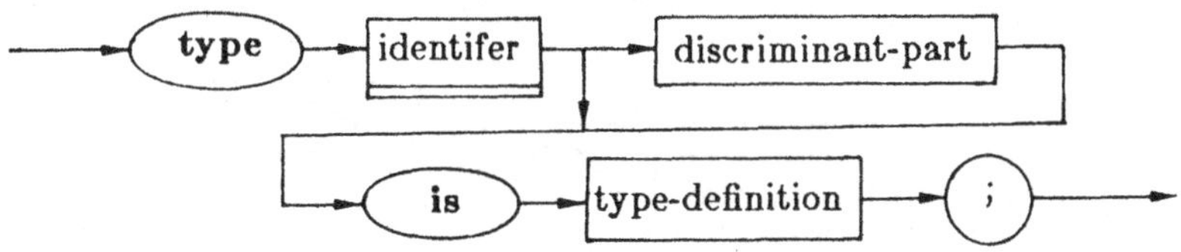

function-call

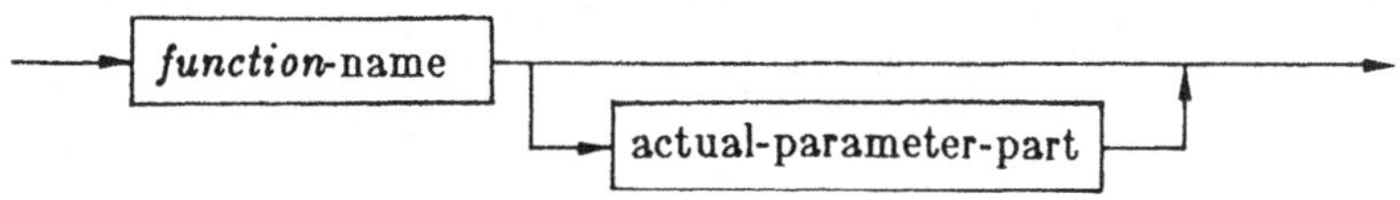

generic-actual-parameter

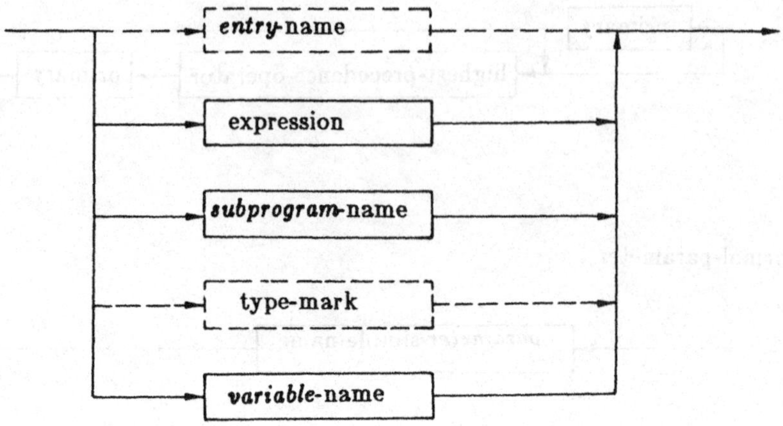

generic-actual-part

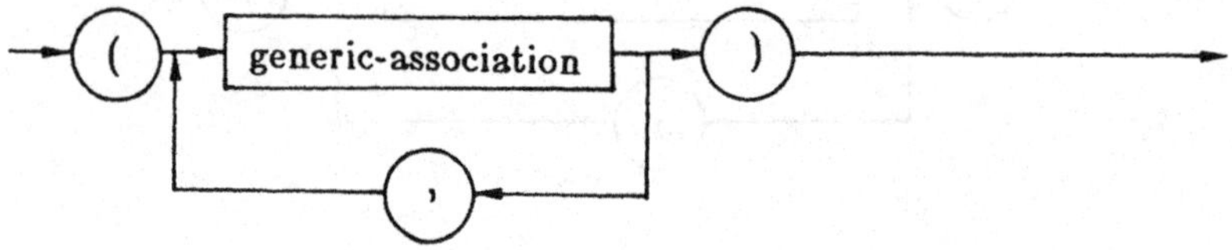

generic-association

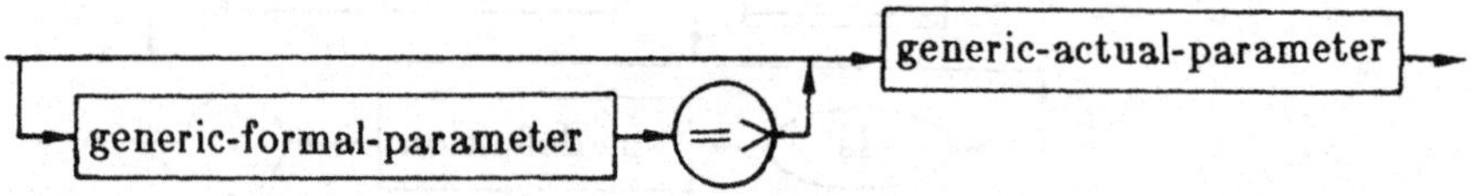

generic-declaration

generic-formal-parameter

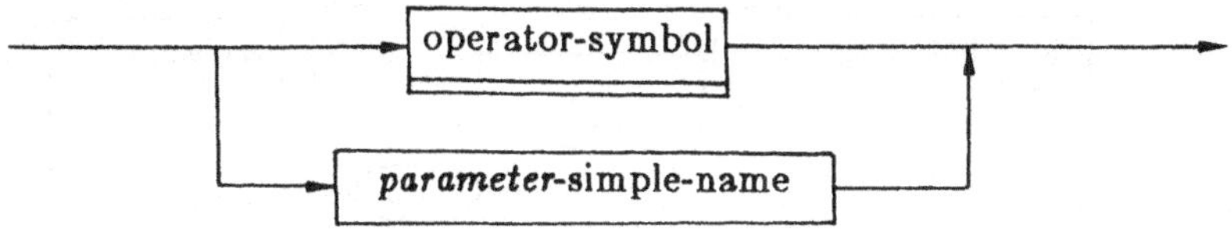

generic-formal-part

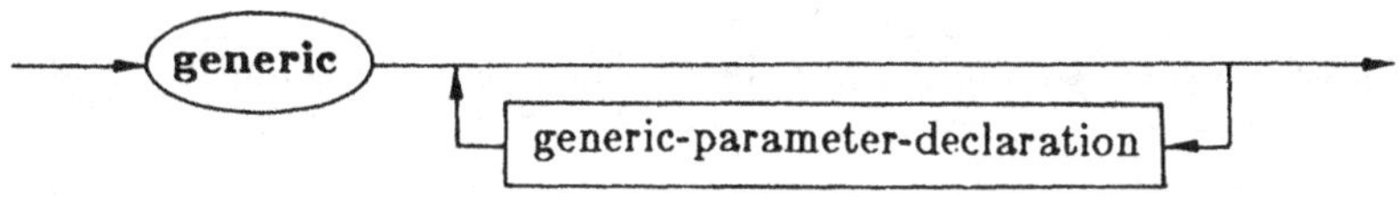

generic-instantiation

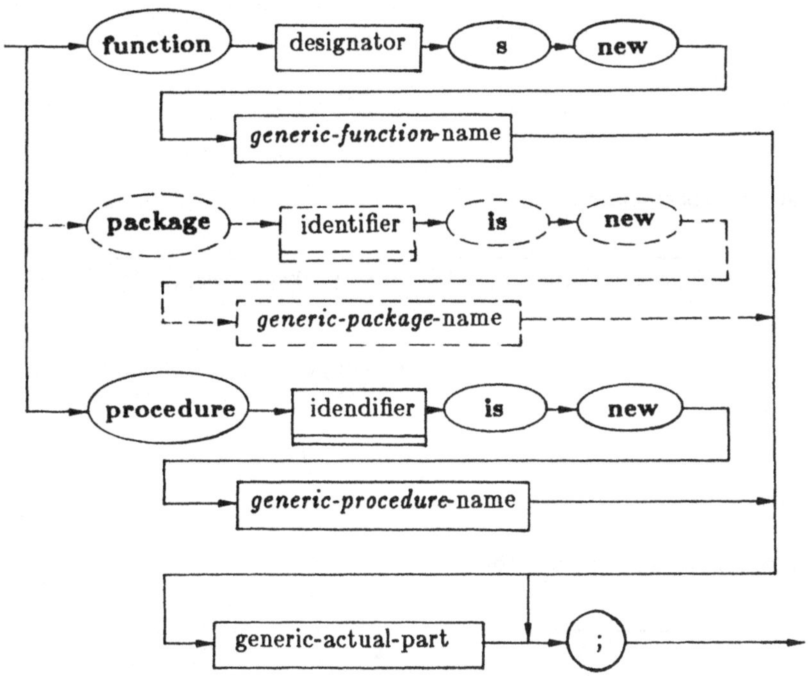

generic-parameter-declaration

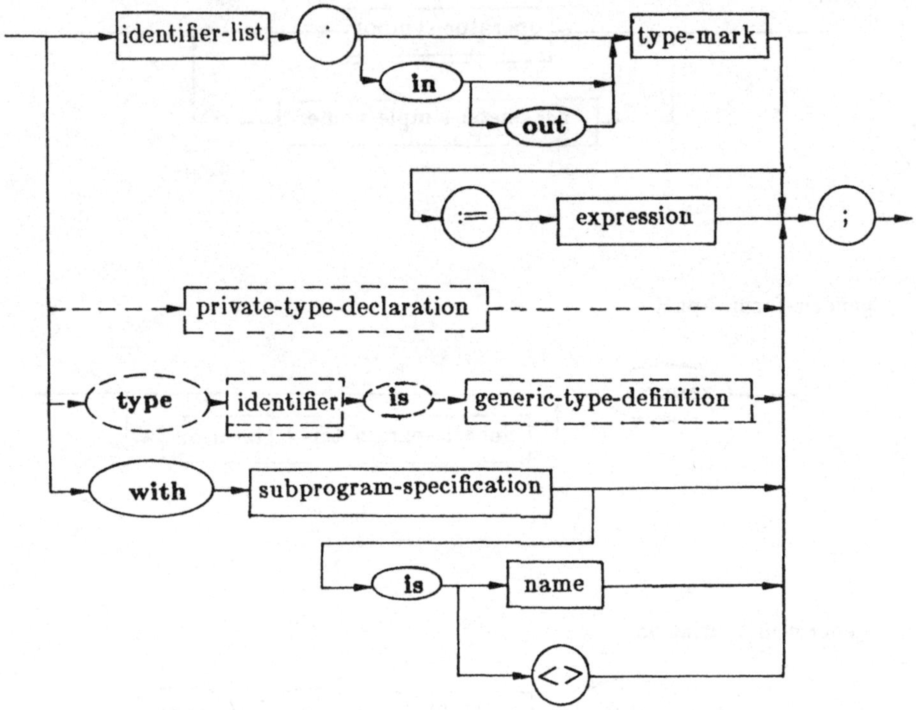

generic-specification

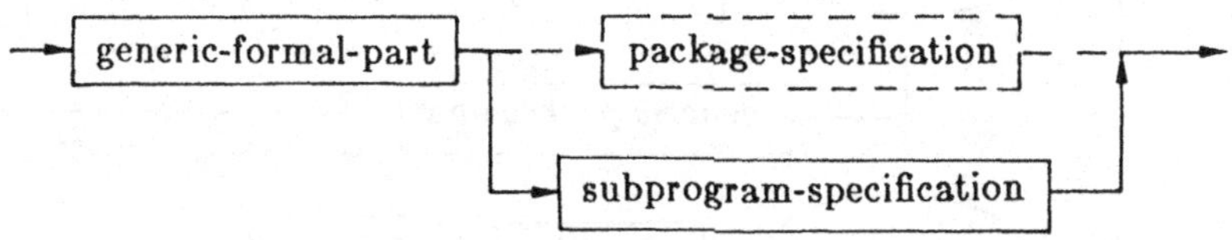

highest-precedence-operator

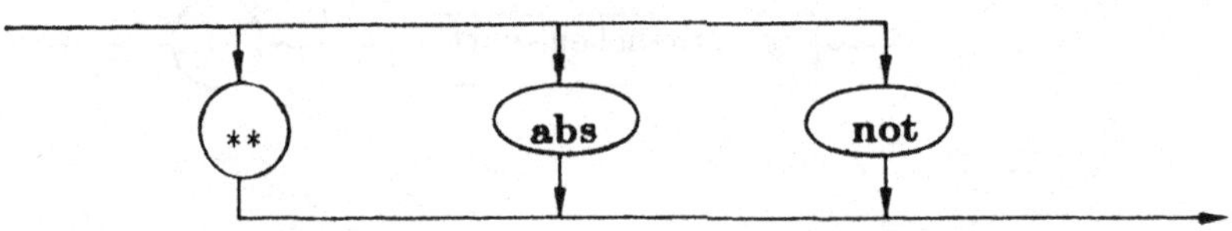

identifier-list

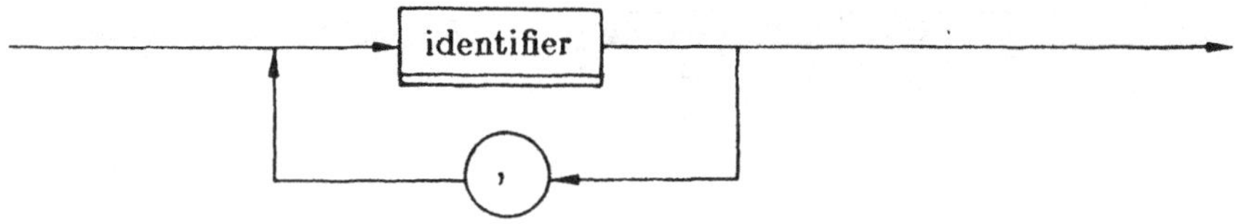

if-statement

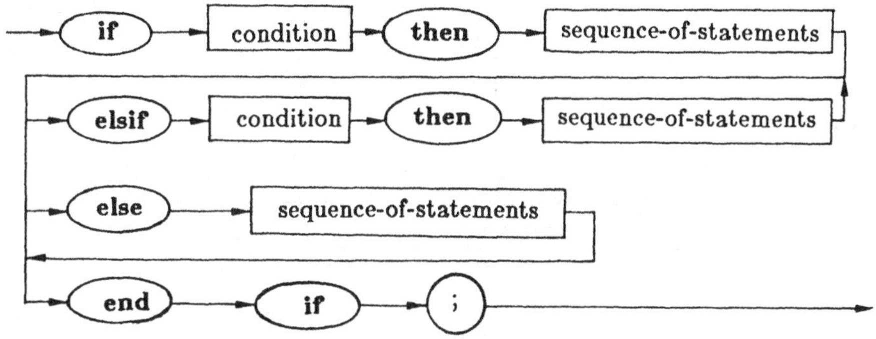

incomplete-type-declaration

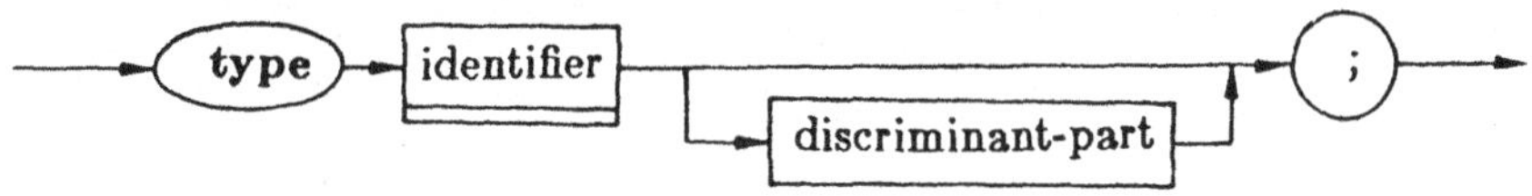

index-constraint

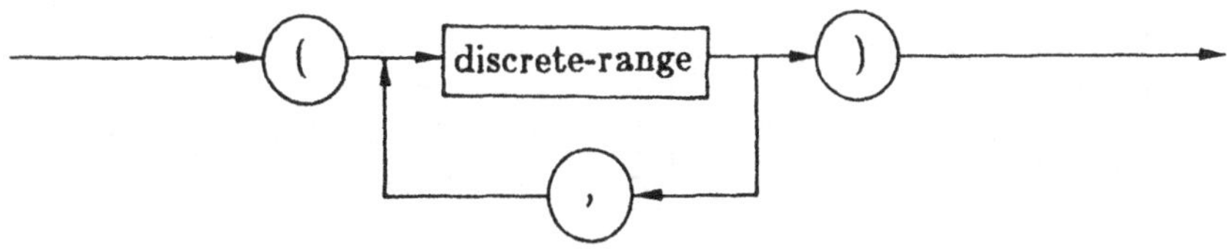

index-subtype-definition

indexed-component

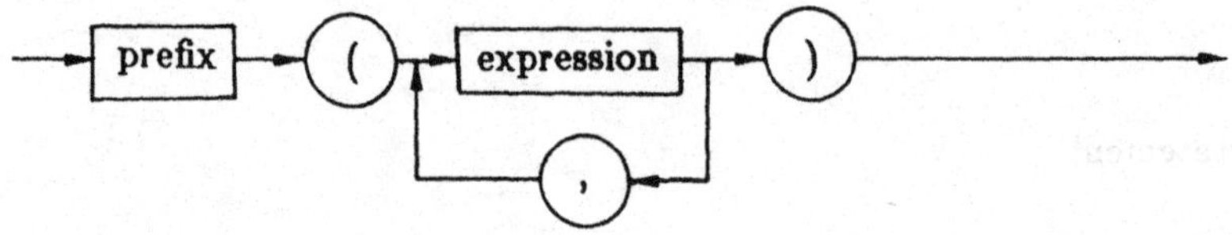

integer-type-definition

iteration-scheme

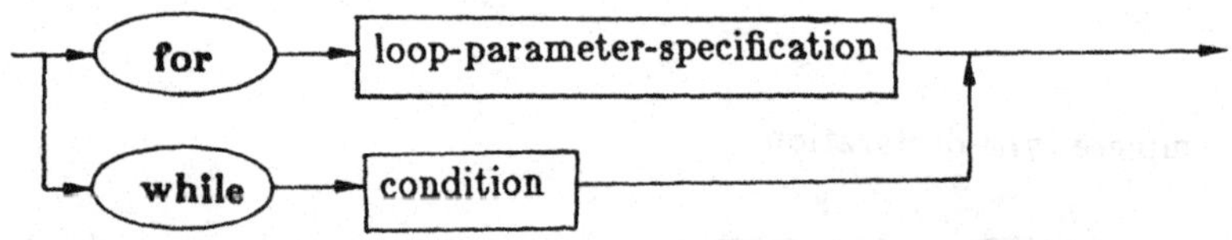

later-declarative-item

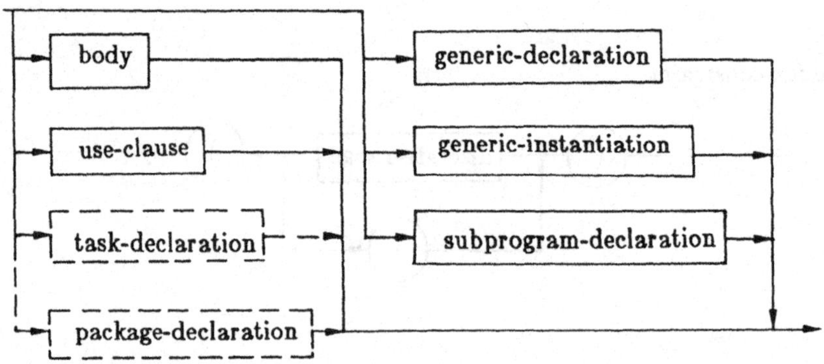

library-unit

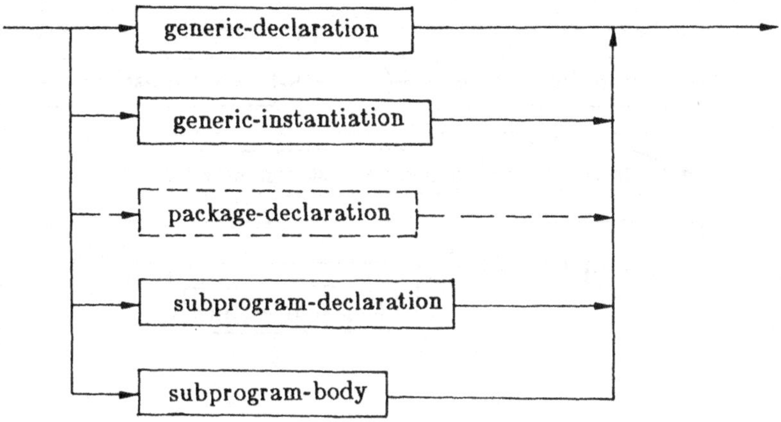

library-unit-body

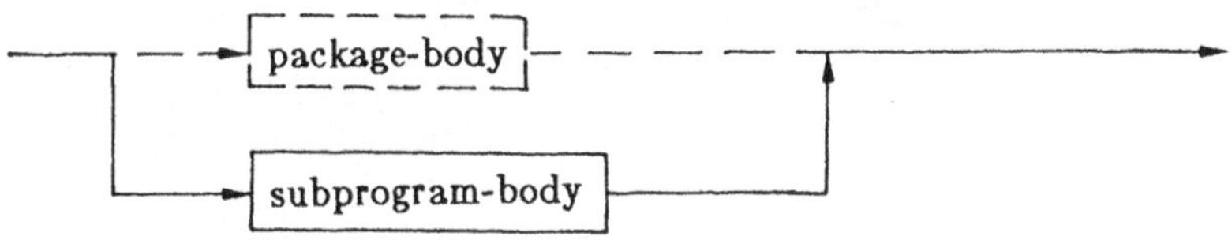

logical-operator

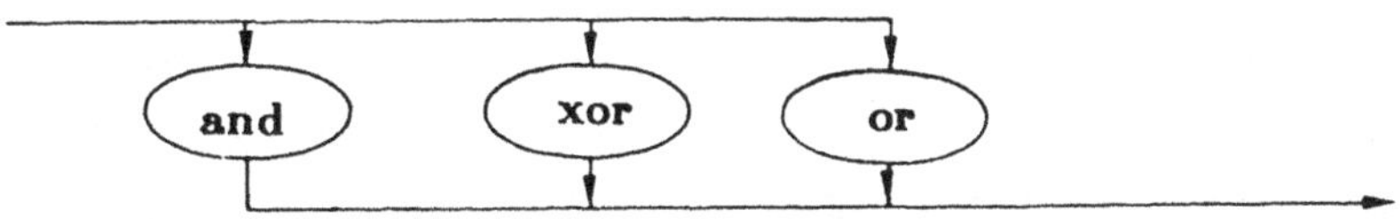

loop-parameter-specification

loop-statement

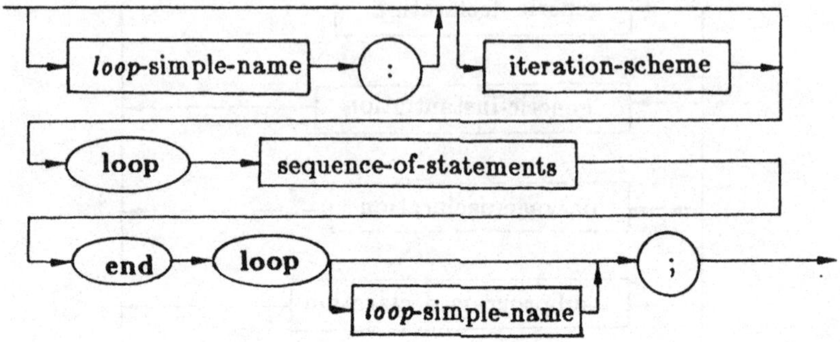

mode

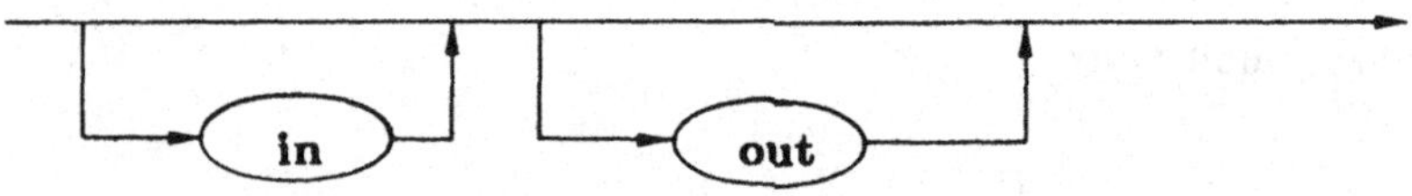

multiplying-operator

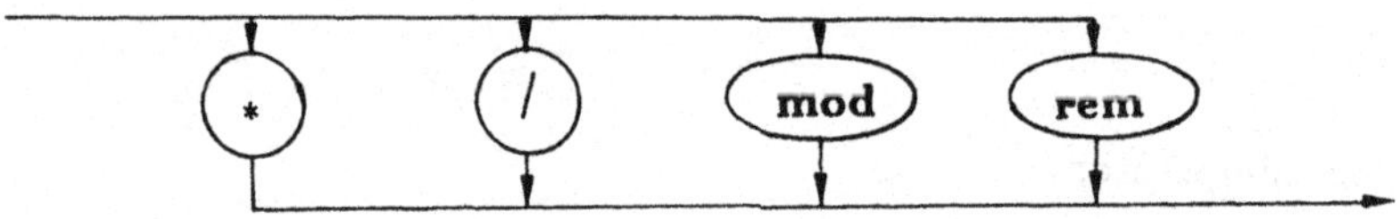

name

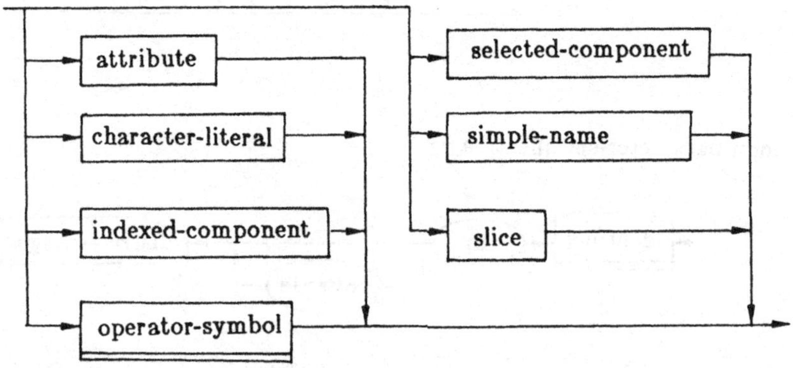

null-statement

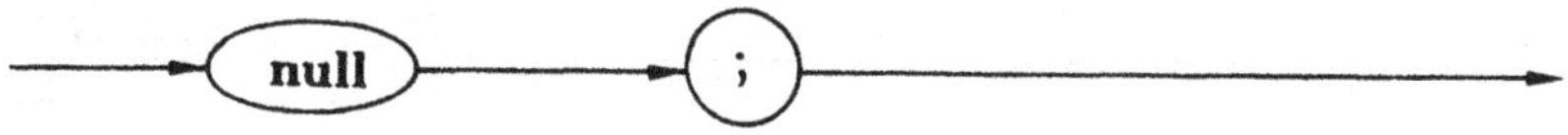

number-declaration

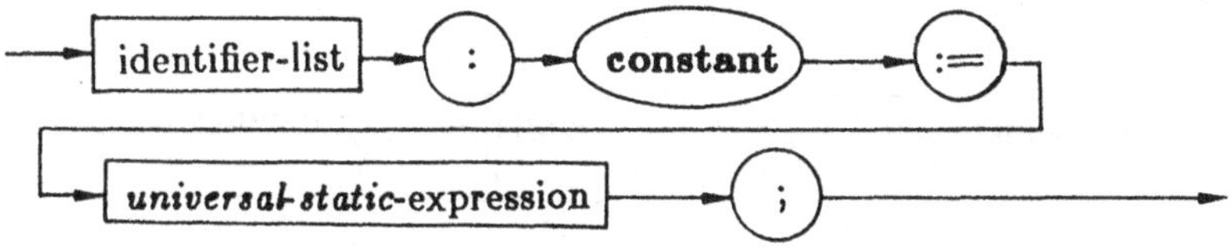

numeric-literal

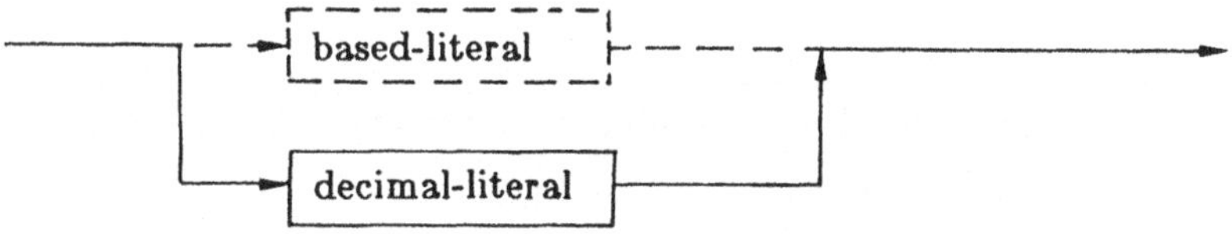

object-declaration

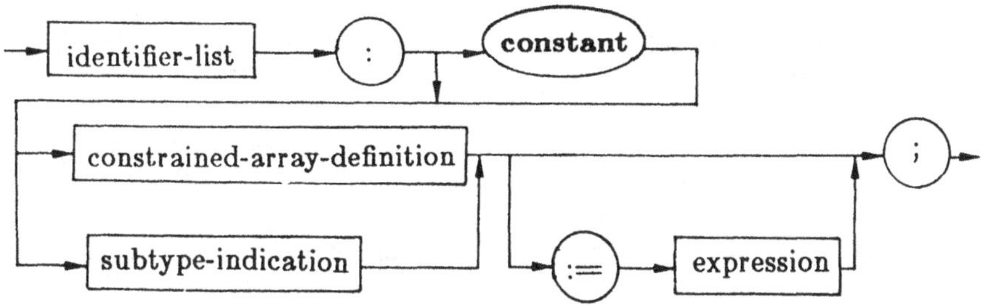

parameter-association

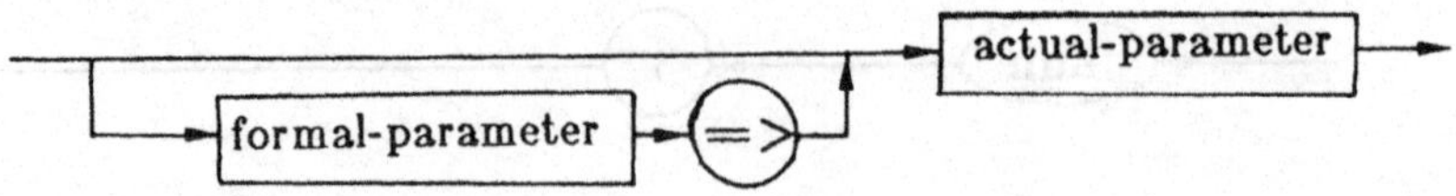

parameter-specification

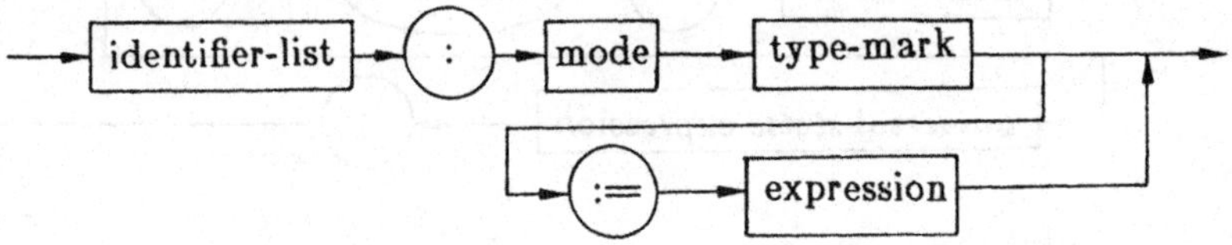

prefix

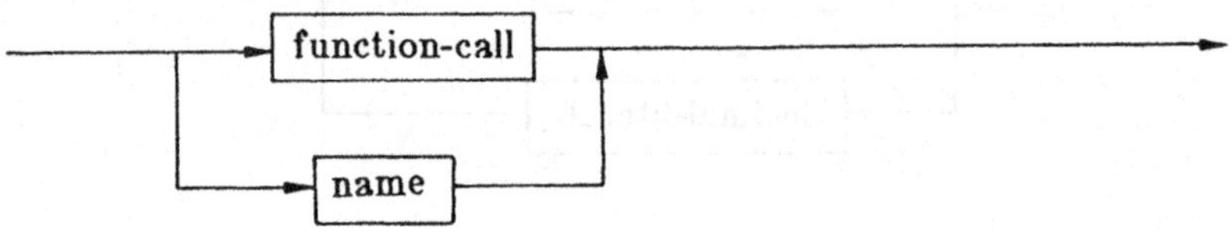

primary

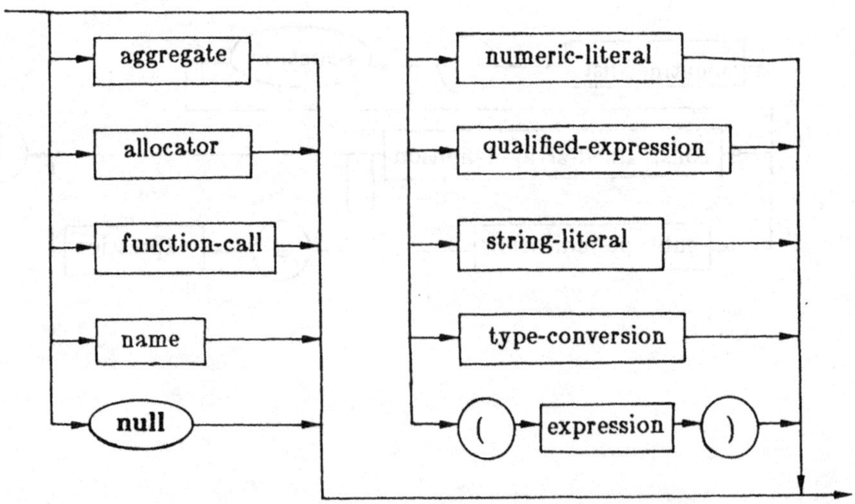

procedure-call-statement

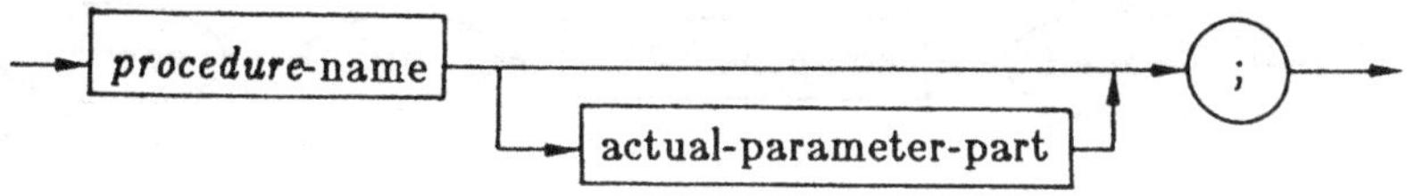

proper-body

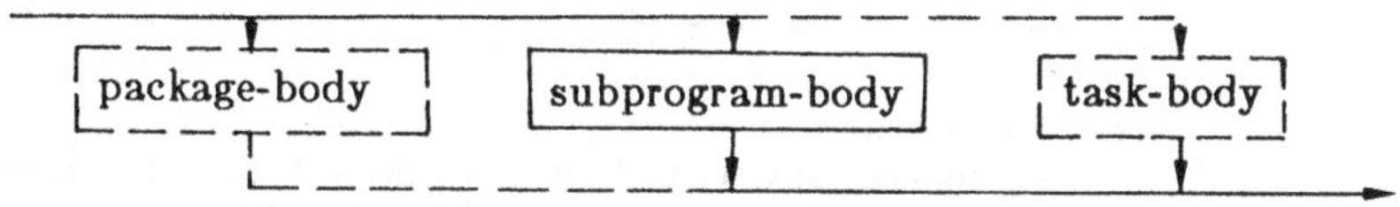

qualified-expression

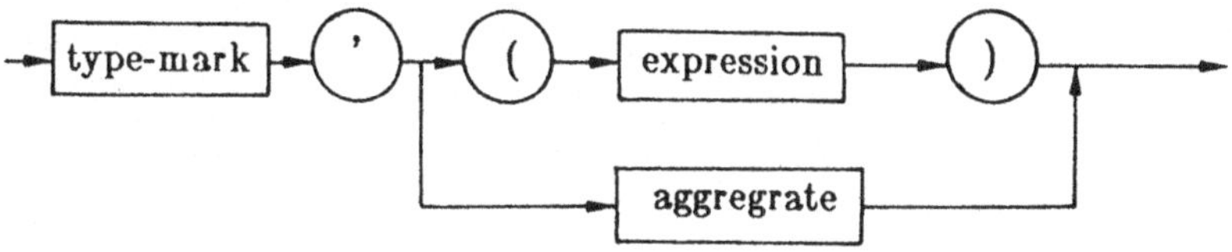

range

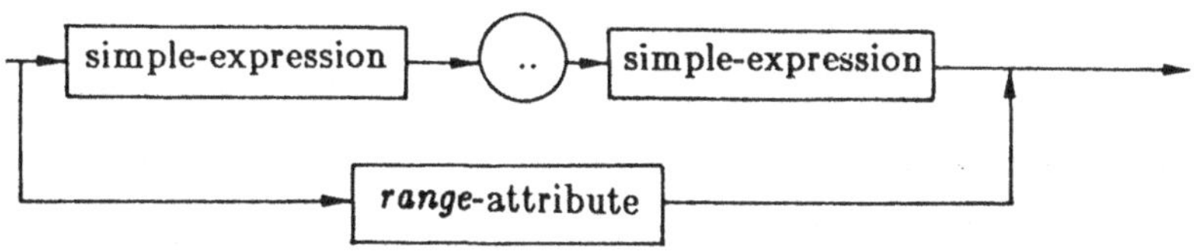

range-constraint

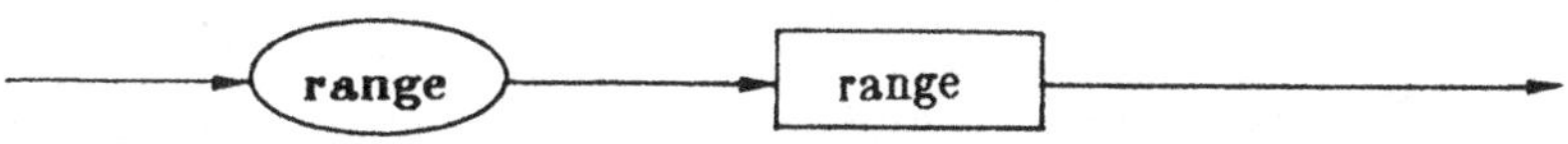

record-type-definition

relation

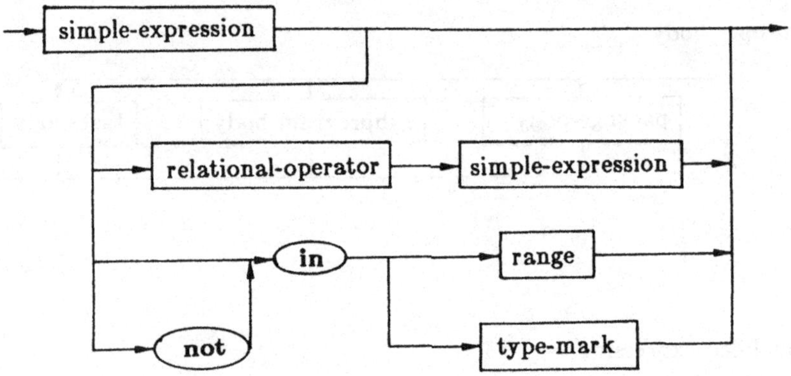

relational-operator

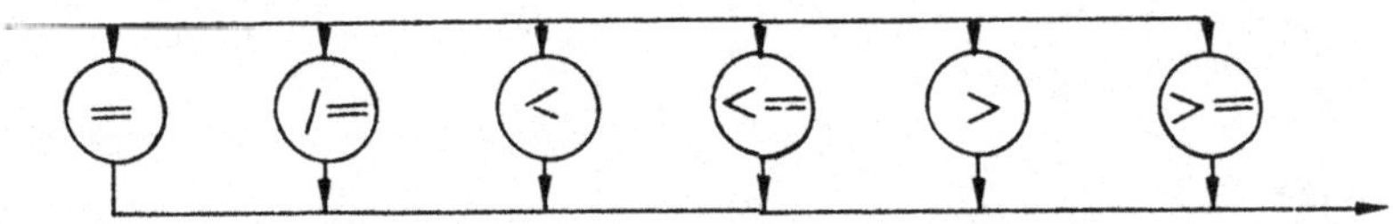

return-statement

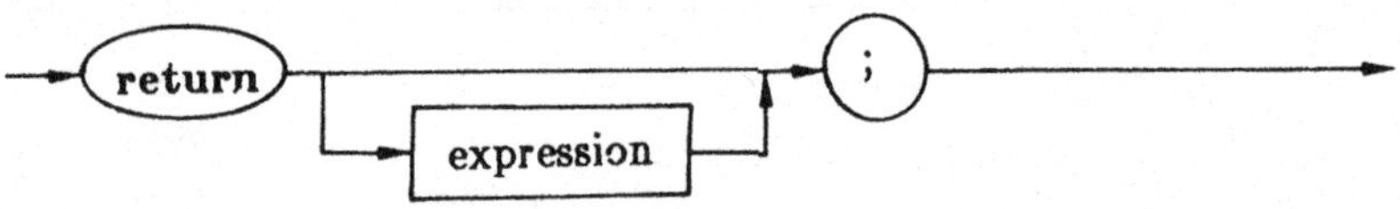

secondary-unit

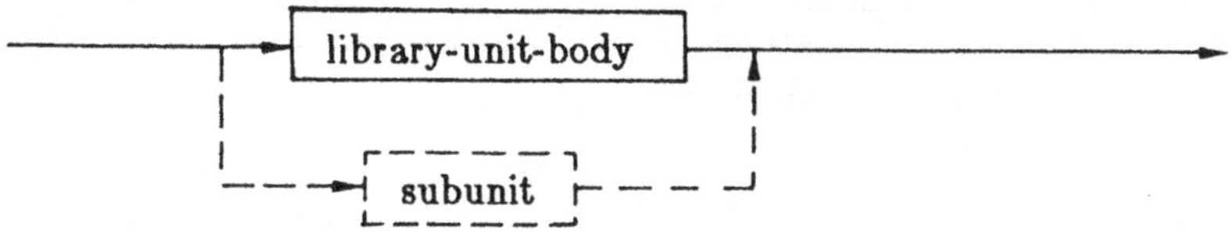

selected-component

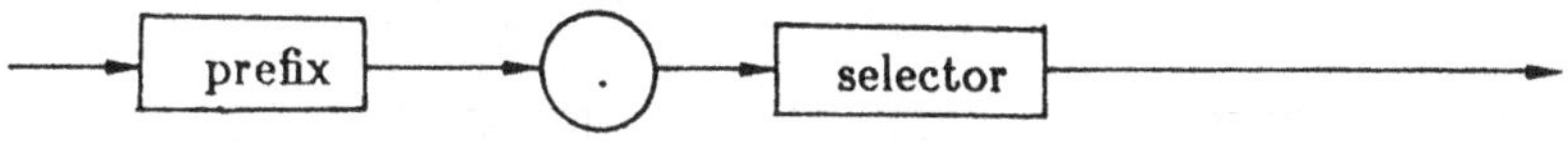

selector

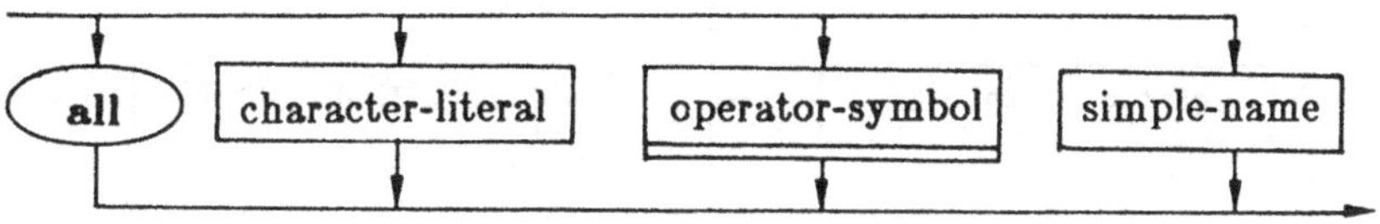

sequence-of-statements

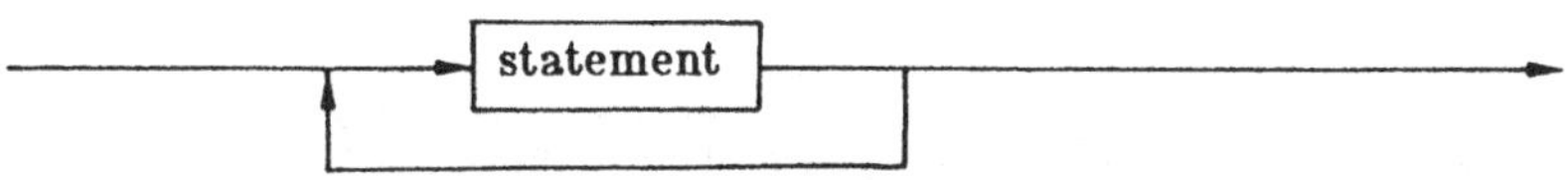

simple-expression

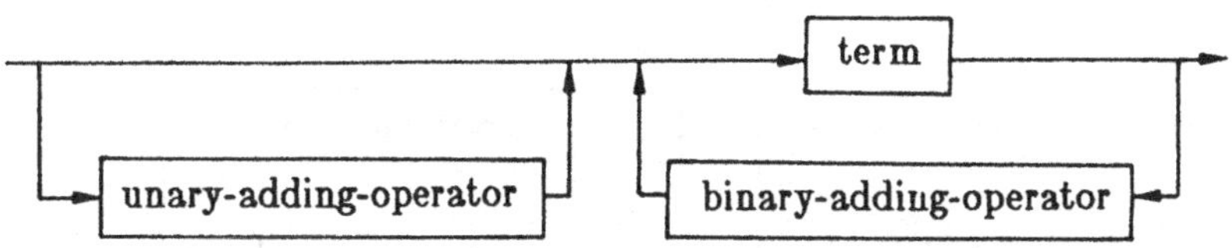

simple-name

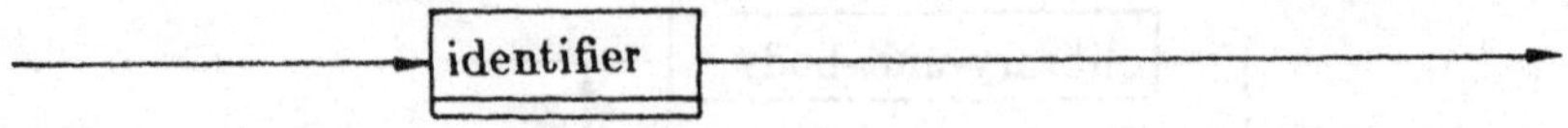

simple-statement

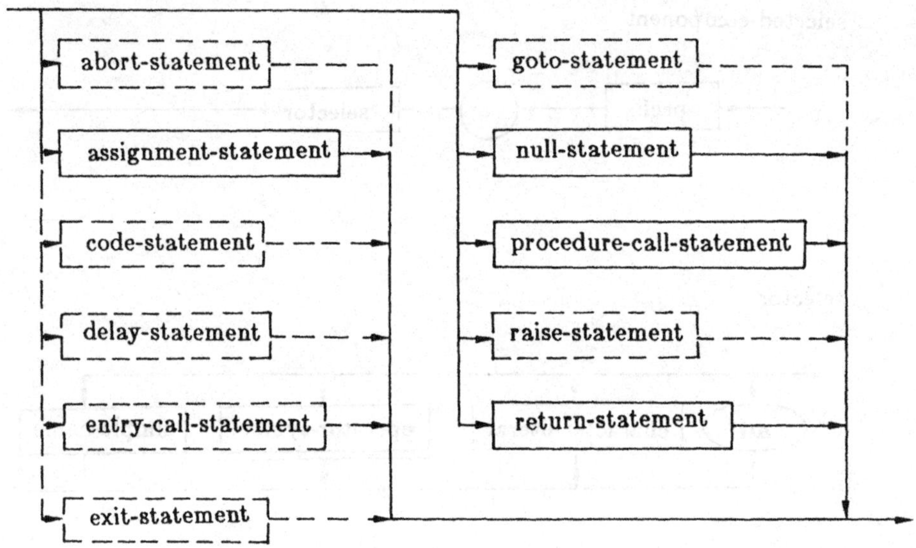

slice

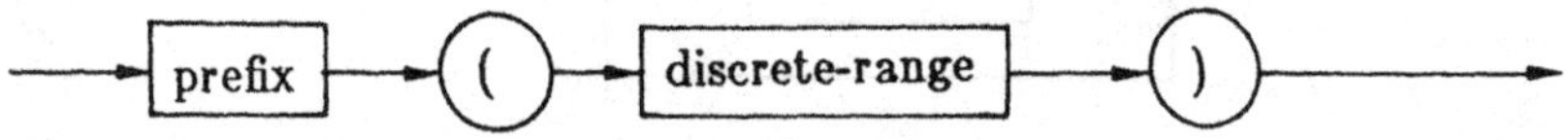

statement

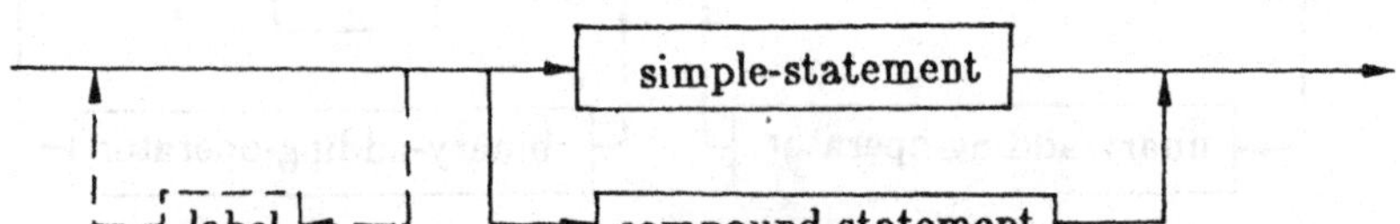

string-literal

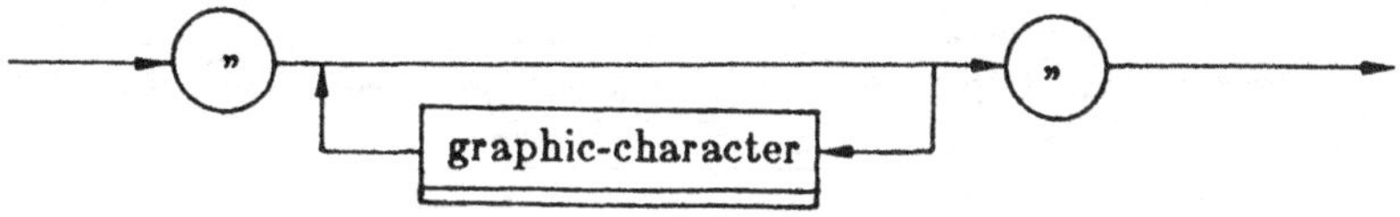

subprogram-body

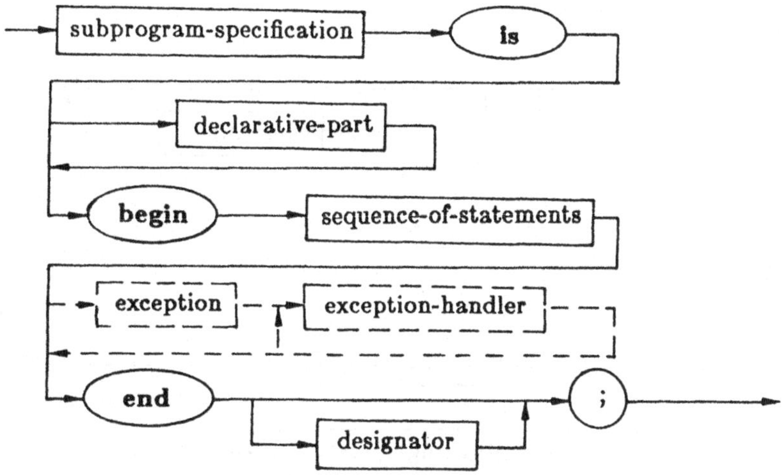

subprogram-declaration

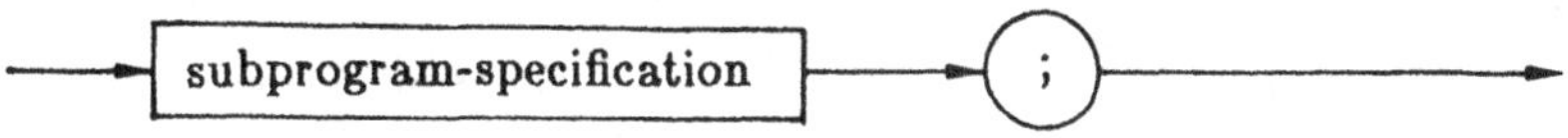

subprogram-specification

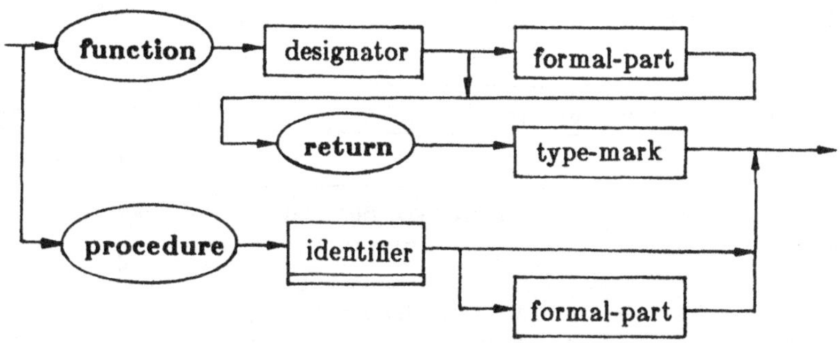

subtype-declaration

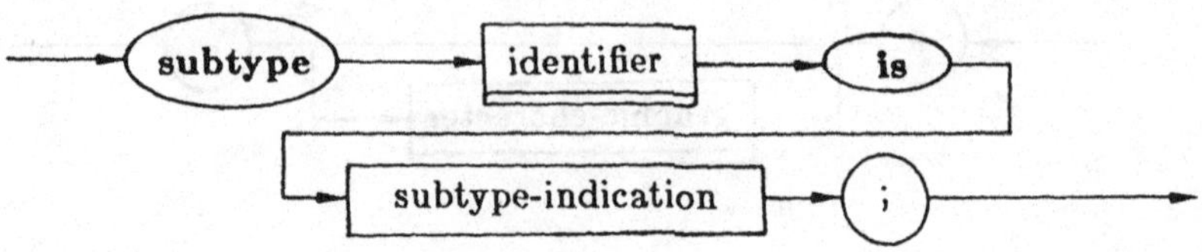

subtype-indication

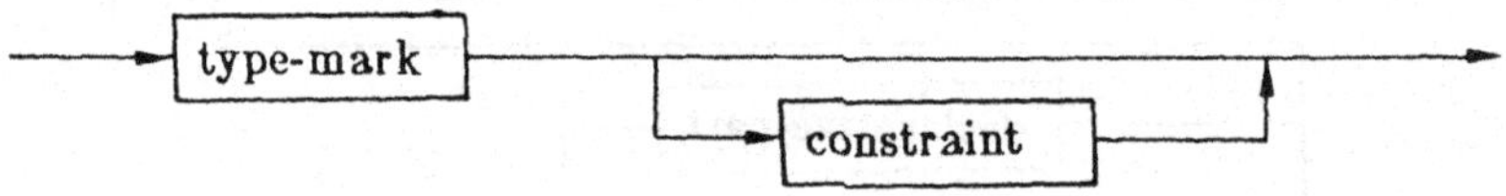

term

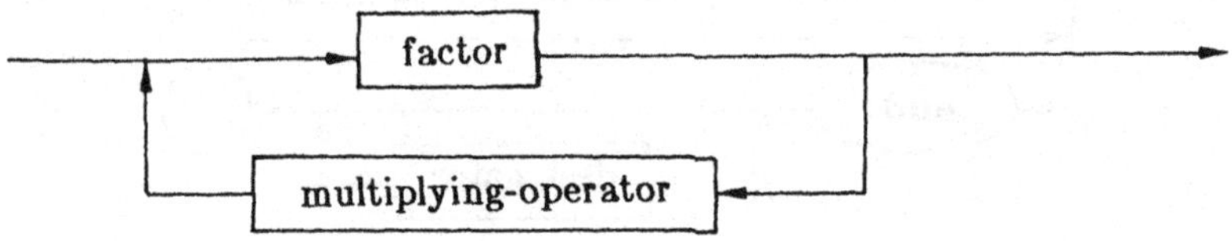

type-conversion

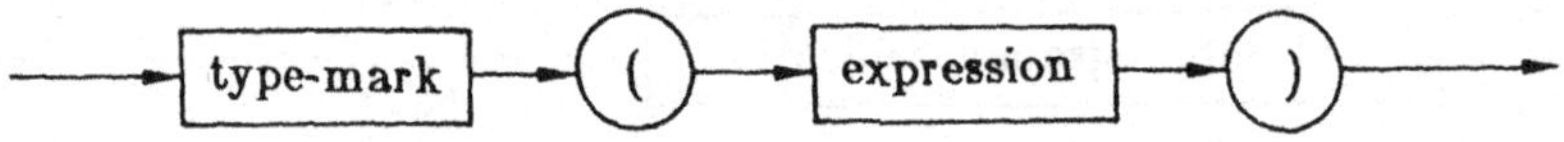

type-declaration

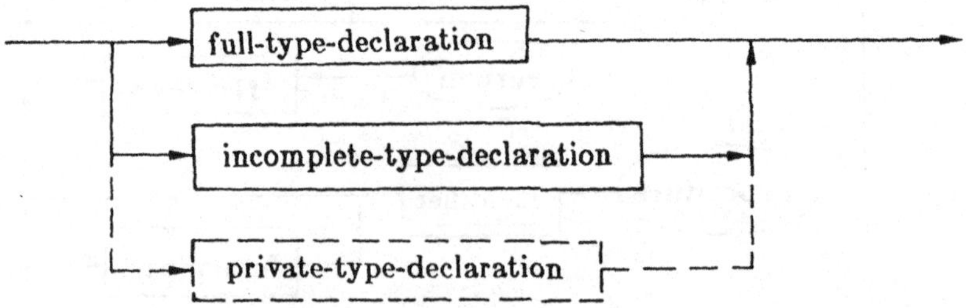

type-definition

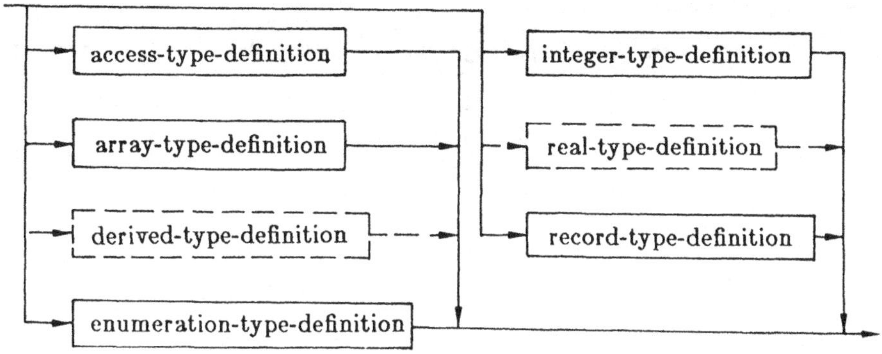

type-mark

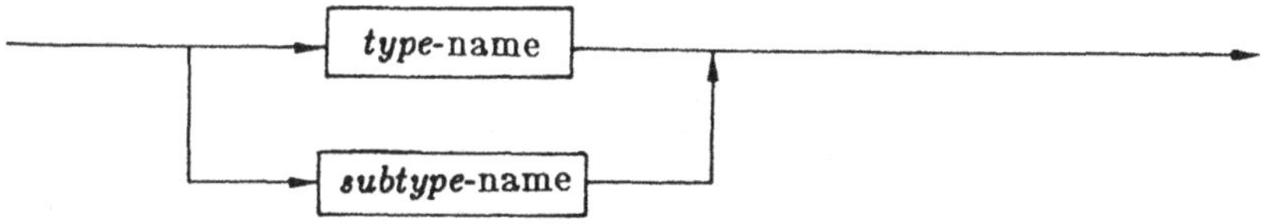

unary-adding-operator

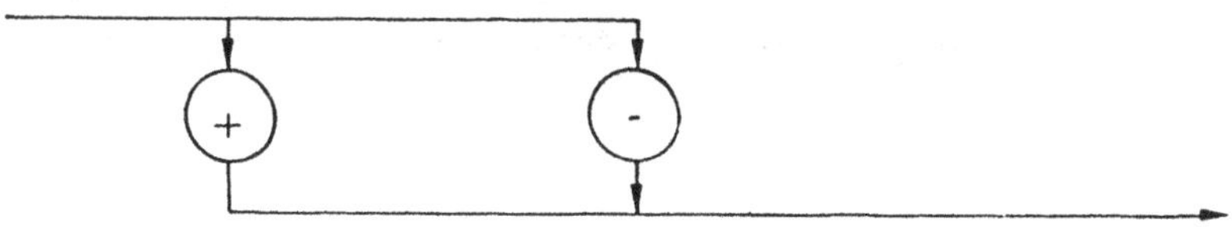

unconstrained-array-definition

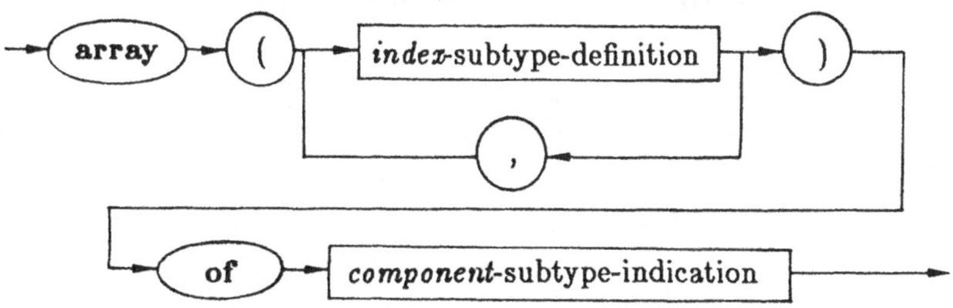

use-clause

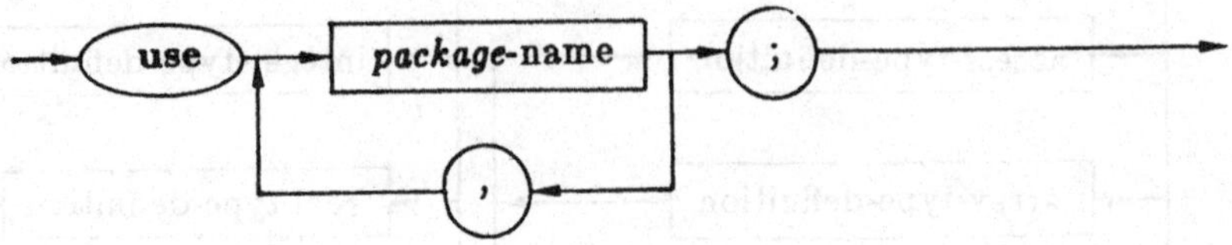

variant

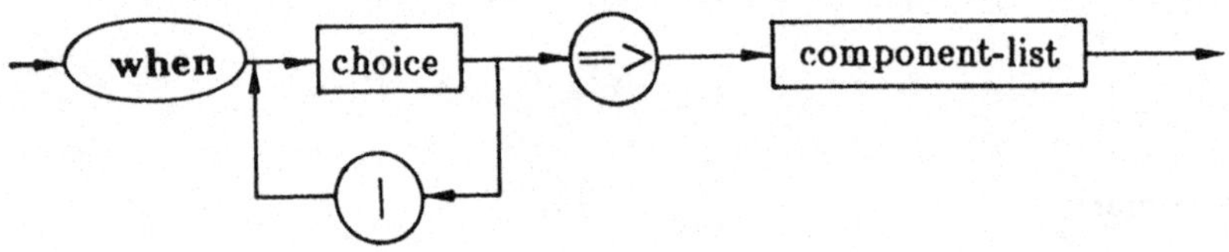

variant-part

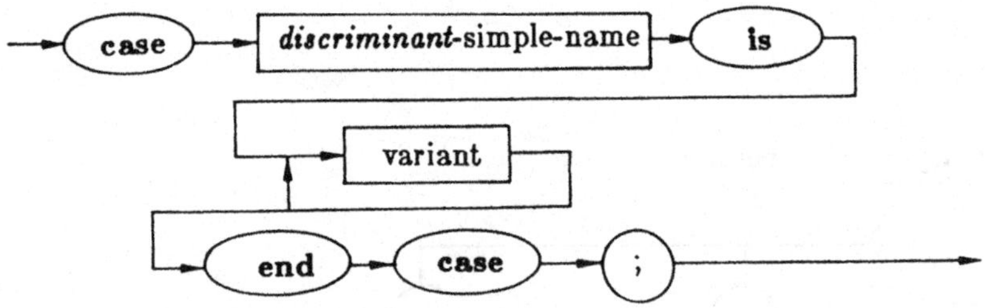

with-clause

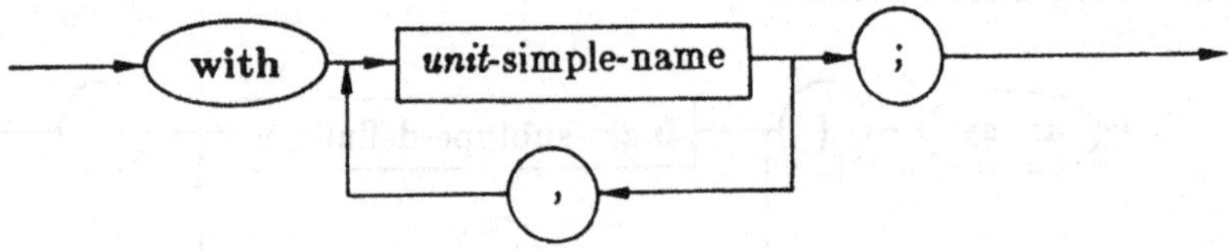

REFERENCES

Generalities

Barron, D.W. An Introduction to the Study of Programming Languages, Cambridge University Press(1977).

Berry, D.M. and *Schwartz, R.L.* Type Equivalence in Strongly Typed Languages: One More Look, SIGPLAN Notices, 14(9), 35-41(1979).

Denvir, B.T. On Orthogonality in Programming Languages, SIGPLAN Notices, 14(7), 18-30, (1979).

Goldberg, A. and *Robson, D.* Smalltalk-80, the Language and its Implementation, Addison-Wesley (1983).

Gordon, M.J.C. The denotational description of programming languages, An introduction, Springer-Verlag, New York (1979).

Hoare, C.A.R. The Emperor's Old Clothes,Comm. of the ACM,24(2),75-83(1981).

Horowitz, E. Fundamentals of Programming languages, Springer-Verlag, Berlin (1983).

Liskov B. - *Snyder, A.* - *Atkinson, R.* and *Schaffert, C.* Abstraction Mechanisms in CLU, Comm. of the ACM, 20(8), 564-576 (1977).

Meek. B. Fortran, PL/1 and the Algols, The MacMillan Press Ltd. (1978).

Shaw, M. - *Almes, G.T.* - *Newcomer, J.M.* - *Reid, B.K.* and *Wulf Wm.A.* A Comparison of Programming Languages for Software Engineering, Software-Practice and Experience, 11, 1-52 (1981).

Shaw, M. (ed). Alphard:Form and Content, Springer-Verlag, New York (1981).

Tanenbaum, A.S. A comparison of Pascal and Algol 68, The Computer Journal, 21(4), 316-323 (1978).

Tennent, R.D. Principles of Programming Languages, Prentice-Hall International, Series in Computer Science (1981).

Tucker, A.B. Programming Languages, McGraw-Hill, Computer Science Series (1977).

Valentine, S.H. Comparative Notes on Algol 68 and PL/1, The Computer Journal, 17(4), 312-325 (1974).

van Wijngaarden, A. Orthogonal Design and Description of a Formal Language, Mathematisch Centrum, Amsterdam, MR76 (1965).

Wexelblat, R.L. (ed). History of Programming Languages, Academic Press (1981).

Wirth, N. Programming in Modula-2, Texts and Monographs in Computer Science, Springer-Verlag, Berlin (1983).

Wirth, N. and *Hoare, C.A.R.* A contribution to the development of Algol, Comm. of the ACM, 9(6), 413-432 (1966).

Wulf, Wm. A. Abstract Data Types: A Retrospective and Prospective View, in Mathematical Foundations of Computer Science, Proceedings of 9th Symposium, Poland, Lecture Notes in Computer Science, 88, Springer-Verlag, Berlin (1980).

Pascal

Addyman, A.M. A Draft Proposal for Pascal, SIGPLAN Notices, 15(4), 1-66 (1980).

Barron, D.W. (ed). Pascal, the Language and its Implementation, John Wiley & Sons (1982).

Brinch Hansen, P. The Architecture of Concurrent Programs, Prentice Hall, Englewood Cliffs, New Jersey (1977).

Habermann, A.N. Critical Comments on the Programming Language pascal, Acta Informatica, 3, 47-57 (1973).

Jensen, K. and *Wirth, N.* Pascal User Manual and Report, Springer, New York (second edition, 1975).

Lecarme, O. and *Desjardins, P.* More Comments on the Programming Language Pascal, Acta Informatica, 4, 231-243 (1975).

Steengaard-Madsen, J. Pascal-Clarifications and Recommended Extensions, Acta Informatica, 12, 73-94 (1979).

Tennent, R.D. Another Look at Type Compatibility in Pascal, Software-Practice and Experience, 8, 429-437 (1978).

Welsh, J. Pascal Plus, another language for Modular Multiprogramming, Software Practice and Experience 9(11), 947-957 (1979).

Welsh, J. - *Sneeringer, J.* and *Hoare, C.A.R.* Ambiguities and Insecurities in Pascal, Software Practice and Experience, 7, 685-696 (1977).

PL/1

American National Standard Programming Language PL/1, ANSI X3.53 1976, American National Standards Institute (1976).

Barnes, R.A. PL/1 for Programmers, North-Holland Publishing Company, New York (1979).

Beech, D. A Structural View of PL/1, Computing Surveys, 2(1), 33-64 (1970).

Conway, R. and *Gries, D.* An Introduction to Programming, A Structural Approach Using PL/1 and PL/C, Winthrop Publishers, Inc., Cambridge (1973).

Holt, R.C. Teaching the Fatal Disease (or) Introductory Computer Programming Using PL/1, SIGPLAN Notices, 8(5), 8-23 (1973).

Holt, R.C. et al. SP/k: A system for Teaching Computer Programming, Comm. of the ACM, 20(5), 301-309 (1977).

Hume, J.N.P. and *Holt, R.C.* Structured Programming Using PL/1 and SP/k, Reston Publishing Company, Inc., (1975).

IBM. OS PL/1 Checkout and Optimizing Compilers: Language Reference Manual, GC33-0009-4, fifth edition (1976).

Algol 68

Brailsford, D.F. and *Walker, A.N.* Introductory Algol 68 Programming, Computers and their Applications 2, Ellis Horwood Publishers (1979).

Branquart, P. - *Lewi, J.* - *Sintzoff, M.* and *Wodon, P.L.* The Composition of Semantics in Algol 68, Comm. of the ACM, 14(11), 697-708 (1971).

Branquart, P. - *Cardinael, J.P.* - *Lewi, J.* - *Delescaille, J.P.* and *Vanbegin, M.* An Optimized Translation Process and Its Application to Algol 68, Lecture Notes in Computer Science, 38, Springer-Verlag, Berlin (1976).

Collin, A.J.T. Programming and Problem-solving in Algol 68, The MacMillan Press Ltd. (1978).

Hoare, C.A.R. Critique of Algol 68, Algol Bulletin, 29, 27-29 (1968).

Lindsay, C. and *van der Meulen, S.G.* Informal Introduction to Algol 68, North-Holland Publishing Company (1971).

McGettrick, A.D. Algol 68, a First and Second Course, Cambridge Computer Science Texts.8, Cambridge University Press (1978).

McGettrick, A.D. Aspects of the Algol 68 Mode Structure, SIGPLAN Notices, 14(7), 62-77 (1979).

Pagan, F.G. A Practical Guide to Algol 68, John Wiley & Sons (1976).

Pagan, F.G. Nested Sublanguages of Algol 68 for Teaching Purposes, SIGPLAN Notices, 15(7,8), 72-81 (1980).

Sintzoff, M. A brief review of Algol 68, Algol Bulletin, 37, 54-62 (1974).

Tanenbaum, A.S. A Tutorial on Algol 68, Computing Surveys, 8(2), 155-190 (1976).

Turski, W.M. Algol 68 Revisited Twelve Years Later of from AAD to ADA, in Algorithmic Languages, De Bakker/van Vliet (eds.), IFIP, North-Holland Publishing Company, 417-431 (1981).

van Wijngaarden, A. et al. Revised Report on the Algorithmic Language Algol 68, Springer-Verlag, Berlin (1976).

Ada

ADA Preliminary ADA Reference Manual, SIGPLAN Notices, 14(6), Part A (1979).

ADA Reference Mnual for the Ada Programming Language, United States Departement of Defense, ANSI/MIL-STD 1815A (1983).

Amoroso, S. Ada, an Introduction to Software Design and Implementation, Pitman (1984).

Barnes, J.G.P. An Overview of ADA, Software Practice and Experience, 10, 851-887 (1980).

Barnes, J.G.P. Programming in Ada, Addison-Wesley Publishing Company, International Computer Science Series (1982).

Ben-Ari, M. and *Yehudai, A.* A Methodology for Modular Use of ADA, SIGPLAN Notices, 16(12), 22-26 (1981).

Bjorner, D. and *Oest, O.* Towards a Formal Description of Ada, Lecture Notes in Computer Science, Springer-Verlag (1980).

Booch, G. Software Engineering with Ada, The Benjamin/Cummings Publishing Company (1983).

Boute, R.T. Simplifying Ada by Removing Limitations, SIGPLAN Notices, 15(2), 17-29 (1980).

Downes, V.A. and *Goldsack, S.J.* Programming Embedded Systems with ADA, Prentice-Hall International,Inc. (1982).

Gehani, N. Ada an Advanced Introduction, Prentice-Hall. Inc. (1984).

Hibbard, P. et al. Studies in ADA style, Springer-Verlag, New York, (1981).

Ichbiah, J.D. et al. Rationale for the Design of the ADA Programming Language, SIGPLAN Notices, 14(6), part B (1979).

Ledgard, H.F. and *Singer, A.* Scaling Down ADA (or Towards a Standard ADA Subset), Comm. of the ACM, 25(2), 121-125 (1982).

Lewis, W.E. Problem Solving Principles for ADA Programming, Hayden Book Company (1982).

Mayoh, B. Problem Solving with Ada, J. Wiley & Sons (1982).

McGettrick, A.D. Program Verification using Ada, Cambridge Computer science Texts. 13, Cambridge University Press (1982).

Nissen, J. and *Wallis, P.* Portability and Style in Ada, Cambridge University Press (1984).

Oysen, S. Ada for programming, Reston (1983).

Pyle, I.C. The Ada Programming Language, Prentice-Hall, Inc. (1981).

Saxon, J. and *Fritz, R.* Beginning Programming with Ada, Prentice Hall, Inc. (1983).

Wegner, P. Programmig with Ada: an Introduction by means of Graduated Examples, Prentice-Hall, Inc. (1980).

Wegner, P. Self-Assessment Procedure VIII, Comm. of the ACM, 24(10), 647-678 (1981).

Wilner, R. and *Simcovec, R.* Programming in Ada, J. Wiley & Sons, (1983).

Young, S. An introduction to Ada, J. Wiley & Sons, (1982).

Index

Made in the USA
Monee, IL
10 June 2026

53048752R00227